T0188403

Wiley Series in Software Design Patterns

The WILEY SERIES IN SOFTWARE DESIGN PATTERNS is designed to meet the needs of today's software architects, developers, programmers and managers interested in design patterns. Frank Buschmann (Series Editor), as well as authors, shepherds and reviewers work collaboratively within the patterns community to strive for high-quality, highly researched, thoroughly validated, classic works, which document accepted and acknowledged design experience. Priority is given to those titles that catalog software patterns and pattern languages with a practical, applied approach in domains such as:

- Distributed systems
- Real time systems
- Databases
- Business information systems
- Telecommunications
- Organizations
- Concurrency
- Networking

Books in the series will also cover conceptual areas of how to apply patterns, pattern language developments and architectural/component-based approaches to pattern-led software development.

TITLES PUBLISHED

- PATTERN-ORIENTED SOFTWARE ARCHITECTURE, Volume 1
Frank Buschmann, Regine Meunier, Hans Rohnert, Peter Sommerlad and Michael Stal

978-0471-95869-7	476pp	1996	Hardback

- PATTERN-ORENTED SOFTWARE ARCHITECTURE, Volume 2
Douglas Schmidt, Michael Stal, Hans Rohnert and Frank Buschmann

978-0471-60695-6	636pp	2000	Hardback

- A PATTERN APPROACH TO INTERACTION DESIGN
Jan Borchers

978-0471-49828-5	250pp	2001	Hardback

- SERVER COMPONENT PATTERNS
Markus Völter, Alexander Schmid, Eberhard Wolff

978-0470-84319-2	462pp	2002	Hardback

- ARCHITECTING ENTERPRISE SOLUTIONS
Paul Dyson, Andy Longshaw

978-0470-85612-3	384pp	2004	Hardback

- PATTERN-ORIENTED SOFTWARE ARCHITECTURE, Volume 3
Michael Kircher, Prashant Jain

978-0470-84525-7	312pp	2004	Hardback

- SECURITY PATTERNS
Markus Schumacher, Eduardo B. Fernandez, Duane Hybertson, Frank Buschmann, Peter Sommerlad

978-0-470-85884-4	600pp	2005	Hardback

Security Patterns in Practice

Security Patterns in Practice

Designing Secure Architectures Using Software Patterns

Eduardo B. Fernandez

WILEY

This edition first published 2013

© 2013 John Wiley & Sons, Ltd.

Registered office

John Wiley & Sons Ltd, The Atrium, Southern Gate, Chichester, West Sussex, PO19 8SQ, United Kingdom

For details of our global editorial offices, for customer services and for information about how to apply for permission to reuse the copyright material in this book please see our website at www.wiley.com.

Wiley also publishes its books in a variety of electronic formats. Some content that appears in print may not be available in electronic books.

Designations used by companies to distinguish their products are often claimed as trademarks. All brand names and product names used in this book are trade names, service marks, trademarks or registered trademarks of their respective owners. The publisher is not associated with any product or vendor mentioned in this book. This publication is designed to provide accurate and authoritative information in regard to the subject matter covered. It is sold on the understanding that the publisher is not engaged in rendering professional services. If professional advice or other expert assistance is required, the services of a competent professional should be sought.

Images on pages page 289, 293, 309 and 316, clockwise from top-left, Teneresa/Shutterstock, gitan100/Shutterstock, dedMazay/Shutterstock

A catalogue record for this book is available from the British Library.

ISBN 978-1-119-99894-5 (hardback)
978-1-119-97049-1 (ebook)
978-1-119-97048-4 (ebook)
978-1-119-97057-6 (ebook)

Printed edition set in 10/12 point Sabon by WordMongers Ltd, Treen, Penzance, Cornwall
Printed in Great Britain by TJ International

To Minjie, Lian and Anna

Publisher's Acknowledgements

Some of the people who helped bring this book to market include the following:

Editorial and Production

VP Consumer and Technology Publishing Director: Michelle Leete
Associate Director – Book Content Management: Martin Tribe
Associate Publisher: Chris Webb
Executive Commissioning Editor: Birgit Gruber
Associate Commissioning Editor: Ellie Scott
Project Editor: Steve Rickaby
Shepherd: Markus Schumacher
Editorial Manager: Jodi Jensen
Senior Project Editor: Sara Shlaer
Editorial Assistant: Annie Sullivan

Marketing

Associate Marketing Director: Louise Breinholt
Marketing Manager: Lorna Mein
Senior Marketing Executive: Kate Parrett
Marketing Assistant: Tash Lee

Composition Services, Printed Edition

Steve Rickaby, WordMongers Ltd

About the Author

Eduardo B. Fernandez (aka Eduardo Fernandez-Buglioni) is a professor in the Department of Computer Science and Engineering at the Florida Atlantic University in Boca Raton, Florida. He is now a visiting professor at Universidad Tecnica Federico Santa Maria, Chile, on leave from FAU. Ed has published numerous papers and four books on authorization models, object-oriented analysis and design and security patterns. He has lectured all over the world at both academic and industrial meetings. His current interests include security patterns, web services, cloud computing security and fault tolerance. He holds an MS degree in Electrical Engineering from Purdue University and a PhD in Computer Science from UCLA. Ed is an active consultant for industry, including assignments with IBM, Allied Signal, Motorola, Lucent, and others. His web page is www.cse.fau.edu/~ed.

About the Foreword Author

Markus Schumacher has served as CEO and Co-Founder of Virtual Forge GmbH since 2006. The company specializes in the security of SAP applications. He was previously a representative of the Fraunhofer Institute for Secure Information Technology (SIT) and worked at SAP as Security Product Manager. Focus topics were secure development, security testing, security response, product certification (Common Criteria) as well as awareness events for the development crew. Markus earned his Doctorate in the field of computer science. He has published numerous articles and coauthored a handful of books, including *Secure ABAP Programming* and *Security Patterns – Volume 1*, and speaks regularly at international conferences.

Contents

Foreword

Security is simple. We use a little bit of cryptography, add some firewalls and passwords – done! In theory...

When I started work in the field of security in the mid 1990s, I met many people who thought they could easily secure their applications. They used certain ingredients of security measures and applied them to whatever problem they had. Even worse: sometimes they didn't use existing ingredients, but build their own – making the same errors made in hundreds of previous projects. And practice proved them wrong: security was never simple – there's always at least one loophole. There's always an unexpected side-effect. There's always something that you miss if you are not an expert. Front page news regularly proves that we obviously never learn.

Key reasons for insecure applications are:

- Lack of time, due to aggressive deadlines and tight budgets
- Lack of knowledge – IT experts are usually not security experts
- Lack of priorities – functionality and performance usually come top

That's why we are literally doomed to failure. Hackers have an easy job entering a system, stealing or changing data and leaving without a trace. Sometimes the victim doesn't even know that something really bad happened until his new designs are somehow copied by a competitor, or supposedly protected customer data is published on public web sites. Or a journalist gets a hint of a fantastic new story. Even worse, modern applications are becoming more and more complex – think of recent trends like mobility and cloud computing. Borders disappear and the means of protecting known areas is difficult.

In traditional engineering we have hundreds of years of knowledge that has evolved over time. We know how to build bridges that survive rain, wind and earthquakes. We know how to build solid cars that give you a good chance of surviving a crash. We know of proven solutions to problems in specific contexts. Written down, these are called a *patterns*, paradigms that have also been applied to software engineering for quite some time. Towards the end of the 1990s we saw work on patterns that were dedicated to security problems. The pattern community came together and collected the work in progress, resulting in one of the first comprehensive security pattern collections, which captured security expertise for getting it done the right way.

It was obvious that the work was not completed by the publication of a few books. Besides mining additional knowledge and writing more patterns, an interesting question is how to apply them effectively. Both of these issues are answered with this new book from Eduardo Fernandez, a pioneer of computer science and security patterns. He has continued the work that we started ten years ago, and I'm honored that I could be his sparring partner while he wrote it.

The result is the most up-to-date guide for software engineers who want to understand how to build reliable applications. It provides guidance for applying the captured expertise of security pattern in your day-to-day work. Security is still not easy, but it is much easier when you understand the benefits, liabilities and dependencies of specific solutions.

Markus Schumacher
Heidelberg, Germany, March 2013

Preface

El que lee mucho y anda mucho, ve mucho y sabe mucho.
(The one who reads a lot and goes around a lot, sees much and knows much.)

Miguel de Cervantes, El ingenioso hidalgo don Quijote de la Mancha

I started working on security when I joined IBM, where I worked for almost nine years doing security research. I coauthored a book on database security while there, one of the first to appear on this topic. I later realized that a large amount of security knowledge was wasted, because practitioners had not read the variety of books and papers that had started to appear; they kept repeating the same mistakes. In particular, software developers knew little about security. Later I participated in a conference about patterns and realized that expressing security knowledge as patterns could be an effective way to spread this knowledge. Around that time, Yoder and Barcalow [Yod97] published a paper about expressing security solutions as patterns that further convinced me that this was a good direction. I found later that security patterns could do more than propagate security knowledge to inexperienced developers; they could also be useful for security experts, to help them apply security in a systematic way to build new applications or products, understand complex standards, audit complex applications and reengineer legacy systems. I was coauthor of a book that published most of the security patterns known up to 2005. However, since that book was published, many more patterns have appeared.

I have written over 80 patterns, most of which are shown in this book. Other authors have presented patterns which complement ours (see Chapter 1). I have listed most of them in the See Also sections of each pattern. Note that they may use a different notation or pattern form to ours.

I did not try to be exhaustive, and I may have left out some useful patterns. I hope to include those discovered later, or that appear later, on the book's web page at http://www.wiley.com/go/securitypatterns or in a new edition of this book. Patterns can be improved after one uses them or understands them better. Some of these patterns were written as long as 15 years ago, while others are still under development. When I looked at the older patterns, I realized that I could write them better now, which delayed the completion of this book. It is not a second volume or a continuation of our 2006 book [Sch06b], but it reflects my own views and my own work. Some of my patterns from the earlier book are included here for completeness; my intention is to eventually produce a complete catalog, although I am not there yet. Other authors have also produced some good patterns, and altogether there is a good quantity of patterns that developers and researchers can use. My audience is mostly made up from software developers who are trying to incorporate security in their work. However, there is material here for researchers and computer science students, as well as for anybody interested in systems security.

A difficult point was to unify the style of patterns produced over a long time span. All the patterns presented here have either been discussed at a pattern conference or presented at a research conference. However, I have reworked all of them for this book, some extensively. I also participated very actively in the original versions, having usually provided the initial ideas, read every line of them and improved their contents. In other words, I am really a full author of this book, not just an editor of past works or a presenter of my students' work.

Patterns alone are not enough: the final objective is to build secure systems. For that purpose, I have been working on a methodology for building secure systems using patterns, of which several examples are shown here. The approach I use is strictly an engineering one. This does not mean avoidance of theory, but I use it only when necessary. It does not mean code either: although I give some code examples, I use mostly models. To handle the complexity of current systems, we need the abstraction power of models. An important value of patterns is that they lead to systems thinking. A system is more than the sum of its parts; looking at isolated code and hardware components is a microscopic view that cannot lead to secure systems.

Patterns can be described from single page ideas to 30-page detailed descriptions. I have chosen an intermediate level, where I give enough detail for a user to understand the meaning of the pattern and evaluate its possibilities. I have found this level of detail the most useful in my work. I have resisted the temptation of adding background material on security: several good textbooks exist (see Chapter 1).

Because I work in a university, I have been accused a few times of not being 'practical enough'. I did work in industry for about ten years, and I occasionally do consulting for companies, so I do have some industrial experience. Some of my students have also provided an important industrial perspective, since many of them were working in local industry when we wrote these patterns. In some respect, this is an interdisciplinary book, in that it connects security to software architecture.

I would greatly appreciate comments or corrections. These patterns encompass all areas of computer systems architecture, and I am sure I may have misunderstood some aspects. I am also particularly interested to hear of any interesting use of security patterns in industrial projects. Write to me at `ed@cse.fau.edu`. Markus Schumacher and I will publish comments on patterns at `securitypatterns.org`.

Book Structure

The book is divided into three parts. The first three chapters describe motivation, experience in using patterns, the objectives of the book, and present my secure development methodology. Part II is a pattern catalog, including patterns for different architectural levels of a computer system. Part III shows some examples of application of the patterns, has tables of patterns, and indicates possible research directions.

Acknowledgements

This work is the result of my work on security over many years, attending security and patterns conferences, listening and talking to many colleagues around the world, all of whom contributed to this work. More specifically, my students, in particular Nelly Delessy, Keiko Hashizume, Ola Ajaj, Juan C. Pelaez and Ajoy Kumar, wrote several versions of these patterns. My colleagues Maria M. Larrondo-Petrie and Mike Van Hilst collaborated in some of the published patterns. My international collaborators included Nobukazu Yoshioka and Hironori Washizaki (Japan), Günther Pernul (Germany), David LaRed (Argentina), Anton Uzunov (Australia), Fabricio Braz (Brazil), Jaime Muñoz Arteaga (Mexico) and Antonio Maña (Spain).

The shepherds and workshop participants in the Pattern Languages conferences (PLoP, EuroPLoP, Asian PLoP and Latin American PLoP) gave valuable comments, in particular Joe Yoder, Fabio Kon, Richard Gabriel, Rosana Braga, Ralph Johnson, Lior Schachter, and others. Craig Heath commented on the first three chapters.

The editorial staff of Wiley UK – Ellie Scott, Birgit Gruber and Sara Shlaer – and Steve Rickaby of WordMongers, were very helpful and encouraging. Markus Schumacher was an ideal shepherd, in that he caught important errors or missing aspects. My thanks to all of them.

Part I

Introduction

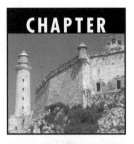

Motivation and Objectives

We will bankrupt ourselves in the vain search for absolute security.

Dwight D Eisenhower

1.1   Why Do We Need Security Patterns?

Most modern applications are distributed and connected by some type of network – often the Internet, but also LANs and other specialized network types. Their platforms may support web interfaces, web services and even agents. The complexity of such systems makes them hard to understand, design and maintain. This complexity also brings vulnerabilities which, when coupled with the fact that these applications may handle valuable information, attract security attacks. The increasing use of mobile devices with improved capabilities and the growing use of sensors make this problem even more acute. Every day the press reports attacks on web sites or databases around the world, which result in millions of dollars of direct or indirect losses. Systems are constantly attacked and often breached. There is also the fear that a hostile adversary may try to disrupt the infrastructure systems of an entire country.

Why do we fail to secure such systems? One important reason is their complexity, which makes errors common and vulnerabilities hard to find. Another important reason is that security is built piecemeal: parts of a system are secured using specific products, but there is rarely a global analysis of the complete system. If done, different models may be used in different parts, for example one for the databases and another for wireless devices. Regrettably, security requires a comprehensive approach if it is to block all possible means of attack. Very secure components cannot make the whole system secure if they do not protect all parts of the system and do not work in a coordinated way. Threat analysis is done locally, but many threats only emerge when different units are interconnected. Further, methodologies for building secure systems focus mostly on new systems, but the majority of the systems in use are legacy systems, often in a state of constant maintenance. Even systems that have been built carefully can suffer from architecture erosion, in which changes made, once in production, can invalidate or weaken security defenses.

We need a way to handle the complexity of new systems and make them secure in a systematic and holistic way. We need a way to reengineer legacy systems to make them more secure, by tracing back code changes so that their impact on security mechanisms can be detected and corrected. Software developers know a particular language and its environment well; however, they may not know much about security, and their systems exhibit many vulnerabilities which can be easily exploited by attackers. They are also under pressure to produce results quickly.

Secure systems need to be built in a systematic way in which security is an integral part of the software lifecycle [Fer04b][How06][McG06]: the same applies to reliability and other quality factors. If when we build applications we also consider the effect of middleware, operating systems and networks as a whole, we can build systems that can withstand a whole spectrum of attacks from external or internal users. We believe that to build secure applications, it is not effective to build a secure platform and then run some application made secure in isolation on it, but rather that the application and its platform should be designed together and the platform match the type of application. In addition, all security and reliability constraints should be defined at the application level, where their semantics are understood and propagated to lower architectural levels [Fer99b] [Fer06b] [Sum97].

Lower levels provide the assurance that the constraints are being followed; that is, they enforce an absence of ways to bypass these constraints. The only way to provide this unification in the presence of myriad implementation details of the component units is to use abstraction. In particular, we can apply abstraction through the use of *patterns*. Patterns are encapsulated solutions to recurrent system problems and define a way to express requirements and solutions concisely, as well as providing a communication vocabulary for designers [Bus96] [Gam94]. The description of architectures using patterns makes them easier to understand, provides guidelines for design and analysis, and can define a way of making their structure more secure. *Security patterns* allow application developers to use security measures without being experts on security. We can also use patterns to evaluate existing systems by examining them to see if they contain the required patterns. Further, we can reengineer legacy systems by using patterns to add missing security features. (I compare the use of patterns to other approaches to producing secure systems below.)

We need to unify the total architecture of the network along horizontal and vertical partitions to apply a holistic approach – specifically, along the system development life-cycle and along its architectural levels [Fer11a]. This book presents a complete pattern-based methodology for building secure systems, covering pure information systems as well as embedded systems. I proposed its main ideas in [Fer06b] and am still refining and extending it. A far-reaching objective is to establish the fact that patterns offer a robust way to build security and reliability into systems. Neumann calls for the need to have 'principled' systems, based on solid conceptual approaches [Neu04]: patterns allow the implicit application of principles. I have done a substantial amount of work in this direction, but further work is still needed to consolidate and extend this. The use of security patterns and other approaches to building secure systems is surveyed in [Uzu12c].

To design a secure system, we first need to understand the possible threats to the system. We have proposed an approach for identifying threats by considering the activities in each use case [Bra08a] [Fer06c]. Such an approach finds threats – as goals of an attacker – that are realized through the lower levels of a system. We need to understand how the specific components of the architecture are compromised, or used by an attacker, to fulfill their objectives. We use the concept of misuse (attack) patterns to model how a misuse is performed [Fer07a].

There is a need for ways to define and enforce standards and regulations; our proposed pattern-based approach can be valuable for that purpose. In fact, some standards – for example HIPAA, FEMA and Sarbanes-Oxley – and regulations are very complex, or even ambiguous; patterns can describe them in a precise way and make them more understandable and usable. Web services and cloud computing have brought about a need for certification of services; patterns could be a good way to achieve this [Dam09].

When we talk about *modeling*, we do not mean yet another authorization model, but rather a model of the integration of security controls for a variety of devices and units in a computer system, fundamental when dealing with complex systems. We can get a measure of completeness by adding patterns to cover all the threats identified in each layer and approach the holistic ideal required to secure systems. We think this is also a good approach to defend against a possible cyber war. Patterns do not provide provable security, but they are a good practical approach to apply to increasingly complex systems.

1.2   Some Basic Definitions

Before we start, we need to define a few basic terms. *Security* is the protection against:

- Unauthorized data disclosure (*confidentiality* or *secrecy*).
- Unauthorized data modification (*integrity*). Unauthorized modification of data may result in inconsistencies or erroneous data. Data destruction may bring all kinds of losses.

- Denial of service: users or other systems may prevent the legitimate users from using their system. Denial of service is an attack on the *availability* of the system.

- Lack of accountability: Users should be responsible for their actions and should not be able to deny what they have done (*non-repudiation*).

The definition of security above describes security as defense against some types of attacks. The generic types of defenses (also known as *countermeasures*) that we can use include:

- *Identification and authentication (I&A).* Identification implies a user or system providing an identity to access a system. Authentication implies providing some proof that a user or system is who or what they claim to be. The result of authentication may be a set of *credentials,* which later can be used to prove identity and may describe some attributes of the authenticated entity. Patterns for identity management and patterns for authentication are described in Chapter 4 and Chapter 5 respectively.

- *Authorization and access control (A & A).* Authorization defines permitted access to resources depending on the accessor (user, executing process), the resource being accessed and the intended use of the resource. Access control is the use of some mechanism to enforce authorization. Chapter 6 describes patterns for access control.

- *Logging and auditing.* These functions imply keeping a record (log) of actions that may be relevant for security and analyzing it later. They can be used to collect evidence for prosecution (*forensics*) and to improve the system by analyzing why an attack succeeded. Logging and auditing is also described in Chapter 6.

- *Hiding of information.* Information hiding is usually performed by the use of cryptography, but steganography is another option (see Chapter 12). The idea is to hide information to protect it.

- *Intrusion detection.* Intrusion Detection Systems (IDS) alert the system in real time when an intruder is trying to attack it. Chapter 10 discusses patterns for networks.

My objective in this book is the construction of complex applications. These include medical systems, financial applications, legal applications, operating systems and others. Such applications are typically implemented with systems that are subject to non-functional requirements such as reliability or fault tolerance. Often they are composed of a variety of software and/or hardware units, some built ad hoc and some bought or outsourced. In such systems the security of the application software itself cannot be separated from the security of the rest of the system.

Another common aspect of such systems is that they frequently must comply with regulatory standards. Systems may include several databases, and usually have Internet access as well as distributed and wireless access. Data is typically accessed using a web application server (WAS) that integrates web and database applications and uses a global enterprise model, usually implemented using components such as J2EE or .NET, applications that are of fundamental value to enterprises and institutions of any type. A systematic approach is required towards building these applications such that they can reach the appropriate level of security. We focus on these applications because they define worst-case scenarios for the application of our patterns methodology.

Security was first studied from a systems viewpoint [Sum97], and standards appeared for evaluating security [cc] [DoD83]. The emphasis then moved to software; numerous papers indicated its importance and gave the impression that software security was the only objective we need to fulfill to produce secure systems [How03]; there is now a considerable effort to improve the security of code [DeW09]. However, things are not so simple: the whole system must be secure, including its hardware and the way the whole system is configured. We need a global and holistic view if we want to produce secure systems. Typical textbooks, for example [Gol06] [Sta12], are very good for discussions of specific topics, but they don't provide a global view. Most research papers study specific mechanisms but rarely look at the complete system. Much work as also been done on stochastic system views of security [Nic04], but while this is an interesting direction for evaluating global aspects of systems, it does not provide constructive solutions for systems security.

In this book we take a systems view of security, for which software architecture is an important basis [Bus07] [Tay10]. Software architecture provides a global view of systems, but until now most studies have not considered the early lifecycle stages or said much about security [Fer12a]; however, the software architecture viewpoint is very important. To apply any methodology, we need a good catalog of patterns: providing that is one of the main objectives of this book.

A related aspect is that of how to apply these patterns through some systematic methodology. We have applied the patterns described here throughout a secure system development methodology based on a hierarchical architecture whose layers define the scope of each security mechanism [Fer04b] [Fer06b]. We discuss this approach in Chapter 3.

1.3   The History of Security Patterns

Yoder and Barcalow wrote the first paper on security patterns [Yod97]. They included a variety of patterns useful in different aspects of security. Before them, at least three papers [Fer93a] [Fer94a] [Ess97] had shown object-oriented models of secure systems without calling them 'patterns', or using one of the standard pattern templates. In 1998, two more patterns appeared: a pattern for cryptography [Bra00] and a pattern for access control [Das98]. After that, several others appeared, and we have now three books on the subject [Bla04] [Sch06b] [Ste05], one of which [Sch06b] was the first to try to categorize and unify a variety of security patterns. Many papers have also appeared, some of which are surveyed here.

Security patterns are now accepted by many companies, Microsoft [msd], Sun [jav] and IBM [IBMb] have papers and web pages on this subject. A general web page for security patterns also exists [sec]. Pattern catalogs include [Ste05][Kie02][Bla04][Dou09], [Sch06b][Ysk06][Haf11][1]. Some surveys of security patterns include [Fer06a][Yos08]

[Uzu12a]. This book extends the ideas of [Sch06b] and adds many new patterns, as well as a methodology for building secure systems.

1.4   Industrial Use of Security Patterns

Most developers don't use models, they just code. However, this situation is slowly changing and design patterns have been successfully applied in many industrial projects, for example [Bec96] [Sch95]. Several major companies now maintain patterns web pages and have published books about them.

Until now, security patterns have not been used as much as design patterns, but some interesting applications exist, such as qmail [Haf08] and BBVA [Mor12]. [ElK09] reports the use of security patterns to enforce security for remote healthcare in *smart homes*. [Ela11] describes a survey of 237 institutions in China to discover their use of security requirements for software construction. One of their most common sources of security knowledge were standards and security patterns.

One of the reasons for the lack of use of security patterns is the lack of a good catalog; we hope to help with this. Another reason could be lack of a methodology, and we expect that our methodology can be of value here.

1.5   Other Approaches to Building Secure Systems

There are several other approaches to building secure systems, of which the most prominent are those based on *secure coding*:

- Microsoft's Security Development Lifecycle (SDL) [How06]. [Lip05] defines activities for all the stages of a lifecycle based on coding with almost no modeling. The analysis stage is almost ignored, and threats are defined with respect to the deployment units of the software.

- OWASP's CLASP is a lightweight process to define requirements for secure software [OWAa]. It also starts from deployment units and analyzes their threats. Similarly to SDL it ignores the semantic aspects of the application.

- Building Security in Maturity Model (BSIMM) is a software security framework, which includes twelve practices organized into the four domains of Governance, Intelligence, SSDL Touchpoints and Deployment [BSI].

DeWin [DeW09] made a detailed comparison of SDL, CLASP and Touchpoints [McG06], looking for similarities and differences, as well as suggesting improvements. Code-based security, while valuable, cannot produce secure systems by itself, but it can be a good complement to model-based methods.

---

[1] Strictly, Haf11 and Ysk06 are not catalogs, they are pattern inventories where they organize existing patterns according to some classification, but do not provide pattern descriptions.

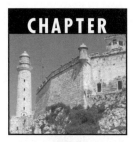

CHAPTER

2

Patterns and Security Patterns

Each problem that I solved became a rule which served
afterwards to solve other problems.

René Descartes, Discourse on Method

2.1   What is a Security Pattern?

A security pattern describes a solution to the problem of controlling (stopping or miti-gating) a set of specific threats through some security mechanism, defined in a given con-text [Sch06b]. This solution needs to resolve a set of *forces*, and can be expressed using UML class, sequence, state and activity diagrams. A set of consequences indicate how well the forces were satisfied; in particular, how well the attacks were handled. A security pattern is not directly related to a vulnerability, but is directly related to a threat. The spe-cific threat may be the result of one or more vulnerabilities, but the pattern is not intended to repair the vulnerability, but to stop or mitigate the threat.

Figure 2.1 shows a generic diagram illustrating the effect of the use of security patterns as deployed in a specific architecture. The sequence diagrams on the left of the figure indicate possible attacks (threats) to a context defined by a deployment diagram. For example, a context may include distributed systems, distributed systems using web services, or operating systems. Typical objects in the deployment diagram (O1, O2, O3) are instantiated from classes in the application class diagram (Classes A, B and C respectively for this example). SP_1 denotes the security pattern solution that is able to stop or mitigate these threats. There may be more than one SP_1 that can handle the threats. Theoretical models of security patterns can be found in [Was09] and in Chapter 8 of [Sch03].

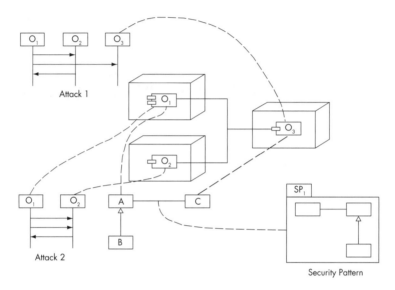

Figure 2.1: A security pattern controlling two attacks

2.2   The Nature of Security Patterns

There are several ways to look at security patterns:

- As an *architectural pattern*. Security patterns can be considered a type of architectural pattern because they usually describe global software architecture concepts; for example, do we need authentication between two distributed units? We prefer this interpretation because security is a global property.

- As a *design pattern*. The fact that security can be considered an aspect of a software subsystem has made some groups consider them design patterns [Bla04] [Dou09]. We think that design patterns are code-oriented and security is an architectural property, but this view can be useful to analyze the effect of code structure on security.

■ As an *analysis pattern*. Security constraints should be defined at the highest possible level, that is, at the conceptual model of the application. For example, we can define which users have which roles and what rights they need to perform their tasks. A conceptual, implementation-free definition of a security mechanism is, in effect, an analysis pattern. We use this approach in our methodology to define system-independent requirements, as described in Chapter 3.

■ As a *special type of pattern*. We can add new sections, remove some sections from the standard template, or we can use a different notation and model. The problem with using special notations is that the designer needs to learn a new language to use the patterns, which is time-consuming and prone to error. This type of pattern is useful for researchers and security experts, but not so much for the average developer.

Can we describe principles as patterns? We agree with [Hey07a] that security principles, for example separation of duty, are in general too broad to be considered patterns. We do not consider less broad concepts, such as confidentiality or integrity, as patterns, because there are many ways to obtain such properties: a pattern should describe a single solution.

Two other interesting points are:

■ Are security patterns styles or architectural patterns?

■ Are security patterns the same as tactics?

Styles are more application-oriented and describe the basic structure of an architecture [Tay10]; should we also have a catalog of security styles? We are not elaborating these points further here: we discuss some of them in [Fer12a].

Other varieties of security patterns include:

■ *Security design patterns.* The Open Group used the style of [Gam94] to build security patterns [Bla04]. They also included some availability patterns in their catalog.

■ A group at CERT took a more literal approach and built *secure design patterns* [Dou09], in which they added security to several of the patterns described in [Gam94].

■ Patterns for enterprise models to define global security concerns [Sch06b]. These patterns include Asset Valuation, Threat Assessment, Security Needs Identification and others. These patterns can be useful for security governance.

■ Some authors, for example [Ray04], consider patterns as parameterized templates or types that are instantiated in applications. The additional precision this provides reduces flexibility in applying the pattern.

■ Jackson's Problem Frames have been used as the basis for patterns for security requirements [Hat07].

- Security and Dependability (S&D) patterns describe implementations of specific security mechanisms, supported by a complete runtime framework [Gal09] [SER] [Spa09].

- Mouratidis uses Secure Tropos, an approach to support multiple views of security, including organizational and external aspects [Mou06] [SeT].

- *Security usability* patterns, patterns oriented to build good user interfaces for security [Mun09].

- [IBMb] describes five security patterns. They are very high-level and do not follow any standard template. They also define a simple methodology for their application.

- *Privacy* patterns: patterns to help users express their privacy concerns [Lob09] [Sad05]. These can be a useful complement to the patterns presented in this book.

- *Enterprise Security Patterns* (ESPs) [Mor12]. Chapter 3 discusses these in more detail.

- [Bas06] presents an approach to building secure systems in which designers specify system models along with their security requirements, and use tools to generate system architectures from the models automatically, including complete, configured access-control infrastructures. Their approach includes a combination of UML-based modeling languages with a security modeling language for formalizing access control requirements. They do not really use patterns, but their models are related to pattern models.

- Two security *antipatterns* are proposed by Kis [Kis02]. An antipattern indicates practices that should be avoided.

Having such variety can be confusing to potential users. Not all of these pattern varieties are mutually exclusive; some can be combined. For example, ESPs include the standard type of security patterns as components.

2.3   Pattern Descriptions and Catalogs

Patterns are usually described using a pattern *template* with predefined sections. This type of description permits systematic use of the pattern and provides a guideline for the pattern writer. The selection of template is an important issue, because it defines the type and characteristics of the information about the pattern. Patterns using ad hoc templates or no templates are difficult to incorporate into existing catalogs, and make the job of comparing and applying patterns much harder. In our patterns we use a template based on that of [Bus96], known as the POSA (Pattern Oriented Software Architecture) template. We show its use in describing a specific pattern below. Other templates used for security patterns include the 'Gang of Four' (GOF) template [Gam94], as used by the Open Group and some authors. That template is intended for design patterns, which are more code-oriented, and does not describe architectural aspects well. Some enhancements of security pattern templates have been proposed, which extend the GOF template with security aspects [Mor12] [Ysk06].

We have tried to provide a reasonable amount of information in our pattern descriptions, aimed at the needs of an application designer, although another audience could be product designers, for example designers of firewalls: our descriptions are probably insufficient for them, although they could be used as initial guidelines. Each pattern is described in an abstract form [Fer08a], independent of implementation details. For some patterns we also show concrete versions, for example for web services. The idea is that one should decide first, in the conceptual model, what security mechanisms are needed, then map them to concrete versions depending on the software choices. In one of our papers we define precise models for the templates that we use for our patterns [Was09]. We used those models to classify security patterns in [Was09] and [Van09].

Some authors describe patterns showing only their main idea, taking about half to one page and using only words. While such patterns may be useful for experienced designers to remind them of possibilities, they are not detailed or precise enough to fulfill the function of communicating experience and knowledge. We think that the solution section of the pattern should be expressed with enough detail and precision to allow a designer to use it. We prefer using an informal description with a diagram, followed by a UML class diagram to describe the information static structure, and several sequence diagrams describing the dynamics of the main use cases. CRC cards can be used to introduce the needed classes, but we don't see them as necessary. Other UML diagrams may be convenient in complex cases, such as state charts and activity diagrams.

Patterns solutions expressed in UML can be implemented readily in appropriate languages such as Java, Smalltalk, C++, XML or C#. Making a solution very precise or formal is against the spirit of patterns, which are suggestions rather than plug-in solutions: a pattern needs to be tailored to satisfy the requirements of the application. If a formal solution is used, it is hard to know if the tailoring has affected the model of the solution. When more formality is needed, we prefer to add OCL annotations to class diagrams [War03a].

2.4   The Anatomy of a Security Pattern

This section uses a Packet Filter Firewall [Sch06b] as an example; each pattern section is preceded by a description of its purpose.

Every pattern starts with a thumbnail – called an 'intent' by some authors – a description of the problem it solves, and optionally a brief description of how it solves the problem.

The Packet Filter Firewall filters incoming and outgoing network traffic in a computer system based on packet inspection at the IP level.

Example

We then give an example of a problem situation where use of this pattern may provide a solution.

Our system has been attacked recently by a variety of hackers, including somebody who penetrated our operating system and stole our clients' credit card numbers. Our employees are wasting time at work by looking at inappropriate sites in the Internet. If we continue like this we will be out of business soon.

Context

We define the context in which the pattern solution is applicable. We may explain relevant characteristics of this context.

Computer systems on a local network connected to the Internet and to other networks with different levels of trust. A host in a local network receives and sends traffic to other networks. This traffic has several layers or levels. The most basic level is the IP level, made up of packets consisting of headers and bodies (payloads). The headers include the source and destination addresses as well as other routing information; the bodies include the message payloads.

Problem

We follow the context with a generic description of what happens when we don't have a good solution. We also indicate the forces that affect the possible solution. (Here we show only a few forces.)

Some of the hosts in other networks may try to attack the local network through their IP-level payloads. These payloads may include viruses or application-specific attacks. We need to identify and block those hosts.

The solution to this problem must resolve the following forces:

- *We need to communicate with other networks, so isolating our network is not an option. However, we do not want to take on a high risk for doing so.*

- *Any protection mechanism should be transparent to the users. Users should not need to perform special actions to be secure.*

- *The cost and overhead of the protection mechanism should be relatively low or the system may become too expensive to run.*

- *The attacks are constantly changing, so it should be easy to make changes to the configuration of the protection mechanism.*

Solution

The solution section describes the idea of the pattern. A descriptive figure may help to visualize the solution.

A Packet Filter Firewall intercepts all traffic coming/going from a port P and inspects its packets (Figure 2.2). Those coming from or going to untrusted addresses are rejected. The untrusted addresses are determined from a set of rules that implement the security policies of the institution. A client from another network can only access the local host if a rule exists authorizing traffic from its address. Specific rules may indicate an address or a range of addresses. Rules may be positive (allow traffic from some address) or negative (block traffic from some address). Most commercial products order these rules for efficiency in checking. Additionally, if a request is not satisfied by any of the explicit rules, then a default rule is applied.

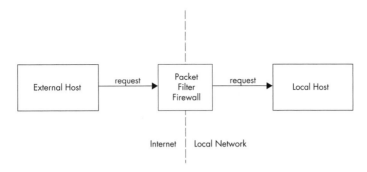

Figure 2.2: The idea of the packet filter firewall

Structure

We next describe the structure (static view) of the solution and some dynamic aspects in the form of sequence diagrams for a use case.

Figure 2.3 shows the class diagram for an external host requesting access to a local host (a server) through a Packet Filter Firewall (PFFirewall). The institution policies are embodied in the objects of class Rule collected by the rule base RuleBase. The rule base includes data structures and operations to manage rules in a convenient way. The rules in this set are ordered and can be explicit or default.

Dynamics

We describe the dynamic aspects of the Packet Filter Firewall using a sequence diagram for one of its use cases (Figure 2.4). There is a symmetrical use case, 'Filtering an outgoing request', which we omit for brevity. We also omit use cases for adding, removing or reordering rules because they are straightforward. (Some authors describe the use case scenario more informally; we also do this at times in this book.)

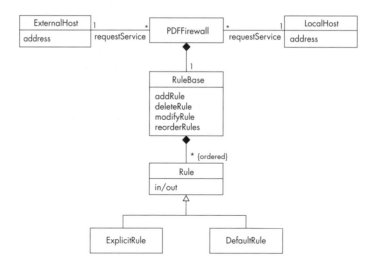

Figure 2.3: Class diagram for Packet Filter Firewall pattern

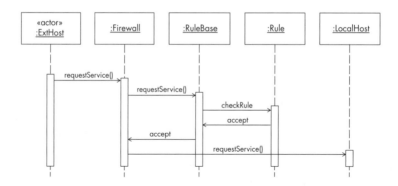

Figure 2.4: Sequence diagram for filtering a client's request

Use Case: *Filtering a Client's Request – Figure 2.4*

Actors   *A host in an external network (client).*

Precondition   *An existing set of rules to filter the request must be in place in the firewall.*

Description   *1   An external host requests access to the local host.*

                 2   A firewall filters the request according to a set of ordered rules. If none of the explicit rules in the rule set allows or denies the request, a default rule is used for making a decision.

3   If the request is accepted, the firewall allows access to the local host.

Alternate flow   The request is denied.

*Postcondition   The firewall has accepted the access of a trustworthy client to the local
host.*

Implementation

The objective of this section is to describe what one should consider when implementing
the pattern. This can be a set of general recommendations, or a sequence of what to do
to use the pattern. It may include some sample code, if appropriate. It is possible to add
details of how some products implement this pattern, for example how a particular firewall is implemented by a specific company.

1   *Define an institution policy about network access, classifying sites according to our
    trust in them.*

2   *Convert this policy into a set of access rules. This can be done manually, which may
    be complex for large systems. An alternative is using an appropriate commercial
    product.*

3   *Write the rules for each firewall. Products such as Solsoft and others automatically
    propagate the rules to each registered firewall.*

4   *Configure the corresponding firewalls according to standard architectures. A
    common deployment architecture is the Demilitarized Zone (DMZ) [Sch06b].*

Now we can see what happens in the example after the pattern solution has been applied.

Example Resolved

*We were able to trace the addresses of our attackers and we got a firewall to block requests
from those addresses from reaching our system. We also made a list of addresses of inappropriate sites and blocked access to them from the hosts in our network. All this reduced
the number of attacks and helped control the behavior of some of our employees.*

Consequences

The Consequences section indicates the benefits and liabilities of the solution embodied
in this pattern. The benefits should match the forces in the Problem section. Benefits that
do not correspond to any force may appear. For our example pattern a truncated list
might be as shown below.

The Packet Filter Firewall Pattern offers the following benefits:

■   *A firewall transparently filters all the traffic that passes through it, thus lowering the
    risk of communicating with potentially hostile networks.*

■   *It is easy to update the rule set to counter new threats.*

- *It is low cost, and is included as part of many operating systems and simple network devices such as routers.*

- *It offers good performance: it only needs to look at the headers of IP packets, not at the complete packet.*

The Packet Filter Firewall Pattern has the following (possible) liabilities:

- *The firewall's effectiveness and speed may be limited due to its rule set (order of precedence). Addition of new rules may interfere with existing rules in the rule set; so a careful approach should be taken to adding and updating access rules.*

- *The firewall can only enforce security policies on traffic that goes through the firewall. This means that one must make changes to the network to ensure that there are no other paths into its hosts.*

- *An IP-level firewall cannot stop attacks coming through the higher levels of the network. For example, a hacker could put malicious commands or data in header data not used for routing, and in the packet contents.*

Known Uses

To accept this solution as a pattern, we should find at least three examples of its use in real systems. We occasionally break this rule, for example when we see that the solution is clearly generic.

This model corresponds to an architecture that is seen in commercial firewall products, such as:

- *ARGuE (Advanced Research Guard for Experimentation), which is based on Network Associates' Gauntlet Firewall.*

- *OpenBSD Packet Filtering Firewall, which is the basic firewall architecture for the Berkeley Software Distribution system.*

- *The Linux Firewall, which is the basic firewall architecture used with the Linux operating system.*

- *The Packet Filter Firewall is also used as an underlying architecture for other types of firewalls that include more advanced features.*

See Also

Finally, we relate our pattern to other known patterns. Those may be complementary patterns, variations of our pattern or extensions of it.

The Authorization pattern [Fer01a] defines the standard security model for the Packet Filter Firewall pattern. This pattern is also a special case of the Single Access Point pattern [Sch06b], and it is the basis for other, more complex, types of firewalls. The DMZ pattern [Sch06b] defines a way to configure this pattern in a network. This pattern can also be combined with the Stateful Inspection Firewall [Sch06b].

We also include a Variants section if appropriate.

2.5 Pattern Diagrams

Figure 2.5 describes the relationships of the patterns described in Chapter 4 using a pattern diagram in which rounded rectangles represent patterns and arrows indicate the contribution of a pattern to another. For example, IDENTITY PROVIDER creates identities to be used by an IDENTITY FEDERATION[1].

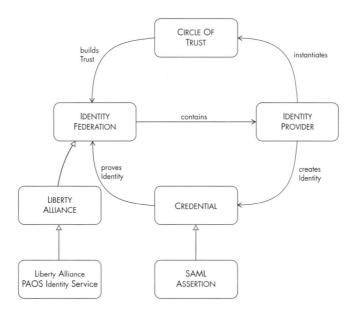

Figure 2.5: Pattern diagram for identity management patterns

This diagram is based on those used in [Bus96], but we have used UML generalization notation to indicate patterns that are specializations of other patterns; for example, SAML ASSERTION is a specialized type of CREDENTIAL. We believe that pattern diagrams offer very important help for designers to select which patterns to use at a given point [Fer06d]. This value was confirmed in the experiment described in [Ysk12]. Their use can be improved by illustrating with a tool that can display them at different stages of design [Fer06d].

2.6 How Can We Classify Security Patterns?

According to [Hey07a], in 2007 about 220 security patterns had been described, but the paper's authors considered only 55% of them to be core patterns. [Haf11] considered 96 patterns to be core patterns. It is not clear how many security patterns have been written,

---

[1] We use this uppercase notation, for example 'IDENTITY PROVIDER', to refer to patterns in this book.

because several are the same pattern with different names, or different patterns with the same name. Patterns can also be defined at different architectural levels, which may lead to several variants of the same pattern. We think of a computer system as a hierarchy of layers, in which the application layer uses the services of the database and operating system layers, which in turn execute on a hardware layer. In fact, this structure (Layers) is a pattern in itself [Bus96], and was reinterpreted as a security pattern in [Fer01a] and [Yod97].

[Avg05] classifies architectural patterns using the type of concerns they address, for example layered structure, data flow, adaptation, user interaction, distribution. We classified security patterns based on architectural levels and concerns [Fer08b]. For example, access control can be defined in the application and propagated to the database and to the operating system. Architecture levels and security concerns are two possible dimensions, both used in this book. Other classifications are discussed in [Haf06].

We refined the basic classifications through the use of a multi-dimensional matrix of concerns [Van09]. Each dimension of the matrix is a distinct list of concerns along a single axis, with a simple concept and a set of distinctions that define the categories. The categories along an axis or dimension should be easily understood and represent widely-used and accepted classifications related to that concept. For example, one dimension would correspond to lifecycle stages, covering domain analysis, requirements, problem analysis, design, implementation, integration, deployment (including configuration), operation, maintenance and disposal. The list of component source types forms another dimension. Types of security response could form yet a third dimension, covering avoidance, deterrence, prevention, detection, mitigation, recovery and investigation (*forensics*). Cells at the intersections of two or more dimensions represent a concern that is more specific than would be expressed by the list of classifications in any one dimension. For example, with two dimensions we can target security patterns for requirements when using COTS for outsourced components. Similarly, we can target security patterns for analysis and design with web services, and of those, more specifically, patterns that address detection or recovery.

Figure 2.6 illustrates a mapping of design patterns in two lifecycle phases and at different levels of architecture. Only a small sample of patterns is shown. While all of the patterns in the figure are applicable to Service Oriented Architecture, some apply more generally to other domains as well. We grouped the patterns within Design along a secondary dimension with Filtering, Access Control and Authentication. In the figure, we show patterns from the domain analysis phase, where the developer would find patterns that explain the domain standards and technologies later used in the design phase. A developer might also navigate to adjoining analysis phase cells (not shown) to look for general patterns on Filtering, Access Control and Authentication. While the patterns are found in these locations in the matrix, understanding their role in a system, and how they relate to one another, still requires a pattern language diagram and other tools and methods for pattern application.

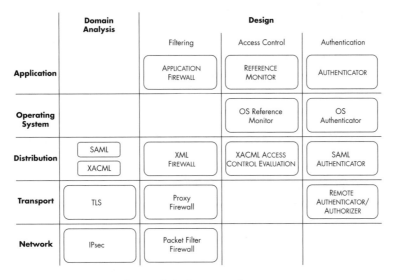

Figure 2.6: A matrix of patterns

The patterns presented in this book are grouped by concern, and within that, by the architectural level at which they would be used.

2.7   Pattern Mining

While applying security patterns in a design may not require a deep knowledge of security, mining security patterns does require such knowledge: you need to understand what mechanisms exist to prevent threats and need some abstraction capability to see the common aspects of such mechanisms. This is how we have found most of our patterns. Designers working on a project where security is an important issue, in addition to using security patterns from a catalog, should also be able to discover new patterns by abstracting recurrent security problems they may encounter.

Schumacher proposes digging into security standards, in particular in the Common Criteria [Sch01], to find patterns by observing the recommendations and approaches to evaluation of this standard. Another approach is to write patterns describing the main aspects of security standards. The justification for this is that standards define generic architectures and all implementations of the standard reflect it. We have produced a variety of standards of this type [Fer12c].

2.8   Uses for Security Patterns

The most common use for security patterns is to help application developers who are not security experts to add security in their designs. With the help of a good catalog and a tool for guidance, developers can select security pattern for a complex application. Other than ours, there are few methodologies that guide designers in selection of security patterns [Bla04] [Mou06].

A set of abstract security patterns can be a good description of the security requirements of a system [Che03] [Fer06c]. Requirements should not include any implementation details, and abstract patterns define the conceptual security needed without deciding about specific implementations.

Another important use is as guidelines for designers of security mechanisms to define the objectives or intended features of their products. For example, a designer of a new XML firewall can find the basic functions for such a device in the corresponding pattern, and use patterns describing security standards to define its support for them in the product.

Another use is in the evaluation of existing systems. This may be the most frequent application of security patterns in practice, when we need to reinforce a legacy system or need to evaluate a system we are acquiring.

Making complex standards understandable is another valuable use. We have distilled the essence of security standards for web services to make them much easier to understand than by reading the corresponding documents [Fer06a] [Fer12c] [Has09b]. We also showed how to use these patterns to simplify the standards for use in mobile devices [Del07c].

Finally, security patterns are a useful tool for teaching security concepts [Fer05a]. Security models and mechanisms must be described in a precise and systematic way. Our experience with formalizing complex access control models has shown that the resulting expressions are not intuitive, require mathematical sophistication, and make it difficult to describe structural properties of the system. On the other hand, UML models are quite intuitive and can conveniently describe structural properties. However, they are less precise than formal methods. We can therefore take a middle ground, integrating formal and informal techniques, describing our models using UML notation enhanced with constraints expressed in OCL.

In the same way that general architectural patterns can be used for recording architectural decisions, we can use security patterns to record decisions we have made about handling security requirements [Fer07e].

The use of patterns for traceability is just starting to be explored.

2.9   How to Evaluate Security Patterns and their Effect on Security

There has been little work on evaluating patterns. How can one define their quality? What makes a good pattern? Patterns are normally evaluated by submitting them to one of the pattern conferences, such as Pattern Languages of Programs (PLoP) or one of its variants, EuroPLoP, Latin American PLoP or Asian PLoP. In these conferences, a pattern paper is developed with the help of a 'shepherd' and then discussed in a workshop. The pattern is then published and exposed for criticism, the intention being to produce a better quality pattern. Of course, the ultimate evaluation comes when developers use such patterns in their designs and find they are useful in producing a robust system. But because security patterns have not been used extensively in practice, it is hard to use experience to evaluate them. [Ysk12] evaluated their use with a student experiment; they added annotations to the patterns to help in their selection and found this useful.

Formal modeling of patterns, combined with model checking, can prove some of the properties of a pattern's solution. Patterns are also evaluated for understandability, how well they fit the context of the problem, how easy it is to tailor them to the requirements and how reusable they are. In practice, the evaluation applies mostly to the solution, but other aspects are just as important. Any pattern that has gone through all these steps is believed to be of good quality: this conclusion applies to security patterns as well.

Halkidis et al. evaluated 13 patterns from the Open Group catalog [Bla04]. They used as criteria how well the patterns followed some principles and the threats they could handle [Hal06]. The quality of pattern documentation is an aspect considered by [Hey07a], which also uses coverage of concerns as a further quality factor. We think that factors such as how well a pattern implies security principles and its coverage of concerns are inherent aspects, while documentation is not related to quality of the pattern itself: a bad pattern cannot be improved, while a bad description can be redone easily [Uzu12a].

The evaluation of how patterns can improve security may be more useful. Security is a quality of system architectures and we need ways to evaluate the effect of patterns on improving this quality. But security is a quality for which there are no numerical measures. It can only be defined in a relative way with respect to another system, or by showing that a system satisfies some predefined security properties. In particular, we are developing a methodology for building secure systems based on adding security patterns along the lifecycle and in all the architectural layers of the system (described in Chapter 3).

Can we show that a system built in this way is secure in some sense? We have explored some issues about evaluating the security of a system built using security patterns [Fer10a]. As far as we know, none of the secure development methodologies [Uzu12c] analyzed the security of a complete system built using their approaches. Later, he evaluated the security risk of systems that used specific security patterns by seeing how well they handled a set of threats (the STRIDE set) [Hal08a].

Yskout et al tried to evaluate the use of patterns by an inventory [Ysk08] and by experiment [Ysk12]. Heyman tried to evaluate whether a pattern was instantiated properly during design and was working appropriately at run time [Hey07a]. [Bre08] used an enterprise metamodel to perform quantitative risk evaluation.

2.10   Threat Modeling and Misuse Patterns

To design a secure system, we first need to understand the possible threats to the system. Without this understanding we may produce a system that is more expensive than necessary and that has a large performance overhead. We have proposed a systematic approach to threat identification, starting from the analysis of the activities in the use cases of the system and postulating possible threats [Fer06c]. This method identifies high-level threats such as 'the customer can be an imposter', but once the system is designed. we need to see how the chosen components could be used by the attacker to reach their objectives.

The misuse pattern describes, from the point of view of the attacker, how a type of attack is performed (what units it uses and how), analyzes ways of stopping the attack by enumerating possible security patterns that can be applied for this purpose, and describes how to trace the attack once it has happened by appropriate collection and observation of forensic data. It also describes precisely the context in which the attack may occur. We have produced several misuse patterns, some of which are described in Chapter 14. Misuse patterns should not be confused with attack patterns [Hog04] [Whi01], which are specific actions to take advantage of a vulnerability, for example producing a buffer overflow. Okubo defined two other types of patterns with similar objectives [Oku11].

2.11   Fault Tolerance Patterns

Reliability and fault tolerance aim to control accidental errors, not intentional attacks. However, some of their aspects are common to security, and of course systems that need security very often also need reliability. We have produced a few patterns of this type [Buc09a] and we are writing a survey of them. We also combined some of them to produce Secure Reliability and Reliable Security patterns [Buc11]. We have not included any of these patterns in this book, but some catalogs of security patterns, such as [Bla04], include several of them.

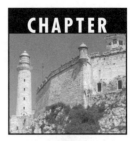

CHAPTER 3

A Secure Systems Development Methodology

By three methods we may learn wisdom: first, by reflection, which is noblest; second, by imitation, which is easiest; and third by experience, which is the bitterest.

Confucius

3.1   Adding Information to Patterns

A big problem for designers is to know where to apply the patterns. For an expert on security this aspect should not be a problem, but for a designer with little experience of security it can be a daunting task. Guiding the designer in the selection of patterns along the development lifecycle is very important in getting patterns accepted and used by developers.

As a possible approach to simplifying the use of patterns by designers, we can define extended patterns that include more information about their use:

■ *Secure semantic analysis patterns* (SSAPs). In this approach a SAP is made secure by adding security patterns after analyzing its use cases and its possible threats. A

SAP is a pattern combining a set of basic use cases [Fer00]. For example, we produced a set of secure functions for law firms [Fer07c]. The work described in [Rod07] is also related to this topic.

■ *Enterprise security patterns* (ESPs) [Mor12]. An enterprise security pattern combines a wide range of items describing generic enterprise security architectures that protect a set of information assets in a specific context. They are a more comprehensive type of pattern that can handle more threats, to facilitate the selection and tailoring of security policies, patterns, mechanisms and technologies for designers when building enterprise security architectures.

■ *Tags* [Ysk12]. Tags include the security objective, the pattern applicability, trade-off labels (impact on other concerns) and relationships between patterns.

Another approach is to define a complete methodology that guides the designer at each step. [Uzu12c] surveys the methodologies that have been proposed up to now. Any methodology should start from some basic principles, of which the two most important are:

■ Security constraints should be defined at the highest layer, where their semantics are clear, and propagated to the lower levels, which enforce them.

■ All the layers of the architecture must be secure.

These principles fit well with the 'security context', defined in [Sch03], a set of lifecycle phases and hierarchical layers.

3.2   A Lifecyle-Based Methodology

There is already consensus that security must be applied throughout the complete lifecycle: adding security at the end of the development lifecycle has been shown to be insufficient. This means that every methodology for building secure systems, using patterns or not, must consider all stages of the lifecycle. We understand the lifecycle to encompass the use of the platform, not just the application levels. Security depends on all levels and must be considered from the beginning. Our use of patterns is guided by these principles. We can define patterns at all levels, which allows a designer to ensure that all levels are secured, and also makes propagating high-level constraints to lower levels easier.

A better approach is extending a development process to incorporate security in all the stages of the lifecycle: this makes it more acceptable to practitioners. The most common lifecycle process approaches are the Rational Unified Process (RUP) and Agile methodologies [Bra10]. Both have several variants. We use the standard RUP as the basis for our approach.

A fundamental idea in our proposed methodology is that security principles must be applied at every development stage, and that each stage can be tested for compliance with those principles. Some approaches to object-oriented development already emphasize tests at every stage.

We first sketch a secure software development cycle that we consider effective for building secure systems, then we discuss each stage in detail. Figure 3.1 shows a secure software lifecycle. The white arrows show where security can be applied, while the black arrows show where we can audit compliance with security policies:

- From the requirements stage we generate secure use cases.
- From the analysis stage we generate authorization rules that apply to the conceptual model.
- From the design stage we enforce rules through the architecture.
- In the implementation, deployment and maintenance stages, language enforcement of the countermeasures and rules is required.

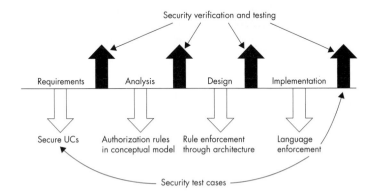

Figure 3.1: Secure software lifecycle

Security verification and testing occurs at every stage of development. We describe the details of each stage below.

- *Domain analysis stage*. Conceptual models to cover areas relevant to the type of applications we are building are defined. Legacy systems are identified and their security implications analyzed. General security or reliability constraints can be applied at this stage.
- *Requirements stage*. Use cases define the required interactions with the system. Applying the principle that security must start from the highest levels, it makes sense to relate attacks to use cases and develop what we call *secure use cases*. We study each action within a use case and see which attacks are possible [Fer06c], then determine which policies would stop these attacks. From the use cases we can also determine the required rights for each actor, and thus apply a need-to-know policy. Note that the set of all use cases defines all the uses of the system; from all the use cases we can determine all the rights for each actor. The security test cases for the complete system can also be defined at this stage. Risk analysis should also be applied at this stage.
- *Analysis stage*. Analysis patterns, and in particular semantic analysis patterns, can be used to build the conceptual model in a more reliable and efficient way [Fer00].

Security patterns describe security models or mechanisms. We can build a conceptual model in which repeated applications of a security pattern realize the rights determined from use cases. In fact, analysis patterns can be built with predefined authorizations according to the roles in their use cases. Then we only need to additionally specify the rights for those parts not covered by patterns. We can then start to define mechanisms (countermeasures) to prevent attacks.

■ *Design stage.* We express the abstract security patterns identified in the analysis stage in the design artifacts; for example interfaces, components, distribution and networking. Figure 3.2 shows some possible attacks to a system. Design mechanisms are selected to stop these attacks. User interfaces should correspond to use cases, and may be used to enforce the authorizations defined in the analysis stage. Secure interfaces enforce authorizations when users interact with the system. Components can be secured by using authorization rules for Java or .NET components.

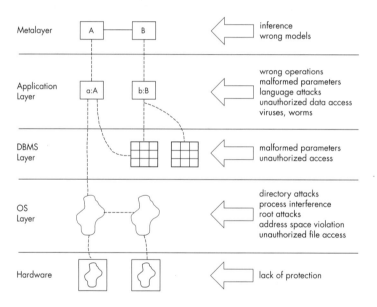

Figure 3.2: Typical attacks to the layers of a system

Distribution provides another dimension to which security restrictions can be applied. Deployment diagrams can define secure configurations to be used by security administrators. A multilayer architecture is needed to enforce the security constraints defined at the application level. In each level we use patterns to represent appropriate security mechanisms. Security constraints must be mapped between levels.

■ *Implementation stage.* This stage requires reflecting in the code the security rules defined in the design stage. Because these rules are expressed as classes, associations and constraints, they can be implemented as classes in object-oriented languages. In this stage we can also select specific security packages or COTS components, for example a firewall product or a cryptographic package.

■ *Deployment and maintenance stages.* Our methodology does not yet address issues in these stages. When the software is in use other security problems may be discovered by users. These problems can be handled by patching, although the amount of patching after applying our approach should be significantly smaller compared to current systems.

If necessary security constraints can be made more precise by using Object Constraint Language (OCL) [War03a] in place of textual constraints. Patterns for security models define the highest level of the architecture. At each lower level we apply the model patterns to specific mechanisms that enforce these models. In this way we can define patterns for file systems, web documents, J2EE components and so on. We can also evaluate new or existing systems using patterns. If a system doesn't contain an embodiment of a correct pattern, it cannot support the corresponding secure model or mechanism.

3.3   Using Model-Driven Engineering

Metamodels describe sets of related concepts that are instantiated together (maybe partially) as part of a methodology or procedure to design a system. The UML class diagrams that describe the solutions of patterns are metamodels that are instantiated to apply security, reliability or some other property to the functional aspects of an application. Metamodels are useful for understanding the security design process and in the implementation of model-driven engineering (MDE) approaches. Alternatives or complements could be the use of ontologies: an *ontology* is a logical theory making precise the intended meaning of a formal vocabulary. Ontologies have been used to organize repositories for security patterns [Dri05].

Figure 3.3 shows a metamodel connecting threats and failures to patterns [Fer11c]. In the diagram, a *threat* can be neutralized by a *security policy.* Similarly, a *failure* can be neutralized by a *reliability policy.* Policies may also include *regulations* and *institution policies.* Security and reliability policies are realized by security and reliability patterns, respectively. A *policy realization pattern* is a pattern that realizes any type of policy and consists of a few classes and associations. Security and reliability patterns are special cases of policy realization patterns.

We have done some work on MDE [Del08], but we need to use it more to make this methodology easier to use, by automating parts of it and adding appropriate tools. [Del08] proposed a metamodel to go from the analysis to a design model. [Ysk08] presented a set of transformations for specific security requirements: delegation of execution, authorization and auditing, using a metamodel tailored for these requirements. A sub-product of MDE is traceability; it now becomes easier to trace back the effect of changes in the code.

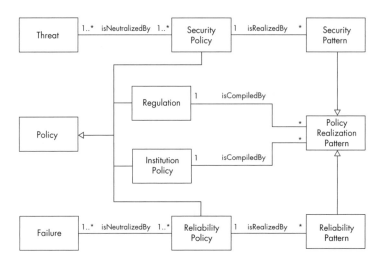

Figure 3.3: Metamodel for requirements and patterns

It is clearly fundamental to have some methodology for applying the patterns. We considered three approaches here:

- Adding more information to each pattern.
- A stage-by-stage approach applied to an existing lifecycle process.
- Model-driven engineering, in which we transform models from stage to stage following metamodels and rules.

Part II

Patterns

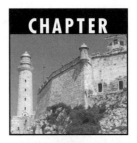

CHAPTER

4

Patterns for Identity Management

He allowed himself to be swayed by his conviction that human beings are not born once and for all on the day their mothers give birth to them, but that life obliges them over and over again to give birth to themselves.

Gabriel García Márquez, 'Love in the Time of Cholera'

'Who are you?' said the Caterpillar. Alice replied, rather shyly, 'I – I hardly know, Sir, just at present – at least I know who I was when I got up this morning, but I think I must have been changed several times since then'.

Lewis Carroll, 'Alice in Wonderland'

4.1   Introduction

The development of software has recently changed significantly. Applications are typically distributed and built from a variety of components, which are themselves developed ad hoc, bought or outsourced. The context for which these applications are intended has also evolved: users have become mobile and access applications from diverse devices that are more vulnerable to theft, eavesdropping or other attacks. In addition, with the ubiquity of computing, users may need to access a wider range of applications, which may not be known to them in advance. The increasing importance of web or cloud services is another important factor. So in many cases there is a need for dynamic trust establishment and identity exchange protocols, and whatever security model is used must support these aspects.

A user may not be known in advance by the resource manager at the time of the request, and consequently their identity may need to be transmitted to the resource's domain. Traditional models don't address the dynamic aspects of identity management. Furthermore, the channels of communication between the participating entities are much more vulnerable than for example in operating system design, or within the boundaries of an organization's computer network.

A decision to grant access must be based on the service's access control rules and the user's degree of trustworthiness. So far there is no accepted way to evaluate this degree of trustworthiness. One solution is to leverage the existing trust relationships between a user and the services that 'know' the user, and propagate identity information about the user to other services [Jos05]. A large amount of work has been done on the propagation of identity information [Bha05] [Mad05] [Rod]. In particular, web services standards have been published that deal with identity management and trust. However, currently web services standards tend to overlap, and how we can integrate them with other components to produce secure applications is not clear. Our patterns may contribute to making the implementation for trust simpler.

Figure 4.1 describes the relationships of the patterns described in this chapter, and associated patterns, using a pattern diagram. We use UML generalization to indicate patterns that are specializations of other patterns; for example, the SAML ASSERTION is a specialized type of CREDENTIAL. A *security domain* is a set of resources in which the administration of security is performed by a unique entity, which typically stores identity information about the subjects[1] of the domain:

- The IDENTITY PROVIDER pattern centralizes the administration of a security domain's users, creating and managing identities for their credentials.

- The CIRCLE OF TRUST pattern represents a federation of service providers that share trust relationships.

- The IDENTITY FEDERATION pattern allows the federation of multiple identities across multiple organizations under a common identity. In web services environ-

---

[1] A subject is an active system component that is able to request resources.

ments, this pattern relies on the SAML ASSERTION pattern, which provides a unifying format for communicating identity information between different security domains [Fer06d].

■ CREDENTIALs carry subjects' identities, and may also carry authorization and descriptive information for that subject.

■ The LIBERTY ALLIANCE IDENTITY FEDERATION pattern describes a specific architecture for an identity federation.

■ The Liberty Alliance PAOS Identity Service pattern further specializes that standard to apply it to wireless systems.

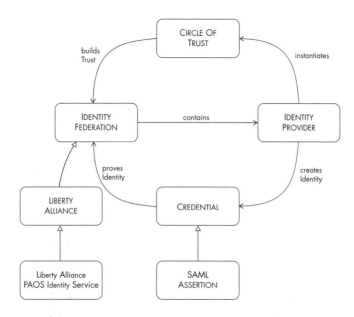

Figure 4.1: Pattern diagram for identity management

All these patterns are described in this chapter with the exception of CREDENTIAL (Chapter 5), SAML ASSERTION (Chapter 11) and Liberty Alliance PAOS Identity Service. The patterns in this chapter were published in [Del06] and [Fer06d]; Nelly Delessy and Maria M. Larrondo-Petrie were coauthors.

We consider CIRCLE OF TRUST, IDENTITY PROVIDER, IDENTITY FEDERATION and CREDENTIAL as *abstract patterns*, independent of any specific platform-oriented implementation (see Chapter 2 and [Fer08a]). LIBERTY ALLIANCE IDENTITY FEDERATION, Liberty Alliance PAOS Identity Service and SAML ASSERTION are concrete patterns that apply to web services. The CREDENTIAL pattern relates this diagram to the patterns in Chapter 5 (Authentication), where we describe how we use identities to validate the user access to a system.

4.2   Circle of Trust

The CIRCLE OF TRUST pattern allows the formation of trust relationships among service providers to allow their subjects to access an integrated and more secure environment.

Example

Our university had different ways to access different services. For each service, one needed a different protocol and to remember a different password. This was cumbersome and prone to error; it was also insecure, because people would write their multiple passwords on their office bulletin boards.

Context

Service providers that provide services to consumers (subjects) over large systems such as the Internet.

Problem

In such large open environments, subjects are typically registered (have accounts) with unrelated services. Subjects may have no relationships with many other services available in the open environment. It may be cumbersome for the subject to deal with multiple accounts, and it may not be secure to build new relationships with other services, since identity theft or violation of privacy can be performed by rogue services. How can we take advantage of relationships between service providers to avoid the inconvenience of multiple log-ins and to select trusted services?

The solution to this problem must resolve the following forces:

■ Service providers are numerous on public networks. It can be cumbersome, indeed impossible, for each service provider to define relations with every other provider.

■ The service providers' infrastructures for their subjects' login may be implemented using different technologies.

Solution

Each service provider establishes business relationships with a set of other service providers. These relationships are materialized by the existence of operational and possibly business agreements between services. Such relationships are trust relationships, since each service provider expects the other to behave according to the operating agreements. Therefore, a circle of trust is a set of service providers that have business and operational relationships with each other – that is, that trust each other. Operational agreements could include information about whether they can exchange information about their subjects, for example, and how and what type of information can be exchanged. Business agreements could describe how to offer cross-promotions to their subjects. Service providers need to agree on operational processes before their users can benefit from the seamless environment.

Structure

Figure 4.2 shows a UML class diagram with an OCL constraint describing the structure of the solution. A `CircleOfTrust` includes several `ServiceProviders`, who trust each other, as described by the OCL expression.

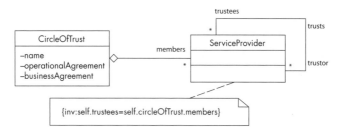

Figure 4.2: Class diagram for the CIRCLE OF TRUST pattern

Implementation

Operational agreements should include a means to concretely enable trust, such as the sharing of a secret key or the secure distribution of certificates. The providers have to exchange credentials through some kind of external channel to trust and recognize each other.

Example Resolved

Our university can now trust the identity providers who are members of our federation, so we do not have to worry that they will misuse our information.

Consequences

The CIRCLE OF TRUST pattern offers the following benefits:

- The subjects can interact more securely with (potentially unknown) trusted services from the circle of trust.
- The services can provide a seamless environment to the subjects, and can exchange information about their users by using operating agreements that describe what common technologies to use.

Liabilities include keeping the participants synchronized in the presence of changes.

Known Uses

- Identity federation systems and models such as the LIBERTY ALLIANCE IDENTITY FEDERATION standard (page 44).
- PayPal has a variety of partners that trust their payment system, including Verifone and Equinox [Pay].

See Also

- IDENTITY PROVIDER (below) and IDENTITY FEDERATION (page 38).
- LIBERTY ALLIANCE IDENTITY FEDERATION (page 44).
- [Niza10] formally discusses the CIRCLE OF TRUST.
- CREDENTIAL (page 62).

4.3   Identity Provider

The IDENTITY PROVIDER pattern allows the centralization of the administration of subjects' identity information for a security domain.

Example

Having applied the CIRCLE OF TRUST pattern, we can trust the identity providers who are members of our federation, but we still have a variety of identities.

Context

One or several resources, such as web services, CORBA services, applications and so on that are accessed by a predetermined set of subjects. The subjects and resources are typically from the same organization.

Problem

Each application or service may implement its own code for managing subjects' identity information, leading to an overloading of implementation and maintenance costs that may lead to inconsistencies across the organization's units.

Solution

The management of the subjects' information for an organization is centralized in an IDENTITY PROVIDER, which is responsible for storing and propagating parts of the subjects' information (that form their identity) to the applications and services that need it.

We define a security domain as the set of resources whose subjects' identities are managed by the IDENTITY PROVIDER. Typically, the IDENTITY PROVIDER issues a set of credentials to each subject that will be verified by the accessed resources. Notice that the security domain is a special kind of CIRCLE OF TRUST within an organization.

Structure

Figure 4.3 shows a UML class diagram describing the structure of the solution. This pattern combines the CIRCLE OF TRUST, making explicit its `Resources` and specializing `ServiceProvider` to the `IdentityProvider`. Subjects are identified using CREDENTIALs given by a specific identity provider.

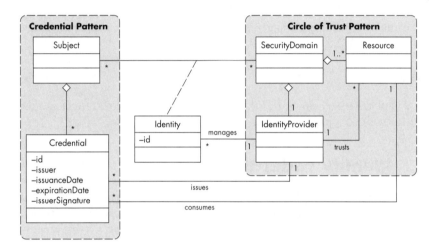

Figure 4.3: Class diagram for the IDENTITY PROVIDER pattern

Example Resolved

Now that we can trust the identity providers who are members of our federation and have a centralized identity managed by a specific identity provider, we do not need multiple identities.

Consequences

The IDENTITY PROVIDER pattern offers the following benefits:

- Maintenance costs are reduced
- The system is consistent in terms of its users

It also suffers from the following liability:

■ The IDENTITY PROVIDER can be a bottleneck in the organization's network.

Known Uses

■ Identity management products, such as IBM Tivoli [IBMc], Sun One Identity Server [SunC], Netegrity's SiteMinder and WSO2 [WSO].

■ SAP NetWeaver Identity Management [SAP] manages user access to applications by providing a central mechanism for provisioning users in accordance with their current business roles. It also supports related processes, such as password management, self-service and approvals workflow.

■ The Empower Identity Manager is oriented to cloud computing [emp]. These products use SAML 2.0 (Chapter 11).

See Also

IDENTITY FEDERATION (below) uses this pattern, as well as the CREDENTIAL (page 62) and CIRCLE OF TRUST (page 34) patterns.

4.4   Identity Federation

The IDENTITY FEDERATION pattern allows the formation of a dynamically created identity within an identity federation consisting of several service providers. Therefore, identity and security information about a subject can be transmitted in a transparent way for the user among service providers from different security domains.

Example

Having a centralized identity is not much good unless we can use it in many places. We need some structure to allow this behavior.

Context

We have several security domains in a distributed environment that trust each other. A security domain is a set of resources (web services, applications, CORBA services and so on) in which administration of security is performed by a unique entity, which typically stores identity information about the subjects known to the domain. Subjects can perform actions in one or more security domains.

Problem

There may be no relationship between some of the security domains accessed by a subject. Thus, subjects may have multiple unrelated identities within each security domain. Consequently, they may experience multiple and cumbersome registrations, authentications and other identity-related tasks prior to accessing the services they need.

How can we avoid the inconvenience of multiple registrations and authorizations across security domains? The solution to this problem must resolve the following forces:

- The identity of a user can be represented in a variety of ways in different domains.

- Parts of a subject's identity within a security domain may include sensitive information that should not be disclosed to other security domains.

- The identity and security-related information in transit between two security domains should be kept confidential, so that eavesdropping, tampering or identity theft cannot be realized.

- A subject may want to access a security domain's resources in an anonymous way.

Solution

Service providers, which are normally part of a security domain in which the local identity of subjects is managed by an identity provider, form identity federations by developing offline operating agreements with other service providers from other security domains. In particular, they can agree about their privacy policies.

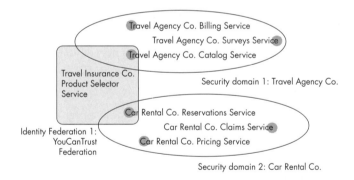

Figure 4.4: Federation and domains

In a security domain, the local identity associated with a user consists of a set of attributes. Some of those attributes can be marked as confidential and should not be passed to other security domains. A federated identity is created gradually and transparently by gathering some of a subject's attributes from its local identities within an identity federation. Therefore, identity and security information about a subject can be transmitted between service providers from the same identity federation transparently to the user. In particular, its authentication status can be propagated to perform single sign-on within the identity federation.

Figure 4.4 illustrates an example of how security domains and identity federations can coexist: a security domain is typically a circle of trust within an organization, whereas an identity federation is a circle of trust whose members can come from different organizations.

Structure

Figure 4.5 shows a UML class diagram with an OCL constraint describing the structure of the solution. An `IdentityFederation` consists of a set of `ServiceProviders` which provide services to `Subjects`. A `Subject` has multiple `LocalIdentities` with some `ServiceProviders`. A `LocalIdentity` can be described as a set of `Attributes` of the `Subject`.

A `Subject` can have several `FederatedIdentities`. This `FederatedIdentity` is composed of a union of attributes from the `LocalIdentities` of the `IdentityFederation`. An `IdentityProvider` is responsible for managing the `LocalIdentities` within a `SecurityDomain`, and can authenticate any `Subjects` on behalf of any `ServiceProvider` of the `IdentityFederation`. A `Subject` has been issued a set of `Credentials` that collect information about its authentication status and its identity within a `SecurityDomain`.

Dynamics

We illustrate the dynamic aspects of the IDENTITY FEDERATION pattern by showing sequence diagrams for two use cases: 'Federate two local identities' (Figure 4.6) and 'Single sign on' (Figure 4.7). The first use case describes how a local entity invites another to join, and their mutual authentication. The second use case shows how a subject, after receiving a credential from an identity provider, uses it to access a new domain.

Implementation

The identity federation can be structured hierarchically or in a peer-to-peer manner. The most basic federation could be based on bilateral agreements between two service providers. In the LIBERTY ALLIANCE IDENTITY FEDERATION pattern (page 44), an `Identity-Federation` has an `IdentityProvider` responsible for managing the federated identity, whereas Shibboleth [Shi] defines a *club* as a set of service providers that has reached some operating agreements.

In the LIBERTY ALLIANCE IDENTITY FEDERATION model, the identity provider proposes incentives for other service providers to affiliate with them and federate their local identities. Furthermore, no attribute can be classified as private: privacy is achieved by letting the user provide their consent each time its identity is federated.

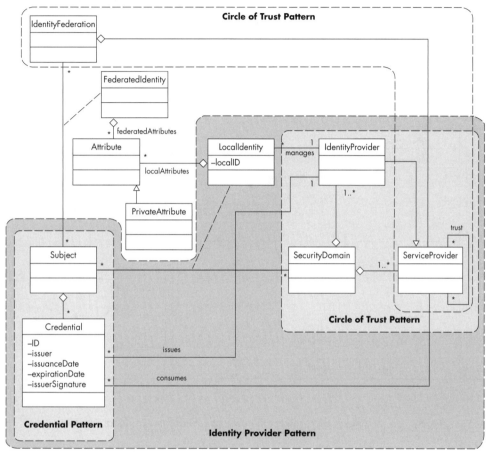

context FederatedIdentity
inv: forall(p | self.federatedAttributes -> includes(p) **implies**
        self.subject.localIdentity.localAttributes -> includes(p))
inv: self.federatedAttributes -> excludes(
        self.subject.localIdentity.localAttributes.oclAsType)
        PrivateAttribute))

Figure 4.5: Class diagram for the IDENTITY FEDERATION pattern

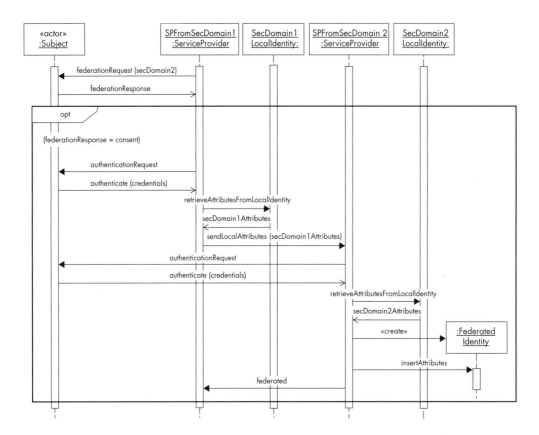

Figure 4.6: Sequence diagram for the use case 'Federate two local identities'

Example Resolved

Having implemented an IDENTITY FEDERATION, we can visit different services using the same identity for all of them.

Consequences

The IDENTITY FEDERATION pattern offers the following benefits:

■ Subjects can access resources within the identity federation in a seamless and secure way without reauthenticating in each new domain.

■ Many different representations of the identity of a user can be consolidated under the same federated identity.

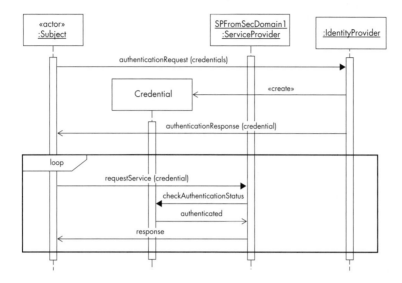

Figure 4.7: Sequence diagram for the use case 'Single sign on'

- Subjects can classify some of their attributes as private. Therefore, an identity provider can identify which attributes it should transmit to other parties and which it should not.

- Parts of the security credentials issued about a subject can be encrypted, so that the subject's privacy can be protected.

- The security credential can be signed, so that its integrity and authenticity is protected and attackers cannot forge security tokens or change some of the subject's attributes.

- A subject can access a security domain's resources in an anonymous way, since not all attributes from a local identity (such as a name) are required to be federated.

The pattern also has some potential liabilities:

- Service providers need to have some kind of agreement before their identities can be federated. They have to exchange credentials through some external channel to trust and recognize each other.

- Even when a subject's sensitive information is classified as private, a security domain can still disclose the subject's private information secretly to other parties, thus violating the subject's privacy.

- A security token can be stolen and presented by an attacker, resulting in identity theft. This is alleviated by the use of expiration dates and unique IDs for credentials.

- In spite of an expiration date and the unique ID feature of a credential, which guarantees its freshness, the unconditional revocation of a credential is not addressed in this solution.

Known Uses

- WS-Federation [Aja13] is a proposed standard allowing web services to federate their identities.
- Liberty Alliance is a standard that allows services to federate into Identity Federations [Liba].
- Microsoft Account (previously Microsoft Wallet, Microsoft Passport, .NET Passport, Microsoft Passport Network and Windows Live ID) is an identity federation that lets users log in to a variety of web sites using only one account [MAJ].
- Shibboleth is an open solution for realizing identity federation among enterprises [Shi].

See Also

- LIBERTY ALLIANCE IDENTITY FEDERATION (below) is a specialization of this pattern.
- CREDENTIAL (page 62).
- A Single Sign On pattern is shown in [Ste05].
- A formal description of identity management patterns is given in [Niza10].

4.5   Liberty Alliance Identity Federation

The LIBERTY ALLIANCE IDENTITY FEDERATION pattern allows merging of identities across multiple organizations under a federated identity and following a common set of rules.

Example

Now that we have centralized identities, we can use them in different places. However, our federation uses a variety of providers, following different standards, and sometimes it is complex to visit some places. We would like to simplify this sharing of resources.

Context

Service providers, such as financial institutions, entertainment companies, Internet portals and so on, that offer services to users. A user typically has accounts with several service providers. Those providers manage a set of attributes of the user, such as a name, date of birth, social security number, preferences and others, that constitute the user's identity. Web services have identities that can be used to access other services.

Problem

There may not be any relationship between service providers, thus users may have multiple unrelated accounts. Consequently, they may experience multiple and cumbersome registrations, authentications and other identity-related tasks prior to accessing the services they need on the Internet.

How can we leverage a federated identity of a user on the Internet? The solution to this problem is affected by the forces of IDENTITY FEDERATION (page 39), and by the following additional forces:

- The identity of a user can be represented in a variety of ways by different services.
- Parts of the user's information may need to be kept confidential and not shown to some service providers.

Solution

Service providers manage local accounts for their clients. They form identity federations by developing offline operating agreements. Among those service providers comprising an identity federation, at least one acts as an identity provider, which is responsible for managing a federated identity. A federated identity is the composite of several local identities. Therefore, identity information about a user or service can be transmitted between service providers in a way that is transparent to the subjects. In particular, their authentication status can be propagated to perform single sign-on within the identity federation. The subject has to provide their consent so that each of their local identities can be federated.

Structure

Figure 4.8 illustrates the solution. An `IdentityFederation` consists of a set of `ServiceProviders` which provide services to `Subjects`. At least one of the `ServiceProviders` acts as the `IdentityProvider`, with which other `ServiceProviders` affiliate. A `Subject` has multiple `LocalIdentities` with some `ServiceProviders`. A `LocalIdentity` can be described as a set of `Attributes` of the `Subject`.

This `Subject` can have several `FederatedIdentities`. Each `FederatedIdentity` is composed of several `LocalIdentities`. The `IdentityProvider` is responsible for managing the `FederatedIdentities`, and can authenticate any `Subject` on behalf of any `ServiceProvider` of the `IdentityFederation`. A `Subject` has a set of `SAMLAuthenticationAssertions` (Chapter 11) that collect information about its authentication status with a `ServiceProvider`.

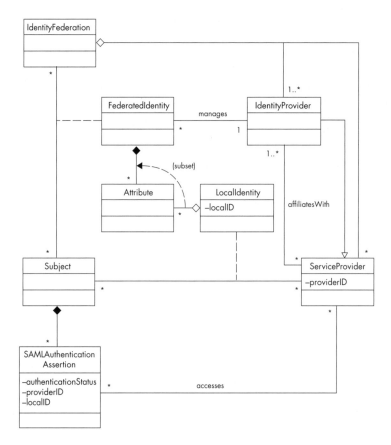

Figure 4.8: Class diagram for the LIBERTY ALLIANCE IDENTITY FEDERATION pattern

Dynamics

We illustrate the dynamic aspects of the LIBERTY ALLIANCE IDENTITY FEDERATION pattern with sequence diagrams for two use cases: 'Federate two local identities' and 'Single sign on'.

Use Case: Federate Two Local Identities – Figure 4.9

Summary   A Subject accesses a ServiceProvider and is asked to allow the federation of its local identities between this ServiceProvider and one of the IdentityProvider.

Actors   Subject, ServiceProvider, IdentityProvider.

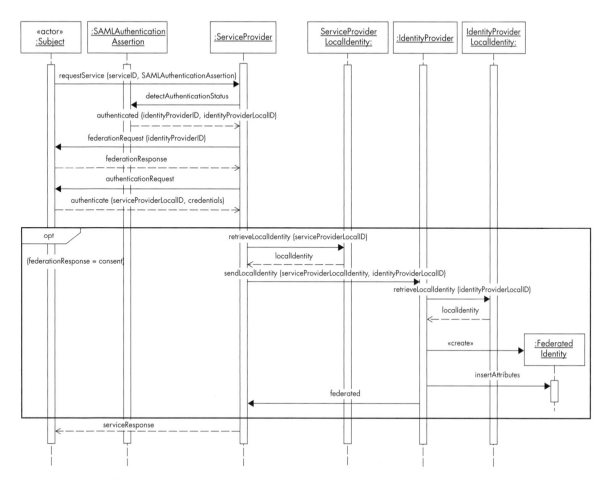

Figure 4.9: Sequence diagram for the use case 'Federate two local identities'

Preconditions   The IdentityProvider and the ServiceProvider are parts of a common identity federation. The Subject has previously agreed to let the IdentityProvider manage its federated identity. The Subject has been authenticated with the IdentityProvider, which has issued a SAMLAuthenticationAssertion.

Description   1   A Subject sends a request to a ServiceProvider.

2   The ServiceProvider accesses the SAMLAuthenticationAssertion previously created by the IdentityProvider, detects that the Subject has been authenticated with the IdentityProvider, and retrieves its IdentityProviderLocalID.

3   The ServiceProvider requests its consent for federating the two local identities of the Subject.

4   The Subject consents to federate these local identities, and is requested to authenticate with the ServiceProvider using its local identity.

5   The ServiceProvider is now able to retrieve the Subject's local identity.

6   The ServiceProvider transmits this identity to the IdentityProvider along with the IdentityProviderLocalID for the Subject.

7   The IdentityProvider retrieves the identity corresponding to the IdentityProviderLocalID.

8   The IdentityProvider creates a FederatedIdentity and inserts the attributes from both the retrieved LocalIdentity and the Identity received from the ServiceProvider.

9   The ServiceProvider transmits its response to the Subject.

Alternate flows   If the Subject does not consent to federate the two identities, the user authenticates with the ServiceProvider as usual and no identity information is exchanged.

Postcondition   A FederatedIdentity, that is the union of the attributes from the two identities, has been created.

Use Case: Single Sign On – Figure 4.10

Summary   A Subject requests access to a ServiceProvider. If the Subject has not been authenticated by an IdentityProvider that is trusted by the ServiceProvider, the ServiceProvider redirects the request to an IdentityProvider that can authenticate the Subject and redirect it to the ServiceProvider.

Actors   Subject, ServiceProvider, IdentityProvider.

Precondition   The Subject has previously established identity federation between the IdentityProvider and the ServiceProvider.

Description   1   A Subject sends a request to a ServiceProvider.

2   The ServiceProvider checks if any SAMLAuthenticationAssertions have been previously created by an IdentityProvider that it trusts.

3   If the Subject has not been authenticated yet, the ServiceProvider redirects the Subject towards IdentityProviders that it trusts, so that the Subject can authenticate itself.

4   The Subject chooses an IdentityProvider and authenticates itself.

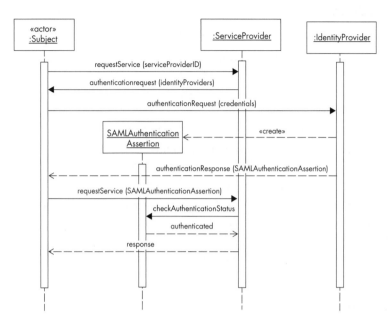

Figure 4.10: Sequence diagram for the use case 'Single sign on'

5   The `IdentityProvider` creates and transfers the `Subject`'s `SAMLAuthenticationAssertion` in an authentication response.

6   The `Subject` transparently resends a request to the `ServiceProvider`, this time including its `SAMLAuthenticationAssertion`.

7   The `ServiceProvider` can verify that the `Subject` has been authenticated and sends its response back to the `Subject`.

Postcondition   The access to the service offered by the `ServiceProvider` has been controlled based on the identity provided by the `IdentityProvider`. If the `Subject` has already been authenticated by the `IdentityProvider`, it does not need to reauthenticate.

Example Resolved

We decided to join the Liberty Alliance Federation. Now all our services are uniform and can be accessed with the same credentials.

Consequences

The LIBERTY ALLIANCE IDENTITY FEDERATION pattern offers the following benefits:

■ Subjects can perform transactions within the identity federation in a seamless and secure way.

■ Many different representations of the identity of a user can be consolidated under the same federated identity.

■ There is no need to reauthenticate in each new domain.

■ Subjects can control whether or not a local identity can be federated. Thus parts of the user's information may be kept confidential.

The pattern also has the following liabilities:

■ Service providers need to have some kind of agreement before their accounts can be federated. They have to exchange credentials through some external channel to be able to trust and recognize each other.

■ Both the subjects and the service providers from the identity federation need to trust the identity provider.

Known Uses

■ Nokia provides a framework for wireless web services based on the LIBERTY ALLIANCE IDENTITY FEDERATION pattern (Nokia web services framework).

■ Several vendors use the LIBERTY ALLIANCE IDENTITY FEDERATION pattern in their access management products: IBM Tivoli Federated Identity Manager [IBMc], Sun Java System Access Manager [SunC].

See Also

■ SAML ASSERTION (page 279) is the fundamental building block for implementing the LIBERTY ALLIANCE IDENTITY FEDERATION pattern [Liba].

■ The AUTHENTICATOR pattern (page 52) is used between the subject and the Identity Provider [Sch06b].

CHAPTER

5

Patterns for Authentication

This above all; to thine own self be true, and it must follow, as the night the day, thou canst not then be false to any man.

William Shakespeare, 'Hamlet'

5.1　Introduction

The previous chapter discussed how users are identified in a system. Before they can perform any activities, both users and other systems must identify themselves and be authenticated – that is, prove to the system that they are who they say they are.

Identification and authentication (I&A) uses some kind of protocol to establish identity. I&A is the basis for authorization and for logging: it provides *accountability*. Once identity is verified, the system may provide a proof of authentication to avoid further authentications.

Figure 5.1 shows how the patterns described in this chapter are interrelated. Once a subject (a user or a system) has identified themselves to the system, we need to verify that their identity is correct. This is the function of the authentication function. AUTHENTICATOR is an abstract pattern, and we show here two concrete versions: REMOTE AUTHENTICATOR/AUTHORIZER and CREDENTIAL. CREDENTIALs may have also authorization properties, discussed later. In distributed systems where users may have access to several systems a Single Sign On service is very convenient[1]. REMOTE AUTHENTICATOR/AUTHORIZER and CREDENTIAL have dual purposes; they can also be used for authorization if they include user rights. Chapter 6 describes how to let users access specific resources once they have been authenticated.

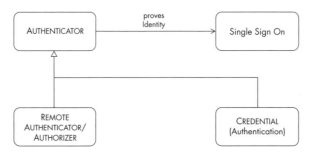

Figure 5.1: Relationships between the patterns in this chapter

AUTHENTICATOR was first published in [Fer03b] and is joint work with John Sinibaldi. Remote Authenticator was first described in [War03a], and was written with Reghu Warrier. CREDENTIAL is joint work with Patrick Morrison [Mor06a].

5.2   Authenticator

When a subject identifies itself to the system, the AUTHENTICATOR pattern allows verification that the subject intending to access the system is who or what it claims to be.

Example

The computer system at Melmac State University has legitimate users who use it to host their files. However, there is no way to ensure that a user who is logged in is a legitimate user. When Melmac was a small school and everybody knew everybody, this was acceptable and convenient. Now the school is bigger and there are many students, faculty members and employees who use the system. Some incidents have occurred in which users impersonated others and gained illegal access to their files.

---

[1] We show this pattern as a variant of AUTHENTICATOR.

Context

Computer systems that contain resources that may be valuable because they include information about business plans, user medical records and so on. We only want subjects that have some reason to gain access to our system to be able to do so.

Problem

How can we prevent imposters from accessing our system? A malicious attacker could try to impersonate a legitimate user to gain access to their resources. This could be particularly serious if the user impersonated has a high level of privilege. How do we verify that a user intending to access the system is legitimate?

The solution to this problem must resolve the following forces:

- *Flexibility.* A variety of users require access to the system and a variety of system units exist with differently sensitive assets. We need to be able to handle all this variety appropriately, or we risk security exposures.

- *Dependability.* We need to authenticate users in a reliable and secure way. This means using a robust protocol and a way to protect the results of authentication. Otherwise, users may skip authentication, or illegally modify its results, exposing the system to security violations.

- *Cost.* There are trade-offs between security and cost: more secure systems are usually more expensive.

- *Performance.* If authentication needs to be performed frequently, performance may become an issue.

- *Frequency.* We should not make subjects authenticate frequently.

Solution

Use a single point of access to receive the interactions of a subject with the system and apply a protocol to verify the identity of the subject. The protocol used may be simple or complex, depending on the needs of the application.

Structure

Figure 5.2 shows the class diagram for this pattern. A `Subject` requests access to the system. The `Authenticator` receives this request and applies a protocol using some `AuthenticationInformation`. If the authentication is successful, the `Authenticator` creates a `ProofOfIdentity`, which is assigned to the subject to indicate that they are legitimate.

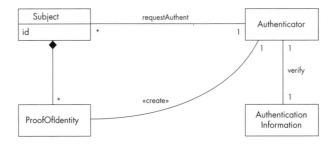

Figure 5.2: Class diagram for the AUTHENTICATOR pattern

Dynamics

Figure 5.3 shows the dynamics of the authentication process. A subject `User` requests access to the system through the `Authenticator`. The `Authenticator` applies some authentication protocol, for example by verifying some information presented by the subject, and as a result a `ProofOfIdentity` is created and assigned to the subject.

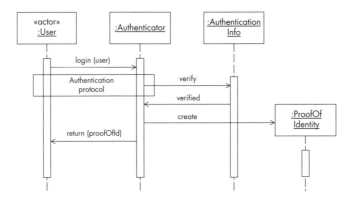

Figure 5.3: Sequence diagram for the use case 'Authenticate subject'

Implementation

In centralized systems, the operating system controls the creation of a session in response to the request by a subject, typically a user. The authenticated user (represented by processes running on their behalf) is then allowed to access resources according to their rights.

Some database systems have their own authentication systems, even when running on top of an operating system. There are many ways to implement authentication protocols, described in specific authentication patterns, for example in REMOTE AUTHENTICATOR/ AUTHORIZER (page 56). Sensitive resource access, for example data in financial systems, requires more elaborate process authentication than systems that handle lower-value assets. Distributed systems may implement this function in specialized servers.

Patterns for selecting authentication approaches are described in [Sch06b].

Example Resolved

Melmac State University implemented an authentication system and now only legitimate users can access their system. Illegal access to files has stopped.

Consequences

The AUTHENTICATOR pattern offers the following benefits:

- *Flexibility.* Depending on the protocol and the authentication information used, we can handle any types of users and we can authenticate them in diverse ways.
- *Dependability.* Since the authentication information is separated, we can store it in a protected area, to which all subjects may have at most read-only access.
- *Cost.* We can use a variety of algorithms and protocols of different strength for authentication. The selection depends on the security and cost trade-offs. Three varieties include something the user knows (passwords), something the user has (ID cards), or something the user is (biometrics).
- Authentication can be performed in centralized or distributed environments.
- *Performance.* We can produce a proof of identity to be used in lieu of further authentication. This improves performance.
- *Frequency.* Using a token means that we do not need to authenticate users.

The pattern also has the following potential liabilities:

- The authentication process takes some time: the overhead depends on the protocol used.
- The general complexity and cost of the system increase with the level of security.
- If the protocol is complex, users waste time and get annoyed.

Variants

Single Sign On. Single Sign On (SSO) is a process whereby a subject verifies their identity and the results of this verification can be used across several domains and for a given amount of time [Kin01]. The result of the authentication is an authentication token, used to qualify all future accesses by the user.

Known Uses

- Commercial operating systems use some form of authentication, typically passwords, to authenticate their users.

- RADIUS (Remote Authentication Dial-In User Service) provides a centralized authentication service for network and distributed systems [Gar02] [Has02] – see REMOTE AUTHENTICATOR/AUTHORIZER below.

- The SSL authentication protocol uses a PKI arrangement for authentication (Chapter 10).

- SAML, a web services standard for security, defines one of its main uses as a way to implement authentication in web services (Chapter 11).

- E-commerce sites such as eBay and Amazon.

See Also

- Distributed Authenticator [Bro99] discusses an approach to authentication in distributed systems.

- The Distributed Filtering and Access Control framework includes authentication [Hay00].

- REMOTE AUTHENTICATOR/AUTHORIZER (see below) provides facilities for authentication and authorization when accessing shared resources in a loosely-coupled distributed system.

- CREDENTIAL (page 62) provides a secure means of recording authentication and authorization information for use in distributed systems.

- Single Access Point and Check Point. See [Sch06b] [Yod97].

5.3   Remote Authenticator/Authorizer

The REMOTE AUTHENTICATOR/AUTHORIZER pattern provides facilities for authentication and authorization when accessing shared resources in a loosely-coupled distributed system.

Example

A multinational corporation may have employees in more than one country, say in the US and Brazil. The user authentication and authorization information necessary to support an employee in the US is stored in the US servers and the information to support that of a Brazilian employee is stored in the Brazil servers. Now assume that an employee from the US is traveling to Brazil and has the need to access some data from the Brazilian database servers.

There are two possible ways to achieve this:

■ Replicate the user information of the employee in the Brazilian server and give them the proper authorizations to access the data.

■ Borrow the user name of an employee in Brazil who has similar rights and use that to access the required information.

Neither of these solutions are satisfactory. The system administrators will be faced with creating and managing coordinated access to user accounts within each of the multiple systems, to maintain the consistency of the security policy enforcement. If the username of another employee is borrowed, accountability is compromised.

Context

Loosely-coupled distributed systems such as the Internet that consist of a variety of computational nodes, and in which some nodes need to share resources. For example, a company with several divisions in different countries.

Problem

A system with centralized authentication is easier to manage and potentially more secure, but it is not flexible enough for distributed systems. How can we provide authentication and authorization in a distributed environment without the need for redundant storage of rights?

The solution to this problem must resolve the following forces:

■ *Non-redundancy.* Storing user authentication and authorization information at multiple locations makes it redundant, difficult to administer and prone to inconsistencies.

■ *Rights transparency.* Although authentication information may be stored anywhere, this location should be transparent to users.

■ *Rights consistency.* Users typically work in the context of some role, and these roles should be standard across a variety of domains, at least within a company or institution.

■ *Accountability.* We need a way to keep users accountable when they are accessing remote resources.

Solution

Set up a single entry point that can transparently redirect the user to the correct server where their user login and access information can be validated.

We can achieve this redirection by using a specialized authentication/authorization server. This server is used for embedded network devices such as routers, modem servers, switches and so on. The authentication servers are responsible for receiving user connection requests, authenticating the user, then returning all configuration information necessary for the client to deliver service to the user.

Structure

Figure 5.4 shows this approach. The `Client` makes a request for a service through a `ProxyAuthenticator/Authorizer` that represents the actual server that contains the user login information. The request is routed to the `Authenticator/Authorizer`, which validates it, based on the role of the subject of the request and the rights of this role with respect to the protection object[1].

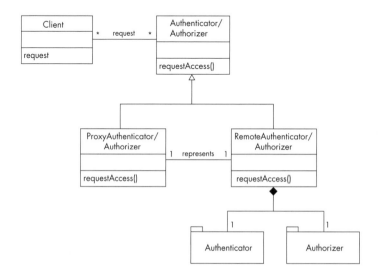

Figure 5.4: Class diagram for the REMOTE AUTHENTICATOR/AUTHORIZER pattern

Dynamics

Typical systems use the following types of messages:

- *Access-request*. Sent by a client to request authentication and authorization for a network access connection attempt.

- *Access-accept*. Sent by a server in response to an access-request message. This message informs the client that the connection attempt is authenticated and authorized.

- *Access-reject*. Sent by a server in response to an access-request message. This message informs the client that the connection attempt is rejected. A server sends this message if either the credentials are not authentic or the connection attempt is not authorized.

---

[1] *Protection object* refers to the object (data item or other resource) being requested by the user.

- *Access-challenge.* Sent by a server in response to an access-request message. This message is a challenge to the client that requires a response.

- *Accounting-request.* Sent by a client to specify accounting information for a connection that was accepted.

- *Accounting-response.* Sent by the server in response to the accounting-request message. This message acknowledges the successful receipt and processing of the accounting-request message.

A message consists of a header and attributes. Each attribute specifies a piece of information about the connection attempt. The scenario of Figure 5.5 illustrates a proxy-based communication between a client and the forwarding and remote servers:

1   A client sends its access-request to the forwarding server.

2   The forwarding server forwards the access-request to the remote server.

3   The remote server sends an access-challenge back to the forwarding server.

4   The forwarding server sends the access-challenge to the client.

5   The client calculates a response for the challenge and forwards it to the forwarding server via a second access-request.

6   The forwarding server forwards the access-request to the remote server.

7   If the response matches the expected response, the remote server replies with an access-accept, otherwise an access-reject.

8   The forwarding server sends the access-accept to the client.

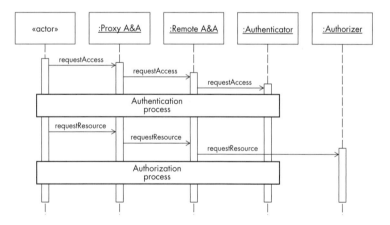

Figure 5.5: Sequence diagram for client authentication

Implementation

For this approach to work:

- Roles and access rights have to be standard across locations.
- Both servers and clients should support the base protocol.

Authorization functions are discussed in Chapter 6: we consider here only authentication aspects. An authentication server can function as both a forwarding server and a remote server, serving as a forwarding server for some realms and a remote server for others. One forwarding server can act as a forwarder for any number of remote servers. A remote server can have any number of servers forwarding to it and can provide authentication for any number of realms. One forwarding server can forward to another forwarding server to create a chain of proxies. A lookup service is necessary to find the remote server.

Figure 5.6 shows an example of a remote authentication dial-in user service (RADIUS) system using a challenge-response approach. (More details of the RADIUS system are shown in the next section.)

Example Resolved

When the US employee travels to Brazil he logs in a remote authenticator/authorizer, which reroutes his request to the US server that stores their login information.

Consequences

The REMOTE AUTHENTICATOR/AUTHORIZER pattern offers the following benefits:

- Roaming permits two or more administrative entities to allow each other's users to dial in to either entity's network for service.
- Storing the user login and access rights at a single location makes it more secure and easy to maintain.
- The user's login ID, password and other details are stored in the internal RADIUS database, or can be accessed from an SQL database.
- The location where the user information is stored is transparent to the user.
- Devices such as active cards [ACS] allow complex request/challenge interactions.

The pattern also has some potential liabilities:

- The additional messages needed increase overhead, thus reducing performance for simple requests. This is not a problem if remote accesses are not very frequent.
- The system is more complex than a system that directly validates clients.

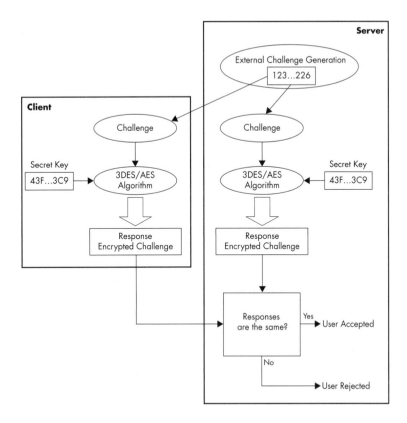

Figure 5.6: RADIUS challenge/response authentication

Known Uses

RADIUS is a widely deployed IETF protocol enabling centralized authentication, authorization and accounting for network access [Has02] [Rig00]. Originally developed for dial-up remote access, RADIUS is now supported by virtual private network (VPN) servers, wireless access points, authenticating Ethernet switches, digital subscriber line (DSL) access and other network access types [Hil].

With proxy RADIUS, one RADIUS server receives an authentication (or accounting) request from a RADIUS client such as a network-attached storage (NAS) system, forwards the request to a remote RADIUS server, receives the reply from the remote server, and sends that reply to the client. A common use for proxy RADIUS is roaming. Roaming permits two or more administrative entities to allow each other's users to dial in to either entity's network for service.

There are many commercially available RADIUS servers in use today. These include:

- *FreeRADIUS*. FreeRADIUS Server [Frea] is a daemon for UNIX operating systems that allows one to set up a RADIUS protocol server, which is usually used for authentication and accounting of dial-up users. FreeRADIUS is an open source product, and has all the benefits open source provides.

- *Steel-Belted Radius*. Steel-Belted Radius is a complete implementation of RADIUS. It provides full user authentication, authorization and accounting capabilities.

  Steel-Belted Radius fully supports proxy RADIUS; it can:

  - Forward proxy RADIUS requests to other RADIUS servers.

  - Act as a target server that processes requests from other RADIUS servers.

  - Pass accounting information to a target server, either to the one performing the authentication or a different one.

- *NavisRadius*. NavisRadius is an implementation of the RFC standard RADIUS protocol that provides authentication, authorization and accounting (AAA) services. NavisRadius provides an integrated network-wide remote access security solution for service providers and carriers. NavisRadius supports the RADIUS standard as defined by the IETF RADIUS RFC 2865 (RADIUS authentication) and 2866 (RADIUS accounting), and is used to provision a wide range of network services.

Earlier authentication servers were used in products from CKS, MyNet and Security Dynamics [CTR96].

See Also

- The whole architecture is an application of the Check Point pattern [Sch06b] [Yod97]. It uses the Proxy pattern [Gam94] as a fundamental component.

- User rights may be defined using a Role-Based Access Control model [Fer01a] [Yod97].

- A pattern for authenticating distributed objects is given in [Bro99].

- The AUTHENTICATOR pattern (page 52) defines its abstract properties.

5.4   Credential

The CREDENTIAL pattern provides a secure means of recording authentication and authorization information for use in distributed systems.

Example

Suppose we are building an instant messaging service to be used by members of a university community. Students, teachers and staff of the university may communicate with each other, while outside parties are excluded. Members of the community may use computers on school grounds, or their own systems, so the client software is made available to the community and is installed on the computers of their choice. Any community member may use any computer with the client software installed.

The client software communicates with servers run by the university in order to locate active participants and to exchange messages with them. In this environment, it is important to establish that the user of the client software is a member of the community, so that communications are kept private to the community. Further, when a student graduates, or an employee leaves the university, it must be possible to revoke their communications rights. Each member needs to be uniquely and correctly identified, and a member's identity should not be forgeable.

Context

Systems in which the users of one system may wish to access the resources of another system, based on a notion of trust shared between the systems.

Problem

In centralized computer systems, the authentication and authorization of a principal can be handled by that system's operating system, middleware and/or application software; all attributes of the principal's identity and authorization are created by and are available to the system. With distributed systems this is no longer the case. A principal's identity, authentication and authorization on one system does not carry over to another system. If a principal is to gain appropriate access to another system, some means of conveying this information must be introduced.

More broadly, this is a problem of exchanging data between trust boundaries. Within a given trust boundary, a single authority is in control, and can authenticate and make access decisions on its own. If the system is to accept requests from outside its own authority/trust boundary, the system has no inherent way of validating the identity or authorization of the entity making that request. How then do we allow external users to access some of our resources?

The solution to this problem must resolve the following forces:

- *Privacy.* The user must provide enough information to grant authorization, without being exposed to intrusive data mining.

- *Persistence.* The information must be packaged and stored in a way that survives travel between systems, while allowing the data to be kept private.

- *Authentication.* The data available must be sufficient for identifying the principal to the satisfaction of the accepting system's requirements, while disallowing others from accessing the system.

- *Authorization.* The data available must be sufficient for determining what actions the presenting principal is permitted to take within the accepting system, while also disallowing actions the principal is not permitted to take.

- *Trust.* The system accepting the credential must trust the system issuing the credential.

- *Generation.* There must be entities that produce the credentials such that other domains recognize them.

- *Tamper freedom.* It should be very difficult to falsify the credential.

- *Validity.* The credential should have an explicit temporal validity.

- *Additional documents.* It might be necessary to use the credential together with other documents.

- *Revocation.* It should be possible to revoke the credential conveniently.

Solution

Store authentication and authorization data in a data structure external to the systems in which the data is created and used. When presented to a system, the data (credential) can be used to grant access and authorization rights to the requester. For this to be a meaningful security arrangement, there must be an agreement between the systems which create the credential (credential authority) and the systems which allow their use, dictating the terms and limitations of system access.

Structure

In Figure 5.7 the `Principal` is an active entity such as a person or a process[1]. The `Principal` possesses a `Credential`, representing its identity and its authorization rights. A `Credential` is a composite describing facts about the rights available to the principal. The `Attribute` may flag whether it is presently enabled, allowing principal control over whether to exercise the right implied by the `Credential`. An expiration date allows control over the duration of the rights implied by the attribute.

A `Credential` is issued by an `Authority`, and is checked by an `Authenticator` or an `Authorizer`. Specialization of a `Credential` is achieved through setting `Attribute` names and values.

Some specializations of `Attributes` are worth mentioning. `Identity`, created by setting an attribute name to, say, 'username' and the value to the appropriate username instance, shows that the subject has been authenticated and identified as a user known to the `Authenticator`. `Privilege`, named after the intended privilege, implies some specific ability granted to the subject. `Group` and `Role` can be indicated in a similar fashion to `Identity`.

Dynamics

There are four primary use cases:

- *Issue credential*, by which a credential is granted to the principal by an authority.

---

[1] The *principal* is the responsible subject.

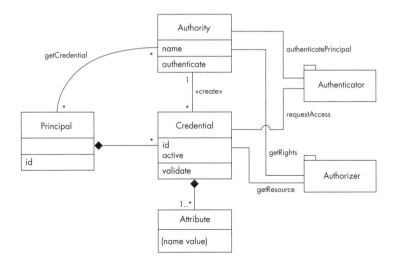

Figure 5.7: Class diagram for the CREDENTIAL pattern

- *Principal authentication*, where an authenticator accepts a credential provided to it by a principal, and makes an access decision based on the credential.
- *Principal authorization*, in which the principal is allowed access to specific items.
- *Revoke credential*, in which a principal's credential are invalidated.

Use Case: Issue Credential – Figure 5.8

The `Principal` presents itself and any required documentation of its identity to an `Authority`. Based upon its rules and what it ascertains about the `Principal`, the `Authority` creates and returns a `Credential`. The returned data may include an identity credential, group and role membership credential attribute, and privilege credential attributes. As a special case, the `Authority` may generate a defined 'public' `Credential` for `Principals` not previously known to the system. This `Credential` is made available to `Authenticators` which reference this `Authority`.

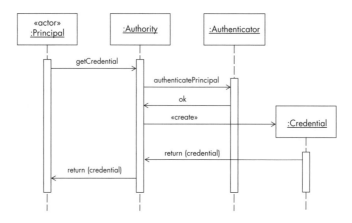

Figure 5.8: Sequence diagram for the use case 'Issue credential'

Use Case: Principal Authentication – Figure 5.9

The `Principal` requests authentication at an `Authenticator`, supplying its name and authentication `Credential`. The `Authenticator` checks the `Credential` and makes an access decision. There are different phases and strengths of check that may be appropriate for this step, discussed in the Implementation section. It is necessary for the `Authenticator` to be established in conjunction with the original authority. Not shown in the sequence diagram, but it is also optionally possible to forward the authentication request and credentials to the authority for verification.

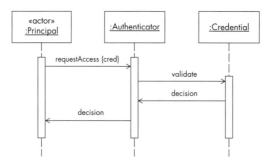

Figure 5.9: Sequence diagram for the use case 'Principal authentication'

Use Case: Revoke Credential

If it is determined that a given principal should no longer have access to the system, or that a principal's credentials have been stolen or forged, the authority can issue a revocation message to each authenticator and authorizer. Once this message has been received, the authentication and authorization subsystems reject future requests from the affected credentials. If the principal is still authorized to use the system, new credentials must be issued.

Implementation

The most significant factor in implementing the CREDENTIAL pattern is to determine the nature of the agreement between the participating systems. This begins with consideration of the functions to be provided by the system to which credentials will give access, the potential users of those functions, and the set of rights that are required for each user to fulfill its role. Once these are understood, a clear representation of the subjects, objects and rights can be developed. This representation forms the basis for storing credentials in some persistent medium and sets the terms of authentication and authorization. It also forms the basis for portability, as persisted data may be placed on portable media for transmission to the location(s) of its use[1].

The problem with a clear representation of security rights is that potential attackers can read them as well as valid participants in the systems in question. In the physical world, anti-forgery devices for credentials use techniques such as embedding the credential data in media that is too expensive to be worth forging for the benefit received: drivers' licenses and other ID cards, passports and currency all are based on the idea that it is too complex and costly for the majority of users to create realistic fakes.

In the digital world, however, copies are cheap. There are two common means of addressing this. One is to require that credentials be established and used within a closed context, and encrypting the communications channels used in that context. The other is to encrypt the credentials when they are issued, and to set up matching decryption on the authenticating system. This further subdivides into 'shared secret' systems, in which the issuing and accepting systems share the cryptographic keys necessary to encrypt and decrypt credentials, and 'public key' systems, in which participating systems can establish means for mutual encryption/decryption without prior sharing. These design choices are part of the terms set by the authority agreement under which the credentials apply. The authenticator must use the same scheme as the authority. Kerberos tokens and X.509 certificates are examples of this that require more specific approaches [Lop04].

As a simple example of 'shared secret' systems, consider a typical online banking authority and authentication setup; at sign-up, the customer verifies their identity to the bank, the authority. As part of the bank's processing, it creates customer data on its website, and allows the customer to create a username and password to gain access to the account. This data is stored on the bank's web server, which serves as the authenticator. The

---

[1] It is important to note that 'portability' is used in a restricted sense here, meaning only that the credential data can be read by a node of the system not directly connected at the time of credential creation, and not necessarily meaning that the data can be transferred for use in other systems.

customer later presents their credentials through a browser to the web server, which authenticates under the authority of the bank.

In implementing the 'principal authentication' use case, there are different phases and strengths of check that may be appropriate. For example, when entering my local warehouse club[1], I need only show a card that looks like a membership card to the authenticator standing at the door. When it comes time to make a purchase, however, the membership card is checked for validity, expiration date and ownership of the person presenting it. In general, the authenticator is responsible for checking the authenticity of the credentials themselves (anti-forgery), whether they belong to their bearer, and whether they constitute valid access to the requested object(s).

Example Resolved

The university created a credential authority, 'IM Registration'. It gave it the responsibility of verifying identity and granting a username and password, in the form of an ID card, to university community members when they join the university community. This login embodies the authority of the granting agency and that of the identity of the subject as verified by the agency. The university defined policies such that members were encouraged to keep their login information private.

The client software is coded to implement an authenticator when someone wants to start a session. Access is granted or denied based on the results of the authentication. Checks on the servers ensure that the member's credential is not expired.

Consequences

The CREDENTIAL pattern offers the following benefits:

- Fine-grained authentication and authorization information can be recorded in a uniform and persistent way.
- A credential from a trusted authority can be considered proof of identity and of authorization.
- It is possible to protect credentials using encryption or other means.

The pattern has the following potential liabilities:

- It might be difficult to find an authority that can be trusted. This can be resolved with chains (trees) of credentials, by which an authority certifies another authority.
- Making credentials tamper-resistant incurs extra time and complexity.
- Storing credentials outside of the systems that use them leaves system authentication and authorization mechanisms open to offline attack.

---

[1] In the US there are 'warehouse clubs', such as Costco and Sam's, whose members can buy goods at a discount.

Known Uses

This pattern is a generalization of the concepts embodied in X.509 Certificates, CORBA Security Service's Credentials [And01], Windows security tokens [Bro05], SAML assertions ([Hug05] and Chapter 11) and the Credential Tokenizer pattern [Ste05]. Capabilities, as used in operating systems, are another implementation of the idea (Chapter 6).

Passports are a non-technical example of the problem and its solution. Countries must be able to distinguish between their citizens, citizens of nations friendly and unfriendly to them, trading partners, guests and unwanted people. There may be different rules for how long visitors may stay, and for what they may engage in while they are in the country. Computer systems share some of these traits: they must be able to distinguish between members and non-members of their user community; non-members may be eligible or ineligible to gain system access or participate in transactions.

See Also

- Metadata-Based Access Control [Pri04] describes a model in which credentials can be used to represent subjects.

- The CREDENTIAL pattern complements Security Session [Sch06b] by giving an explicit definition of that pattern's 'session object', as extracted from several existing platforms.

- The Authenticator pattern [Bro99] and the REMOTE AUTHENTICATOR/AUTHORIZER pattern ([War03b], also page 56) describe types of authenticator.

- An Authorizer is a concrete version of the abstract concept of Reference Monitor ([Sch06b] and Chapter 6).

- Delegation of credentials is discussed in [Wei06a].

- [Ste05] describes a Session Object pattern that 'abstracts encapsulation of authentication and authorization credentials that can be passed across boundaries'. They seems to be talking about access rights rather than credentials: credentials abstract authentication and authorization rights.

- The CIRCLE OF TRUST pattern (page 34) allows the formation of trust relationships among service providers in order for their subjects to access an integrated and more secure environment. CREDENTIALs can be used for identification in a circle of trust.

CHAPTER

6

Patterns for Access Control

With the Berlin (defense) I was able to set up a fortress
that he could come near but not breach.

Vladimir Kramnik (ex-world chess champion)

6.1   Introduction

Once a subject has been granted access to a system, we need to control their access to specific resources. The rights of the subjects of the system are defined using some model of access control and expressed in the form of authorization rules. Security models are a more precise and detailed expression of policies and are used as guidelines to build and evaluate systems, usually are described in a formal or semi-formal way.

Models can be discretionary or mandatory. In a discretionary access control (DAC) model, users can be owners of data and can transfer their rights at their discretion: that is, in a DAC model, there is no clear separation of use and administration; users can be owners of the data they create and act as their administrators. In a mandatory access control (MAC) model, only designated users are allowed to grant rights, and users cannot transfer them. Users and data are classified by administrators, and the system applies a set of built-in rules that users cannot circumvent.

Orthogonal to this classification, there are several models for information access control that differ in how they define and enforce their policies [Gol06], [Sum97]. The most common are:

- An *Access Matrix* describes access by subjects (actors, entities) to protected objects (data/resources) in specific ways (access types) [Gol06] [Har76] [Sum97]. It is more flexible than the multilevel model and it can be made even more flexible and precise using predicates and other extensions. However, it is intrinsically a discretionary model in which users own the data objects and may grant access to other subjects. It is not clear who owns the information in companies and institutions, and the discretionary property reduces security. This model is usually implemented using *access control lists* (lists of the subjects that can access a given object) or *capabilities* (tickets that allow a process to access some objects).

- *Role-Based Access Control* (RBAC) collects users into roles based on their tasks or functions and assigns rights to each role [San96]. Some of these models [San96], [Tho98] have their roles structured as hierarchies, which may simplify administration. RBAC has been extended and combined in many ways.

- *Attribute-Based Access Control* (ABAC). This model controls access based on properties (attributes) of subjects or objects. It is used in environments where subjects may not be pre-registered [Pri04].

- The *Multilevel Model* organizes data using security levels. This model is usually implemented as a mandatory model in which its entities are labeled indicating their levels. The multilevel model is able to achieve a high degree of security, although it can be too rigid for some applications. Usually it is not possible to structure the variety of entities involved in complex applications into strictly hierarchical structures.

While these basic models may be useful for specific domains or applications, they are not flexible enough for the full range of policies present in some of these applications [DeC02] [DeC05]. This is manifested in the large variety of ad hoc RBAC variations that have been proposed, most of which add specialized policies to a basic RBAC model. For example, some models have added content or context-dependent access [Cha01], delegation [Zha02], task-based access [Tho97] and relationships between role entities [Bar99]. All these models effectively incorporate a set of built-in access control policies and cannot handle situations not considered by these policies, which means that a complex system may need such models for specific users or divisions. The variety of access control models makes it difficult for software developers to select an appropriate model for the application they build.

The contents of the rules are defined by institution policies. Policies are high-level guidelines defining the way an institution conducts its activities in its business, professional, economic, social and legal environment. The *institution security policy* includes laws, rules and practices that regulate how an institution uses, manages and protects resources.

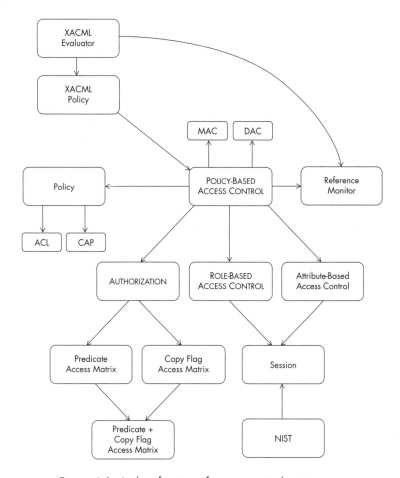

Figure 6.1: A classification of access control patterns

We present here several patterns for access control that correspond to the models described on page 72 and some of their extensions or generalizations. Figure 6.1 starts from the basic components of access control to provide a more general approach to developing access control models. This diagram can be the starting point that allows a designer to select the type of access control they need in their application. Once this abstract level is clear, we need to go to a software-oriented level, where we can choose more specific approaches. The center of this diagram is POLICY-BASED ACCESS CONTROL (PBAC, page 84) which indicates that the rules represent access policies, which are in turn defined by a Policy pattern (see Figure 6.1). The POLICY-BASED ACCESS CONTROL pattern decides whether a subject is authorized to access an object according to policies defined in a central policy repository. The enforcement of these policies is defined by a Reference Monitor pattern. Depending on its administration, PBAC can be mandatory or discretionary. XACML is a type of PBAC-oriented Service-Oriented Architectures (SOA) [Del07a], shown here as two patterns to separate its aspects of rule definition and evaluation. Policies can be implemented as access control lists (ACLs) or capabilities. The Reference Monitor may use a policy enforcement point (PEP), a policy decision point (PDP), and other patterns to describe the administrative structure of enforcement.

Authorization, RBAC, and multilevel patterns appeared in [Sch06b]; we have revised and updated them. Policy-Based Authorization, Access Control List and Capability are from [Del07a]. The Reified Reference Monitor pattern is from [Fer09c], while the Controlled Access Session pattern is from [Fer06e]. The Security Logger/Auditor pattern comes from [Fer11d].

6.2   Authorization

Also known as Access Matrix

The AUTHORIZATION pattern describes who is authorized to access specific resources in a system, in an environment in which we have resources whose access needs to be controlled. The model indicates, for each active subject, which resources the subject can access and what it can do with them.

Example

In a medical information system we keep sensitive information about patients. Unrestricted disclosure of this data would violate the privacy of the patients, while unrestricted modification could jeopardize their health.

Context

A computing environment that has resources that have value for its users or their institution.

Problem

We need a way to control access to resources, otherwise any active entity (user, process) could access any resource and we could have confidentiality and integrity problems, as well as misuse of network bandwidth or peripheral devices.

How can we describe who is authorized to access specific resources in a system? The solution to this problem must resolve the following forces:

- *Independence.* The resource control structure must be independent of the type of resources and must apply to all of them.
- *Flexibility.* The resource control structure should be flexible enough to accommodate different types of subjects and resources.
- *Modifiability.* It should be easy to modify the rights of active entities in response to changes in their duties or responsibilities.
- *Security.* The resource control structure should be protected against tampering.

Solution

Indicate, for each active subject that can access resources – objects or *protection objects* (see page 58) – which resources it can access and how (access type).

Structure

Figure 6.2 shows a class diagram of the entities involved. The `Subject` class describes an active entity that attempts to access a resource (`ProtectionObject`) in some way. The association between the `Subject` and the `ProtectionObject` defines an authorization, from which the pattern gets its name. The association class `Right` describes the access type (for example read, write) the subject has to the corresponding object. Through this class one can check the rights that a subject has on some object, or who is allowed to access a given object.

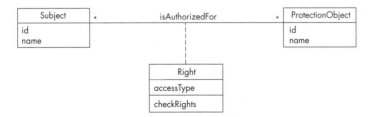

Figure 6.2: Class diagram for the AUTHORIZATION pattern

Dynamics

Use cases include 'Add a rule', 'Delete a rule', 'Modify a rule', 'Create user' and so on. We do not show their sequence diagrams here because they are very simple.

Implementation

An organization, according to its policies, should define all the required accesses to resources. The most common policy is *need-to-know*, in which active entities receive access rights according to their needs (see the Least Privilege pattern [Fer11d]). The AUTHORIZATION pattern is abstract and many implementations of it are possible: the two most common approaches are access control lists and capabilities. Access control lists (ACLs) are kept with the protected objects to indicate who is authorized to access them, while capabilities are assigned to processes to define their execution rights. Access types should be application-oriented.

Example Resolved

A hospital using an authorization system can define rules that allow only doctors or nurses to modify patient records, and only medical personnel to read patient records. We can also define specific types of access for finer control, for example `readMedicine` for an assistant nurse.

Consequences

The AUTHORIZATION pattern offers the following benefits:

- *Independence.* The pattern applies to any type of resource. Subjects can be executing processes, users, roles, user groups. Protection objects can be transactions, data, memory areas, I/O devices, files or other resources. Access types are individually definable and can be application-specific in addition to the usual read and write. It is easy to add or remove authorizations.

- *Security.* Some systems separate administrative authorizations from user authorizations for further security, on the principle of *separation of duties* [Sum97]. Authorization rules can be protected in the same way as other data structures such as relations.

- *Flexibility.* The rules apply to any type of subject or object.

- *Modifiability.* It is easy to add new rules to reflect policy changes.

- An access request may not need to specify the exact object in the rule: the object may be implied by an existing protected object [Fer75]. Subjects and access types may also be implied. This reduces the number of rules, at the cost of some extra processing time to deduce the specific rule needed.

The pattern also has the following potential liabilities:

- If there are many users or many objects, a large number of rules must be written. This makes administration difficult and error-prone.

- It may be hard for the security administrator to realize why a given subject needs a right, or the implications of a new rule. There is no semantic relation between subjects and objects.

- Defining authorization rules is not enough, we also need an enforcement mechanism.

Variants

AUTHORIZATION is usually represented by an access matrix model, which is the model usually described in textbooks, and may also include:

- Predicates or guards, which may restrict the use of the authorization according to specific conditions, or provide content-dependent authorization.

- Delegation of some of the authorizations by their holders to other subjects through the use of a Boolean 'copy' flag [Sum97].

- Packet Filter Firewall [Sch06b] implements a variety of this pattern in which the subjects and objects are defined by Internet addresses.

Figure 6.3 extends AUTHORIZATION to include those aspects. A `Right` now includes not only the type of access allowed, but also a predicate that must be true for the authorization to hold, and a copy flag that can be true or false, indicating whether or not the right can be transferred. `CheckRights` is an operation to determine the rights of a subject or to find who has the rights to access a given object.

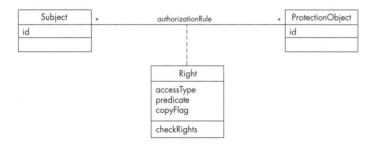

Figure 6.3: Access matrix with predicates and copy flag

Known Uses

This pattern defines the most basic type of authorization rule, from which more complex access-control models can be built. It is based on the concept of the access matrix, a fundamental security model [Gol06] [Sum97]. Its first object-oriented form appeared in [Fer93b]. Subsequently, it has appeared in several other papers and products. It is the basis for the access control systems of most commercial operating system and database products, such as UNIX, Windows, Oracle and many others.

See Also

- ROLE-BASED ACCESS CONTROL (below) is a specialization of this pattern.
- The Reference Monitor pattern complements the AUTHORIZATION pattern by defining how to enforce the defined rights.
- There is a discussion of authorization in [Fer81].

6.3   Role-Based Access Control

The ROLE-BASED ACCESS CONTROL pattern describes how to assign rights based on the functions or tasks of users in an environment in which control of access to computing resources is required.

Context

Any environment in which we need to control access to computing resources and in which there is a large number of users and information types, or a large variety of resources.

Problem

For convenient administration of authorization rights, we need to have a means of factoring out rights. Otherwise, the number of individual rights is just too large; granting rights to individual users would require storing many authorization rules, and it would be hard for administrators to keep track of these rules. It is also hard to associate semantic meanings to the rules. How can we reduce the number of rules and make their semantics clearer?

The solution to this problem must resolve the following forces:

- *Complexity.* We would like to make the work of the security administrator as simple as possible.

- *Semantics.* In most organizations people are assigned specific functions or tasks. Their rights should correspond to those tasks.

- *Policy.* We need to define rights according to organizational policies.

- *Commonality.* People performing the same tasks should have the same rights.

- *Policy enforcement.* We want to help the organization to define precise access rights for its members according to a need-to-know policy.

- *Flexibility.* People joining, leaving and changing functions should not require complex rights manipulation.

Solution

Most organizations have a variety of job functions that require different skills and responsibilities. Users should be assigned rights based on their job functions or their designated tasks. This corresponds to the application of the *need-to-know* principle, a fundamental security policy [Sum97]. Job functions can be interpreted as roles that people play in performing their duties. In particular, web-based systems have a variety of users: company employees, customers, partners, search engines and so on.

Structure

Figure 6.4 shows a class diagram for ROLE-BASED ACCESS CONTROL. The User and Role classes describe registered users and their predefined roles respectively. Users are assigned to roles, roles are given rights according to their functions. The association class Right defines the access types that a user within a role is authorized to apply to the protection object. The combination Role, ProtectionObject and Right is an instance of the AUTHORIZATION pattern.

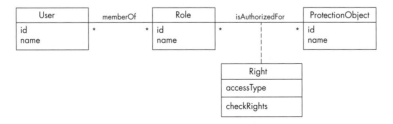

Figure 6.4: Class diagram for the ROLE-BASED ACCESS CONTROL pattern

Dynamics

Use cases include 'Add a rule', 'Delete a rule', 'Modify a rule', 'Assign user to role', 'Assign rights to role' and so on. We do not show their sequence diagrams here because they are very simple.

Implementation

Roles may correspond to job titles, for example 'manager', 'secretary'. A finer-grained approach is to make them correspond to tasks. For example, a professor has the roles of 'thesis advisor', 'teacher', 'committee member', 'researcher' and so on. An approach to defining role rights is described in [Ful07].

There are many possible ways to implement roles in a software system. [Kod01] considers the implementation of the data structures needed to apply an RBAC model. Concrete implementations can be found in operating systems, database systems and web application servers.

Example Resolved

The hospital now assigns rights to the roles of doctors, nurses and so on. The number of authorization rules has decreased dramatically as a result.

Consequences

The ROLE-BASED ACCESS CONTROL pattern offers the following benefits:

- *Semantics*. We can make the rights given to a role correspond to tasks.
- *Complexity.* It allows administrators to reduce the complexity of security. Because there are many more users than roles, the number of roles becomes much smaller.
- *Policy.* Organization policies about job functions can be reflected directly in the definition of roles and the assignment of users to roles.
- *Commonality.* People performing the same tasks can be given the same rights.
- *Flexibility.* It is very simple to accommodate users joining, leaving or being reassigned. All these use cases require only manipulation of the associations between users and roles.
- *Structure*. Roles can be structured into hierarchies for further flexibility and reduction of rules.
- *Role separation*. Users can activate more than one session at a time for functional flexibility: some tasks may require multiple views or different types of actions. Role separation is also important to avoid conflicts of interest: we can add UML constraints to indicate that some roles cannot be used in the same session or given to the same user (*separation of duties*).

The following potential liability may arise from applying this pattern:

- Some institutions may not have clearly defined roles in their organization, and some work must therefore be done to define these roles.

Variants

The model shown in Figure 6.5 additionally considers composite roles and objects: it is an application of the Composite pattern [Gam94]. The figure also includes the concept of a session, which defines a context for the use of a role, may restrict the number of roles used together at execution time, and can be used to enforce role exclusion at execution time.

Known Uses

The RBAC pattern represents in object-oriented form a model described in terms of sets in [San96]. That model has been the basis of most research papers and implementations of this concept. RBAC is implemented in a variety of commercial systems, including Sun's J2EE, Microsoft's Windows 2000 and later, Microsoft's .NET [Fen06], IBM's WebSphere, and Oracle, among others. The basic security facilities of Java's JDK 1.2 have been shown to be able to support a rich variety of RBAC policies. The NIST has developed a standard for RBAC [Fer01b]. We have used RBAC to describe access to physical structures [Fer07f].

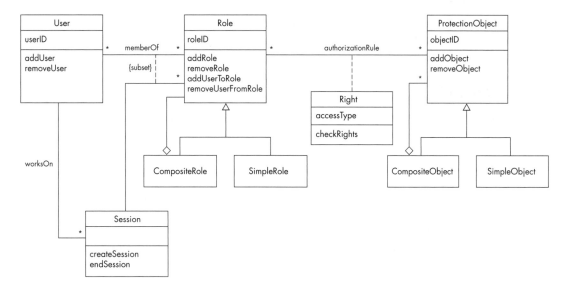

Figure 6.5: Class diagram for the Extended RBAC model

See Also

Earlier versions of this pattern appeared in [Fer93b] and [Yod97], and a pattern language for its software implementation appears in [Kod01], although this paper does not consider composite roles, groups and sessions.

The pattern whose class diagram is shown in Figure 6.5 includes AUTHORIZATION and Composite. A session object is used to provide execution context (see Variants).

6.4   Multilevel Security

In some environments data and documents may have critical value and their disclosure could bring serious problems. The MULTILEVEL SECURITY pattern describes how to categorize sensitive information and prevent its disclosure. It describes how to assign classifications (*clearances*) to users and classifications (sensitivity levels) to data, and how to separate different organizational units into categories. Access of users to data is based on policies, while changes to the classifications are performed by trusted processes that are allowed to violate the policies.

Example

The general command of an army has decided on a plan of attack in a war. It is extremely important that this information is not known outside a small group of people, or the attack may be a failure.

Context

In some environments data and documents may have critical value and their disclosure could bring serious problems.

Problem

How can you control access in an environment with sensitive documents so as to prevent leakage of information?

The solution to this problem must resolve the following forces:

- We need to protect the confidentiality and integrity of data based on its sensitivity.

- Users have to be allowed to read documents based on their position in the organization.

- There should be a way to increase or decrease the ability of users to read documents and the sensitivity of the documents. Otherwise, people promoted to higher positions, for example, will not be able to read sensitive documents, and we will end up with a proliferation of sensitive and obsolete documents.

Solution

Assign classifications (as clearances) to users and classifications (as sensitivity levels) to data. Separate different organizational units into categories. For example, classifications may include levels such as 'top secret', 'secret' and so on, and categories may include units such as engDept, marketingDept and so on. For confidentiality purposes, access of users to data is based on policies defined by the Bell-LaPadula model [Gol06], while for integrity the policies are defined by Biba's model [Sum97]. Changes to the classifications are performed by trusted processes that are allowed to violate the policies of these models.

Structure

Figure 6.6 shows the class diagram of the MULTILEVEL SECURITY pattern. The `UserClassification` and `DataClassification` classes define the active entities and the objects of access respectively. Both classifications may include categories and levels. Trusted processes are allowed to assign users and data to classifications, as defined by the `Assignment` class.

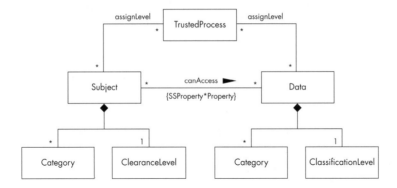

Figure 6.6: Class diagram for the MULTILEVEL SECURITY pattern

Implementation

Data classification is a tedious task, because every piece of information or document must be examined and assigned a classification tag. New documents may get automatic tags based on their links to other documents. User classifications are based on users' rank and units of work and are only changed when they change jobs. It is hard to classify users in commercial environments in this way: for example, in a medical system it makes no sense to assign a doctor a higher classification than a patient, because a patient has the right to see their record.

Example Resolved

The group involved in planning attacks, as well as all the related documents it produces, are given a classification of 'top secret'. This will prevent leakage towards lower-level army staff.

Consequences

The MULTILEVEL SECURITY pattern offers the following benefits:

- The classification of users and data is relatively simple and can follow organization policies.
- This model of the pattern can be proved to be secure under certain assumptions [Sum97].
- The pattern is useful to isolate processes and execution domains.

The following potential liabilities may arise from applying this pattern:

- Implementations should use labels in data to indicate their classification. This assures security: if not done, the general degree of security is reduced.

- We need trusted programs to assign users and data to classifications.

- Data must be able to be structured into hierarchical sensitivity levels and users should be able to be structured into clearances. This is usually hard, or even impossible, in commercial environments.

- This model can handle only secrecy and prevention of leakage of information. A dual model is needed to also handle integrity.

- Covert channels may break the assumed security.

Variants

It is possible to define a similar pattern to control integrity in multilevel models according to the Biba rules [Gol06].

Known Uses

This pattern has been used by several military-sponsored projects and in a few commercial products, including DBMSs (Informix, Oracle) and operating systems (Pitbull [Arg] and HP's Virtual Vault [HP]).

See Also

The concept of roles can also be applied when implementing this pattern, role classifications replacing user classifications.

6.5   Policy-Based Access Control

The POLICY-BASED ACCESS CONTROL pattern describes how to decide whether a subject is authorized to access an object according to policies defined in a central policy repository.

Example

Consider a financial company that provides services to its clients. Their computer systems can be accessed by clients, who send orders to the company for buying or selling commodities (stocks, bonds, real estate, art and so on) via e-mail or through their website. Brokers employed by the company can carry out the clients' orders by sending requests to the systems of various financial markets, or by consulting information from financial news websites. A government auditor visits periodically to check for compliance with laws and regulations.

All of these activities are regulated by policies with various granularities within the company. For example, the billing department can have the rule 'Only registered clients whose account status is in good standing may send orders', the technical department can decide that 'E-mails with attachments bigger than x Mb won't be delivered', the company security policy can state that 'Only employees with a broker role can access the financial market's web services' and that 'Only the broker or custodian of a client can access its transaction information', whereas the legal department can issue the rule that 'Auditors can access all transaction information', and so on.

All of these policies are enforced by different components of the company's computer system (e-mail server, file system, web service access control component, and financial application). This approach has several problems: the policies may be described in different syntaxes, and it is difficult to have a global view of which policies apply to a specific case. Moreover, two policies can be conflicting, and there is no way to combine them in a clear way. In summary, this approach could be error-prone and complex to manage.

Context

Consider centralized or distributed systems with a large number of resources (objects). A large number of subjects may access those objects. Rules are defined to control access to objects. The rules defined by the organization are typically designed by different actors (technical, organizational, legal and so on), and each set of rules designed by a specific policy designer can concern overlapping sets of objects and/or subjects.

Problem

Enforcing these rules for a particular access request may be complex, and thus error-prone, because there is no clear view of which rules to apply to a request.

How can we enforce access control according to the predefined rules in a consistent way? The solution to this problem must resolve the following forces:

- Objects may be frequently added or removed.
- The solution should be able to implement a wide variety of access control models, such as access matrix, RBAC.
- Malicious users can attempt unauthorized access to objects.
- There should be no direct access to objects: every request must be mediated.

Solution

Most access control systems are based on the AUTHORIZATION pattern (page 74), in which the access of a subject to an object depends only on the existence of a positive applicable rule. If no such rule exists, the access is denied.

In our case, the situation is more complicated: the existence of a positive applicable rule should not necessarily imply that access should be granted. All the rules must be taken into account, and a final decision must be made from the set of applicable rules and some meta-information about the way they should be combined. Part of that meta-information is located in a policy object. This policy object aggregates a set of rules, and specifies how those rules must be combined. For more flexibility about the combination of rules, a composite object regroups the rules into policies and *policy sets*. Policy sets aggregate policies, and include information about how to combine rules from different policies. To be able to select all applicable rules easily, they should be stored in a unique repository for the organization and administered in a centralized way.

At access time, all requests are intercepted by policy enforcement points (PEPs), a specific type of Reference Monitor [Sch06b]. The repository is accessed by a unique policy decision point (PDP), which is responsible for computing the access decision by cooperating with a policy information point (PIP), which may provide information about the subject or the resource accessed. The rules and policies are administered through a unique policy administration point (PAP).

Finally, because rules and policies are designed by different teams, possibly for the same objects and subjects, this scheme does not guarantee that a conflict between rules in different policy components would never occur. In that case, the PDP may have a *dynamic policy conflict resolver* to resolve the conflict, which would need to use meta-rules. A complementary *static policy conflict resolver* may be a part of the PAP, and should detect conflicts between rules at the time they are entered into the repository.

Structure

Figure 6.7 illustrates the solution. A `Subject`'s access requests to particular objects are intercepted by `PEPs`, which are a part of the security infrastructure that is responsible for enforcing the organization `Policy` about this access. `PEPs` query another part of the security infrastructure, the `PDP`, which is responsible for computing an access decision. To compute the decision, the `PDP` uses information from a `PIP`, and retrieves the applicable `Policy` from the unique `PolicyRepository`, which stores all of the `PolicyRules` for the organization.

The `PolicyRepository` is also responsible for retrieving the applicable rules by selecting those rules whose `subjectDescriptor`, `resourceDescriptor` and `environmentDescriptor` match the information about the subject, the resource and the environment obtained from the `PIP`, and whose `accessType` matches the required `accessType` from the request. The `PAP` is a unique point for administering the rules. In case the evaluation of the `Policy` leads to a conflict between the decisions of the applicable `Rules`, a part of the `PDP`, the `DynamicPolicyConflictResolver`, is responsible for producing a uniquely determined access decision. Similarly, a `StaticPolicyConflictResolver` is a part of the `PAP` and is responsible for identifying conflicting rules within the `PolicyRepository`.

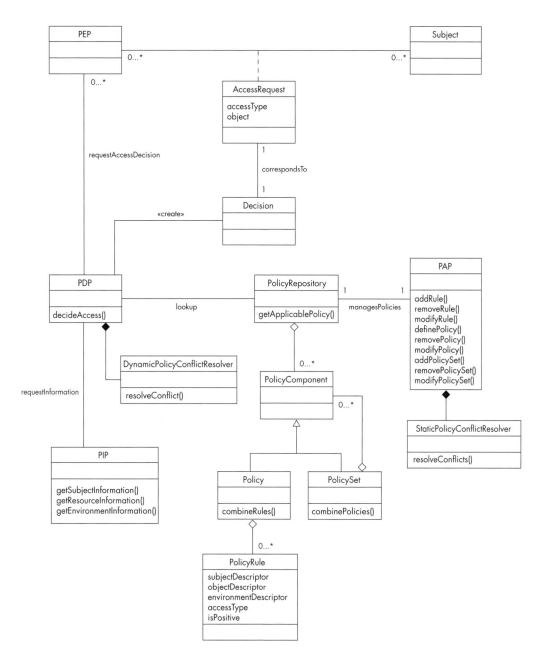

Figure 6.7: Class diagram for the POLICY-BASED ACCESS CONTROL pattern

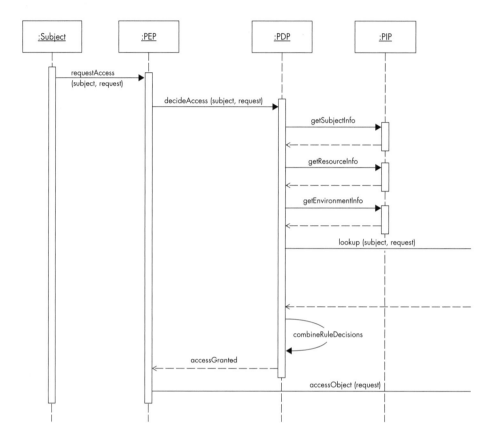

Figure 6.8: Sequence diagram for the use case 'Request access to an object'

Dynamics

Figure 6.8 shows a sequence diagram describing the most commonly used case of 'Request access to an object'. The Subject's request for accessing an Object is intercepted by a PEP, which forwards the request to the PDP. The PDP can retrieve information about the Subject, the Object and the current environment from the PIP. This information is used to retrieve the applicable Rules from the PolicyRepository.

The PDP can then compute the access decision by combining the decisions from the Rules forming the applicable policy and can finally send this decision back to the PEP. If the access has been granted by the PDP, the PEP forwards the request to the Object.

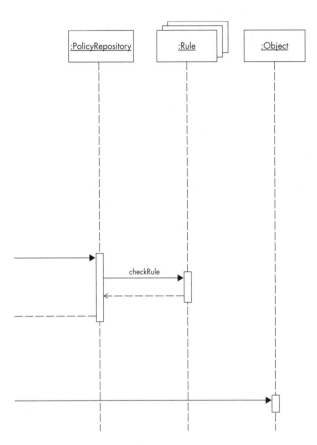

Figure 6.8 (continued)

Example Resolved

Use of the POLICY-BASED ACCESS CONTROL pattern allows the company to centralize its rules. Now the billing department, as well as the technical department, the legal department and the corporate management department can insert their rules in the same repository, using the same format. The different components of the computer system that used to enforce policies directly (that is, e-mail server, file system, web service access control component and financial application) just need to intercept the requests and redirect them to the central policy decision point. To do that, each of them runs a policy enforcement point, which interfaces with the main policy decision point.

The rules could be grouped in the following way: a unique company policy set might include all other policies and express the fact that all policies coming from the corporate management should dominate all other policies. Each department would have their own policy, composed of rules from that department, and combined according to each department's policy.

Finally, a simple dynamic conflict resolver could be configured to enforce a closed policy in case of conflict. The rules can be managed easily, since they are written to the same repository, conflicts can be resolved, and there is a clearer view of the company's security policy.

Consequences

The POLICY-BASED ACCESS CONTROL pattern offers the following benefits:

- Since the access decisions are requested in a standard format, an access decision becomes independent of its enforcement. A wide variety of enforcement mechanisms can be supported and can evolve separately from the policy decision point.

- The pattern can support the access matrix, RBAC or multilevel models for access control.

- Since every access is mediated, illegal accesses are less likely to be performed.

The pattern also has some potential liabilities:

- It could affect the performance of the protected system, since the central PDP/PolicyRepository/PIP subsystem may be a bottleneck in the system.

- Complexity.

- We need to protect the access control information.

Known Uses

- XACML (eXtensible Access Control Markup Language), defined by OASIS, uses XML for expressing authorization rules and for access decision following this pattern.

- Symlabs' Federated Identity Access Manager Federation is an identity management that implements identity federation. Its components include a PDP and PEPs.

- Components Framework for Policy-Based Admission Control, a part of the Internet 2 project, is a framework for the authentication of network components. It is based on five major components: Access Requester (AR), Policy Enforcement Point (PEP), Policy Decision Point (PDP), Policy Repository (PR) and the Network Detection Point (NDP).

- XML and Application firewalls [Del05] also use policies.

- SAML (Security Assertion Markup Language) is an XML standard defined by OASIS for exchanging authentication and authorization data between security domains. It can be used to transmit the authorization decision.

See Also

- XACML patterns [Del05] is an implementation of this pattern (Chapter 11).
- The ACCESS CONTROL LIST (below) and CAPABILITY (page 96) patterns are specific implementations of this pattern.
- The PEP is just a Reference Monitor [Fer01a].
- This pattern can implement the Access Matrix and ROLE-BASED ACCESS CONTROL patterns.

A general discussion of security policies, including some IETF models that resemble patterns, is given in [Slo02].

6.6   Access Control List

The ACCESS CONTROL LIST (ACL) pattern allows controlled access to objects by indicating which subjects can access an object and in what way. There is usually an ACL associated with each object.

Example

We are designing a system in which documents should be accessible only to specific registered users, who can either retrieve them for reading or submit modified versions. We need to verify that a specific user can access the document requested in a rapid manner.

Context

Centralized or distributed systems in which access to resources must be controlled. The systems comprise a policy decision point and policy enforcement points that enforce the access policy. A system has subjects that need to access resources to perform tasks. In the system, not every subject can access any object: access rights are defined and can be modeled as an access matrix, in which each row represents a subject and each column represents an object. An entry in the matrix is indexed by a specific subject and a specific object, and lists the types of actions that this subject can execute on this object.

Problem

In some systems the number of subjects and/or objects can be large. In this case, the direct implementation of an access matrix can use significant amounts of storage, and the time used for searching this large matrix can be significant.

In practice, the matrix is sparse. Subjects have rights on few objects and thus most of the entries are empty.

How can we implement the access matrix in a space- and time-efficient way? The solution to this problem must resolve the following forces:

- The matrix may have many subjects and objects. Finding the rule that authorizes a specific request to an object may take a lot of time, as entries are unordered.

- The matrix can be very sparse: storing it as a matrix would require storing many empty entries, thus wasting space.

- Subjects and objects may be frequently added or removed. Making changes in a matrix representation is inefficient.

- The time spent for accessing a centralized access matrix may result in an additional overhead.

- A request received by a policy enforcement point indicates the requester identity, the requested object and the type of access requested. The requester identity, in particular, is controlled by the requester, and so may be forged by a malicious user.

Solution

Implement the access matrix by associating each object with an access control list (ACL) that specifies which actions are allowed on the object, by which authenticated users. Each entry in the list comprises a subject's identifier and a set of rights. Policy enforcement points enforce the access policy by requesting the policy decision point to search the object's ACL for the requesting subject identifier and access type. For the system to be secure, the subject's identity must be authenticated prior to its access to any objects. Since the ACLs may be distributed, like the objects they are associated with, several policy administration points may be responsible for creating and modifying the ACLs.

Structure

Figure 6.9 illustrates the solution. To be protected, an `Object` must have an associated `ACL`. This `ACL` is made up of `ACLEntries`, each of which contains a set of `Rights` permitted for a specific authenticated `Subject`. An authenticated `Subject` accesses an `Object` only if a corresponding `Right` exists in the `Object`'s ACL. For security reasons, only the `PDP` can create and modify `ACLs`. At execution time, the `PDP` is responsible for searching an `Object`'s ACL for a `Right` in order to make an access decision.

Dynamics

Figure 6.10 shows a sequence diagram describing the typical use case for 'Request object access'. The authenticated `Subject`'s request for access to an `Object` is intercepted by a `PEP`, which forwards the request to the `PDP`. It can then check that the `ACL` corresponding to the `Object` contains an `ACLEntry` which corresponds to the `Subject` and which holds the `accessType` requested by the `Subject`.

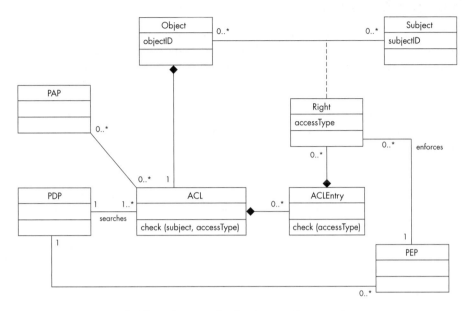

Figure 6.9: Class diagram for the ACCESS CONTROL LIST pattern

Implementation

A decision must be made regarding the granularity of the ACLs. For example, it is possible to regroup users, such as the minimal access control lists in UNIX. It is also possible to have a finer-grained access control system. For example, the extended access control lists in UNIX allow specified access not only for the file's owner and owner's group, but also for additional users or groups.

The choice of access types can also contribute to a finer-grained access control system. For example, Windows defines over ten different permissions, whereas UNIX-like systems usually define three.

A creation/inheritance policy must also be defined: what should the ACL look like at the creation of an object? From what objects should it inherit its permissions?

ACLs are pieces of information of variable length. A strategy for storing ACLs must be chosen. For example, in the Solaris UFS file system, each `inode` has a field called `i_shadow`. If an `inode` has an ACL, this field points to a shadow `inode`. On the file system, shadow `inodes` are used like regular files. Each shadow `inode` stores an ACL in its data blocks. Linux and most other UNIX-like operating systems implement a more general mechanism called *extended attributes* (EAs). Extended attributes are name/value pairs associated permanently with file system objects, similar to the environment variables for a process [Gru03].

Example Resolved

To enforce access control, we create a policy decision point and its corresponding policy enforcement points, which are responsible for intercepting and controlling accesses to the documents. For each document, we provide the policy decision point with a list of the users authorized to access the document and how (read or write). At access time, the policy decision point is able to search the list for the user. If the user is on the list with the proper access type, it can grant access to the document, otherwise it will refuse access.

In our distributed system, we make sure that only authenticated users – that is, users who provided a valid credential – can make requests.

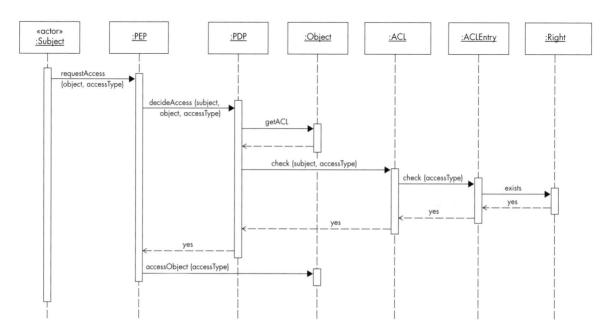

Figure 6.10: Sequence diagram for use case 'Request object access'

Consequences

The ACCESS CONTROL LIST pattern offers the following benefits:

- Because all authorizations for a given object are kept together, we can go to the requested object and find out if a subject is there. This is much quicker than searching the whole matrix.

- The time spent accessing an ACL is less than the time that would have been spent accessing a centralized matrix.

■ Access to unauthorized objects using forged requests on behalf of legitimate subjects is not possible, because we make sure that the requests are from only authenticated subjects.

The pattern also has the following potential liabilities:

■ The administration of the subjects is rendered more difficult: the deletion of a subject may imply a scan of all ACLs, although this can be done automatically.

■ When the environment is heterogeneous, it needs to be adapted to each type of PEPs. PDPs and PAPs must be implemented in a different way, adding an additional development cost.

Known Uses

■ Operating systems such as Microsoft Windows (from NT/2000 on), Novell's NetWare, Digital's OpenVMS and UNIX-based systems use ACLs to control access to their resources.

■ In Solaris 2.5, file ACLs allow a finer control over access to files and directories than the control that was possible with the standard UNIX file permissions. It is possible to specify specific users in an `ACLEntry`. It is also possible to modify ACLs for a file `testfile` by using the `setfacl` command in a similar way to the `chmod` command used for changing standard UNIX permissions:

```
setfacl -s u::rwx,g::---,o::---,m:rwx,u:user1:rwx,u:user2:rwx
testfile
```

■ IBM Tivoli Access Manager for e-businesses uses ACLs to control access to the web and application resources [IBMc].

■ Cisco IOS, Cisco's network infrastructure software, provides basic traffic filtering capabilities with ACLs [Cisa].

See Also

■ The PEP and PDP come from the previous pattern in this chapter. The CAPABILITY pattern (below) is another way to implement the Access Matrix.

■ Access Matrix and RBAC [Fer01a] are models that can be implemented using ACLs.

■ PEP is just a Reference Monitor [Fer01a].

■ A variant exists oriented to centralized systems, Policy Enforcement, which leverages ad hoc data structures to enhance efficiency [Zho02].

■ Acegi is a security framework for Java, used to build ACLs [Sid07].

6.7   Capability

The CAPABILITY pattern allows controlled access to objects by providing a credential or ticket to a subject to allow it to access an object in a specific way. Capabilities are given to the principal.

Example

We are designing a system that allows registered users to read or modify confidential documents. We need to verify that a specific user can access a confidential document in an efficient and secure manner. In particular, we worry that if the parts of our system that deal with access control are too large and/or distributed, they may be compromised by attackers.

Context

Distributed systems in which access to resources must be controlled. The systems have a policy decision point and its corresponding policy enforcement points that enforce the access policy. A system is composed of subjects that need to access resources to perform their tasks. In the system, not every subject can access any object: access rights are defined and can be modeled as an access matrix, in which each row represents a subject and each column represents an object. An entry of the matrix is indexed by a specific subject and a specific object, and lists the types of actions that this subject can execute on this object. The system's implementation is vulnerable to threats from attackers that may compromise its components.

Problem

In some of these systems the number of subjects and/or objects can be large. In this case, the direct implementation of the access matrix can use significant amounts of storage, and the time to search a large matrix can be significant.

In practice, the matrix is sparse. Subjects have rights on few objects and thus most of the entries are empty. How can we implement the access matrix in a space- and time-efficient way?

The solution to this problem must resolve the following forces:

- The matrix may have many subjects and objects. Finding the rule that authorizes a specific request to an object may take a lot of time (unordered entries).

- The matrix can be very sparse, and storing it as a matrix would require storing many empty entries, thus wasting space.

- Subjects and objects may be frequently added or removed. Making changes in a matrix representation is inefficient.

- The time spent for accessing a centralized access matrix may result in an additional overhead.

- A request received by a policy enforcement point indicates the requester identity, the requested object and the type of access requested. The requester identity, in particular, is controlled by the requester, and so may be forged by a malicious user.

- The size of the units that can create and/or modify the policies (such as policy administration points) has an impact on the security of the system. Minimizing their size will reduce their chance of being compromised by attackers.

Solution

Implement the access matrix by issuing a set of *capabilities* to each subject. A capability specifies that the subject possessing the capability has a right on a specific object. Policy enforcement points and the policy decision point of the system enforce the access policy by checking that the capability presented by the subject at the access time is authentic, and by searching the capability for the requested object and access type. Trust a minimum part of the system – create a unique capability issuer that is responsible for issuing the capabilities. The capabilities must be implemented in a way that allows the policy decision point to verify their authenticity, so that a malicious user cannot forge one.

Structure

Figure 6.11 illustrates the solution. In order to protect the `Objects`, a `CapabilityProvider`, the minimum trusted part of our system, issues a set of `Capabilities` to each `Subject` by using a secure channel. A `Capability` contains a set of `Rights` that the `Subject` can perform on a specific `Object`. A `Subject` accesses an `Object` only if a corresponding `Right` exists in one of the `Subject`'s `Capabilities`. At execution time, the PDP is responsible for checking the `Capability`'s authenticity and searching the `Capability` for both the requested `Object` and the requested `accessType` in order to make an access decision.

Dynamics

Figure 6.12 shows a sequence diagram describing the typical use case of 'Request object access'. The `Subject` requests access to an `Object` by including a corresponding `Capability`. The request is intercepted by a PEP, which forwards the request to the PDP. It can then check that the `Capability` holds the `accessType` requested by the `Subject`.

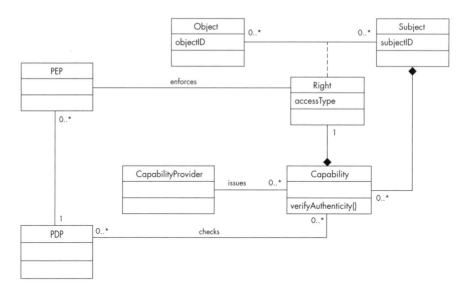

Figure 6.11: Class diagram for the CAPABILITY pattern

Implementation

Since a capability must be unforgeable and unmodifiable, it can be implemented as hardware or software:

- As hardware:
    - *Tags*. Tagging allows for the categorization of each word as data or a capability. Then no copying should be allowed from capability to data or vice versa, no arithmetic operation should be allowed on capabilities. A disadvantage of this method is the memory waste by using tags.
    - *Segmentation*. Whole segments of memory are used exclusively for capabilities or for data. No operation should be allowed between partitions of different types. A disadvantage of this is that many processes may need two segments.
- As software:
    - *Cryptography*. Usually used, the capabilities may be encrypted by the capability issuer's key.

Example Resolved

To enforce access control, we create a policy decision point and its corresponding policy enforcement points that are responsible for intercepting and controlling accesses to confidential documents. When a user logs on to the system, a robust token issuer provides a

set of tokens that indicate which confidential documents are authorized. Tokens are digitally signed so that they can't be created or modified by users. At request time, a user
wishing to access a confidential document presents its token to the policy enforcement
point, and then to the policy decision point, which grants them access to the document.
If a user does not present a token corresponding to the document and the access mode,
access is refused.

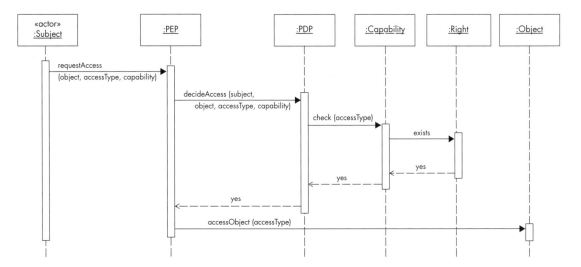

Figure 6.12: Sequence diagram for the use case 'Request object access'

Consequences

The CAPABILITY pattern offers the following benefits:

- Because the capability is sent together with the request, the time spent for accessing
  an authorization is much less than the time that would have been spent searching a
  whole matrix, or searching an access control list (ACL).

- The time spent accessing a capability at request time is less than the time that would
  have been spent accessing a centralized matrix.

- The part of the system that we need to trust is minimal. The capability provider is
  only responsible for issuing capabilities to the right users at an initial time.

- It is harder for malicious users to forge or modify capabilities, since a capability
  provides a way to verify its authenticity.

The pattern also has some potential liabilities:

- The administration of the objects is more difficult: The addition of an object implies the issuing of capabilities to every authorized user.

■ When the environment is heterogeneous, the administration of the rights is more complex. There is no straightforward way to revoke a right, since users are in control of the capabilities they have acquired. A solution could be to add a validity time to each capability, or through indirection, or by using virtual addresses [And08].

■ The right is transferable: that is, a capability can be stolen and replayed by (or given to) a malicious user. (This is not the case in OSs in which accesses to the capabilities are also controlled by the TCB, but those need the support of special hardware.)

Known Uses

■ Most of the capability-based systems are operating systems. Usually hardware assistance is needed; for example, capabilities are placed in special registers and manipulated with special instructions (Plessey P250), or they are stored in tagged areas of memory (IBM 6000).

■ Many distributed capability-based systems have been researched and described [Joh85] [Don76] [San96] [Amo96]. Among those, Amoeba [Amo96] is a distributed operating system in which multiple machines can be connected together. It has a microkernel architecture. All objects in the system are protected using a simple scheme. When an object (representing a resource) is created, the server doing the creation constructs a capability in the form of an 128-bit value and returns it to the caller. Subsequent operations on the object require the user to send its capability to the server to both specify the object and to prove the user has permission to manipulate the object. Capabilities are protected cryptographically to prevent tampering. The Symbian operating system uses capabilities [Hea06].

See Also

■ The PEP and PDP are from the ACCESS CONTROL LIST pattern (page 91). The ACCESS CONTROL LIST pattern is another way to implement the access matrix.

■ Capabilities can be implemented into the VAS (virtual address space) using segmentation.

■ The PEP is just a Reference Monitor [Fer01a].

■ Access Matrix, RBAC [Fer01a] are models that can be implemented using ACLs. Credentials [Mor06a] are a type of capability.

6.8   Reified Reference Monitor

Also known as Intercepting Filter, Application Controller

The REIFIED REFERENCE MONITOR pattern describes how to force authorizations when a subject requests a protection object and provide the subject with a decision.

In a computational environment in which users or processes make requests for data or resources, this pattern describes how to define an abstract process that intercepts all requests for resources from subjects and checks them for compliance with authorizations.

Context

A multiprocessing environment in which subjects request protection objects to perform their functions and access resources based on a decision made by a reference monitor.

Problem

Not enforcing the defined authorizations is the same as not having them: subjects can perform all types of illegal actions. Any user could read any file, for example. How can we control the subjects' actions?

Also, an access decision can be sometimes more complex than a Boolean response; for example, when a user wants to access a database type: they may be authorized to access a subset of the data requested as per the rules. In this case, the reference monitor communicates with the subject and the decision is not Boolean – 'yes' or 'no': it can be either a display on the screen, some statement, or maybe negation. In many cases there is also the need to keep decisions in memory. If the same subject requests the same object again, the system should not spend time in re-deciding, as it affects performance.

The solution to this problem must resolve the following forces:

■ Defining authorization rules is not enough: they must be enforced whenever a subject makes a request for a protection object.

■ There are many possible implementations: we need an abstract model of enforcement.

■ Decisions should be sent to the subject, as they can be more complex than mere Boolean decisions. By defining set of attributes for decisions, we can make the reference monitor more flexible.

Solution

Define an abstract process that intercepts all requests for resources, checks them for compliance with authorizations, makes decisions based on these authorization rules, and stores the decisions, including their attributes (Figure 6.13).

Figure 6.14 shows the class diagram for a reified Reference Monitor. In this figure `SetofAuthorizationRules` denotes a collection of authorization rules organized in some convenient way. Figure 6.15 shows a sequence diagram illustrating how checking is performed. An executing subject (`ActualSubject`) requests some type of access to a `ProtectionObject`. The `ReferenceMonitor` intercepts the request and searches in the set of authorization rules for a matching `Authorization` (rule). After the search a `Decision` is created. If positive, the request proceeds to access the `ProtectionObject`.

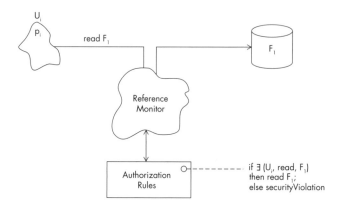

Figure 6.13: The concept of the Reference Monitor

Consequences

The REIFIED REFERENCE MONITOR pattern offers the following benefits:

- If all requests are intercepted we can make sure that they comply with the rules.
- The subject has better understanding of the decision made by the reference monitor to grant or deny its request.
- Implementation has not been constrained by using this abstract process.

The pattern also has the following potential liabilities:

- Specific implementations (concrete Reference Monitors) are needed for each type of resource. For example, a file manager controls requests for files.
- Checking each request and making decision may result in unacceptable performance loss. We may need to perform some checks at compile time, for example, and not repeat them at execution time. Another possibility is to factor out checks, for example when opening a file, or having trusted processes that are not checked.
- We may have to keep decisions in memory, so that when the same subject requests the same protection object, we already know the decision and do not compromise performance in making it again.

Known Uses

Most modern operating systems implement this concept, for example Solaris 9, Windows 2000, AIX and others. The Java Security Manager is another example.

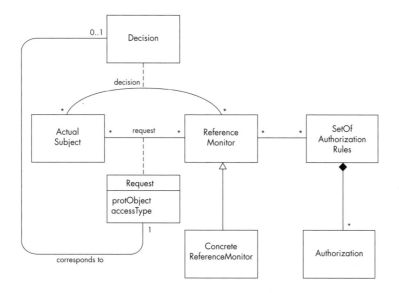

Figure 6.14: Class diagram for the REIFIED REFERENCE MONITOR pattern

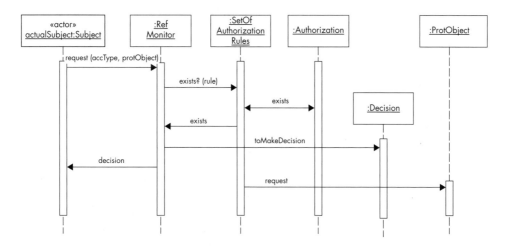

Figure 6.15: Sequence diagram for enforcing security of requests

See Also

■ This pattern is a generalization of the Reference Monitor pattern we described in [Sch06b]. Some patterns combine it with the AUTHORIZATION, ROLE-BASED ACCESS CONTROL or DAC patterns [Kim06], but we feel that it is better to separate it so that it can be combined with other models for the authorization rules.

■ The Java community has rediscovered this pattern and call it Intercepting Filter [Rad04] or Application Controller [OWAb].

6.9   Controlled Access Session

The CONTROLLED ACCESS SESSION pattern describes how to provide a context in which a subject (user, system) can access resources with different rights without need to reauthenticate every time they access a new resource.

Example

Lisa is a secretary in a medical organization who sometimes helps with patient tests in the laboratory. As a secretary she has access to patients' information such as name, address, social security number and so on. This is necessary so that she can bill them and their insurance companies. In the lab she has access to anonymized patient test results. Combining the accesses provided by her two jobs in one window allows her to associate test results and patients' names, which violates patient privacy.

Context

Any environment in which we need to control access to computing resources and in which users can be classified according to their jobs, groups, departments, assignments or tasks.

Problem

A given user may be authorized to access a system because they need to perform several functional activities. However, for a particular access, only those privileges should be active that are necessary to perform the intended task. This is an application of the principle of *least privilege*, and is necessary to prevent the user from misusing the system, either intentionally, accidentally by performing an error, or without knowledge and tricked to do so, for example through a Trojan Horse attack. Additionally, it potentially restricts damage in the case of session hijacking: a successful attack process would not have all the privileges of a user available, only the active subset.

The solution to this problem must resolve the following forces:

■ Subjects may have many rights directly or indirectly through the execution contexts they need for their tasks. Using all of them at one time may result in conflicts of interest and security violations. We need to restrict the use of those rights depending on the application or task the subject is performing.

- In the context of an interaction we can make access to some functions implicit, thus facilitating the use of the system and preventing errors that may result in vulnerabilities. For example, some editors or other tools could be implicitly available in some sessions.

- It is not convenient to make subjects reauthenticate every time they request a new resource. Once the subject is authenticated, this condition should remain valid during the whole session.

Solution

Define a unit of interaction, a *session*, which has a limited lifetime, for example between login and logoff of a user, or between the beginning and the end of a transaction. When a user logs on and after authentication, the session activates some execution contexts with only a subset of the authorizations they possess. This should be the minimum subset that is needed for the user or transaction to perform the intended task. Only those rights are available within the session. A subject can be in several sessions at the same time; however, in every session only the necessary rights are active.

Structure

Figure 6.16 shows the class model of the CONTROLLED ACCESS SESSION pattern. The classes Subject and Session have obvious meanings. The class ExecutionContext contains the set of active rights that the subject may use within the session.

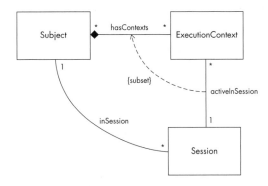

Figure 6.16: Class model for the CONTROLLED ACCESS SESSION pattern

Dynamics

Figure 6.17 shows the use case 'Open (activate) a session'. A subject logs on and the logon interface authenticates it. The box with a double arrow indicates some authentication dialog or protocol. After the subject is authenticated, the interface creates a session object and returns a handle to the subject.

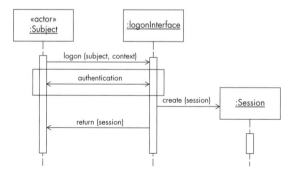

Figure 6.17: Sequence diagram for the use case 'Open a session'

Implementation

Based on institution and application policies, define which contexts (implying specific rights) should be used in each task and grant them to the corresponding subject. The rights should be selected using the least privilege principle, and there should be no contexts with excessive rights; for example, the administrator rights should be divided into smaller sets.

Example Resolved

Lisa can log on a secretary *or* as a lab assistant, but she cannot combine these activities in one session. Now she cannot relate test results to patients' names.

Consequences

The CONTROLLED ACCESS SESSION pattern offers the following benefits:

- We can give only the necessary rights to each execution context, according to its function, and we can invoke in a session only those contexts that are needed for a given task.
- We can exclude combinations of contexts that might result in possible access violations or conflicts of interest.
- Any functions can be made implicit in a session.
- Once a subject starts a session it doesn't have to be reauthenticated: its status is kept by the session.

The pattern also has the following potential liabilities:

- If we need to apply fine-grained access, it might be inefficient to include many contexts in order to perform complex activities.
- Using sessions may be confusing to the users.

Known Uses

- Session Access is part of the RBAC standard proposal by NIST, which has been adopted by the American National Standards Institute, International Committee for Information Technology Standards (ANSI/INCITS) as ANSI INCITS 359-2004 [Fer01b].
- Multics [Sum97] used execution contexts (based on projects) to limit access rights.
- Session Access is implemented in the security module CSAP [Dri03] of the Webocrat system in conjunction with an RBAC policy.
- Views in relational databases can be used to define sets of rights. Controlling the use of views by users can control their use of rights in sessions. This is done for example in Oracle and DB2, where SQL can be used to define restricted views [Elm03].

See Also

- The Access Session pattern is used in the SESSION-BASED ROLE-BASED ACCESS CONTROL pattern (page 107) and Attribute-Based Access Control [Pri04] patterns.
- The Session pattern of [Yod97] created a session object that defined a namespace to hold all the variables that need to be referenced by many objects.
- Peter Sommerlad remade this pattern as a Security Session [Sch06b], intended to prevent a user having to be reauthenticated every time they access a new object.
- Abstract Session [Pry00] is a pattern with a similar objective to Security Session: when an object's services are invoked by clients, the server object may have to maintain state for each client. The server creates a session object that encapsulates state information for the client, and returns a pointer to the session object.

However, none of these patterns considers limitation of rights. Our pattern is an extension of these patterns, concentrating all its security functions and emphasizing the function of a session as a limiter of rights.

6.10   Session-Based Role-Based Access Control

The SESSION-BASED ROLE-BASED ACCESS CONTROL pattern allows access to resources based on the role of the subject, and limits the rights that can be applied at a given time based on the roles defined by the access session.

Example

John is a developer on a project. He is also a project leader for another project. As a project leader he can evaluate the performance of the members of his project. He combines his two roles and adds several flattering evaluations about himself in the project where he is a developer. Later, his manager, thinking that the comments came from the project leader of the project on which John is a developer, gives John a big bonus.

Context

Any environment in which we need to control access to computing resources, in which users can be classified according to their jobs or their tasks, and in which we assign rights to the roles needed to perform those tasks.

We assume the existence of a Session pattern that can be used for the solution.

Problem

In an organization a user may play several roles. However, for each access the user must act only within the authorizations of a single role (that is, within the context of the role) or combinations of roles that do not violate institution policies. How can we force subjects to follow the policies of the institution when using their roles?

In addition to the forces defined for the CONTROLLED ACCESS SESSION pattern, the solution to this problem must resolve the following forces:

■ People in institutions have different needs for access to information, according to their functions. They may have several roles associated with specific functions or tasks.

■ We want to help the institution to define precise access rights for its members so that the least privilege policy can be applied when they perform specific tasks.

■ Users may have more than one role and we may want to enforce policies such as *separation of duty*, where a user cannot be in two or more specific roles in the same session.

Solution

A subject may have several roles. Each role collects the rights that a user can activate at a given moment (execution context), while a session controls the way in which roles are used, and can enforce role exclusion at execution time.

Structure

The structure of the SESSION-BASED ROLE-BASED ACCESS CONTROL pattern is shown in the class diagram in Figure 6.18. The class `Role` is an intermediary between `Subject` and `Object`, holding all authorizations a user possesses while performing the role, and acts here as an execution context. Within a `Session`, only a subset of the roles assigned to a `Subject` may be activated, just those necessary to perform the intended task. Roles may be composed according to a Composite pattern [Gam94], in which higher-level roles acquire (inherit) rights from lower-level roles.

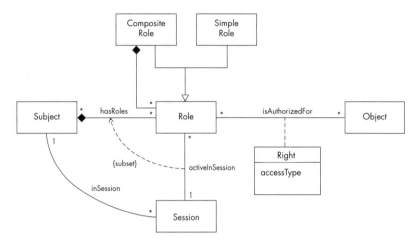

Figure 6.18: Class diagram for the SESSION-BASED ROLE-BASED ACCESS CONTROL pattern

Dynamics

Figure 6.19 shows a sequence diagram for the use case 'Request access to an object'. A `Subject` has already opened a `Session` (see Figure 6.17 on page 106) and requests access to an object in a specific way (`accessType`). The session uses the corresponding `ReferenceMonitor`, which in turn checks whether the rights of the `Session` roles allow the access. If so, the access is permitted.

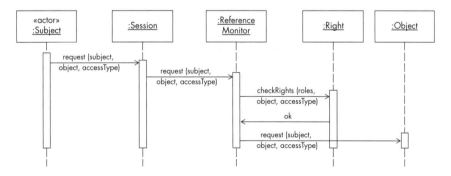

Figure 6.19: Sequence diagram for the use case 'Request access to an object'

Implementation

1   Determine the roles the system should contain (role catalog), according to the user functions or tasks.

2   Collect lists of incompatible roles and use these lists when a session is started (static constraints). These constraints can be defined using OCL or some other formal language as additions to the class diagram of the pattern.

3   Determine the number of roles which may be active within a session (dynamic constraints).

4   When a user opens a session, they must declare what roles they intend to use, and the system will open the corresponding session, or refuse to do so in the case of conflicts.

See [Fer06e] for an example of a real implementation.

Example Resolved

When John logs on in the project where he is a developer, he only gets the rights for a developer and cannot add evaluations. When he logs on in the project where he is a project leader he can only evaluate the members of his group. He cannot combine the rights of his role in the same session, and now he only gets legitimate evaluations.

Consequences

In addition to the benefits mentioned for CONTROLLED ACCESS SESSION (page 104), additional benefits of the SESSION-BASED ROLE-BASED ACCESS CONTROL pattern are:

■   Sessions may include all needed roles for those subjects authorized for some task.

■   Users can activate more than one session at a time for functional flexibility (some tasks may require multiple roles).

■   Fine-grained rights can be assigned to roles to enforce a need-to-know policy.

■   When a session is open, we can exclude roles that violate institution policies.

The pattern has the following potential liabilities

■   Additional conceptual complexity is required to define which roles can be used together and which should be mutually exclusive.

■   User confusion if they have to use several roles to perform their work.

Known Uses

■   The structure and dynamics of a Session-Based RBAC are implemented in the security module CSAP [Dri03] of the Webocrat system. Webocrat is a portal supporting

E-Democracy which was developed within the European Webocracy project (FP5-IST-1999-20364) between 2000-2003.

■ Views in relational databases can be used to define sets of rights. Controlling the use of views by roles can control the use of rights in sessions. In both Oracle and DB2 SQL can be used to define restricted views based on roles [Elm03].

See Also

This pattern is a combination of the CONTROLLED ACCESS SESSION pattern (page 104) and the RBAC pattern [Sch06b]. As indicated earlier, structuring of roles can be represented by a Composite pattern. A Reference Monitor pattern is needed to enforce the use of rights during execution.

6.11   Security Logger and Auditor

Also known as Audit Trail

The SECURITY LOGGER AND AUDITOR pattern describes how to keep track of users' actions in order to determine who did what and when. It logs all security-sensitive actions performed by users and provides controlled access to records for audit purposes.

Example

A hospital uses RBAC to define the rights of its employees. For example, doctors and nurses can read and write medical records and related patient information (lab tests and medicines). When a famous patient came to the hospital, one of the doctors, who was not treating him, read his medical record and leaked this information to the press. When the leak was discovered there was no way to find out which doctor had accessed the patient's records.

Context

Any system that handles sensitive data, in which it is necessary to keep a record of access to data.

Problem

How can we keep track of users' actions in order to determine who did what and when? The solution to this problem must resolve the following forces:

■ *Accuracy.* We should faithfully record what a user or process has done with respect to the use of system resources.

- *Security.* Any information we use to keep track of what the users have done must be protected. Unauthorized reading may reveal sensitive information. Tampering may erase past actions.

- *Forensics.* When a misuse of data occurs, it may be necessary to audit the access operations performed by users to determine possible unauthorized actions, and maybe trace the attacker or understand how the attack occurred.

- *System improvement.* The same misuses may keep occurring; we need to learn from past attacks.

- *Compliance.* We need a way to verify and to prove to third parties that we have complied with institution policies and external regulations.

- *Performance.* We need to minimize the overhead of logging.

Solution

Each time a user accesses some object, we record this access, indicating the user identifier, the type of access, the object accessed and the time when the access happened.

The database of access entries must have authentication and authorization systems, and possibly an encryption capability.

Structure

In Figure 6.20 User operations are logged by the LoggerAuditor. The LoggerAuditor keeps the Log of user accesses, in which each access is described by a LogEntry. The security administrator (SecAdmin) activates or deactivates the Log. The Auditor can read the Log to detect possible unauthorized actions.

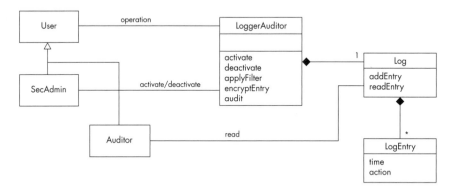

Figure 6.20: Class diagram of the SECURITY LOGGER AND AUDITOR pattern

Dynamics

Possible use cases include 'Log user access', 'Audit log', 'Query log database'.

A sequence diagram for the use case 'Log user access' is shown in Figure 6.21. The User performs an operation to apply an access type on some object: operation (accessType, object). The LoggerAuditor adds an entry with this information, and the name of the user, to the Log. The Log creates a LogEntry, adding the time of the operation.

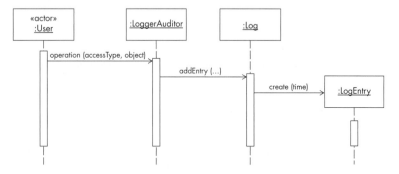

Figure 6.21: Sequence diagram for the use case 'Log user access'

Implementation

The class diagram shown in Figure 6.20 provides a clear guideline for implementation, since its classes can be directly implemented in any object-oriented language. We need to define commands to activate or deactivate logging, apply filters, indicate devices to be used, allocate amount of storage and select security mechanisms. One can filter some logging by selecting users, events, importance of events, times and objects in the filters. Administrative security actions, for example account creation/deletion, assignment of rights and others, must also be logged.

Logging is performed by calling methods on the LoggerAuditor class. Every non-filtered user operation should be logged. Logged messages can have levels of importance associated with them.

Audit is performed by an auditor reading the log. This can be complemented with manual assessments that include interviewing staff, performing security vulnerability scans, reviewing application and operating system access controls and analyzing physical access to the systems [sau]. The Model-View-Controller pattern can be used to visualize the data using different views during complex statistical analysis of the log data.

Example Resolved

After the incident, the hospital installed a SECURITY LOGGER AND AUDITOR, so in the future such violations can be discovered.

Consequences

The SECURITY LOGGER AND AUDITOR pattern offers the following benefits:

- *Security.* It is possible to add appropriate security mechanisms to protect recorded data, for example access control and/or encryption.

- *Forensics.* The pattern enables forensic auditing of misused data objects. Records of access can be used to determine whether someone has maliciously gained access to data. This pattern can also be used to log access to data objects by system processes. For example, malicious code planted in the system can be tracked by finding processes that have misused objects.

- *System improvement.* By studying how past attacks happened, we can improve the system security.

- *Compliance.* Auditing a log can be used to verify and prove that institutional and regulatory policies have been followed.

- *Performance.* We can reduce overhead by parallel or background logging. We can also not log some events not considered significant. Finally, we can merge this log with the recovery log, needed for possible rollback.

The pattern has the following potential liabilities:

- It can incur significant overhead, since each object access has to be logged.

- A decision must be made by software designers as to the granularity at which objects are logged. There is a trade-off between security and performance.

- It is not easy to perform forensic analysis, and specialists are required.

- Protecting the log adds some overhead and cost.

Variants

Most systems have a system logger, used to undo/rollback actions after a system crash. That type of logger has different requirements, but sometimes is merged with the security logger [SAP09]. System logs are of interest to system and database administrators, while security logs are used by security administrators, auditors and system designers.

Another variant could include the automatic raising of alarms by periodic examination of the log, searching records that match a number of rules that characterize known violations. For example, intrusion detection systems use this variant.

We can also add logging for reliability, to detect accidental errors.

Known Uses

- Most modern operating systems, including Microsoft Windows [Smi04], AIX [aix10], Solaris and others have security loggers.

- SAP uses both a security audit log and a system log [SAP09].

See Also

- The Secure Logger is a pattern for J2EE [Ste06]. It defines how to capture application-specific events and exceptions to support security auditing. This pattern is mostly implementation-oriented and does not consider the conceptual aspects discussed in our pattern. It should have been called a 'security logger', because it does not include any mechanisms to protect the logged information.

- Martin Fowler has an Audit Log analysis pattern [Fow] for tracking temporal information. The idea is that whenever something significant happens, you write some record indicating what happened and when it happened.

- Patterns for authentication (Chapter 5): how can we make sure that a subject is who they say they are?

- AUTHORIZATION (page 74) describes how we can control who can access to which resources, and how, in a computer system.

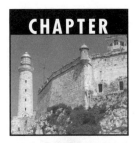

CHAPTER

7

Patterns for Secure Process Management

Music is given to us with the sole purpose of establishing an order in things, including, and particularly, the coordination between man and time.

Igor Stravinsky

7.1   Introduction

Operating systems are fundamental to the provision of security to computing systems. The operating system supports the execution of applications, and any security constraints defined by applications must be enforced by the operating system. The operating system must also protect itself, because compromise would give access to all the user accounts and all the data in their files. A weak operating system would allow hackers access not only to data in the operating system files, but data in database systems that use the services of the operating system. The operating system enables this protection by protecting processes from each other and protecting the permanent data stored in its files [Sil05]. For this purpose, the operating system controls access to resources such as memory address spaces and I/O devices. Most operating systems use an access matrix or the ROLE-BASED ACCESS CONTROL pattern (page 78) as a security model. For example, an access matrix defines which processes (subjects in general) have what types of access to specific resources (resources are represented as objects in modern operating systems).

In a computer system processes typically collaborate to perform some activity or call each other to request services. Process invocations occur through local or remote procedure calls; these operations are supported at the kernel level through send/receive operations, which may be direct or indirect (using mailboxes) [Sil05]. The operation name used for invocation, plus the number, type, and length of the parameters in the call is called the procedure *signature*. The controlled interaction of processes in a computing environment is fundamental to its security and reliability. Processes can be attacked by other processes or by external clients; errors in one process can propagate to others. Executing processes in a computing system need to be protected from attacks from other processes. Many of those attacks come from the invocation of unprotected (no access control) or wrong entry points, or using the wrong type or size of parameters in these calls.

Computer system functionality can be divided between the kernel (or operating system proper) components and user-oriented utilities such as browsers, media players and so on. Typically, an operating system includes the following functional components:

- *Process management*: handles creation and deletion of processes, communication and scheduling.

- *Memory management*: keeps track of which parts of memory are used by which processes; allocates and deallocates memory.

- *File management*: handles creation and deletion of files and directories, file searches, and mapping files to secondary storage.

- *I/O management*: provides interfaces to hardware device drivers, as well as handling mass memory management components including buffering, caching and spooling.

- *Networking*: controls communication paths between two or more systems.

- *Protection system*: includes authentication of users and file and memory protection.

- *User interface*: communicates between user and operating system, including command interpreters.

Operating systems authenticate users when they first log in. A user then executes an application composed of several concurrent processes. Processes are usually created through system calls to the operating system. A process that needs to create a new process gets the operating system to create a child process that is given access to some resources.

Executing applications need to create objects for their work. Some objects are created at program initialization, while others are created dynamically during execution. The access rights of processes with respect to objects must be defined when these processes are created. Applications also need resources such as I/O devices and others that may come from resource pools; when these resources are allocated, the application must be given rights for them. These rights are defined by authorization rules or policies that must be

enforced when a process attempts to access an object. This means that we need to intercept every access request; this is done by the REIFIED REFERENCE MONITOR (page 100).

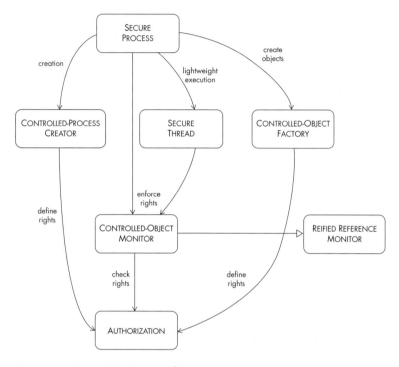

Figure 7.1: Patterns for secure process management

In this chapter we present patterns for secure process management. Figure 7.1 shows
how these patterns work together. They include:

- *SECURE PROCESS/THREAD.* How can we make sure that a process does not interfere
  with other processes or misuse shared resources? A process is a program in execution; a secure process is also a unit of execution isolation as well as a holder of
  rights to access resources, and has a separate virtual address space. A thread is a
  lightweight process. A variant, called Secure Thread, is a lightweight process with
  controlled access to resources.

- *CONTROLLED-PROCESS CREATOR.* How can we define the rights to be given to new
  processes? Define the rights of a new process as part of their creation.

- *CONTROLLED-OBJECT FACTORY.* How can we specify the rights of processes with
  respect to a new object? When a process creates a new object through a Factory, the
  request includes the features of the new object. These features include a list of rights
  to access the object.

- *CONTROLLED-OBJECT MONITOR.* How can we control access by a subject to an object? A specialized Reference Monitor can intercept access requests from processes. The Reference Monitor checks whether the process has the requested type of access to the object.

We also included in this chapter two patterns that are useful for process isolation:

- *PROTECTED ENTRY POINTS.* This pattern forces a call from one process to another to go through only pre-specified entry points where the correctness of the call is checked and other access restrictions can be applied.

- *PROTECTION RINGS.* This pattern assigns processes to a set of hierarchical rings that control how processes call each other and how they access data. Crossing of rings is done through *gates* that check the rights of the crossing process. A process calling another process or accessing data in a higher ring must go through a gate.

Patterns for process scheduling [wik1] and resource management [Kir04] also exist, but are not relevant to security and so are not discussed here.

The Controlled-Process Creator, the Controlled-Object Factory and the Controlled-Object Monitor patterns were published in [Fer03b], coauthored by John C. Sinibaldi. The Secure Process/Thread pattern was published in [Fer06f], coauthored with Tami Sorgente and Maria M. Larrondo-Petrie. The Protected Entry Points pattern appeared in [Fer08c], coauthored with David LaRed. Some of these patterns are updated versions of the ones in Chapter 8 of [Sch06b].

7.2   Secure Process/Thread

The SECURE PROCESS/THREAD pattern describes how to make sure that a process does not interfere with other processes or misuse shared resources. A process is a program in execution; a secure process is also a unit of execution isolation as well as a holder of rights to access resources, and has a separate virtual address space. A thread is a lightweight process. A variant, called Secure Thread, is a thread with controlled access to resources.

Example

A group of designers in Company X built an operating system and did not include any mechanisms to control the actions of processes. This resulted in processes being able to access the address space and resources of other processes. In this environment we cannot protect the shared information, nor assure the correct execution of any process – their code and stack sections may be corrupted by other processes. While its performance was good, nobody wanted to use this operating system once its poor security was known.

Context

Typically, operating systems support a multiprogramming environment, with many user-defined and system processes active at a given time. During execution it is essential to maintain all information regarding a process, including its current *status* (the value of the program counter), the contents of the processor's registers, and the process stack containing temporary data (subroutine parameters, return addresses, temporary variables and unresolved recursive calls). All this information is called the *process context*. When a process needs to wait, the operating system must save the context of the first process and load the next process for execution; this is a *context switch*. The saved process context is brought back when a suspended process resumes execution.

Problem

We need to control the resources accessed by a process during its execution and protect its context from other processes. The resources that can be accessed by a process define its *execution domain*, and the process should not break the boundaries of this domain. The integrity of a process' context is essential, not only for context switching, but also for security, so that it cannot be controlled by another process, and for reliability, to prevent a rogue process from interfering with other processes.

The solution to this problem must resolve the following forces:

- If processes have unrestricted access to resources, they can interfere with the execution of other processes and misuse shared resources. We need to control what resources they can access.

- Processes should be given only the rights they need to perform their functions (*need to know* or *least privilege* principle ([Gol06], Chapter 3).

- The rights assigned to a process should be fine-grained, otherwise we cannot apply the least privilege principle.

- Each process requires some data, a stack, and space for temporary variables to store the status of its devices and other information. All this information resides in its address space and needs to be protected.

Solution

Assign to each process a set of authorization rights to access the resources they need. Assign to the process a unique address space to store its context and execution-time data. This protects processes from interference from other processes, assuring confidentiality and integrity of the shared data and proper use of shared resources. In the *process descriptor*, a data structure containing all the information a process needs for its execution, add rights to make access to any resource explicitly authorized. Ensure that every access to a resource is intercepted and checked for authorization.

It may also be possible to add resource quotas, to avoid denial of service problems, but this requires some global resource usage policies.

Structure

Figure 7.2 shows the class diagram for the SECURE PROCESS/THREAD pattern. In the figure, each `ProcessDescriptor` has `ProcessRights` for specific `Resources`. Additional security information indicates the owner of the process. The `ProcessRights` are defined by the AUTHORIZATION pattern (page 74; the `ProcessDescriptor` acts as subject in this pattern) and are enforced by the REIFIED REFERENCE MONITOR pattern (page 100), which intercepts request for resources and checks them for authorization. More than one `ProcessDescriptor` can be created, describing different processes and corresponding to multiple executions of `ProgramCode`. A separate `VirtualAddressSpace` is associated with each process (defined by the VIRTUAL ADDRESS SPACE ACCESS CONTROL pattern (page 146). The process context is stored in the `VirtualAddressSpace` of the process, while the `ProgramCode` can be shared by several processes.

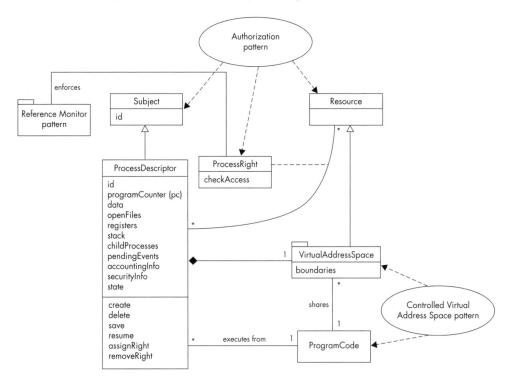

Figure 7.2: Class diagram for the SECURE PROCESS pattern

Dynamics

Figure 7.3 shows a sequence diagram for the use case 'Access a resource'. A `requestResource` operation from a process includes the process ID and the intended type of access. The request is intercepted by the `ReferenceMonitor`, which determines whether it is authorized (the `checkAccess` operation in the `Right` class). If so, the access proceeds.

Other related use cases (not shown) include 'Assign a right to a process' and 'Remove a right from a process'.

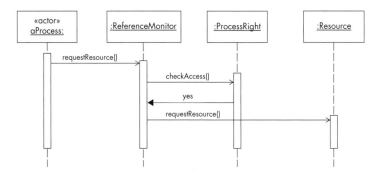

Figure 7.3: Sequence diagram for the use case 'Access a resource'

Implementation

The process descriptor is typically called a *process control block* (PCB), or *task control block* (TCB), and includes references (pointers) to its code section, its stack and other required information. There are different ways of implementing data structures: records (structs in C) are typically used for the process descriptor. The process descriptors of the processes in the same state are usually linked in a double-linked list. The hardware may include registers for some of the attributes of the process descriptor; for example, the Intel X86 Series includes registers for typical attributes. There are various ways of associating a virtual address space to a process, described in Chapter 9. There are also various ways to associate rights with a new process; see the CONTROLLED-PROCESS CREATOR pattern (page 126). The hardware architecture normally implements the virtual address space, and restricts access to the sections (segments) allocated to each process using appropriate mechanisms.

The patterns as shown describe models where subjects have rights described by an access matrix or according to ROLE-BASED ACCESS CONTROL (page 78). Some operating systems use multilevel (typically mandatory) models in which the access of a process is determined by its level with respect to the resource being accessed [Sch06b]. In the latter case, the process, instead of being given a right, has a tag or label that indicates its level. Resources have similar tags and the reference monitor compares both tags.

Example Resolved

Company X solved its problem by adding rights to a process representation. Now each process is constrained to access only those resources for which it has rights. This protects processes from each other, as well as the confidentiality and integrity of shared data and other resources. While other security problems may still persist, the general security of the operating system increased significantly.

Consequences

The SECURE PROCESS/THREAD pattern offers the following benefits:

- It is possible to give specific rights for resources to each process which restricts them to access only authorized resources.

- It is possible to apply the least privilege principle for execution.

- The process' contexts can be protected from other processes, because they are restricted to access only authorized resources.

- The virtual address space of a process can be protected by the hardware and its memory manager.

The pattern has the following potential liabilities:

- There is some overhead in using a Reference Monitor to enforce accesses.

- It may not be clear what rights to assign to each process.

- Having a separate address space implies a slow context switch, which affects performance. Because of this, kernel processes usually share an address space.

- There are other security problems not controlled by this pattern, such as denial of service, users taking control in administrator mode, or virus propagation. Those problems require complementary security mechanisms, some of which are described by other patterns [Sch06b].

Known Uses

- Linux uses records for process descriptors. One of the entries defines the process credentials (rights) that define its access to resources [Nut03] [Sil05]. Other entries describe its owner (subject) and process ID. A more elaborated approach using execution domains is used in Selinux, a secure version of Linux [Sel].

- Windows NT and 2000. Resources are defined as objects (actually, as classes). The process ID is used to determine access to objects [Sil05]. Each file object has a security descriptor that indicates the owner of the file, and an access control list that describes the access rights for the processes to access the file.

- Solaris threads have controlled access to resources defined in the application, for example when using the POSIX standard [Sil05].

- Operating systems running on Intel architectures can protect thread stacks, data and code by placing them in special segments of the shared address space, with hardware-controlled access.

Variant

- *Secure Thread*. Because of the slow context switching of processes, most operating systems use *threads*, which have a smaller context. How can we make the execution of a thread secure? A secure thread is a thread with controlled access to resources. Figure 7.4 represents the addition of the `ThreadDescriptor` to the secure process. One process may have multiple threads of execution. Each thread is represented by a `ThreadDescriptor`. A unique `VirtualAddressSpace` is associated with a process and shared by peer threads. `ThreadRights` define access rights to the `VirtualAddressSpace`.

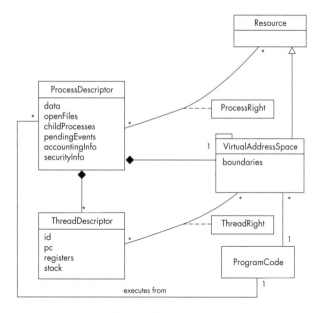

Figure 7.4: Class diagram for the SECURE THREAD pattern

Thread status typically includes a stack, a program counter and some status bits. There are various ways of associating threads with a process [Sil05]; typically, several threads are collected into a process. Threads can be created with special packages, for example PTHREADS in UNIX, or through the language, as in Java or Ada. Rights can be added explicitly, or we can use the hardware architecture's enforcement of the proper use of the process areas (see Known Uses).

See Also

- CONTROLLED-PROCESS CREATOR (below): at process creation time, rights are assigned to the process.
- VIRTUAL ADDRESS SPACE ACCESS CONTROL (page 146). A virtual address space is assigned to each process that can be accessed according to the rights of the process.
- AUTHORIZATION (page 74), which defines the rights to access resources.
- The REIFIED REFERENCE MONITOR pattern (page 100), used to enforced the defined rights.
- Processes run at rebooting are critical for security [Loh10].

7.3   Controlled-Process Creator

The CONTROLLED-PROCESS CREATOR pattern describes how to define the rights to be given to new processes, by defining the rights as part of the process' creation.

Example

The UNIX operating system creates a process with the same rights as its parent. If a hacker can trick UNIX into creating a child of the supervisor process, this runs with all the rights of the supervisor.

Context

An operating system in which processes or threads need to be created according to application needs. Users execute applications composed of several concurrent processes. Processes are normally created through system calls to the operating system.

Problem

A computing system uses many processes or threads. Processes need to be created according to applications' needs, and the operating system itself is composed of processes. If processes are not controlled, they can interfere with each other and access data illegally. Their rights to resources should be carefully defined according to appropriate policies, for example *need to know*.

The solution to this problem must resolve the following forces:

- There should be a convenient way to select a policy to define process' rights. Defining rights without a policy brings contradictory and unsystematic access restrictions that can be easily circumvented.

- The child process may need to run with its parent process' rights for specific actions, but this should be carefully controlled, otherwise a compromised child could leak information or destroy data.

- The number of children created by a process must be restricted, or *process spawning* could be used to perform denial-of-service attacks.

- There are situations in which a process needs to act with more than its normal rights, for example to get data from a file to which it doesn't normally have access.

Solution

Because new processes are created through system calls or messages to the operating system, we have a chance to control the rights given to the new process. Typically, operating systems create a new process as a child process. There are several policies for granting rights to a child process. For example:

- The child process can inherit all the rights of its parent, or a subset of them.

- Allow the parent assign a specific set of rights to its children (more secure).

Structure

Figure 7.5 shows the class diagram for this pattern. The `ControlledProcessCreator` is the part of the operating system in charge of creating processes. The `CreationRequest` contains the access rights that the parent defines for the created child. These access rights must be a subset of the parent's access rights.

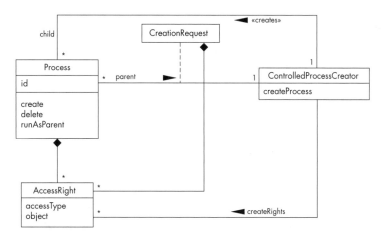

Figure 7.5: Class diagram for the CONTROLLED-PROCESS CREATOR pattern

Dynamics

Figure 7.6 shows the dynamics of process creation. A `Process` requests the creation of a new `Process`. The access rights passed in the creation request are used to create the `AccessRights` for the new process.

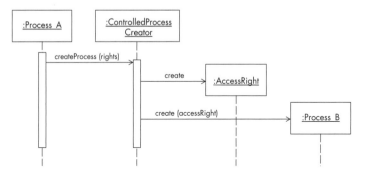

Figure 7.6: Process creation dynamics

Implementation

For each required application of kernel processes or threads, define their rights according to their intended function.

Example Resolved

There is now no automatic inheritance of rights in the creation of child processes, so creating a child process confers no advantage for a hacker.

Consequences

The CONTROLLED-PROCESS CREATOR pattern offers the following benefits:

- It is possible to define rights to use an object according to its sensitivity.
- Objects allocated from a resource pool can have rights attached dynamically.
- The operating system can apply ownership policies: for example, the creator of an object may receive all possible rights for the objects it creates.
- The created process can receive rights according to predefined security policies.
- The number of children produced by a process can be controlled. This is useful to control denial of service attacks.
- The rights may include the parent's ID, allowing the child to run with the rights of its parent.

The following potential liability may arise from applying this pattern:

■ Explicit rights transfer takes more time than using a default transfer.

Known Uses

In many operating systems, for example UNIX, rights are inherited as a full set from the parent. Some hardened operating systems, such as Hewlett Packard's Virtual Vault, do not allow inheritance, and a new set of rights must be defined for each child [HP].

See Also

The CONTROLLED EXECUTION DOMAIN pattern (page 151) could use this pattern to define the execution domain of new processes.

7.4 Controlled-Object Factory

The CONTROLLED-OBJECT FACTORY pattern describes how to specify the rights of processes with respect to a new object. When a process creates a new object through a Factory, the request includes the features of the new object. Among these features it includes a list of rights to access the object.

Example

In many operating systems the creator of an object gets all possible rights to the object. Other operating systems apply predefined sets of rights: for example, in UNIX all the members of a file owner's group may receive equal rights for a new file. These approaches may result in unnecessary rights being given to some users, violating the principle of *least privilege* (see Chapter 6 and [Fer11d]).

Context

A computing system that needs to control access to the objects it creates because of their different degrees of sensitivity. Rights for these objects are defined by authorization rules or policies that should be enforced when a process attempts to access an object.

Problem

In a computing environment, executing applications need to create objects for their work. Some objects are created at program initialization, while others are created dynamically during execution. The access rights of processes with respect to objects must be defined when these processes are created, or there may be opportunities for the processes to misuse them. Applications also need resources such as I/O devices and others that may come from resource pools: when these resources are allocated, the application must be given rights to them.

The solution to this problem must resolve the following forces:

■ Applications create objects of many different types, but we need to handle them uniformly with respect to their access rights, otherwise it would be difficult to apply standard security policies.

■ We need to allow objects in a resource pool to be allocated and have their rights set dynamically; not doing so would be too rigid.

■ There may be specific policies that define who can access a new object, and we need to apply them when creating the rights for an object. This is a basic aspect of security.

Solution

Whenever a new object is created, define a list of subjects that can access it, and in what way.

Structure

The class diagram for this pattern is shown in Figure 7.7. When a `Process` creates a new object through a `Factory`, the `CreationRequest` includes the features of the new object. Among these features is a list of rights defining rights for a `Subject` to access the created `Object`. This implies that we need to intercept every access request: this is done by an implementation of the CONTROLLED-OBJECT MONITOR pattern (page 132).

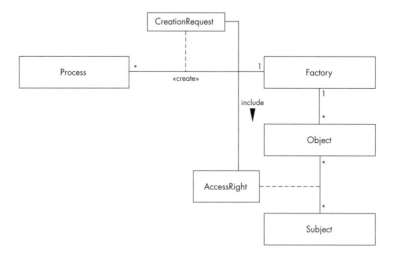

Figure 7.7: Class diagram for the CONTROLLED-OBJECT FACTORY pattern

Dynamics

Figure 7.8 shows the dynamics of object creation. A `Process` creating an `Object` through a `Factory` defines the rights for other subjects with respect to this object.

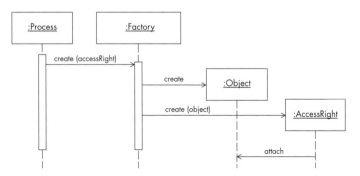

Figure 7.8: Object creation dynamics

Implementation

Each object may have an associated access control list (ACL). This will list the rights each subject (represented by a process) has for the associated object. Each entry specifies the rights that any other object within the system can have. In general, each right can be an 'allow' or a 'deny'. These are known as *access control entries* (ACE) in the Windows environment [Har01] [Mic00]. The set of access rules is also known as the *access control list* (ACL) in Windows and most other operating systems.

Capabilities are an alternative to an ACL. A capability corresponds to a row in an access matrix. This is in contrast to the ACL, which is associated with the object. The capability indicates to the secure object that the subject does indeed have the right to perform the operation. The capability may carry some authentication features in order to show that the object can trust the provided capability information. A global table can contain rows that represent capabilities for each authenticated user [And08], or the capability may be implemented as a list for each user which indicates to which object they have access.

Example Resolved

Our users can now be given only the rights to the created objects that they need. This prevents them from having too many (possibly unnecessary) object rights: many misuses occur through processes having too many rights.

Consequences

The CONTROLLED-OBJECT FACTORY pattern offers the following benefits:

- There can be no objects that have default access rights because somebody forgot to define access rights for them.
- It is possible to define access rights for an object based on its sensitivity.
- Objects allocated from a resource pool can have rights attached to them dynamically.
- The operating system can apply ownership policies: for example, the creator of an object may receive all possible rights to the objects it creates.

The following potential liabilities may arise from applying this pattern:

- There is a process creation overhead.
- It may not be clear what initial rights to define.

Known Uses

The Win32 API allows a process to create objects with various `create()` system calls using a structure containing access control information (DACL) passed as a reference. When the object is created the access control information is associated with the object by the kernel: the kernel returns a handle to the caller to be used for access to the object. Other operating systems apply predefined sets of rights: for example, all the members of the owner's group in UNIX may receive equal rights for a new file.

See Also

Builder and other creation patterns [Gam94].

7.5   Controlled-Object Monitor

The CONTROLLED-OBJECT MONITOR pattern allows control of access by a subject to an object, using a specialized Reference Monitor to intercept access requests from processes. The Reference Monitor checks whether the process has the requested type of access to the object.

Example

Our operating system does not check all user requests for access to resources such as files or areas of memory. A hacker discovered that some accesses are not checked, and was able to steal customer information from our files. He also left a program that randomly overwrites memory areas and creates serious disruption for other users.

Context

A computing system that needs to control access to its created objects because of their different degrees of sensitivity. Rights for these objects are defined by authorization rules or policies that should be enforced when a process attempts to access an object.

Problem

When objects are created we define the rights of processes over them. These authorization rules or policies must be enforced when a process attempts to access an object.

The solution to this problem must resolve the following forces:

- There may be many objects with different access restrictions defined by authorization rules; we need to enforce these restrictions when a process attempts to access an object.
- We need to control different types of access, or the object may be misused.

Solution

Use a specialized reference monitor to intercept access requests from processes. The reference monitor checks whether the process has the requested type of access to the object according to some access rule.

Structure

Figure 7.9 shows the class diagram for this pattern. This is a more specific implementation of the Reference Monitor pattern ([Sch06b]). The modification shows how the system associates the rules to the secure object in question.

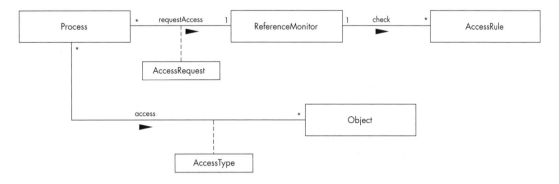

Figure 7.9: Class diagram for the CONTROLLED-OBJECT MONITOR pattern

Dynamics

Figure 7.10 shows the dynamics of secure subject access to a secure `Object`. Here the request is sent to the `ReferenceMonitor`, where it checks the `AccessRules`. If the access is allowed, it is performed and the result returned to the subject. Note that here, a handle or ticket is returned to the subject, so that future access to the secure `Object` can be performed directly, without additional checking.

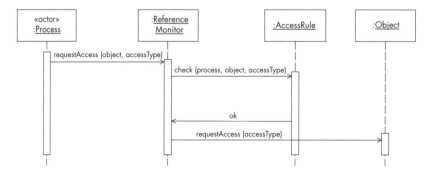

Figure 7.10: Sequence diagram for validating an access request

Implementation

A possible implementation would be as follows:

1   A user is authenticated when they log on.

2   Created objects inherit the original user's ID that is contained within a token. This token associates with the user process to be used by the operating system to resolve access rights. Only those authorized may have the desired access to the secure object.

3   Each object that a user wishes to access may have an associated access control list (ACL). This will list what right each user has for the associated object.

4   Each entry specifies what right any other object within the system can have. In general, each right can be an 'allow' or a 'deny'. These are also known as access control entries (ACE) in the Windows environment [Har01] [Mic00]. The set of access rules is also known as the access control list (ACL) in Windows and most operating systems (see Chapter 6).

Capabilities are an alternative to the ACL. A capability corresponds to a row in an access matrix. This is in contrast to the ACL, which is associated with the object. The capability indicates to the secure object that the subject does indeed have the right to perform the operation. The capability may carry some authentication features in order to show that the object can trust the provided capability information. A global table can contain rows that represent capabilities for each authenticated user [And08], or the capability may be implemented as a list corresponding to each user, indicating what objects the user can access.

Example Resolved

A reference monitor mediates all requests. There are now no unchecked requests, so a hacker cannot get access to unauthorized files or memory areas.

Consequences

The CONTROLLED-OBJECT MONITOR pattern offers the following benefits:

- The access rules can implement an access matrix defining different types of access for each subject.
- Each access request can be intercepted and accepted or rejected depending on the authorization rules.

Potential liabilities include:

- The need to protect the authorization rules. However, the same mechanism that protects resources can also protect the rules.
- The overhead of controlling each access. Some accesses may be compiled for efficiency.

Known Uses

Windows NT. The Windows NT security subsystem provides security using the patterns described here. It has the following three components (see [Har01] [Kel97] [Mic00]):

- Local Security Authority
- Security Account Manager
- Security Reference Monitor

This implementation is described in detail on page 153.

Java 1.2 Security. The Java security subsystem provides security using the patterns described here. The Java access controller builds access permissions based on permission and policy. It has a `checkPermission` method that determines the codesource object of each calling method and uses the current policy object to determine the permission objects associated with it. Note that the `checkPermission` method will traverse the call stack to determine the access of all calling methods in the stack. The `java.policy` file is used by the security manager and contains the grant statements for each codesource.

7.6   Protected Entry Points

The PROTECTED ENTRY POINTS pattern describes how to force a call from one process to another to go through only prespecified entry points where the correctness of the call is checked and other access restrictions may be applied.

Example

ChronOS is a company building a new operating system, including a variety of plug-in services such as media players, browsers and others. In their design, processes can call each other in unrestricted ways. This makes process calls fast, which results in generally good performance, and everybody is satisfied. However, when they test the system, an error anywhere produces problems, because it propagates to other processes, corrupting their execution. Also, many security attacks are shown to be possible. It is clear that when their systems are in use they will acquire a bad reputation and ChronOS will have problems selling it. They need to have a system that provides resilient service in the presence of errors, and which is resistant to attacks.

Context

Executing processes in a computing system. Processes need to call other processes to ask for services or to collaborate in the computation of an algorithm, and usually share data and other resources. The environment can be centralized or distributed. Some processes may be malicious or contain errors.

Problem

Process communication has an effect on security, because if a process calls another using entry points without appropriate checks, the calling process may read or modify data illegally, alter the code of the executing process, or take over its privilege level. If the checks are applied at specific entry points, some languages, such as C or C++, let the user manipulate pointers to bypass those entry points. Process communication also has a major effect on reliability, because an error in a process may propagate to others and disrupt their execution.

The solution to this problem must resolve the following forces:

- Executing processes need to call each other to perform their functions. For example, in operating systems user processes need to call kernel processes to perform I/O, communications and other system functions. In all environments, process may collaborate to solve a common problem, and this collaboration requires communication. All this means that we cannot use process isolation to solve this problem.

- A call must go to a specified entry point or checks could be bypassed. Some languages let users alter entry point addresses, allowing input checks to be bypassed.

- A process typically provides services to other processes, but not all services are available to all processes. A call to a service not authorized to a process can be a security threat or allow error propagation.

- In a computing environment we have a variety of processes with different levels of trust. Some are processes that we normally trust, such as kernel processes; others may include operating system utilities, user processes and processes of uncertain origin. Some of these processes may have errors or be malicious. All calls need to be checked.

- The number, type and size of the passed parameters in a call can be used to attack a process, for example by producing a buffer overflow. Incorrect parameters may produce or propagate an error.

Solution

Systems that use explicit message passing have the possibility of checking each message to see if it complies with system policies. For example, one security feature that can be applied when calling another process is *protected entry points*. A process calling another process can only enter the called process at predesigned entry points, and only if the signature used is correct (name, number of parameters, type and size of parameters). This prevents bypassing entry checks and avoids attacks such a buffer overflows.

Structure

Figure 7.11 shows the class diagram of the solution. `CallingProcess` and `CalledProcess` are roles of processes in general. When a `CallingProcess` makes a request for a service to another process, the request is handled by an `EntryPoint`. This `EntryPoint` has a name and a list of parameters with predefined numbers, types, and size limits that can be used to check the correctness of the call signature. It can optionally add access control checks by using a Reference Monitor pattern or other input data tests.

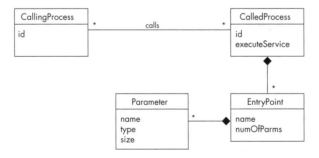

Figure 7.11: Class diagram for the PROTECTED ENTRY POINTS pattern

Dynamics

Figure 7.12 shows a `CallingProcess` performing a service call. The call must use a proper signature: that is, if the name of the service (`opName`) or the names of the parameters are incorrect, and the type or length of the parameters is not correct, it is rejected (this is checked by operation `checkParmList`).

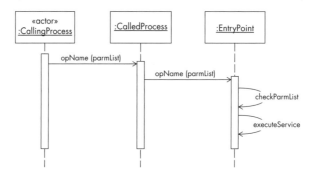

Figure 7.12: Sequence diagram for a process making a service call

Implementation

Kernels support calls as direct calls or through mailboxes. In the first case, the called process must check that the call is correct; in the second case, the mailbox must do the checking.

Entry points must be expressed as references as in Java, and not as pointers, as in C or C++ (as pointers allow arithmetic operations). In languages that use pointers, it is necessary to restrict their use in procedure calls; for example by disallowing pointer arithmetic.

Example Resolved

If the parameters of all calls are validated through protected entry points, many security and reliability problems can be avoided. Additional checks, such as access control and data value checks, can also be applied.

Consequences

The PROTECTED ENTRY POINTS pattern offers the following benefits:

- If we can check all the calls of one process to another, we can check that the calls are for appropriate services and apply checks for security or reliability purposes.

- Checking the number, type and length of the parameters passed in a call can prevent a variety of attacks and stop the propagation of some errors.
- If we know the level of trust of processes, we can adjust the number of checks; for example, we can apply more checks to suspicious processes.

Known Uses

- Multics.
- Systems that use ring architectures, for example the Intel Series 86 and Pentium.
- Systems that use capabilities, such as IBM S/6000.
- A specific use can be found in a patent for PC BIOS [Day91].

See Also

- This pattern can be seen as a specific realization of the abstract principle *validate input parameters*.
- The PROTECTION RINGS pattern (see below).
- Multilevel Secure Partitions; see [Fer08c].
- The CAPABILITY pattern (page 96).
- Access control and distributed access control (Chapter 6). These checks can be applied in specific entry points to control access to resources.

7.7 Protection Rings

The PROTECTION RINGS pattern allows control of how processes call other processes and how they access data. Crossing of rings is done through *gates* that check the rights of the crossing process. A process calling another process or accessing data in a higher ring must go through a gate.

Example

The ChronOS designers found that for applications that use programs with a variety of origins, there is a high overhead in applying elaborate checks to all of them. It would be more efficient to apply the checks selectively, depending on how much they trust the programs making the calls, but this is not usually known at execution time. If they could find a way to classify processes according to trust, they could improve the application of checks. It is not enough to rely on program features to enforce entering the right entry points, because applications may come in a variety of languages, some of which may allow skipping entry points.

Context

Executing processes in a computing system. Processes need to call other processes to ask for services or to collaborate in the computation of an algorithm, and usually share data and other resources. Some processes may be malicious or contain errors that may affect process execution. This pattern applies only to centralized environments, as opposed to distributed systems.

Problem

Defining a set of protected entry points is not enough if we cannot enforce their use. How can we prevent a process from calling another on an entry point that has no checks? We cannot rely on language features unless we only use a restricted set of languages, which is not practical in general. If all processes are alike we also need to apply the same checks to all of them, which may be overkill.

The solution to this problem must resolve the following forces:

- We want to be able to enforce the application of protected entry points, at least for some processes. In this way, requests from suspicious processes can always be controlled.

- We would like to separate processes according to their level of trust, and check only calls from a low-level to a higher-level process. This can reduce execution-time overhead considerably.

- In each higher level we can check signature validity, as well as control access or apply reliability tests. These actions should result in a more secure execution environment.

Solution

Define a set of hierarchical protection domains, called *protection rings* (typically 4 to 32) with different levels of trust. Assign processes to rings based on their level of trust. Ring crossing is performed through gates that enforce protected entry points: a process calling a higher-level process or accessing data at a higher level can only call this process or access data at predesigned entry points with controlled parameters. Additional checks for security or reliability can be applied at the entry points.

Structure

Figure 7.13 shows a class diagram for this pattern. The `CallingProcess` requests services from a `CalledProcess`. To do so, it must enter a `CallGate`, which applies protected entry points that check the correct use of signatures. `CallRules` define the requirements for inter-level calls. The `CallingProcess` can access `Data` according to a set of `DataAccessRules`.

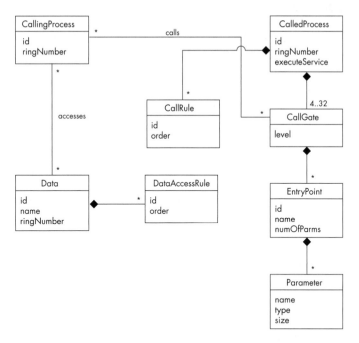

Figure 7.13: Class diagram for the PROTECTION RINGS pattern

Dynamics

Figure 7.14 shows a sequence diagram for a call to a higher-privilege ring. If the call fails an exception may be raised.

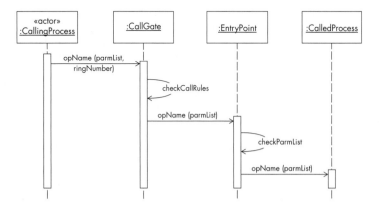

Figure 7.14: Sequence diagram for a successful call to a higher-privilege ring

Implementation

The call rules and the data access rules are usually implemented in the call instruction microcode [int99]. Figure 7.15 shows a typical use of rings. Processes are assigned to rings based on their level of trust; for example, we could assign four rings in decreasing order of privilege and trust, to supervisor, utilities, trusted user programs, untrusted user programs.

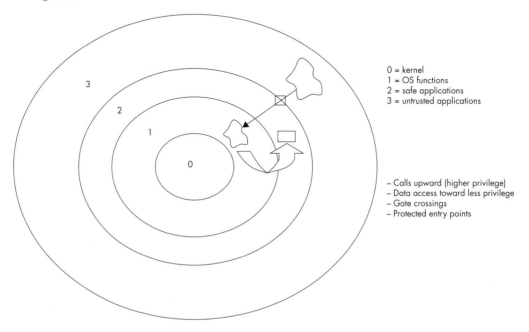

0 = kernel
1 = OS functions
2 = safe applications
3 = untrusted applications

– Calls upward (higher privilege)
– Data access toward less privilege
– Gate crossings
– Protected entry points

Figure 7.15: Assignment of protection rings

The program status word of the process indicates its current ring, and data descriptors also indicate their assigned rings. The values of the calling and called processes are compared to apply the transfer rules.

The Intel X86 architecture [int99] applies two rules:

■ Calls are allowed only in a more privileged direction, with possible restriction of a minimum calling level.

■ Data at level p can be accessed only by a program executing at a more privileged level ($<= p$).

Another possibility for improving security is to allow calls only within a range of rings: in other words, jumping many rings is considered suspicious. Multics defined a *call bracket*, where calls are allowed only within rings in the bracket. More precisely, for a call from procedure i to a procedure with bracket (n1, n2, n3) the following rules apply:

- If n2<i<=n3, the call is allowed to specific entry points.
- If i>n3, the call is not allowed.
- If i < n1, any entry point is valid.

This extension only makes sense for systems that have many rings.

Example Resolved

Now we can preassign processes to levels according to their trust. All calls to processes of higher privilege are checked. Processes of low trust get more checks.

Consequences

The PROTECTION RINGS pattern offers the following benefits:

- We can separate processes according to their level of trust.
- Level transfers happen only through gates where we can apply the PROTECTED EN-TRY POINTS pattern; that is, we have enforced protected entry points for upward calls.
- We can control procedure calls as well as data access across levels.

The pattern also has some potential liabilities:

- Crossing rings take time. Because of this delay, some operating systems use fewer rings. For example, Windows uses two rings, IBM's OS/2 uses three rings [wik2]. Using fewer rings improves performance at the expense of security.
- Without hardware support the crossing ring overhead is unacceptable, which means that this approach is only practical for operating systems and for centralized environments.

Variants

- Rings don't need to be strictly hierarchical; partial orders are possible and convenient for some applications. For example, a system that includes a secure database could assign a level to the database equal to but separated from system utilities; the highest level is for the kernel, and the lowest level is for user programs. This was done in a design involving an IBM 370 [Fer78].
- In some systems, such as the MV8000, rings are associated with memory locations.
- Multics used the concept of the *call bracket*, where a call can be made within a range of rings.

Known Uses

- Multics introduced this concept and used 32 rings, as well as call brackets [Gra68].
- The Intel Series X86 and Pentium [int99].
- MV8000 [mv] [Wal81].
- Hitachi HITAC.
- ICL 2900, VAX 11 and MARA, described in [Fro85], which also describes Multics and the Intel series.
- [Shi00] shows a use of rings to protect against malicious mobile code.
- An IBM S/370 was modified to have non-hierarchical rings [Fer78].
- Rings have been used for fault-tolerant applications [Oza88].

See Also

- A combination (process, domain) corresponds to a row of the Access Matrix [Sch06b].
- Multilevel Secure Partitions [Fer08c] is an alternative for distributed environments, in which processes are assigned levels based on multilevel security models.
- PROTECTED ENTRY POINTS (page 136).

CHAPTER

8
Patterns for Secure Execution and File Management

The severity of the laws prevents their execution.

Charles de Montesquieu

8.1　Introduction

In this chapter we present patterns for the secure execution of processes:

- ■ *VIRTUAL ADDRESS SPACE ACCESS CONTROL*. How can we control access by processes to specific areas of their virtual address space (VAS) according to a set of predefined access types? Divide the VAS into segments that correspond to logical units in the programs. Use special words (*descriptors*) to represent access rights for these segments.

- ■ *EXECUTION DOMAIN*. How can we define an execution environment for processes, indicating explicitly all the resources a process can use during its execution, as well as the type of access for the resources? Attach a set of descriptors to the process that represent the rights of the process.

- *CONTROLLED EXECUTION DOMAIN.* How can we define an execution environment for processes? Attach a set of descriptors to each process that represents the rights of the process. Use the Reference Monitor pattern to enforce access.

- *VIRTUAL ADDRESS SPACE STRUCTURE SELECTION.* How can we select the virtual address space for operating systems that have special security needs? Some systems emphasize isolation, others information sharing, yet others good performance. The organization of each process' virtual address space (VAS) is defined by the hardware architecture and has an effect on performance and security. Consider all the hardware possibilities and select according to need.

Assume here that resources are represented as objects, as it is common in modern operating systems. Figure 8.1 shows how these patterns are organized into a pattern language. For example, authentication is needed for file access and for controlled object access, a subject must be authorized to access some object in a specific way, and we need to make sure that the requester is not an imposter. The other three patterns complete the definition of the controlled execution domain, where the creation and access to objects are now controlled.

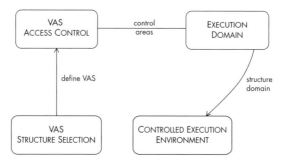

Figure 8.1: Patterns for secure process execution

The first three patterns come from [Fer02], the last one from [Fer05c].

8.2 Virtual Address Space Access Control

The VIRTUAL ADDRESS SPACE ACCESS CONTROL pattern allows control of access by processes to specific areas of their virtual address space (VAS) according to a set of predefined access types.

Context

Multiprogramming systems with a variety of users. Processes executing on behalf of these users must be able to share memory areas in a controlled way. Each process runs in its own address space. The total virtual address space (VAS) at a given moment includes the union of the VASs of the individual processes, including user and system processes. Typical allowed accesses are read, write, and execute, although finer access typing is possible.

Problem

Processes must be controlled when accessing memory, otherwise they could overwrite each other's memory areas or gain access to private information. While relatively small amounts of data can be directly compromised, illegal access to system areas could allow a process to get a higher execution privilege level and thus access files and other resources.

The solution to this problem must resolve the following forces:

- There is a need for a variety of access rights for each separate logical unit (*segment*) of the VAS. In this way security and controlled sharing are possible.

- There is a variety of virtual memory address space structures: some systems use a set of separate address spaces, others a single-level address space. Further, the VAS may be split between the users and the operating system. We would like to control access to all of these types of virtual memory in a uniform manner.

- For any approach to be efficient, hardware support is necessary. This implies that an implementation of the solution will require a specific hardware architecture. However, the solution must be hardware-independent.

Solution

Divide the VAS into segments that correspond to logical units in the programs. Use special words (*descriptors*) to indicate access rights as the starting address of the accessible segment, the limit of the accessible segment and the type of access permitted (read, write, execute).

Figure 8.2 shows a class diagram of the solution. A `Process` must have a `Descriptor` to access a segment in the `VAS`.

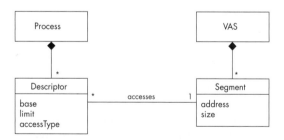

Figure 8.2: Class diagram for the VIRTUAL ADDRESS SPACE ACCESS CONTROL pattern

Implementation

Some implementation aspects include:

- The limit check when accessing an address must be done by the instruction micro-code, or the overhead would be unacceptable. This check is part of an instance of the REIFIED REFERENCE MONITOR pattern (page 100).

- The same idea applies to purely paging systems, except that the limit in the descriptor is defined by the page size. In paged systems pages do not correspond to logical units and cannot perform a fine-granularity security control.

- There are two basic ways to implement this pattern:
  - *Proper descriptor systems.* The descriptors are loaded at process creation by the operating system, handled through special registers, and disappear at the end of execution.
  - *Capability systems.* A special trusted portion of the operating system distributes capabilities to programs. Programs own these capabilities: to use them, the operating system loads them into special registers or memory segments. In both cases, access to files is derived from their ACLs.

Consequences

The VIRTUAL ADDRESS SPACE ACCESS CONTROL pattern offers the following benefits:

- The pattern provides the required segment protection, because a process cannot access a segment without a descriptor for it. Two processes with descriptors with the same base–limit pair can conveniently share a segment.

- The pattern applies to any type of virtual address space: single, segregated or split.

- If all resources are mapped to the virtual address space, the pattern can control access to any type of resource, including files.

- The solution can be implemented in different ways.

The pattern also has the following potential liabilities:

- Segmentation makes storage allocation inefficient because of external fragmentation [Sil03]. In most systems segments are paged for convenient allocation.

- Hardware support is needed, which makes the implementation of this solution hardware-dependent.

- In systems that use separate address spaces, it is necessary to add an extra identifier to the descriptor registers to indicate the address space number.

Known Uses

The Plessey 250 [Ham73], Multics [Gra68], IBM S/38, IBM S/6000, Intel X86 [Chi84] and Intel Pentium use some type of descriptors for memory access control. The operating systems in these machines must use this approach for memory management.

See Also

This pattern is a direct application of the AUTHORIZATION pattern (page 74) to the processes' address space.

8.3   Execution Domain

The EXECUTION DOMAIN pattern describes how to define an execution environment for processes, indicating explicitly all the resources a process can use during its execution, as well as the type of access for the resources.

Context

A process executes on behalf of a user, group or role (a subject). During execution a process must posses the access rights to resources that were defined for its subject. The set of access rights given to a process define its execution *domain*. At times the process may also need to enter other domains to perform its work; for example, to access data from a file in another domain. Frequently, users structure their domains as a tree of nested domains.

Problem

Restricting a process to a specific set of resources is a basic step to control malicious behavior. Otherwise, unauthorized processes could destroy or modify information in files or databases, with obvious results, or could interfere with the execution of other processes.

The solution to this problem must resolve the following forces:

■   There is a need to restrict the actions of a process during its execution, otherwise it could perform illegal actions.

■   Resources typically include memory and I/O devices, but can also be system data structures and special instructions. Although resources are heterogeneous, we want to treat them uniformly.

■   A process needs the flexibility to create multiple domains and to enter inner domains for specific purposes.

■   There should be no restrictions on how the domain is implemented.

Solution

Attach a set of descriptors to the process that represent the rights of the process. In Figure 8.3, the class `Domain` represents domains, and, in conjunction with the Composite pattern [Gam94], describes nested domains. Operation `enter()` in class `Domain` lets a `Process` enter a new `Domain`. A `Domain` includes a set of descriptors that define rights for resources.

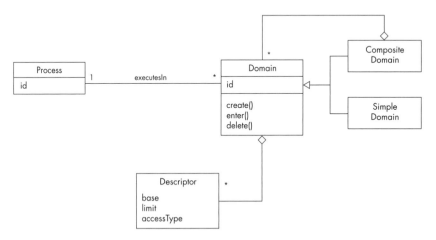

Figure 8.3: Class diagram for the EXECUTION DOMAIN pattern

Consequences

The EXECUTION DOMAIN pattern offers the following benefits:

- It lets users apply the principle of least privilege to processes: they can be given only the rights they need to perform their functions.
- It can be applied to describe access to any type of resource if the resource is mapped to a specific memory address.
- Processes may have several execution domains, either peer or nested.
- The model does not restrict the implementation of domains. A domain could be represented in many ways. For example, the Plessey 250, IBM S/38 and IBM S/6000 use capabilities. The Intel X86 and Pentium series (and their corresponding operating systems) use descriptors for memory access control.
- Special domains with predefined rights or types of rights can be defined. For example, Multics and the Intel X86 series use protection rings, where each ring is assigned to a type of program: supervisor, utilities, user programs, and external programs. The rings are hierarchically structured, based on their level of trust. Descriptors are used to cross rings in program calls.

- The descriptors refer to VAS segments, which is the most usual implementation. However, they could indicate resources not mapped to memory.

This pattern also has the following potential liabilities:

- Extra complexity: special hardware may be needed to accelerate processing.

- Performance overhead in setting up domains and in entering and leaving domains. Because of this, some operating systems for Intel processors use only two rings, improving performance but reducing security.

- The way to set up the execution domain is implementation-dependent. In descriptor systems the operating system creates a descriptor segment with the required descriptors. In capability systems the descriptors are part of the process code and are enabled during execution.

Known Uses

- The concept of domains comes from Multics [Gra68]. Segments or pages (as in EROS [Sha02]) are structured as tree directories.

- The Plessey 250 and the IBM S/6000 running AIX [Cam90] are good examples of the use of this pattern.

- The Java Virtual Machine defines restricted execution environments in a similar way [Oak01].

8.4   Controlled Execution Domain

The CONTROLLED EXECUTION DOMAIN pattern allows control of access to all operating system resources by processes, based on user, group or role authorizations.

Example

When Jim discovered that the customer files had authorizations and could not be accessed directly, he tried another approach. He realized that processes were not well controlled and could access memory and other resources belonging to other users. He systematically searched areas of memory and I/O devices being used by other processes until he could scavenge a few credit card numbers that he could use in his illicit activities.

Context

A system in which a process executes on behalf of a user or role (a subject). A process must have access rights to use these resources during execution. The set of access rights given to a process define its execution *domain*. Processes must be able to share resources in a controlled way. The rights of the process are derived from the rights of its invoker.

Problem

Even if direct access to files is restricted, users can use 'tunneling' to attack them through a lower level. If the process execution environment is uncontrolled, processes can scavenge information by searching memory and accessing disk drives. They might also take control of the operating system itself, in which case they have access to everything.

The solution to this problem must resolve the following forces:

- We need to constrain the execution of processes and restrict them to use only resources that have been authorized based on the rights of the subject that activated the process.

- Subjects can be users, roles or groups. We want to deal with them uniformly.

- Resources typically include memory and I/O devices, but can also be files and special instructions. We want to consider them in a uniform way.

- A subject may need to activate several processes, and a process may need to create multiple domains. Execution domains may need to be nested. We want flexibility for our processes.

- Typically, only a subset of a subject's rights needs to be used in a specific execution. We need to provide to a process only the rights it needs during its execution (using the principle of *least privilege*).

- The solution should put no constraints on implementation.

Solution

Figure 8.4 shows the class diagram of the CONTROLLED EXECUTION DOMAIN pattern. This model combines the AUTHORIZATION (page 74), EXECUTION DOMAIN (page 149) and REIFIED REFERENCE MONITOR (page 100) patterns to let processes operate in an environment with controlled actions based on the rights of their invoker.

Process execution follows the EXECUTION DOMAIN pattern (page 149): as a process executes it creates one or more `Domains`. `Domains` can be recursively composed. The descriptors used in the process' domains are a subset of the `Authorizations` that the subject has for some `ProtectionObjects` (defined by an instance of the AUTHORIZATION pattern). `ProtectionObject` is a superclass of the abstract `Resource` class, and `ConcreteResource` defines a specific resource. `Process`' requests go through a `ReferenceMonitor` that can check the domain descriptors for compliance.

Figure 8.5 (page 154) shows a sequence diagram showing the use of a right after entering a domain. Here x denotes a segment requested by the `Process`. An instance of the Reference Monitor pattern controls the process requests. This diagram assumes that the descriptors of the domain have been previously set up.

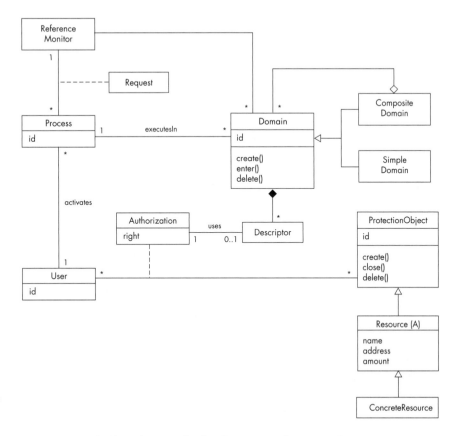

Figure 8.4: Class diagram for the CONTROLLED EXECUTION DOMAIN pattern

Implementation

Windows NT. The Windows NT security subsystem provides security using this and others of the patterns described here, including REIFIED REFERENCE MONITOR (page 100), AUTHENTICATOR (page 52) and ACCESS CONTROL LIST (page 91). It has the following three components [Har01] [Kel97] [Mic00]:

- Local Security Authority (LSA)
- Security Account Manager (SAM)
- Security Reference Monitor (SRM)

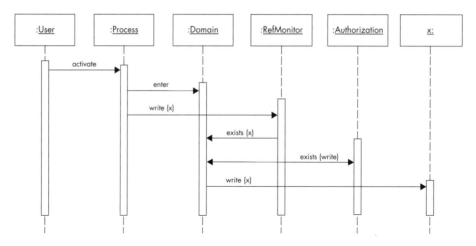

Figure 8.5: Sequence diagram for entering a domain and using a right in that domain

The LSA and SAM work together to authenticate the user and create the user's access token. The security reference monitor runs in kernel mode and is responsible for the enforcement of access validation. When access to an object is requested, a comparison is made between the file's security descriptor and the secure ID (SID) information stored in the user's access token. The security descriptor is made up of access control entries (ACE) included in the object's access control list (ACL). When an object has an ACL, the SRM checks each ACE in the ACL to determine whether access is to be granted. After the SRM grants access to the object, further access checks are not needed, as a handle to the object that allows further access is returned the first time.

Types of object permissions are 'no access', 'read', 'change', 'full control' and 'special access'. For directory access, the following are added: 'list', 'add' and 'read'.

Windows use the concept of a handle for access to protected objects within the system. Each object has a security descriptor (SD) that contains a *discretionary access control list* (DACL) for the object. Each process has a security token that contains an SID that identifies the process. This is used by the kernel to determine whether access is allowed. The ACL contains access control entries (ACEs) that indicate what access is allowed for a particular process SID. The kernel scans the ACL for the rights corresponding to the requested access.

A process requests access to an object when it asks for a handle using, for example, a call to `CreateFile()`, which is used both to create a new file or open an existing file. When the file is created, a pointer to an SD is passed as a parameter. When an existing file is opened, the request parameters, in addition to the file handle, contain the desired access, such as `GENERIC_READ`. If the process has the desired rights for the access, the request succeeds and an access handle is returned; this allows different handles to the same object to have different accesses [Har01]. Once the handle is obtained, additional access to read a file will not require further authorization. The handle may also be passed to another trusted subject for further processing.

Java 1.2 Security. The Java security subsystem provides security using the patterns described here. The Java access controller builds access permissions based on permission and policy. It has a `checkPermission` method that determines the codesource object of each calling method and uses the current policy object to determine the permission objects associated with it. Note that the `checkPermission` method will traverse the call stack to determine the access of all calling methods in the stack. The `java.policy` file is used by the security manager and contains the grant statements for each codesource.

Example Resolved

A new operating system was installed, with mechanisms to make processes operate with the rights of their activator. Jim did not have access to customer files, which made his processes also unable to access these files. Now he could not scavenge in other users' areas and his illicit actions were thwarted.

Consequences

The CONTROLLED EXECUTION DOMAIN pattern offers the following benefits:

- We can apply the least privilege principle to processes based on the rights of their activators. This also provides accountability.
- It can be applied with any type of resource.
- Subjects may activate any number of processes, and processes may have several execution domains.
- The model is abstract and does not restrict possible implementations.
- Execution domains are defined according to the EXECUTION DOMAIN pattern (page 149) and may include any subset of the subject's rights.

This pattern also has the following potential liabilities:

- Some extra complexity and performance overhead.
- Dependence on the hardware architecture.

Known Uses

The IBM S/38, the IBM S/6000 running AIX, the Plessey 250 [Ham73] and EROS [Sha02] have applied this pattern using capabilities. Proper descriptor systems such as the Intel architectures may use this approach, although their operating systems do not always do so. Recent uses of this pattern include Adobe Reader Protected Mode [Ark10] and Chromium Sandbox [Chr].

See Also

This pattern uses the AUTHORIZATION (page 74), EXECUTION DOMAIN (page 149) and REIFIED REFERENCE MONITOR (page 100) patterns. The VIRTUAL ADDRESS SPACE ACCESS CONTROL pattern (page 146) may be used indirectly by the EXECUTION DOMAIN pattern.

8.5   Virtual Address Space Structure Selection

The VIRTUAL ADDRESS SPACE STRUCTURE SELECTION pattern describes how to select the virtual address space for operating systems that have special security needs. Some systems emphasize isolation, others information sharing, others good performance. The organization of each process' virtual address space (VAS) is defined by the hardware architecture and has an effect on performance and security. The pattern enables all the hardware possibilities to be considered and selected according to need.

Example

We have a system running applications using images that require large graphic files. The application also has stringent security requirements, because some of the images are sensitive and should be only accessed by authorized users. We need to decide on an appropriate VAS structure.

Context

Virtual memory allows the total size of the memory used by processes to exceed the size of physical memory. Upon use, the virtual address is translated by the address translation unit (usually the memory management unit (MMU) in microprocessors) to obtain a physical address that is used to access physical memory. To execute a process, the kernel creates a per-process virtual address space. We have a multiprogramming system with a variety of users and applications. Processes execute on behalf of users and at times must be able to share memory areas, at other times must be isolated, and in all cases we need access control. Performance may also be an issue.

Problem

We need to select the virtual address space for processes depending on the majority of the applications we intend to execute, otherwise we can have mismatches that may result in poor security or performance.

The solution to this problem must resolve the following forces:

■ Each process needs to be assigned a relatively large VAS to hold its data, stack, space for temporary variables, variables to keep the status of its devices, and other information.

■ In multiprogramming environments processes have diverse requirements; some require isolation, others information sharing, others good performance.

■ Data typing is useful to prevent errors and improve security. Several attacks occur by executing data and modifying code [Gol06].

■ Sharing between address spaces should be convenient, otherwise performance may suffer.

Solution

Select from four basic approaches that differ in their security features:

■ *One address space per process* (Figure 8.6). The supervisor (kernel plus utilities) and each user process get their own address spaces. Using one VAS per process has the following trade-offs:

   ■ Good process isolation.

   ■ Some protection against possible illegal actions by a compromised operating system.

   ■ Simplicity.

   ■ Sharing is complex (special instructions to cross spaces are needed).

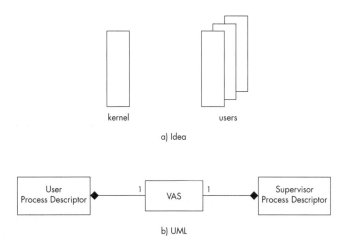

Figure 8.6: One address space per process

- *Two address spaces per process* (Figure 8.7). Each process gets a data and a code (program) virtual address space. Use of two VASs per process has the following trade-offs:

  - Good process isolation.

  - Some protection against possible illegal actions by a compromised operating system.

  - Data and instructions can be separated for better protection (some attacks take advantage of execution of data or modification of code). Data typing is also good for reliability.

  - A disadvantage is complex sharing, plus poor address space utilization.

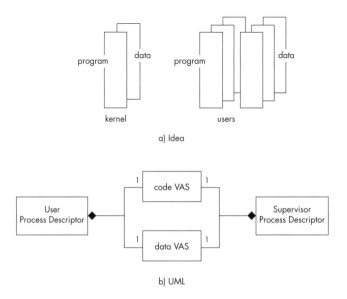

Figure 8.7: Two address spaces per process

- *One address space per user process, all of them shared with one address space for the operating system* (Figure 8.8). The operating system (supervisor) can be shared between all processes. This scheme has the following trade-offs:

  - Good process isolation.

  - Good sharing of resources and services.

  - Suboptimal with respect to security (the supervisor has complete access to the user processes, and it must be trusted).

  - The address space available to each user process has been halved.

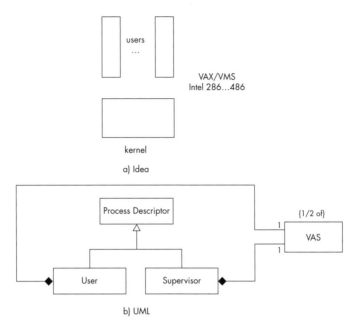

a) Idea

b) UML

Figure 8.8: One address space per user process, all of them shared with one address space for the operating system

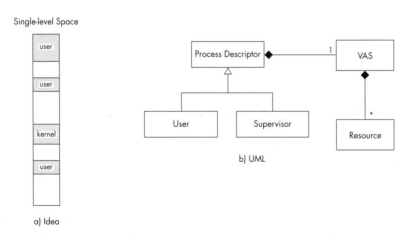

a) Idea

b) UML

Figure 8.9: A single-level address space

- *A single-level address space* (Figure 8.9). Everything, including files, is mapped to one memory space. Use of a single-level address space has the following trade-offs:

  - Good process isolation.

  - Logical simplicity.

  - Uniform protection (all I/O is mapped to memory).

  - Offers the most elegant solution (only one mechanism to protect memory and files), and is potentially the most secure if capabilities are also used.

  - Hard to implement in hardware due to the large address space required.

Implementation

The VAS is implemented by the hardware architecture. The operating system designer can choose one of the architectures based on the requirements of the applications, according to the trade-offs discussed above. In a particular case, the choice may be influenced by company policies, cost, performance and other factors, as well as security.

Consequences

In addition to the specific benefits described as part of the solution (trade-offs), the VIR-TUAL ADDRESS SPACE STRUCTURE SELECTION pattern has the following general liabilities:

- Without hardware support it is not feasible to separate the virtual address spaces of the processes. Most processors use register pairs or descriptors that indicate the base (start) of a memory unit (segment) and its length or limit [Sil08].

- If the mix of applications is not well-defined, it is hard to select the best solution. Considerations other than security then become more important.

Known Uses

- *One address space per process.* The NS32000, WE32100 and Clipper microprocessors [Fer85]. Several versions of UNIX were implemented in these processors.

- *Two address spaces per process.* Used in the Motorola 68000 series. The Minix 2 operating system uses this approach [Tan06].

- *One address space per user process, all of them shared with one address space for the operating system.* Used in the VAX series and in Intel processors. Windows runs in this type of address space.

- *Single-level address space.* Multics, IBM S/38, IBM S/6000 and HP PA-RISC use this approach. Multics had its own operating system. IBM AIX ran in S/6000 [Cam90]. The PA-RISC architectures ran a version of UNIX.

See Also

- SECURE PROCESS/THREAD (page 120). The interaction between processes depends strongly on the virtual address space configuration, which can affect security, performance and sharing properties of the processes.

- VIRTUAL ADDRESS SPACE ACCESS CONTROL (page 146) [Fer02] [Sch06b]. A VAS is assigned to each process that can be accessed according to the rights of the process. The VIRTUAL ADDRESS SPACE STRUCTURE SELECTION pattern is applied first to select the appropriate structure. Once selected, the VAS is secured using the Controlled Virtual Address Space pattern.

- The Secure Storage pattern for rebooting is discussed by [Loh10].

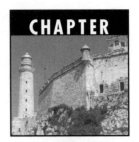

CHAPTER

9

Patterns for Secure OS Architecture and Administration

A great building must begin with the immeasurable, must go through measurable means when it is being designed, and in the end must be unmeasured.

Louis Kahn

9.1   Introduction

Operating systems act as an intermediary between the user of a computer and its hardware. The purpose of an operating system is to provide an environment in which users can execute programs in convenient and efficient manner [Sil08]. They control and coordinate the available resources to present an abstract machine with convenient features to the user. The architecture of the operating system organizes components to structure its functional and non-functional aspects. The security of operating systems is very critical, since they support the execution of all applications. Most of the reported attacks occur through the operating system. The security of individual execution-time actions such as process creation and memory protection is very important, and we presented patterns for these functions in Chapter 7 and Chapter 8. However, the general architecture of the operating system is also very important to the system's ability to provide a secure execution environment.

Most operating systems use five basic architectures [Sil08] [Tan08]. One, the *monolithic* architecture, has little value for security and it is only mentioned as a possible variant of the modular architecture. We present here patterns representing these four architectures (Figure 9.1):

- MODULAR OPERATING SYSTEM ARCHITECTURE. Separate the operating system's services into modules, each representing a basic function or component. The basic core kernel only has the required components to start itself and the ability to load modules. The core is the one module always in memory. Whenever the services of any additional modules are required, the module loader loads the appropriate module. Each module performs a function and may take parameters.

- LAYERED OPERATING SYSTEM ARCHITECTURE. The overall features and functionality of the operating system are decomposed and assigned to hierarchical layers. This provides clearly defined interfaces between each section of the operating system and between user applications and the system functions. Layer i uses services of a lower layer i-1 and does not know of the existence of a higher layer, i+1.

- MICROKERNEL OPERATING SYSTEM ARCHITECTURE. Move as much of the operating system functionality as possible from the kernel into specialized servers, coordinated by a microkernel. The microkernel itself has a very basic set of functions. Operating system components and services are implemented as external and internal servers.

- VIRTUAL MACHINE OPERATING SYSTEM ARCHITECTURE. Provide a set of replicas of the hardware architecture (virtual machines) that can be used to execute multiple and possibly different operating systems with strong isolation between them.

We also include two other related patterns in this chapter:

- ADMINISTRATOR HIERARCHY. Many attacks come from the unlimited power of administrators. How can we limit the power of administrators? Define a hierarchy of system administrators with rights controlled using a ROLE-BASED ACCESS CONTROL (RBAC, page 78) pattern and assign rights according to their functions.

- FILE ACCESS CONTROL. How can we control access to files in an operating system? Apply the AUTHORIZATION pattern (page 74) to describe access to files by subjects. The protection object is now a file component that may be a directory or a file.

The four secure architectures appeared as patterns in [Fer05c], coauthored with Tami Sorgente. The Administrator Hierarchy pattern appeared in [Fer06f], coauthored with Tami Sorgente and Maria M. Larrondo-Petrie. Finally, the File Access Control pattern appeared in [Fer03b], coauthored with John Sinibaldi.

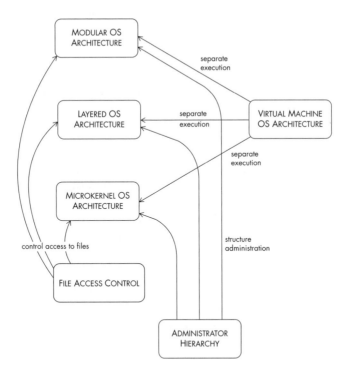

Figure 9.1: Pattern diagram of OS architectures, administration and file systems

9.2   **Modular Operating System Architecture**

The MODULAR OPERATING SYSTEM ARCHITECTURE pattern describes how to separate operating system services into modules, each representing a basic function or component. The basic core kernel only has the required components to start itself and the ability to load modules. The core is the one module always in memory. Whenever the services of any additional modules are required, the module loader loads the appropriate module. Each module performs a function and may take parameters.

Example

Our group is building a new operating system that should support various types of devices requiring dynamic services with a wide variety of security requirements. We want to dynamically add operating system components, functions and services, as well as tailor their security aspects according to the type of application. For example, a media player may require support to prevent copying of its contents, or a module for which a vulnerability alert has been issued could be removed.

Context

A variety of applications with diverse requirements that need to execute together, sharing hardware resources.

Problem

We need to be able to add or remove functions easily so that we can accommodate applications with a number of security requirements. How can we structure the operating system functions for this purpose?

The solution to this problem must resolve the following forces:

- Operating systems for PCs and other types of uses require a large variety of plugins. New plugins appear frequently, and we need the ability to add and remove them without disrupting normal operation.

- Some of the plugins may contain malware; we need to isolate their execution so they do not affect other processes.

- We would like to hide security-critical modules from other modules to avoid possible attacks.

- Modules can call each other, which is a possible source of attacks.

Solution

Define a core module that can load and link modules dynamically as needed.

Structure

Figure 9.2 shows a class diagram for this pattern. The KernelCore is the core of the modular operating system. A set of LoadableModules is associated with the KernelCore, indicating the modules that can be loaded according to their applications and the functions required. Any LoadableModule can call any other LoadableModule.

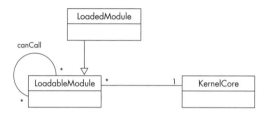

Figure 9.2: Class diagram for the MODULAR OPERATING SYSTEM ARCHITECTURE pattern

Implementation

1   Separate the functions of the operating system into independent modules according to whether:

- They are complete functional units.
- They are critical with respect to security.
- They should execute in their own process for security reasons, or their own thread for performance reasons.
- They should be isolated during execution because they may contain malware.

2   Define a set of loadable modules. New modules can be added later, according to the needs of specific applications.

3   Define a communication structure for the resultant modules. Operations should have well-defined call signatures and all calls should be checked.

4   Define a preferred order for loading some basic modules. Modules that are critical for security should be loaded only when needed to reduce exposure to attacks.

Example Resolved

We structured the functions of our system following the MODULAR OPERATING SYSTEM ARCHITECTURE pattern. Because each module could have its own address space, we can isolate its execution. Because each module can be designed independently, they can have different security constraints in their structure. This structure gives us flexibility with a good degree of security.

Consequences

The MODULAR OPERATING SYSTEM ARCHITECTURE pattern offers the following benefits:

- Flexibility to add and remove functions contributes to security, in that we can add new versions of modules with better security.
- Each module is separate and communicates with other modules over known interfaces. We can introduce controls in these interfaces.
- It is possible to partially hide critical modules by loading them only when needed and removing them after use.
- By giving each executing module its own address space we can isolate the effects of a rogue module.

This pattern also has the following potential liabilities:

- Any module can 'see' all the others and potentially interfere with their execution.

■ Uniformity of call interfaces between modules makes it difficult to apply stronger security restrictions to critical modules.

Variants

Monolithic Kernel. The operating system is a collection of procedures. Each procedure has a well-defined interface in terms of parameters and results and each one is free to call any other [Tan08]. There is no organization relating the operating system, components, services and user applications: all the modules are at the same level. The difference between monolithic and modular operating system architectures is that in the monolithic approach, all the modules are loaded together at installation time, instead of on demand. This approach is not very attractive for secure systems.

Known Uses

■ The Solaris 10 operating system (Figure 9.3) is designed following this pattern. Its kernel is dynamic and composed of a core system that is always resident in memory [Sun04a]. The various types of Solaris 10 loadable modules are shown in Figure 9.3 as loaded by the kernel core: the diagram does not represent the communication links between individual modules.

■ ExtremeWare from Extreme Networks [Ext].

■ Some versions of Linux use a combination of modular and monolithic architectures.

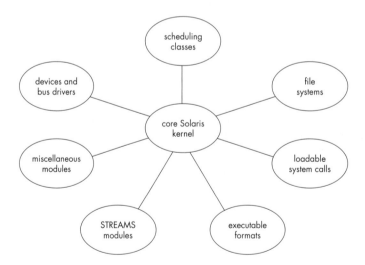

Figure 9.3: The modular design of the Solaris 10 operating system [Sil08]

See Also

The CONTROLLED EXECUTION DOMAIN pattern (page 151) can be used to isolate executing modules.

9.3 Layered Operating System Architecture

The LAYERED OPERATING SYSTEM ARCHITECTURE pattern allows the overall features and functionality of the operating system to be decomposed and assigned to hierarchical layers. This provides clearly defined interfaces between each section of the operating system and between user applications and the operating system functions. Layer i uses the services of a lower layer i-1 and does not know of the existence of a higher layer, i+1.

Example

Our operating system is very complex and we would like to separate different aspects in order to handle them in a more systematic way. Complexity brings vulnerability. We also want to control the calls between operating system components and services to improve security and reliability. Finally, we would like to hide critical modules. We tried a modular architecture, but it did not have enough structure to do all this systematically.

Context

A variety of applications with diverse requirements that need to execute together sharing hardware resources.

Problem

Unstructured modules, as in the MODULAR OPERATING SYSTEM ARCHITECTURE pattern (page 165), have the problem that all modules can reach all other modules, which facilitates attacks. We need to conceal the existence of some critical modules.

The solution to this problem must resolve the following forces:

- Interfaces should be stable and well-defined. Going through any interface could imply authorization checks.

- Parts of the system should be exchangeable or removable without affecting the rest of the system. For example, we could have modules that perform more security checks than others.

- Similar responsibilities should be grouped, to help understandability and maintainability. This contributes indirectly to improved security.

- We should control module visibility to avoid possible attacks from other modules.

- Complex components need further decomposition. This makes the design simpler and clearer and also improves security.

Solution

Define a hierarchical set of layers and assign components to each layer. Each layer presents an abstract machine (a set of operations) to the layer above it, hiding the implementation details of the lower layers.

Structure

Figure 9.4 shows a class diagram for the LAYERED OPERATING SYSTEM ARCHITECTURE pattern. LayerN represents the highest level of abstraction, and Layer1 is the lowest level of abstraction. The main structural characteristic is that the services of LayerN are used only by LayerN+1. Each layer may contain complex entities consisting of different components.

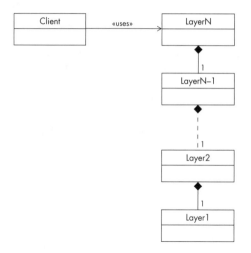

Figure 9.4: Class diagram for LAYERED OPERATING SYSTEM ARCHITECTURE pattern

Dynamics

Figure 9.5 shows the sequence diagram for the use case 'Open and read a disk file':

- A user sends an openFile() request to the OSInterface.
- The OSInterface interprets the openFile() request.
- The openFile() request is sent from the OSInterface to the FileManager.
- The FileManager sends a readDisk() request to the DiskDriver.

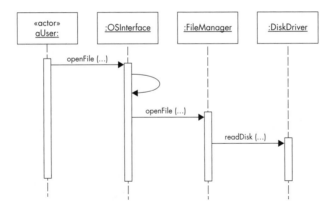

Figure 9.5: Sequence diagram for the use case 'Open and read a disk file'

Implementation

1   List all units in the system and define their dependencies.

2   Assign units to levels such that units in higher levels depend only on units of lower levels.

3   Once the modules in a given level are assigned, define a language (set of commands) for the level. This language includes the operations that we want to make visible to the next level above. Add well-defined operation signatures and security checks in these operations to assure the proper use of the level.

4   Hide those modules that control critical security functions in lower levels.

Example Resolved

We structured the functions of our system as in shown in Figure 9.6, and now we have a way to control interactions and enforce abstraction. For example, the file system can use the operations of the disk drivers and enforce similar restrictions in the storage of data.

The user of a file cannot take advantage of the implementation details of the disk driver to attack the system.

Consequences

The LAYERED OPERATING SYSTEM ARCHITECTURE pattern offers the following benefits:

■   Lower levels can be changed without affecting higher layers. We can add or remove security functions as needed.

■   There are clearly defined interfaces between each operating system layer and the user applications, which improves security.

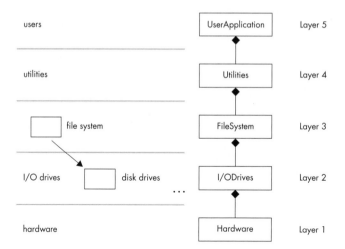

Figure 9.6: An example of the use of a layered OS architecture

- Control of information is possible using layer hierarchical rules and enforcement of security policies between layers.

- The fact that layers hide implementation aspects is useful for security, in that possible attackers cannot exploit lower-level details.

The pattern also has the following potential liabilities:

- It may not be clear what to put in each layer. In particular, related modules may be hard to allocate. There may be conflicts between functional and security needs when allocating modules.

- Performance may decrease due to the indirection of calls through several layers. If we try to improve performance, we may sacrifice security.

Known Uses

- The Symbian operating system (Figure 9.7) uses a variation of the layered approach [Sym01].

- The UNIX operating system (Figure 9.8) is separated into four layers, with clear interfaces between the system calls to the kernel and between the kernel and the hardware.

- IBM's OS/2 also uses this approach [OS2].

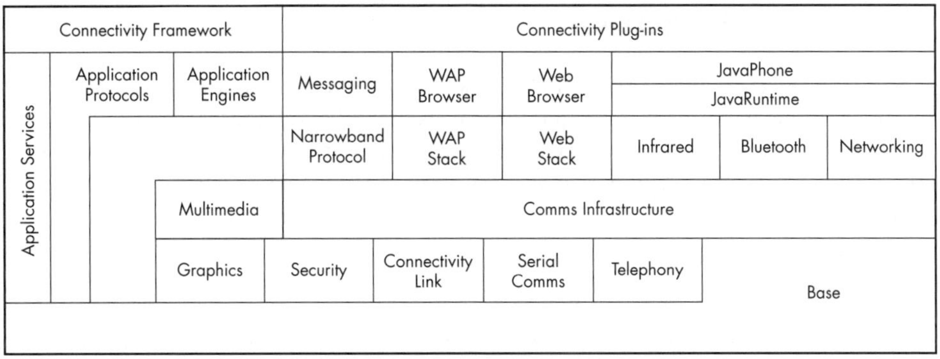

Connectivity Framework			Connectivity Plug-ins					
Application Protocols	Application Engines	Messaging	WAP Browser	Web Browser	JavaPhone			
					JavaRuntime			
		Narrowband Protocol	WAP Stack	Web Stack	Infrared	Bluetooth	Networking	
	Multimedia		Comms Infrastructure					
	Graphics	Security	Connectivity Link	Serial Comms	Telephony	Base		

(left vertical label: Application Services)

Figure 9.7: Symbian operating system layered architecture [Sym01]

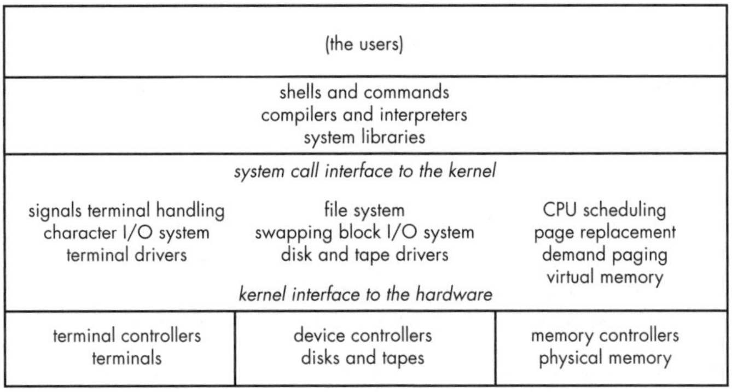

(the users)
shells and commands compilers and interpreters system libraries
system call interface to the kernel
signals terminal handling   file system   CPU scheduling character I/O system   swapping block I/O system   page replacement terminal drivers   disk and tape drivers   demand paging   virtual memory
kernel interface to the hardware
terminal controllers   device controllers   memory controllers terminals   disks and tapes   physical memory

Figure 9.8: UNIX layered architecture [Sil08]

Variant

Layer skipping. In this architecture there are special applications that are able to skip layers for added performance. This structure requires a trade-off between performance and security. By deviating from the strict hierarchy of the layered system, there may not be enforcement of security policies between layers for such applications.

See Also

This pattern is a specialization of the Layers architectural pattern [Bus96]. Security versions of the Layers pattern have appeared in [Fer02] [Sch06b] [Yod97].

9.4   Microkernel Operating System Architecture

The MICROKERNEL OPERATING SYSTEM ARCHITECTURE pattern describes how to move as much of the operating system functionality as possible from the kernel into specialized servers, coordinated by a microkernel. The microkernel itself has a very basic set of functions. Operating system components and services are implemented as external and internal servers.

Example

We are building an operating system to support a range of applications with different reliability and security requirements and a variety of plugins. We would like to provide operating system versions with different types of modules: some more secure, some less so.

Context

A variety of applications with diverse requirements that need to execute together sharing hardware resources.

Problem

In general-purpose environments we need to be able to add new functionality with variation in security and other requirements, as well as provide alternative implementations of services to accommodate different application requirements.

The solution to this problem must resolve the following forces:

■ The application platform must be able to cope with continuous hardware and software evolution: these additions may have very different security or reliability requirements.

■ Strong security or reliability requirements indicate the need for modules with well-defined interfaces.

■ We may want to perform different types of security checks in different modules, depending on their security criticality.

■ We would like a minimum of functionality in the kernel, so that we have a minimum of processes running in supervisor mode. A simple kernel can be checked for possible vulnerabilities, which is good for security.

Solution

Separate all functionality into specialized services with well-defined interfaces, and provide an efficient way to route requests to the appropriate servers. Each server can be built with different security constraints. The kernel mainly routes requests to servers and has minimal functionality.

Structure

The `Microkernel` is the central communication for the operating system. There is one `Microkernel` and several `InternalServers` and `ExternalServers`, each providing a set of specialized services (Figure 9.9). In addition to the servers, an `Adapter` is used between the `Client` and the `Microkernel` or an external server. The `Microkernel` controls the internal servers.

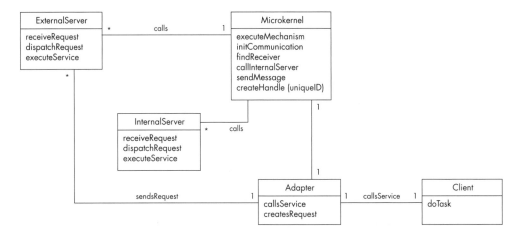

Figure 9.9: Class diagram for MICROKERNEL OPERATING SYSTEM ARCHITECTURE pattern

Dynamics

A client requests a service from an external server using the following sequence (Figure 9.10):

1   The `Adapter` receives the request from the `Client` and asks the `Microkernel` for a communication link with the `ExternalServer`.

2   The `Microkernel` checks for authorization to use the server, determines the physical address of the `ExternalServer` and returns it to the `Adapter`.

3   The `Adapter` establishes a direct communication link with the `ExternalServer`.

4   The `Adapter` sends the request to the `ExternalServer` using a procedure call or a remote procedure call (RPC). The RPC can be checked for well-formed commands, correct size and type of parameters (that is, we can check signatures).

5   The `ExternalServer` receives the request, unpacks the message and delegates the task to one of its own methods. All results are sent back to the `Adapter`.

6   The `Adapter` returns to the `Client`, which in turn continues with its control flow.

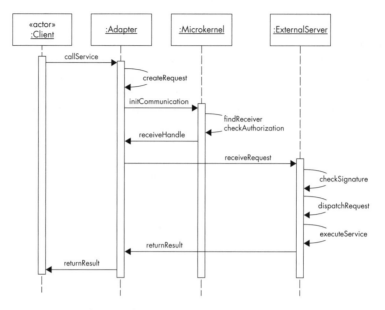

Figure 9.10: Sequence diagram for an operating system call through the microkernel

Implementation

1 Identify the core functionality necessary for implementing external servers and their security constraints. Typically, basic functions of the operating system should be internal servers; utilities, or user-defined services should go into external servers. Each server can use the patterns from [Fer02] and [Fer03b] for their secure construction.

2 Define policies to restrict access to external and internal servers. Clients may be allowed to call only specific servers.

3 Find a complete set of operations and abstractions for every category of server identified.

4 Determine strategies for request transmission and retrieval.

5 Structure the microkernel component. The microkernel should be simple enough to ensure its security properties; for example, it should be impossible to infect it with malware.

6 Design and implement the internal servers as separate processes or shared libraries. Add security checks in each server using the PROTECTED ENTRY POINTS pattern (page 136).

7   Implement the external servers. Add security checks in each service provided by the servers using AUTHORIZATION (page 74) and AUTHENTICATOR (page 52).

Example Resolved

By implementing our system using a microkernel, we can have several versions of each service, each with different degrees of security and reliability. We can replace servers dynamically if needed. We can also control access to specific servers and ensure that they are called in the proper way.

Consequences

The MICROKERNEL OPERATING SYSTEM ARCHITECTURE pattern offers the following benefits:

- Flexibility and extensibility: if you need an additional function or an existing function with different security requirements, you only need to add an external server. Extending the system capabilities or requirements also only requires addition or extension of internal servers.

- The microkernel mediates all calls for services and can apply authorization checks. In fact, the microkernel is in effect a concrete realization of a reference monitor (page 100).

- The well-defined interfaces between servers allow each server to check every request for their services.

- It is possible to add even more security by putting fundamental functions in internal servers.

- Servers usually run in user mode, which further increases security.

- The microkernel is very small and can be verified or checked for security.

The pattern also has the following potential liability:

- Communication overhead, since all messages must go through the Microkernel.

Known Uses

- The PalmOS Cobalt (Figure 9.11) operating system has a preemptive multitasking kernel that provides basic task management. Many applications in PalmOS do not use the microkernel services; they are handled automatically by the system. The microkernel functionality is provided for internal use by system software or for certain special-purpose applications [Pal].

- The QNX Microkernel (Figure 9.12) is intended mostly for communication and process scheduling in real-time systems [QNX]. It will be used in the new RIM systems, adopting a layered architecture [Qwi].

- Mach and Windows NT also use some form of microkernels [Sil08].

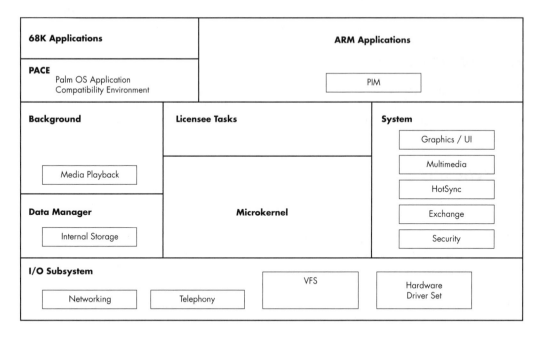

Figure 9.11: PalmOS Microkernel combined with layered OS architecture [Pal]

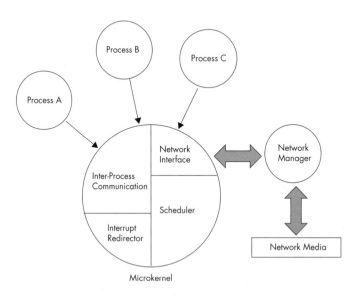

Figure 9.12: QNX microkernel architecture [QNX]

Variant

Layered Microkernel. The MICROKERNEL OPERATING SYSTEM ARCHITECTURE pattern can be combined with the LAYERED OPERATING SYSTEM ARCHITECTURE pattern. In this case, servers can be assigned to levels and a call is accepted only if it comes from a level above the server level.

See Also

This pattern is a specialization of the Microkernel pattern [Bus96]. As indicated, the microkernel itself can be considered as a concrete version of the REIFIED REFERENCE MONITOR pattern (page 100).

9.5   Virtual Machine Operating System Architecture

The VIRTUAL MACHINE OPERATING SYSTEM ARCHITECTURE pattern describes how to provide a set of replicas of the hardware architecture (virtual machines) that can be used to execute multiple and possibly different operating systems with strong isolation between them.

Example

A web server is hosting applications for two competing companies. These companies use different operating systems. We want to ensure that neither of them can access the other company's files or launch attacks against the other system.

Context

Mutually suspicious sets of applications that need to execute in the same hardware. Each set requires isolation from the other sets.

Problem

Sometimes we need to execute different operating systems on the same hardware. How can we keep those operating systems isolated in such a way that their executions don't interfere with each other?

The solution to this problem must resolve the following forces:

- Each operating system needs to have access to a complete set of hardware features to support its execution.

- Each operating system has its own set of machine-dependent features, such as interrupt handlers. In other words, each operating system uses the hardware in different ways.

- When an operating system crashes or it is penetrated by a hacker, the effects of this situation should not propagate to other operating systems running on the same hardware.

- There should be no way for a malicious user in one virtual machine to get access to the data or functions of another virtual machine.

Solution

Define an architectural layer that is in control of the hardware and supervises and coordinates the execution of each operating system environment. This extra layer, usually called a *virtual machine monitor* (VMM) or *hypervisor*, presents to each operating system a replica of the hardware. The VMM intercepts all system calls and interprets them according to the operating system from which they came.

Structure

Figure 9.13 shows a class diagram for the VIRTUAL MACHINE OPERATING SYSTEM ARCHITECTURE (VMOS) pattern. The VMOS contains one VirtualMachineMonitor (VMM) and multiple virtual machines (VM). Each VM can run a local operating system (LocalOS). The VirtualMachineMonitor supports each LocalOS and is able to interpret its system calls. As a LocalProcess runs on a LocalOS, the VM passes the operating system calls to the VMM, which executes them in the hardware.

Dynamics

Figure 9.14 shows the sequence diagram for the use case 'Perform an OS call on a virtual machine'. A local process wishing to perform a system operation uses the following sequence:

1   A LocalProcess makes an operating system call to the LocalOS.

2   The LocalOS maps the operating system call to the VMM (by executing a privileged operation).

3   The VMM interprets the call according to the local operating system from which it came, and it executes the operation in hardware.

4   The VMM sends return codes to the LocalOS to indicate successful instruction execution, as well as the results of the instruction execution.

5   The LocalOS sends the return code and data to the LocalProcess.

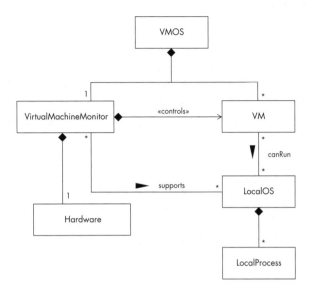

Figure 9.13: Class diagram for the VIRTUAL MACHINE OPERATING SYSTEM ARCHITECTURE pattern

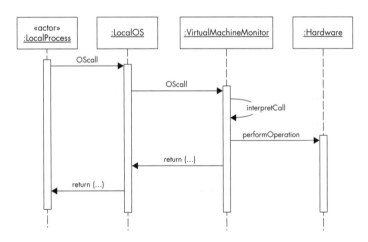

Figure 9.14: Sequence diagram for the use case 'Perform an OS call on virtual machine'

Implementation

1 Select the hardware that will be virtualized. All of its privileged instructions must trap when executed in user mode (this is the usual way to intercept system calls).

2 Define a representation (data structure) for describing operating system features that map to hardware aspects, such as meaning of interrupts, disk space distribution, and so on, and build tables for each operating system to be supported.

3 Enumerate the system calls for each supported operating system and associate them with specific hardware instructions.

Example Resolved

In the example shown in Figure 9.15, two companies using UNIX and Linux can execute their applications in different virtual machines. The VMM provides strong isolation between these two execution environments.

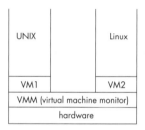

Figure 9.15: Virtual Machine operating system example

Consequences

The VIRTUAL MACHINE OPERATING SYSTEM ARCHITECTURE pattern offers the following benefits:

- The VMM intercepts and checks all system calls. The VMM is in effect a reference monitor and provides total mediation for the use of the hardware. This can provide strong isolation between virtual machines [Ros05].

- Each environment (virtual machine) does not know about the other virtual machine(s), this helps prevent cross-VM attacks.

- There is a well-defined interface between the VMM and the virtual machines.

- The VMM is small and simple and can be checked for security.

- The architecture defined by this pattern is orthogonal to the other three architectures discussed earlier, and can execute any of them as local operating systems.

The pattern also has the following potential liabilities:

- All the virtual machines are treated equally. If virtual machines with different security categories are required, it is necessary to build specialized versions. This approach is followed in KVM/370 (see Variants).

- Extra overhead in the use of privileged instructions.

- It is complex to let virtual machines communicate with each other, if this is needed.

Variants

- The architecture defined by this pattern is orthogonal to the other three architectures discussed earlier, and can execute any of them as local operating systems.

- KVM/370 was a secure extension of VM/370 [Gol79]. This system included a formally verified security kernel, and its virtual machines executed in different security levels, for example top secret, confidential, and so on. In addition to the isolation provided by the VMM, this system also applied the multilevel model described in Chapter 6.

Known Uses

- IBM VM/370 [Cre81]. This was the first VMOS, and provided virtual machines for an IBM 370 mainframe.

- VMware [Nie00]. This is a current range of products that provide virtual machines for Intel X86 hardware.

- Solaris 10 [Sun04a] calls the virtual machines 'containers', and one or more applications execute in each container.

- Connectix [Cona] produces virtual PCs to run Windows and other operating systems.

- Xen is a VMM for the Intel x86 developed as a project at the University of Cambridge, UK [Bar00].

- Some smart phone operating systems use virtual machines to separate users' private system from their work environment. These include the L4 Microvisor and RIM's BlackBerry 10 OS [Qwi].

See Also

- REIFIED REFERENCE MONITOR (page 100). The VMM is a concrete version of a reference monitor.

- The operating system patterns in [Fer02] and [Fer03b] can be used to implement the structure of a VMOS architecture.

9.6   Administrator Hierarchy

Many attacks come from the unlimited power of administrators. The ADMINISTRATOR HIERARCHY pattern allows the power of administrators to be limited, by defining a hierarchy of system administrators with rights controlled using a ROLE-BASED ACCESS CONTROL (RBAC) model, and assigns them rights according to their functions.

Example

UNIX defines a superuser who has all possible rights. This is expedient: for example, when somebody forgets a password, but allows hackers to totally control the system through a variety of implementation flaws. Through gaining access to the administrator rights, an individual can create new administrator and user accounts, restrict their privileges and quotas, access their protected areas, or remove their accounts.

Context

An operating system with a variety of users, connected to the Internet. There are some commands and data that are used for system administration, and access to them needs to be protected. This control is usually applied through special interfaces. There are at least two roles required to properly manage privileges, *Administrator* and *User*.

Problem

Usually, the administrator has rights such as creating accounts and passwords, installing programs and so on. This creates a series of security problems. For example, a rogue administrator can perform all the usual functions, and even erase the log to hide their tracks. A hacker that takes over administrative power can do similar things. How can we curtail the excessive power of administrators to control rogue administrators or hackers?

The solution to this problem must resolve the following forces:

- Administrators need to use commands that permit management of the system, for example define passwords for files, define quotas for files, and create user accounts. We cannot eliminate these functions.

- Administrators need to be able to delegate some responsibilities and privileges to manage large domains. They also need the right to take back these delegations, otherwise the system is too rigid.

- Administrators should have no control of system logs, or no valid auditing would be possible.

- Administrators should have no access to the operational data in the users' applications. Or, if they do, their accesses should be logged.

Solution

Separate the different administrative rights into several hierarchical roles. The rights for these roles allow the administrators to perform their administrative functions and no more. Critical functions may require more than one administrative role to participate. Use the principle of *separation of duty* (Chapter 6), where a user cannot perform critical functions unless in conjunction with other users.

Structure

Figure 9.16 shows a hierarchy for administration roles. This follows the Composite pattern [Gam94]; that is, a role can be simple or composed of other roles, defining a tree hierarchy. The top-level `Administrator` can add or remove administrators of any type and initialize the system, but should have no other functions. Administrators in the second level control different aspects, for example security, or use of resources. Administrators can further delegate their functions to lower-level administrators. Some functions may require two administrators to collaborate.

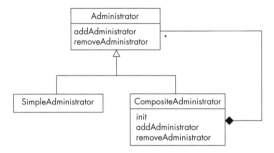

Figure 9.16: Class diagram for the ADMINISTRATOR HIERARCHY pattern

Implementation

1   Define a top-level administrative role with only the functions of setting up and initializing the system. This includes definition of administrative roles, assignment of rights to roles and assignment of users to roles.

2   Separate the main administrative functions of the system and define an administrative role for each one of them. These define the second level of the hierarchy.

3   Define further levels to accommodate administrative units in large systems, or for breaking down rights into functional sets.

Figure 9.17 shows a class diagram describing a typical administrator hierarchy. Here the `SystemAdministrator` starts the system and does not perform further actions. The second-level administrators can perform set up and other functions; the `SecurityAdmin-`

istrator defines security rights. `SecurityDomainAdministrators` define security in their domains.

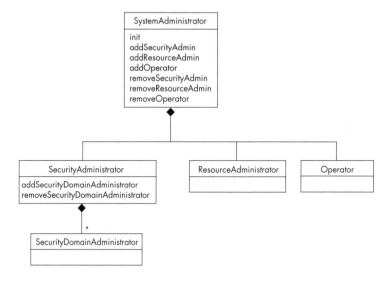

Figure 9.17: A typical administration hierarchy

Example Resolved

Now the superuser only starts the system. During normal operation the administrators have restricted powers. If a hacker takes over their functions they can do only limited damage.

Consequences

The ADMINISTRATOR HIERARCHY pattern offers the following benefits:

- If an administrative role is compromised, the attacker gets only limited privileges, so the potential damage is limited.
- The reduced rights also reduce the possibility of misuse by the administrators.
- The hierarchical structure allows taking back control of a compromised administrative function.
- The advantages of the RBAC model apply: simpler and fewer authorization rules, flexibility for changes, and so on [Sch06b].
- This structure is useful not only for operating systems, but also for servers, databases systems or any systems that require administration.

The pattern also has the following potential liabilities:

- Extra complexity for the administrative structure.

- Less expediency: performing some functions may involve more than one administrator.

- Many attacks are still possible: if someone misuses an administrative right, this pattern only limits the damage. Logging can help misuse detection.

Known Uses

- AIX [Cam90] reduces the privileges of the system administrator by defining five partially-ordered roles: superuser, security administrator, auditor, resource administrator and operator.

- Windows NT uses four roles for administrative privileges: standard, administrator, guest and operator. A user manager has procedures for managing user accounts, groups and authorization rules.

- Trusted Solaris [Sun04a]. This operating system is an extension of Solaris 8, using the concept of *trusted roles* with limited powers.

- Argus Pitbull [Arg]. In this operating system, *least privilege* is applied to all processes, including the superuser. The superuser is implemented using three roles: systems security officer, system administrator and system operator.

See Also

- This pattern applies the principles of *least privilege* and *separation of duty*, which some people consider also to be patterns. Each administrator role is given only the rights it needs to perform its duties and some functions may require collaboration.

- Administrative rights are usually organized according to a ROLE-BASED ACCESS CONTROL model (page 78).

9.7   File Access Control

The FILE ACCESS CONTROL pattern allows control of access to files in an operating system. Authorized users are the only ones that can use a file in specific ways.

Example

In a laboratory researchers used to share all their files: they were working on common projects and they trusted each other. However, the laboratory grew and inexperienced or unknown colleagues started to work. Now it is not such a good idea to share everything.

Context

The users of operating systems need to use files to store permanent information. These files can be accessed by different users from different workstations, and access to the files must be restricted to authorized users who can use them in specific ways. Because of the needs of the institution, some (or all) of the files must be shared by these subjects.

Use cases for a file system include creation and deletion of files, opening and closing of files, reading and writing files, copying files and so on. A subject has a home directory for each authorized workstation, but the same home directory can be shared among several workstations or among several subjects. The home directory is used to search the files for which a subject has rights. Files are organized using directories, usually in a tree-like structure of directories and files. This facilitates the search for specific files.

Problem

How can we control access to files in an operating system and ensure that only authorized users can use files in specific ways?

The solution to this problem must resolve the following forces:

- There may be different types of subjects, for example users, roles and groups. The rights for users in groups or roles are derived from the group or role's rights (that is, they are implicit rights). Groups of groups are possible, which makes deducing access even harder. All these subjects must be handled uniformly.

- Subjects may be authorized to access files or directories, and to exercise their file access rights from specific workstations. To prevent illegal actions, we may need ways to apply these two types of authorization.

- Each operating system implements file systems in a different way. We need to abstract out implementation details.

- Not all operating systems use workstations, groups or roles. We need a modular system in which features not used can be removed easily from the model.

Solution

We apply the AUTHORIZATION pattern (page 74) first to describe access to files by subjects. Typically, file systems use ACCESS CONTROL LISTS (page 91) consisting of sets of authorizations. The protection object is now a file component that may be a directory or a file. To reflect the fact that files may be accessed only from some workstations, we use the AUTHORIZATION pattern again, with the same subject and with workstations as protection objects. The tree structure of files and directories can be conveniently described by applying the Composite pattern [Gam94].

Structure

The class diagram in Figure 9.18 combines two versions of the AUTHORIZATION pattern with a Composite pattern. File access is an extension of that pattern by replacing `Pro-tectionObject` by `FileComponent` and `Right` by `AccessControlListEntry` (ACLE), and workstation access is defined by a similar application of the AUTHORIZATION pattern.

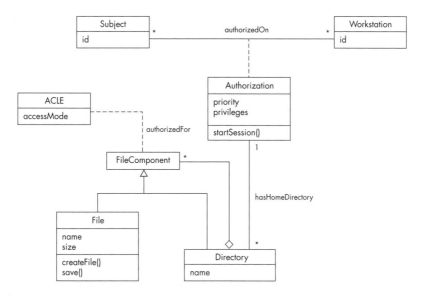

Figure 9.18: Class diagram for the FILE ACCESS CONTROL pattern

Dynamics

The sequence diagram in Figure 9.19 shows the use case 'Open and write to a file'. A user actor opens the file, the directory locates it and when found, opens it. Opening results in the file access permission being set up for future reference[1]. When the user later tries to write to the file, their rights to write the file are checked and the write operation proceeds if authorized.

Example Resolved

A new operating system is installed that has authorization controls for its files. Now a need-to-know policy is set up, where only users that need access to specific files are given such access. This is the end of erroneous or unauthorized activities.

---

[1] In some systems, opening a file also requires a specific authorization. Figure 9.19 assumes that this is not the case, although the pattern does not preclude this possibility.

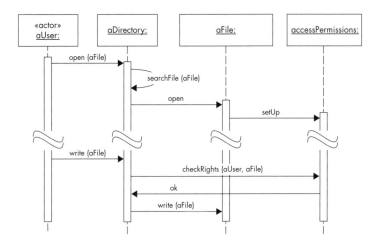

Figure 9.19: Sequence diagram for the use case 'Open and write to a file'

Consequences

The FILE ACCESS CONTROL pattern offers the following benefits:

■ The subjects can be users, roles and groups by proper specialization of the class Subject. Roles and groups can be structured recursively (see Chapter 6); for example, role and group hierarchies permit more flexibility in the assignment of rights.

■ The protection objects can be single files, directories, or recursive structures of directories and files.

■ Most operating systems use read/write/execute as access types, but higher-level types of access are possible. For example, a file representing students in a university could be accessed with commands such as list, order alphabetically, and so on.

■ Implied authorization is possible; for example, access to a directory may imply similar type of access to all the files in the directory [Fer94b]. This approach allows an administrator to write fewer authorization rules, because some access rights can be deduced from others.

■ Workstation access is also controlled – workstations can be homes for directories.

■ This is a conceptual model that doesn't restrict implementation approaches.

■ Workstation authorization is separated from file authorization; systems that do not need workstation authorization can just ignore the relevant classes.

■ In some operating systems, for example Inferno [Rau97], all resources are represented as files. Other systems represent resources by objects with access control lists. This means that this pattern could be used to control all the resources of such operating systems.

The pattern also has the following potential liabilities:

■ Implementations of the pattern are not forced to follow the access matrix model. For example, UNIX uses a pseudo-access matrix that is not appropriate for applying the need-to-know policy[1]. However, constraints can be added to the pattern to force all the instances of the pattern to conform to an access matrix model.

■ Typically, access permissions are implemented as access control lists (ACLs) [Gol06] [Sil08]. These are data structures associated with a file in which each entry defines a subject that can access the file and its permitted access modes. The pattern models the entries of the ACLs, but not the fact that they are associated with the file components.

Other aspects include:

■ Some systems use the concept of *owner*, who has all rights on the files they create. The owner in this model corresponds to a special type of subject. When roles are used, there are no owners, and when groups are used, ownership is not inherited in subgroups.

■ In some systems, files are mapped to the virtual memory address space. The FILE ACCESS CONTROL pattern still applies to this case, although a more uniform solution is then possible (see the VIRTUAL ADDRESS SPACE ACCESS CONTROL pattern, page 146).

■ In some systems, a directory is not strictly a tree, because it is possible to have links between files in different subtrees [Sil08]. Modeling this case would require adding some associations in the model of Figure 9.18.

Known Uses

This pattern can be found in most current operating systems, such as Windows, UNIX, Linux. Not all these systems use all the concepts of the pattern.

See Also

■ This pattern uses the AUTHORIZATION pattern (page 74).

■ If roles are used, then the ROLE-BASED ACCESS CONTROL pattern (page 78) is also relevant.

■ The file structure uses a Composite pattern [Gam94]. It can use the CONTROLLED EXECUTION DOMAIN pattern (page 151) for its implementation.

---

[1] Some versions of UNIX, for example IBM AIX, extend this model to support a full access matrix.

10

Security Patterns for Networks

Thus, what is of supreme importance in war is to attack the enemy's strategy.

Sun Tzu

As network administrator I can take down the network with one keystroke. It's just like being a doctor but without getting gooky stuff on my paws.

Scott Adams ('Dogbert')

10.1   Introduction

The Internet protocol suite, also referred to as TCP/IP, defines a reference model for networks that includes four layers [Sta03]: Application, Transport, Internet and Link. One can apply security to any of these layers, where two secure protocols are commonly used:

■ The IPSec protocol, which provides cryptographic functions at the Internet (IP) layer [For04b] [Sta06].

■ The Transport Layer Security (TLS) protocol, which provides similar functions at the transport (TCP) layer [For04b] [Sta06]. This protocol is based on the Secure Sockets Layer (SSL) protocol.

Figure 10.1 shows the layers and the security protocols used in each of the layers. The Application layer has different protocols based on the type of application. The Transport layer uses TLS as the security protocol, while the IP layer uses IPSec as the security protocol. Application protocols such as HTTP, LDAP and SOAP need to use the lower layers to support typical application tasks such as displaying web pages or running e-mail services; they use their own version of security protocols such as HTTPS, LDAPS (Secure LDAP) and WSS (Web Service Security) respectively.

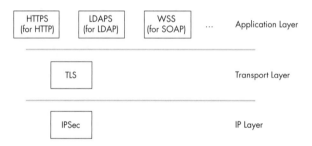

Figure 10.1: Network layers and security protocols

These secure protocols can be used directly in applications, or can be prepackaged to provide secure channels, in the form of *virtual private networks* (VPN).

Figure 10.2 shows a pattern diagram that puts the different types of secure network protocols into perspective. The ABSTRACT VIRTUAL PRIVATE NETWORK pattern defines the basic functions and threats of a VPN, independently of the protocol over which it operates. An abstract pattern defines only fundamental, implementation-independent functions and threats [Fer08a]. Concrete patterns add functionalities and threats and take into account the characteristics of their specific concrete environment. In this case, the abstract functions are realized by concrete VPNs which operate according to the rules of specific protocols: IPSec VPN and TLS VPN.

We present here patterns for the Abstract VPN, IPSec VPN and TLS VPN. Figure 10.2 also shows patterns for the TLS and IPSec protocols, which in turn use patterns for authentication ([Sch06b] and page 52) and Secure Channel [Bra00] (not shown in the figure).

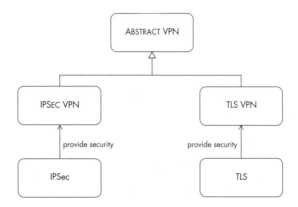

Figure 10.2: Pattern diagram for network security patterns

One can also apply security defenses at the network boundaries, where networks enter the computational nodes. Two security mechanisms are normally used at network boundaries:

- Firewalls, which filter input and output traffic according to predefined rules. We have previously written patterns for firewalls at the IP (packet filter) and TCP (proxy firewall) layers [Sch06b], as well as the (User) Application layer [Del04]. See also Chapter 11.

- Intrusion detection systems (IDS), which try to detect attacks in real time [Bie01]. IDSs can be signature-based or behavior-based.

We present the VPN patterns first, followed by the TLS protocol pattern, and finally the IDS patterns. These patterns have been coauthored with Ajoy Kumar and have been published in [Fer05d] [Kum10] [Kum12a] [Kum12b].

10.2   Abstract Virtual Private Network

The ABSTRACT VIRTUAL PRIVATE NETWORK pattern describes how to set up a secure channel between two endpoints using cryptographic tunneling, with authentication at each endpoint. An endpoint is an interface exposed by a communicating unit (user site or network).

Example

Our company has employees all over the world. Because of cost, we decided to use the Internet to communicate. However, we are having problems because their orders are hacked and the attackers get access to customers' credit card numbers and other details.

Our staff want to be sure they are talking to other employees, and must be able to send secure messages to discuss prices, discounts and so on.

Context

Users scattered in many fixed locations, who need to communicate securely with each other using the Internet or some other insecure network. In such a network attackers may intercept messages and try to read, modify or replay them.

Problem

In today's world, companies have offices all over the world and a lot of people work remotely. They need a secure connection to other specific nodes so that confidential work can be performed securely. Their communication can be intercepted by attackers, who may get access to private information and may even modify the messages. How can we establish a secure channel for the end users of a network so that they can exchange messages through fixed points using an insecure network?

The solution to this problem must resolve the following forces:

- We need to use the Internet or other insecure networks to reduce cost, but in turn subjecting our network to numerous threats.
- Only registered users should access the institution's endpoints.
- We need to make sure that the users with which we are communicating are the right ones, otherwise confidentiality may be compromised.
- The number of users remotely connected may be growing: the system should be scalable.
- Because different users or institutions require different levels of security, the system should be flexible enough to accommodate different ways of providing security and different degrees of security.
- In some cases we also need to support authorization to access specific resources in the endpoints.
- The system should be easy to set up and use, otherwise users and administrators will not want to use it.
- The system should not impose a heavy performance penalty, otherwise it will not be used all the time.
- The pattern should be adaptable to the needs and constraints of different protocol layers.

Solution

Protect communications by establishing a cryptographic tunnel between endpoints on one of the layers of the communication protocol. Add authentication functions at each endpoint. Figure 10.3 shows the case in which site A is talking to site B over the Internet using routers R1 and R2, respectively. The secure connection is established through one of the Internet layers.

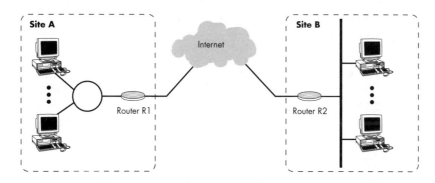

Figure 10.3: Two sites communicating through the Internet [For04b]

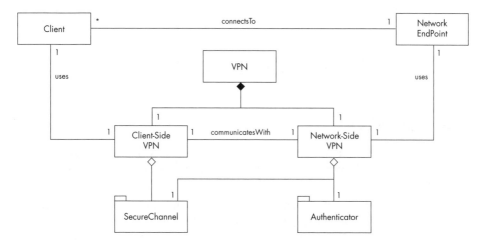

Figure 10.4: Class diagram for the ABSTRACT VIRTUAL PRIVATE NETWORK pattern

Structure

Figure 10.4 shows the class diagram for the ABSTRACT VIRTUAL PRIVATE NETWORK pattern, in which a `SecureChannel` can be established between a `Client` and a `NetworkEndPoint`. `EndPoints` communicate with other `EndPoints`. A user is authenticated by an AUTHENTICATOR pattern (page 52). AUTHENTICATOR and Secure Channel [Bra00] are patterns, composed typically of several classes, and are shown using the UML symbol for package.

Dynamics

The sequence diagram of Figure 10.5 shows a use case in which an end user tries to access an endpoint in a network, endPoint2, from another endpoint, endPoint1. The Authenticator at endPoint1 authenticates the user. The Authenticator creates a Token as proof of authentication, which can be used to establish a SecureChannel. This channel allows secure access to endPoint2.

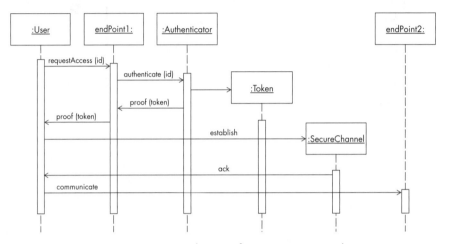

Figure 10.5: Sequence diagram for accessing an endpoint

Implementation

1 First define the endpoints which the VPN will reach. Consider the architectural layer where the communications should be secured, according to the needs of the applications.

2 After this decision, use the concrete VPN pattern at the corresponding level, IP or TCP. See the corresponding patterns (IPSec VPN, page 200, and TLS VPN, page 202) for help in making this decision. Both endpoints must share a public key system for authentication and must have appropriate software packages running on them.

Example Resolved

Now the users can be authenticated at the endpoints, which ensures that they are communicating with their own employees. User messages are now protected from external attacks when sent over the secure channel.

Consequences

The ABSTRACT VIRTUAL PRIVATE NETWORK pattern offers the following benefits:

- We can use the Internet or other insecure networks to reduce cost.

- Cryptography can protect our messages from being read or modified by attackers.

- Authentication at endpoints ensures that only registered users can access the secure channel.

- Mutual authentication between end users is possible.

- The system can accommodate new links for new users by just replicating the access software.

- We can use any cryptographic algorithm to establish the secure channel, which allows us to make trade-offs between security and cost.

- We can add authorization to access specific resources at each endpoint.

- We can add a logging system for the users logging in at the endpoints for use in audits.

- The VPN is transparent to the users, who are authenticated by their local endpoints.

- The VPN is a client-server architecture that is easy to configure.

- We can have different versions of the pattern that can use the specific features of each protocol layer.

The pattern also has the following potential liabilities:

- If the VPN connection is compromised, the attacker could get full access to the internal network. Authorization can restrict this access, however.

- Because of encryption, VPN traffic is invisible to IDS monitoring. If the IDS probe is outside the VPN server, as is often the case, then the IDS cannot see the traffic within the VPN tunnel. Therefore, if a hacker gains access to the end node of the VPN, they can attack the internal systems without being detected by the IDS.

- In the case of VPN with a private end user, the remote computer used by the private user is vulnerable to outside attacks, which in turn can attack the network to which it is connected.

- There is some overhead in the encryption process.

Variants or Concrete Patterns

Virtual private networks can be established at the application layer (XML or application VPN); TLS (SSL) VPNs are established at the transport layer. IPSec VPNs are established at the IP layer. Because of their importance, we describe the latter two below as separate patterns.

Known Uses

- Citrix provides a site-to-site SSL VPN connection for remote users to log into the secure network, as well as access applications on the company (secure) network [Cit].
- Cisco VPN uses an IPSec VPN and provides authorization [Cisb].
- Nokia provides a VPN connection for Nokia mobile users.

See Also

- Firewalls can be added to each endpoint to filter inputs [Sch06b]. They can protect against some types of attacks coming from untrusted sources.
- IDSs can be added in each of the network layers to detect attacks in real time [Fer05d].
- The VPN uses the Secure Channel pattern that in turn uses cryptography to protect its messages [Bra00].
- The Authenticator pattern[Sch06b] can authenticate users and nodes.
- Access Control/Authorization can be added at each site to control access to specific resources [Sch06b].

10.3   IPSec VPN

The IPSEC VPN pattern describes how to set up a secure channel between two endpoints using cryptographic tunneling through the IP layer, with authentication at each endpoint.

Context

Users scattered in many predefined locations, who need to communicate securely with each other, using the Internet or another insecure network.

Problem

Assuming that we need to communicate using the IP protocol, how can we establish a secure channel for the end users of a network so that they can exchange messages through some fixed points?

The solution to this problem must resolve the following forces:

- The number and required speed of the communications must decide the type of protection we use. The use of IPSec would provide higher speed between fixed physical locations [Sta03].
- Communication at the IP level includes the network, servers and routers. Messages should be protected while going through all of them.

Solution

Implement the cryptographic tunnel at the IP level using the facilities of IPSec.

Structure

The class diagram for the IPSEC VPN pattern is similar to the one shown in Figure 10.4 on page 197.

Implementation

Designing the architecture of the IPSec protocol includes appropriate host placement (for host-to-host architectures) and/or gateway placement (for host-to-gateway and gateway-to-gateway architectures)[Qu02]. Both sides must share a public key system for authentication and must have appropriate software packages running on them.

The packet filter firewall determines which types of traffic should be permitted and denied, and what protection and compression measures (if any) should be applied to each type of permitted traffic (for example, ESP tunnel using AES for encryption and HMAC-SHA-1 for integrity protection; LZS for compression). HMAC stands for Hash-based Message Authentication Code, and SHA-1 is a specific hash algorithm [For04b] [Sta06]; they are used for protecting message integrity.

Encapsulating Security Payload (ESP) is a sub-protocol of IPSec that provides confidentiality, data origin authentication, integrity and replay protection [Sta03]. AES is the Advanced Encryption Standard [For04b].

Consequences

The IPSEC VPN pattern offers the following benefits:

- IPSec is supported by most operating systems.
- The VPN is transparent to clients in gateway-to-gateway architectures.
- We can use a variety of authentication protocols.

The pattern also has the following potential liabilities:

- It can only protect IP-based communications.
- It requires client software to be configured (and installed on hosts without a built-in client) for host-to-gateway and host-to-host architectures.
- It does not protect communications between clients and the IPSec gateway in gateway-to-gateway architectures.
- IPSec VPNs require large software packages, typically 6–8 MB, and may be difficult to configure.

Variants

We can add authorization for the end users.

Known Uses

- Cisco has an IPSec VPN and they also provide authorization [Cisb].
- Cyberoam offers an identity-based IPSec VPN [Cyb].
- Check Point's VPN Software Blade is an IPSec VPN that integrates access control, authentication and encryption [Che].

See Also

- Firewalls can be added to each endpoint to filter inputs [Sch06b]. They can protect against some types of attacks coming from untrusted sources.
- IDSs can be added in each of the network layers to detect attacks in real time [Fer05d].
- The VPN uses the Secure Channel pattern, which in turn uses cryptography to protect its messages.
- The Authenticator pattern [Sch06b] can authenticate users and nodes.
- Access Control/Authorization can be added at each site to control access to specific resources [Sch06b].

10.4   TLS Virtual Private Network

Also known as SSL VPN

The TLS VIRTUAL PRIVATE NETWORK pattern describes how to set up a secure channel between two endpoints using cryptographic tunneling through the transport layer, with authentication and authorization at each endpoint.

Example

Our company has a web-based e-commerce site. We need to assure the customers that they are interacting with the proper application and that they can send their financial information securely when buying items.

Context

A large number of users, in many locations, need to communicate securely with each other, using the Internet or another insecure network. Most of the interactions occur through web sites.

Problem

How can we establish a secure channel through the transport layer for the end users of a network so that they can exchange messages through fixed points?

The solution to this problem must resolve the following forces:

■ Messages will go from one process to another process, through servers and routers. A message should maintain its security during this communication.

■ The performance should be good at both normal and peak loads.

Solution

Use TLS reverse proxy servers (commonly referred to as *SSL proxy servers*) to connect remote users. A remote user who needs to access the organization's applications uses the main URL for the proxy server in their web browser, and connects to it through TLS-protected HTTP. The user then authenticates to the proxy server. Once authenticated, the user can access designated applications, as specified in the proxy server's access controls.

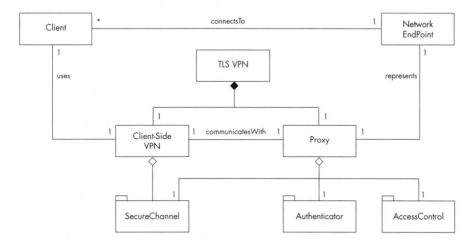

Figure 10.6: Class diagram for the TLS VIRTUAL PRIVATE NETWORK pattern

Structure

Figure 10.6 shows the class diagram for the TLS VIRTUAL PRIVATE NETWORK pattern. A `Proxy` represents the endpoint and has the functions of authentication, secure channel and access control (authorization).

Implementation

An authentication algorithm is implemented at the server which authenticates the server to the client [Hey07b]. A secure channel is established over the public network using a suitable cryptographic algorithm that allows users to communicate securely with the servers. Some TLS VPNs provide hardware accelerators. Both the client and the server must have preloaded VPN software.

Example Resolved

The SSL proxy server can authenticate the server to the user and establishes a secure channel so that remote users can send their financial information in encrypted form, thus protecting it from eavesdropping attacks.

Consequences

The TLS VIRTUAL PRIVATE NETWORK pattern offers the following benefits:

- If access is needed only for web-based applications, the solution is very convenient for users, and easier to deploy and maintain than remote access solutions that involve client installation or configuration.

- The proxy server can authenticate users before they can gain any access to applications, as opposed to allowing users to connect directly to individual applications' login screens. This adds another layer of security by only allowing authenticated users to see what applications are being served.

- Since the client systems connect above the network layer, they are not on the same network layer as the IPSec client. This severely reduces their ability to attack or misuse systems in the organization's networks.

- The proxy server can authenticate itself to the user by means of a certificate.

- Logging is now more convenient: it is just another function of the proxy.

The pattern also has the following potential liabilities:

- Non-web-based applications, and applications that are more challenging to proxy, (such as those that use multiple dynamic ports) typically require additional software and services such as terminal servers and special client software. This makes the solution more resource-intensive to deploy and less convenient to use.

- Compromise of the proxy server could allow an attacker to intercept data and authentication credentials for many different applications at once.

- TLS (SSL) is a complex protocol that has been found to have security problems in some implementations. This means that the degree of security achievable with this pattern may not be as high as with the IPSEC VPN pattern.

Known Uses

- Citrix provides a site-to-site SSL VPN connection for remote users to log into the secure network and access applications on the company's (secure) network [Cit].
- SonicWALL acquired Aventail and its TLS VPN. This product includes authentication and network access control [Son10].
- Cyberoam has an identity-based TLS VPN [Cyb].
- Aventail, Cisco, Juniper, Microsoft and Nokia also provide TLS VPNs.

See Also

- Firewalls can be added to each endpoint to filter inputs [Sch06b]. They can protect against some types of attacks coming from untrusted sources.
- IDSs can be added on each of the network layers to detect attacks in real time [Fer05d].
- The VPN uses the Secure Channel pattern, which in turn uses cryptography to protect its messages [Bra00].
- The Authenticator pattern [Sch06b] can authenticate users and nodes.
- Authorization can be added in each site to control access to specific resources [Sch06b].
- Proxy is a pattern in [Gam94]. In this case it intercepts requests going to the endpoints and performs the required checks.

10.5   Transport Layer Security

The TRANSPORT LAYER SECURITY pattern describes how to provide a secure channel between a client and a server by which application messages are communicated over the transport layer of the Internet. The client and the server are mutually authenticated and the integrity of their data is preserved.

Example

A bank customer may want to check their account balance on line. The bank uses the transport layer to transfer its confidential data. We need to protect this communication, as this confidential data is vulnerable to attack. The customer also has to ensure that the transactions are with the bank and not with an imposter, while the bank may need to verify that access is by a legitimate customer.

Context

Users using applications that exchange sensitive information, such as web browsers for e-commerce or similar activities. The transport layer in TCP/IP provides end-to-end communication services for applications within a layered architecture of network components and protocols, and specifically convenient services such as connection-oriented data stream support, flow control and multiplexing.

Problem

The messages communicated between applications and servers on the transport layer are vulnerable to attack by intruders, who may try to read or modify them. Either the server or the client may be imposters.

The solution to this problem must resolve the following forces:

- *Confidentiality and integrity.* The data transferred in the transport layer between the client and the server could be intercepted and read, or modified illegally.
- *Authenticity.* Either the server or the client could be an imposter, which may allow security breaches. A 'man-in-the-middle' attack is also possible, in which an attacker poses both as the client to the server and as the server to the client.
- *Flexibility.* Security protocol should be flexible and configurable, to be able to handle new attacks.
- *Transparency.* The security measures of the protocol should be transparent to users.
- *Configurability.* The protocol should allow users to select different degrees of security.
- *Overhead.* The overhead should be minimal, or users will not want to use the protocol.

Solution

Establish a cryptographic secure channel between the client and the server using algorithms that can be negotiated between the client and the server. Provide the means for client and server to authenticate each other. Provide a way to preserve the integrity of messages.

Structure

Figure 10.7 shows a class diagram for the basic architecture of the TRANSPORT LAYER SECURITY pattern. A `Client` requests some `Service` from the `Server`. The `TLSProtocol` controller conveys this request using an `Authenticator` to mutually authenticate the

Server and the Client, and creates a Secure Channel between them. AUTHENTICATOR and Secure Channel are patterns (see Variants on page 212).

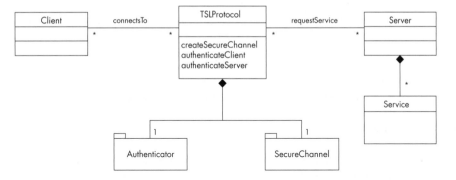

Figure 10.7: Class diagram for the TRANSPORT LAYER SECURITY pattern

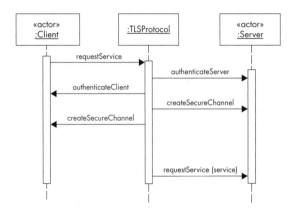

Figure 10.8: Sequence diagram for the use case 'Request a service'

Dynamics

We describe the dynamic aspects of the TRANSPORT LAYER SECURITY pattern using a sequence diagram for the following use case:

Use Case: Request a Service – Figure 10.8

Summary	A Client requests a service and the TLSProtocol authenticates the request and creates a secure channel.
Actors	Client, Server.
Precondition	The security parameters of the secure exchange have been predefined.

Description   *1* The `Client` makes a service request to the `Server`.

              2 The `TLSProtocol` authenticates the `Server` to the `Client` and the `Client` to the `Server`.

              3 The `TLSProtocol` creates a secure channel between the `Server` and the `Client`.

Alternate Flows ■ The authentication can fail.

              ■ The creation of a secure channel can fail.

Postcondition   The `Server` accepts the request and grants the service.

Implementation

One of the protocols that is dominant today for providing security at the transport layer is Secure Sockets Layer (SSL). The SSL protocol is a transport layer security protocol that was proposed and developed Netscape Communications in the 1990s. Transport Layer Security (TLS) is an IETF version of the SSL protocol, which has become a standard [Yas04]. Much implementation advice can be found in [Sel12].

The TLS protocol is partitioned into two main protocol layers, the TLS Record Protocol and the TLS Handshake Protocol, executing above the TCP transport layer protocol, as shown in Figure 10.9 [Elg06] [Sta12]. There are other minor protocols at the handshake protocol layer, such as the Cipher Change Protocol, Alert Protocol and Application Protocol.

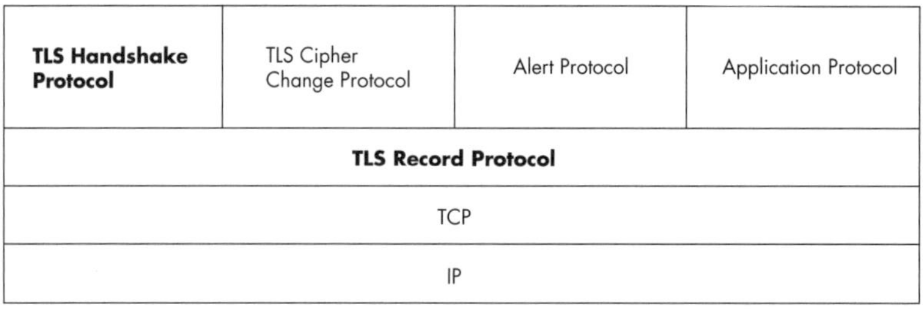

TLS Handshake Protocol	TLS Cipher Change Protocol	Alert Protocol	Application Protocol
TLS Record Protocol			
TCP			
IP			

Figure 10.9: TLS layers

- *Record Protocol.* The TLS Record Protocol provides encryption and message authentication for each message. A connection is created using symmetric cryptography data encryption. The keys for this symmetric encryption are generated uniquely for each connection and are based on a secret negotiated by another protocol (such as the TLS Handshake Protocol). Messages include a message integrity check using a keyed message authentication code (MAC), computed using hash functions [Sta03].

- *Handshake Protocol.* A TLS handshake supplies the authentication and key exchange operations for the TLS protocol. The security state agreed upon in the handshake is used by the TLS Record Protocol to provide session security. This protocol allows the server and client to authenticate each other and to negotiate an encryption algorithm and cryptographic keys before the application protocol transmits or receives any data. The TLS Handshake Protocol provides connection security where the peers' identities can be authenticated using asymmetric cryptography. This authentication can be made optional, but is generally required for at least one of the peers.

A TLS session is an association between a client and a server, created by the handshake protocol. Sessions define a set of cryptographic security parameters, which can be shared among multiple connections. Sessions are used to avoid the expensive negotiation of new security parameters for each connection.

A session state is defined by the following parameters:

- *Session identifier*. This is generated by the server to identify a session with a chosen client.
- *Peer certificate*. The X.509 certificate of the peer.
- *Compression method*. A method used to compress data prior to encryption.
- *Algorithm specification or CipherSpec*. Specifies the encryption algorithm that encrypts the data and the hash algorithm used during the session.
- *Master secret*. 48-byte data, being a secret shared between the client and server.
- *'resumable'*. A flag indicating whether the session can be used to initiate new connections.

The handshake protocol consists of the following four phases:

1 In the first phase, an initial connection is established to start the negotiation. The client and server exchange 'hello' messages that are used to establish security parameters used in the TLS session, and settings used during the handshake, such as the key exchange algorithm.

2 During the second phase, authentication, the server sends a certificate message to the client: this may include a server certificate when an RSA key exchange is used, or Diffie-Hellman parameters when a Diffie-Hellman key exchange is used. The server may also request a certificate from the client, using the certificateRequest message.

3 During the third phase, the client, if asked, may send its certificate to the server in a certificate message, along with a certificateVerify message, so that the server can verify certificate ownership (if the server requested a client certificate during the second phase). This phase includes the establishment of the security parameters such as the encryption key. The client must send either a pre-master secret encrypted using the server's public key, or public Diffie-Hellman parameters in the clientKeyExchange message, so that the client and server can compute a shared master secret.

4   In the fourth phase, the client and server finish the handshake, which implies that the client and server are mutually authenticated and have completed the required key exchange operations.

Structure and Dynamics of the Handshake Protocol

The structure of the handshake protocol is shown in the class diagram in Figure 10.10. The `Client` requests a service from the `Server` at the Transport layer. The `TLSHandshakeProtocolController` uses client and server certificates to mutually authenticate the `Client` and the `Server`, then performs the `clientKeyExchange`.

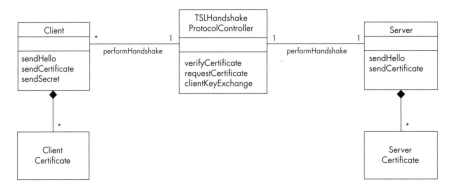

Figure 10.10: Class diagram for the TLS handshake protocol.

We describe the dynamic aspects of the TLS handshake using the sequence diagram shown in Figure 10.11.

Summary	A TLS handshake supplies the authentication and key exchange operations for the TLS protocol.
Actors	`Client`, `Server`.
Precondition	The `Client` has made a request for a service from the host `Server` and an initial connection has already been established. The `Client` and `Server` need to have a digital certificate, issued by some Certificate Authority.
Description	1 The `Client` and `Server` exchange initial Hello messages.
	2 The `ProtocolController` requests the certificate from the `Server` and the `Server` sends the certificate.
	3 The server certificate is verified.
	4 The `Server` requests the certificate from the `Client` (optional).
	5 If asked, the `Client` sends the certificate to the `Server`.
	6 The client certificate is verified.

7   The `Client` sends the predefined secret encrypted using the `Server`'s public key which is the client key exchange.

8   The `Client` and the `Server` complete mutual handshake and the initial encryption parameters.

Alternate Flows ■   Authentication of the `Server` or `Client` can fail. A certificate can be expired or outdated.

          ■   The `Client` could lose the encryption key while exchanging with the `Server`.

Postcondition   `Client` and `Server` can start exchanging data at the transport layer.

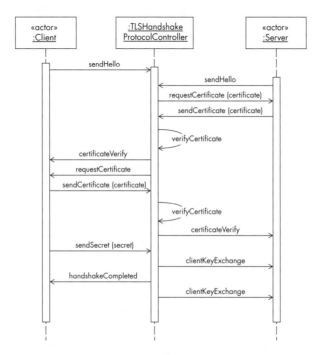

Figure 10.11: Sequence diagram for the TLS handshake use case

The other minor protocol layers from Figure 10.9 are discussed below:

■ *Cipher Change Protocol.* This protocol signals transitions in cipherSpec, which is a session parameter explained above.

■ *Alert Protocol.* This protocol raises alerts for the communication. This record should normally not be sent during normal handshaking or application exchanges. However, this message can be sent at any time during the handshake and up to the closure of a TLS session. If this record is used to signal a fatal error, the session will be closed immediately after sending the record. If the alert level is flagged as a warning, the remote partner can decide whether or not to close the session.

■ *Application Protocol.* Now the handshake is completed and the application protocol is enabled. This marks the start of data exchange between the server and the client.

Example Resolved

When a request is made to the bank's server by an online client at the transport layer, the bank's server is authenticated to the customer, the customer is authenticated to the server and a secure channel is created between them. Now the client knows that online bank transactions are secure.

Consequences

The TRANSPORT LAYER SECURITY pattern offers the following benefits:

■ *Confidentiality and integrity.* A secure channel is established between the server and the client, which can provide data confidentiality and integrity for the messages sent. We could add a logging system for the client at its endpoint for future audits.

■ *Authenticity.* Both client and server can be mutually authenticated. Man-in-the-middle attacks can be prevented by mutual authentication.

■ *Flexibility.* We can easily change the algorithms for encryption and authentication protocols.

■ *Transparency.* The users don't need to perform any operation to establish a secure channel.

■ *Configurability.* Users can select algorithms to obtain different degrees of security.

The pattern also has the following potential liabilities:

■ *Overhead.* As seen from Figure 10.11, the overhead is significant for short sessions: many messages are needed.

■ SSL/TLS is a two-party protocol; it is not designed to handle multiple parties. However the MTLS variant can handle multiple parties.

Variants

■ *WTLS.* A modified version of TLS, called WTLS (Wireless TLS protocol) has been used in mobile systems. WTLS is based on TLS and is similar in some aspects [Bad04]. WTLS has been superseded in the WAP (Wireless Application Protocol) 2.0 standard by the End-to-End Transport Layer Security specification.

■ *MultipleTLS* (MTLS). This is an application-level protocol running over the TLS Record protocol. The MTLS provides application multiplexing over a single TLS session. Therefore, instead of associating a TLS session with each application, this protocol allows several applications to protect their communication over a single TLS session [Bad09].

Some different versions of TLS are given below.

- *TLS 1.0*. TLS 1.0 is an upgrade of SSL Version 3.0 and is an IETF version of SSL. The differences between this protocol and SSL 3.0 are not large, but they are significant enough that TLS 1.0 and SSL 3.0 do not interoperate. TLS 1.0 does include a means by which a TLS implementation can downgrade the connection to SSL 3.0, but this weakens security.

- *TLS 1.1*. TLS 1.1 is an update of TLS version 1.0. Significant differences include:

  - Added protection against cipher block chaining (CBC) attacks. In CBC mode, each block of plaintext is XORed with the previous cipher text block before being encrypted.

    - The implicit Initialization Vector (IV) was replaced with an explicit IV.

    - Change in handling of padding errors.

  - Support for registration of parameters.

- *TLS 1.2*. This is a revision of the TLS 1.1 protocol, which contains improved flexibility, particularly for negotiation of cryptographic algorithms. The major changes are:

  - The MD5/SHA-1 combination in the pseudorandom function (PRF) has been replaced with cipher-suite-specified PRFs. All cipher suites in this document use P_SHA256.

  - The MD5/SHA-1 combination in the digitally-signed element has been replaced with a single hash. Signed elements now include a field that explicitly specifies the hash algorithm used.

  - Substantial cleanup to the client's and server's ability to specify which hash and signature algorithms they will accept.

  - Addition of support for authenticated encryption with additional data modes.

  - Tightening up of a number of requirements.

  - Verification of data length now depends on the cipher suite (default is still 12) [wik3].

- *EAP-TLS* is a wireless authentication protocol for TLS [EAP].

Known Uses

- Mozilla Firefox versions 2 and above support TLS 1.0 [Moz].

- Internet Explorer (IE) 8 in Windows 7 and Windows Server 2008 support TLS 1.2 [MS].

- Presto 2.2, used in Opera 10, supports TLS [Rut].

See Also

- The Authenticator pattern describes how to mutually authenticate a client and a server [Sch06b].
- The Secure Channel pattern describes a cryptographic channel used to communicate secure data [Bra00].

10.6   Abstract IDS

The ABSTRACT IDS pattern allows monitoring of all traffic as it passes through a network, and its analysis it to detect possible attacks and trigger an appropriate response.

Example

Our company has a firewall to control traffic from the Internet. However we are still plagued by viruses and other attacks that penetrate the firewall. The attacks can be existing attacks or new attacks. We need to improve our defense against such attacks.

Context

Nodes for local systems that need to communicate with each other using the Internet or another insecure network.

Problem

An attacker may try to infiltrate our system through the Internet and misuse our information by reading or modifying it. We need to know when an attack is happening and take appropriate response.

The solution to this problem must resolve the following forces:

- *Communication.* The system is usually more secure if we have a closed network. However in today's world it is better and more realistic to use the Internet or other insecure network to reduce costs, which may subject our network to security threats.
- *Real time behavior.* Attacks should be detected before the attack completes its purpose, so that we can preserve our assets and save time and money. It is difficult to detect an attack when it is happening, but such detection is imperative if we are to react timely and appropriately.
- *Incomplete security.* Security measures such as encryption, authentication and so on may not protect all our systems, because they do not cover all possible attacks.
- *Non-suspicious users.* Protecting our system through a firewall is quick and easy. However, request coming from a non-suspicious address (that is, one permitted by a firewall) could still be harmful and should be monitored further.

- *Flexibility.* Hard-coding the type of attack can be done easily. But it will be hard and time-consuming to adapt to attack patterns that change constantly.

Solution

Each request to access the network is analyzed to check whether it conforms to the definition of an attack. If we detect an attack, an alert is raised and some countermeasures maybe taken.

The ABSTRACT IDS pattern defines the basic features of any intrusion detection system (IDS). An abstract pattern defines only fundamental, implementation-independent functions and threats [Fer08a]. Concrete patterns add functionalities and threats, and take into account the characteristics of their specific concrete environment. In this case, the abstract functions are realized by concrete IDSs that operate based on known attack signatures, or based on abnormal behavior or anomaly in the network: SIGNATURE-BASED IDS or BEHAVIOR-BASED IDS. We present here patterns for all these three types of IDS.

Figure 10.12: Possible placement of network IDS to complement a firewall

Figure 10.12 shows the typical placement of an IDS in a network, complementing a firewall. The firewall filters requests for services, and the IDS further checks for suspicious patterns in request sequences. If a suspicious pattern is detected, the network operator is alerted and the firewall may block some or all traffic.

Structure

Figure 10.13 shows the class diagram for the ABSTRACT IDS pattern. A `Client` requests some service from the `Server`. The `IDS` intercepts this request and sends it to an `Event-Processor`. The `EventProcessor` processes the event so that the `AttackDetector` can analyze the event and implement some method of detection using information from `AttackInformation`. When an attack is detected, a `Response` is created.

Dynamics

We describe the dynamic aspects of the ABSTRACT IDS pattern using a sequence diagram for the following use case.

Use Case: Detect an Intrusion – Figure 10.14

Summary   The `Client` requests a service from the `Host`. The `IDS` intercepts the message and checks whether the request is an attack or not and raises a response.

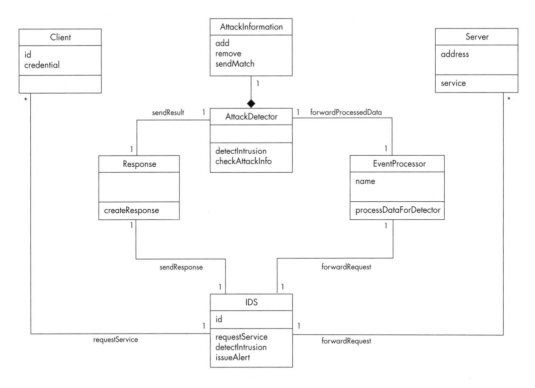

Figure 10.13: Class diagram for the ABSTRACT IDS pattern

Actors   Client, Server.

Precondition We have attack information available.

Description   1 A Client makes a service request to the Host.

2 The IDS send the request event to an EventProcessor.

3 The EventProcessor processes the event data so that the AttackDetector can interpret the event.

4 The AttackDetector tries to detect whether this request is an attack or not by comparing with the available information in the Attack-Information.

5 If an attack is detected, a Response is created.

Alternate Flows ■ The AttackInformation may not be able to detect an attack (a false negative).

■ The AttackInformation may indicate an attack when no attack is present (a false positive).

Postcondition If an attack is detected, suitable preventive measures may be applied.

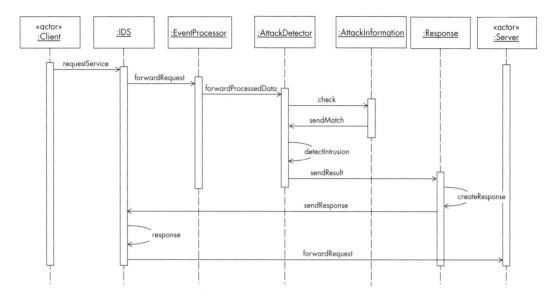

Figure 10.14: Sequence diagram for the use case 'Detect an intrusion'

Implementation

We need to create a database with attack information so that we can check against this database and decide whether an attack is happening. The incoming event is compared against the database and a decision is made whether the incoming event is an attack or not. The concrete versions of this pattern use different types of information to detect attacks.

The Common Intrusion Detection Framework (CIDF) is a working group created by DARPA in 1998 that is mainly oriented towards creating a common framework in the IDS field. CIDF defined a general IDS architecture based on the consideration of four types of functional modules as shown in Figure 10.15 [Gar09].

- *E blocks* ('event-boxes'). This block is composed of sensor elements that monitor the target system, thus acquiring information events to be analyzed by other blocks.

- *D blocks* ('database-boxes'). These are elements intended to store information from E blocks for subsequent processing by A and R boxes.

- *A blocks* ('analysis-boxes'). Processing modules for analyzing events and detecting potential hostile behavior.

- *R blocks* ('response-boxes'). The main function of this type of block is the execution, if any intrusion occurs, of a response to thwart the detected menace.

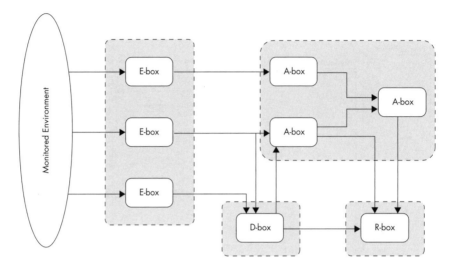

Figure 10.15: General CIDF architecture for IDS systems (from [Gar09])

Consequences

The ABSTRACT IDS pattern offers the following benefits:

- *Communication.* If we can detect most attacks, we can safely use the Internet or other insecure networks to access other systems.

- *Real time behavior.* Attacks can be detected when the attack happens and the system alerted, which saves the both time and money in recovery measures, and may prevent misuse of assets. Attacks can be detected in real time if they have sufficient and appropriate information.

- *Incomplete security.* The IDS provides be an added layer of security in addition to encryption, authentication and so on.

- *Non-suspicious users.* A request coming from a non-suspicious address (permitted by a firewall) is further inspected and analyzed.

- *Flexibility.* The detection information can be modified to include new attacks or new behavior.

The pattern also has the following potential liabilities:

- Some attacks may be so fast that it may be hard to recognize them in real time.

- Attack patterns are closely tied to a given environment (operating system, hardware architecture and so on) and cannot be applied easily to other systems. This means we need to define detection information tailored to an environment.

- There is some overhead in the addition of IDSs to a system.

- The concrete versions of these systems have additional liabilities.

Variants (Concrete Patterns)

- IDS can be either behavior (rule) based or can be based on anomalies (abnormal behavior). There are significant differences in the use and effectiveness of these two approaches. The patterns for both the SIGNATURE-BASED IDS and BEHAVIOR-BASED IDS are described next.

- A hybrid model of both the signature based and behavior based IDS together is now available: a behavior-based IDS detects the anomalies in traffic and then compares the anomalies with an attack signature in a signature-based IDS.

- According to the resources they monitor, IDS systems are divided into two categories: *host-based IDS* systems and *network-based IDS* systems. Host-based IDS systems are installed locally on host machines and evaluate the activities and access to key servers within the host. Network-based IDS systems inspect the packets passing through the network [Ozg05]. This classification is out of the scope of this book and is not discussed here.

Known Uses

NID is a freely-available hybrid intrusion detection package. It monitors network traffic and scans for the presence of known attack signatures, as well as deviations from normal network behavior [Gra00].

See Also

- Firewalls can be added to complement the IDS [Sch06b]. Firewalls usually deny requests made by unknown addresses. They can protect against attacks coming from distrusted sources and can block the addresses from where an attack originates.

- The response class could be implemented as a Strategy pattern [Gam94].

10.7   Signature-Based IDS

Also known as Rule Based IDS, Knowledge-Based IDS

The SIGNATURE-BASED IDS pattern describes how to check every request for access to the network against a set of existing attack signatures, to detect possible attacks and trigger an appropriate response.

Example

Our company has a firewall to control traffic from the Internet. However we are still plagued by viruses and other attacks that penetrate the firewall. We need to improve our defense against such attacks.

Context

Distributed systems executing applications that may provide services to remote nodes. Access to the network can be from the Internet or from other external networks.

Problem

Whenever data is accessed from the distrusted networks, there is always a possibility that this access can be harmful to the local node. We need to detect possible attacks while they are occurring. Security techniques such as authentication and firewalls are usually implemented to provide security, but we need additional defenses to detect whether an access request is a possible attack or not. The solution to this problem must resolve the following forces:

- *Known attacks.* It is easier to protect the system against known attacks. Many attacks are new instances of known attacks and have a well-defined attack signature.
- *Completeness.* If we have a complete collection of known attacks and their signatures, it is easier to detect an attack exhibiting one of these signatures.
- *Flexibility.* Hard-coding the type of attack can be done easily, but it will be hard and time-consuming to adapt to attack patterns that keep changing constantly.

Solution

Detect the occurrence of attacks by matching the current attack signature against the signature of previously known attacks.

Structure

Figure 10.16 shows the class diagram of this pattern. The IDS intercepts an access request for a service. An EventProcessor processes the information and feeds this processed information to a AttackDetector, which tries to match the sequence of requests to the signatures in the AttackSignatureInformation and decides whether or not the request is an intrusion. If an attack is detected by getting a match of signatures, some appropriate Response is raised.

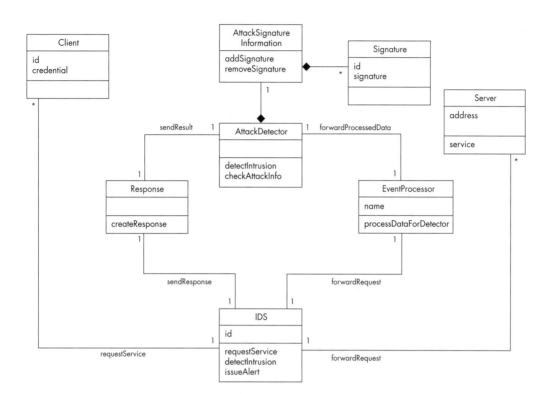

Figure 10.16: Class diagram for the SIGNATURE-BASED IDS pattern

Dynamics

We describe the dynamic aspects of the SIGNATURE-BASED IDS pattern using a sequence diagram for the following use case.

Use Case: Detect an Intrusion – Figure 10.17

Summary   The Client requests a service from the Host. The Signature-Based IDS intercepts the message and determines whether the signature of the event matches an existing attack signature. If the request is an attack, appropriate response is raised.

Actors   Client, Server.

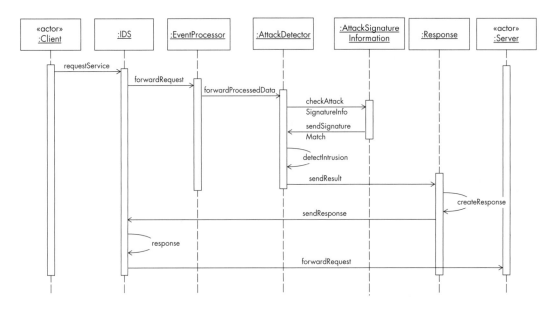

Figure 10.17: Sequence diagram for the use case 'Detect an intrusion'

Precondition   Information about attack signatures is available.

Description   1   A `Client` makes a service request for a service to the `Host`.

2   The `IDS` send the request event to an `EventProcessor`.

3   The `EventProcessor` processes the event as required by the `Attack-Detector` and passes the processed event data to the `AttackDetector`.

4   The `AttackDetector` tries to detect whether this request is an attack or not by comparing the signature of the event with the available signatures in the `AttackSignatureInformation`.

5   If a match is detected, a `Response` is created.

Alternate Flows   ■ The `AttackSignatureInformation` may not be able to detect an attack (a false negative).

■ The `AttackSignatureInformation` can match and may indicate an attack when no attack is present (a false positive).

Postcondition   If an attack is detected while it is happening, suitable preventive measures can be adopted.

Implementation

We first need to create a database with a set of all the known or expected attack patterns. We then select a detection algorithm. Some possible detection algorithms are:

- *Expression matching.* The simplest form of misuse detection involves searching the event stream for known attack pattern expressions [Ver02].

- *State transition analysis.* The whole process is a network of states and transitions. Every observed event is applied to finite state machine instances (each representing an attack scenario), possibly causing transitions[Ver02].

- *Dedicated languages.* Some IDS implementations describe intrusion signatures using specialized languages varying from compiled expressions to programming languages such as Java. A signature takes the form of a specialized program, with raw events as input. Any input triggering a filtering program, or input that matches internal alert conditions, is recognized as an attack [Ver02].

- *Genetic algorithms.* A genetic algorithm is used to search for the combination of known attacks (expressed as a binary vector, each element indicating the presence of a particular attack) that best matches the observed event stream [Ver02].

Example Resolved

We added an intrusion detection system beside the existing firewall to the system. Now any request authorized by the firewall is checked against known attack signatures to detect whether the access request is a possible attack. If we detect an attack, an alert can be raised and the firewall can block the request.

Consequences

The SIGNATURE-BASED IDS pattern offers the following benefits:

- *Known attacks.* Detection can be effective against known attacks.

- *Completeness.* If all known attack signatures are available in the database, attacks can be detected in real time.

- *Flexibility.* It is relatively easy to add new attacks to the detection set.

The pattern also has the following potential liabilities:

- It only works for known attacks: a new attack will not be detected. We have to constantly update the database with new attack signatures.

- Some attacks don't have well-defined signatures, or the attacker may disguise the signatures. This may lead to false positives and false negatives.

- Some attacks may be so fast that it may be hard to recognize them in real time.

- Attack patterns are closely tied to a given environment (operating system, hardware architecture, and so on) and cannot be applied easily to other systems.

Known Uses

- An IDS can be combined with a firewall, as is done in Nokia's network systems [Nok01].

- Cisco IDS utilizes detection techniques including stateful pattern recognition, protocol parsing, heuristic detection and anomaly detection [Cisb].

- LIDS is a signature-based intrusion detection/defense system for the Linux kernel [Lid].

- RealSecure [Rs] by Internet Security Systems is an IDS adapted by IBM for intrusion detection packages. It can monitor TCP, UDP and ICMP traffic and, if a match is found, countermeasures can be implemented along with read/write server locking, IP blocking and other measures. This product is bundled with CheckPoint Software's Firewall [Che].

See Also

- This pattern is a special (concrete) case of the Reference Monitor pattern [Fer01a].

- The patterns for firewalls in [Sch06b] complement this pattern.

- The response class could be implemented as a Strategy pattern [Gam94].

10.8   Behavior-Based IDS

Also known as Anomaly-Based IDS

The BEHAVIOR-BASED IDS pattern describes how to check every request for access against patterns of network traffic in order to detect possible deviations from normal behavior (anomaly) that may indicate an attack and trigger appropriate responses.

Example

A company uses a public network for its applications. The network is exposed to security threats, especially a variety of unknown attacks. Their business could be in jeopardy if their customers realize that their system is not secure enough.

Context

Any network application where the temporal behavior of network traffic is repetitive and predictable.

Problem

Whenever data is accessed from the Internet or other external networks, there is always a possibility that this access can be harmful to the network. We need to detect possible attacks while they are occurring.

The solution to this problem must resolve the following forces:

- *New attacks.* In today's world networks are constantly bombarded with new attacks that do not have a specific attack signature. We need to detect these kinds of attacks.

- *Real-time.* We need to detect attacks in real time while they are happening, and not after the attack has happened and it is too late to recover from it.

- *Increased vulnerability.* Some networks, such as mobile networks, are more vulnerable to unknown attacks because of their mobile nature.

Solution

Observe the traffic over a network and try to find deviations from normal or expected behavior. Any deviation from normal behavior is treated as a sign of intrusion.

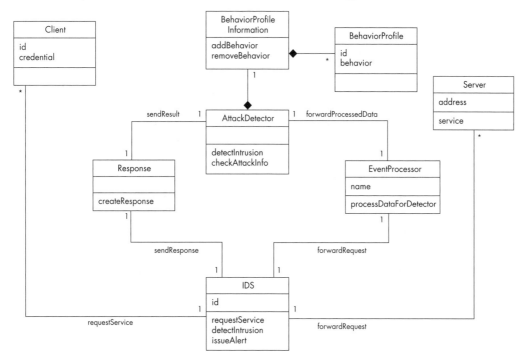

Figure 10.18: Class diagram for the BEHAVIOR-BASED IDS pattern

Structure

Figure 10.18 shows the class diagram for this pattern. A `Client` requests some service from the system. The `IDS` intercepts this request and sends it to an `EventProcessor`. The `EventProcessor` processes the event data as needed by the `AttackDetector`, which involves establishing profiles of normal behavior that can be compared with the current behavior in `BehaviorProfileInformation`, and passes the processed data to the `AttackDetector`. When an attack is detected, a `Response` is created.

Dynamics

We present the dynamic aspects of the BEHAVIOR-BASED IDS pattern using sequence diagrams for the following use case.

Use Case: Detect an Intrusion – Figure 10.19

Summary	The `Client` requests a service from the `Host`. The behavior-based IDS intercepts the message and determines whether the behavior of the request matches a normal behavior profile. If it does not, an attack is suspected and a response is raised.
Actors	`Client`, `Server`.
Precondition	A set of normal behavior profiles is available.
Description	1 `Client` makes a service request to the `Host`.
	2 The `IDS` send the request event to an `EventProcessor`.
	3 The `EventProcessor` processes the event as required by the `Attack-Detector` and passes the processed event data to the `AttackDetector`.
	4 The `AttackDetector` tries to detect whether this request is an attack or not by comparing the behavior profile of the request with the available behavior profiles in the `BehaviorProfileInformation`.
	5 If a match is detected, a `Response` is created.
Alternate Flows	■ The `BehaviorProfileInformation` may not be able to detect an attack (a false negative).
	■ The `BehaviorProfileInformation` can match and may indicate an attack when no attack is present (a false positive).
Postcondition	If an attack is detected while it is happening, suitable preventive measures can be adopted.

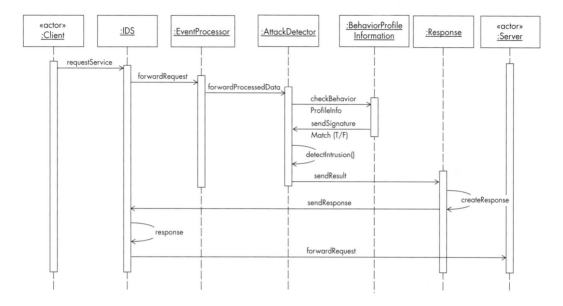

Figure 10.19: Sequence diagram for the use case 'Detect an intrusion'

Implementation

Examples of techniques used for anomaly detection in practice are:

- *Genetic algorithms.* In this approach, applications are modeled in terms of system calls for different conditions, such as normal behavior, error conditions and attack conditions. A typical genetic algorithm involves two steps. The first step involves coding the input population of the algorithm. The second step involves finding a fitness function to test each individual of the population against some evaluation criteria. In the learning process each event sequence of node behavior forms a gene. Fitness is calculated for a collection of genes. If genes with required fitness cannot be found in the current generation, new sets of genes are evolved through crossover and mutation. The process of evolution continues until genes with the required fitness are found. The detection process involves defining vectors for event data and methods of testing whether the vector indicates an intrusion or not [Kis10].

- *Protocol verification.* The basis for this approach is the fact that most intruders use irregular or unusual protocol fields, which are not handled properly by application systems [Ver02].

- *Statistical models.* These can be either multivariate models or models based on available statistics such as threshold measures, or mean and standard deviations of the profile. Clustering analysis where clusters represent similar activities or user patterns is also sometimes used [Ver02].

Example Resolved

We added an intrusion detection system to our network. Now all traffic is checked against a normal behavior profile to see whether the access request is an anomaly and hence a possible attack. We are now able to detect many new attacks that do not have a known signature and prevent them.

Consequences

The BEHAVIOR-BASED IDS pattern offers the following benefits:

- *New attacks.* Detection can be effective against new attacks that could cause abnormal behavior in the network traffic. For example, we can identify an attack with a specific behavior, such as when a usually passive web server tries to connect to a large number of addresses, it could be the result of a worm attack.
- *Real time.* This kind of IDS works well with network traffic that exhibits a normal behavior and where it will be easier to detect an abnormal behavior pattern for the network.
- *Increased vulnerability.* This kind of IDS is usually good in wireless networks, which are more vulnerable due to their mobile nature.

The pattern also has the following potential liabilities:

- It generates a lot of false positives. Many anomalies detected are not attacks, but could be just unusual behaviors of users.
- It cannot be implemented in networks that do not have a predictable traffic pattern.
- The technology adopted for one network is not easily portable to another system, and can be different from system to system in a network, as normal behavior for one system is usually not the normal behavior for another system.
- If the attacker carries out an attack by mimicking regular traffic or normal behavior, the attack may go undetected.

Known Uses

- Cisco IPS 4200 Series utilizes detection techniques including stateful pattern recognition, protocol parsing, heuristic detection and anomaly detection [Cisb].
- AirTight's wireless IPS automatically detects, classifies, blocks and locates wireless threats using behavior analysis. They use a genetic algorithm to establish normal behaviors [Air].

Some other uses of anomaly-based IDSs are given in Table 10.1 [Gar09].

NAME	MANUFACTURER	HYBRID	RESPONSE	ANOMALY-RELATED TECHNIQUES
AirDefense Guard	AirDefense, Inc.	Y	Y	Detection, correlation and multi-dimensional detection
Barbedwire's IDS Softblade	Barbedwire Technologies	Y	Y	Protocol analysis, pattern matching
BreachGate WebDefend	Breach Security	Y		Behavior-based analysis, statistical analysis, Using correlation functions.
Bro	Lawrence Berkeley National Laboratory	Y	Y	Application level semantics, event analysis, pattern matching, protocol analysis.

Table 10.1 Network-based IDS platforms with anomaly detection functionalities, according to the manufacturer's information [Gar09]

The Hybrid column indicates hybrid detection, and the Response column indicates that some kind of response mechanism is also available.

See Also

- This pattern is used in conjunction with the SIGNATURE-BASED IDS pattern (page 219).

- Firewalls are usually used together with the IDS in a network: the patterns for firewalls in [Sch06b] complement this pattern.

- The response class could be implemented as a Strategy pattern [Gam94].

CHAPTER

11

Patterns for Web Services Security

You are what you do, not what you say you'll do.

Carl Gustav Jung

11.1 Introduction

Service-oriented architectures (SOAs) and web services are special cases of distributed systems. Distributed systems are typically heterogeneous systems that are accessible to a wide variety of institution partners, customers or mobile employees, and introduce a new variety of security threats. To protect its assets, an organization needs to define security policies, which are high-level guidelines that specify the states in which the system is considered to be secure. These policies need to be enforced by security mechanisms. In large organizations, the policies may be issued by different actors, making their management difficult. Moreover, they need to be enforced for a variety of resources. To make things more difficult, they may have to follow government or institution regulations. One way to allow interoperability, apply security, and enforce compliance with regulations is through

231

the use of standards that define architectures to guarantee that all participants will follow the same rules in their interactions.

There are many web services security standards, which are rather complex and sometimes overlap; representing them as patterns makes them easier to understand and to compare with other patterns. This chapter presents our work on security patterns for web services and their standards. Many patterns have been identified in the web services community, at various level of granularity. For example, [Ben02] and [Zir04] propose patterns for web services composition, while [Ima03] and [Tat04] identify security patterns.

However, most of the proposed web services security patterns are low-level patterns. They are effectively implementation patterns that give solutions to concrete problems in terms of specific technologies. Erl has written a whole book on patterns for web services [Erl09]. However, his patterns are rather abstract, for example Brokered Authentication, and do not consider any aspects of standards: they are also mostly descriptive. At present, only our patterns deal with the security of web service standards. We have also written web service reliability patterns [Buc09b], as well as misuse patterns for web services [Mun11]. A survey of our work is given in [Fer12c].

Web services standards tend to be complex and verbose, and it is not easy for designers and users to understand their key points. Web services standards are typically long documents: for example, the XACML 3.0 Core Specification run to 150 pages, and is written to be comprehensive but not to be easy to understand. It uses a combination of XML, UML and natural language [Mos05]. By expressing web services security mechanisms and standards as patterns, we can verify whether an existing product implementing a given security mechanism supports some specific standard [Fer06d]. Conversely, a product vendor can use the standards to guide the development of the product. By expressing standards as patterns, we can also compare them and understand them better, and discover overlapping and inconsistent aspects between them. A standard defines a generic architecture, and this is a basic feature of any pattern; it can then be confirmed as a best practice by looking at products that implement the standard (and implicitly the pattern). There are many security standards for web services [Fer10b] defined by several committees, including W3C, OASIS and IETF.

The patterns described here are specialized versions of more fundamental and more general patterns. For example, XACML [Del05] is a specialization of the AUTHORIZATION pattern. As such it carries the general properties of an AUTHORIZATION pattern and adds aspects specific to XML access control. The new aspects may themselves be patterns; for example, the Composite pattern [Gam94] appears frequently in these models to indicate recursive composition. Identifying patterns as part of a more complex pattern makes it easier to understand the functions of the complex model.

The pattern diagram shown in Figure 11.1 shows the relationships between our patterns for web services standards.

- WS-SECURITY (page 330) describes how to send secure and authenticated messages by leveraging a standard for XML Encryption, and how to authenticate messages by using the XML Signature standard [Has09c].

- Authorization to access specific parts of an XML document is defined by the XAC-ML standard, which is composed of rule definition (XACML Policy) and rule enforcement (XACML Evaluation) [Del05].

- Authorization and authentication assertions can be conveyed to different domains by using SAML [Fer06d].

- General policies are described using WS-POLICY, which is used in turn to define trust among entities (WS-TRUST).

We describe patterns for all these standards except WS-Federation and WS-Secure Conversation. We also include patterns for application and XML firewalls [Del04]. All these patterns were written with Nelly Delessy and Ola Ajaj [Aja10a][Aja10b].

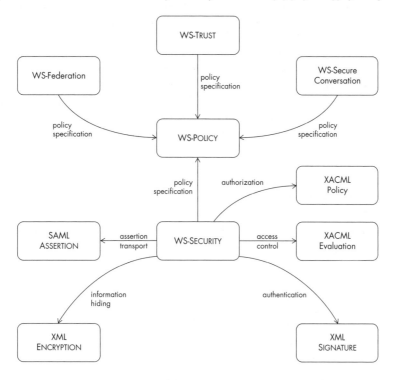

Figure 11.1: Pattern diagram for web services standards

11.2   Application Firewall

Also known as Content Firewall

The APPLICATION FIREWALL pattern allows filtering of calls and responses to/from enterprise applications, based on an institution's access control policies.

Example

Consider an application for handling medical records in a hospital. One of the services it provides is to allow patients to look up their personal medical records from home. To ensure that only patients can access this service, a user must first be identified as a patient and must then be authenticated. Finally, the application must ensure that only the medical records belonging to the patient are returned (that is, it must match the name in the medical record with that of the user).

One way to provide this security is to let the application maintain a list of all valid patients with their authentication credentials, and implement the code for blocking unauthorized access. This approach has several problems. In the future, if the hospital decides to give patients the ability to schedule appointments, it will have to repeat the implementation of the access control code for the scheduling application as well. Furthermore, if there are changes in hospital business policies – for example, to allow external primary care physicians to access the medical records of their own patients – these applications will have to be rewritten. In this changing scenario, a new access control list for authorized primary care physicians will have to be added to the medical record application, and a list of patients will have to be associated with each physician to indicate the patients belonging to a specific doctor. Such application modifications are time-consuming, difficult to manage, expensive and error-prone.

Context

Enterprise applications executing in distributed systems accessed from a local network, the Internet, or other external networks. These distributed systems typically include packet filter and/or proxy-based firewalls.

Problem

Enterprise applications in an organization's internal network are accessed by a broad spectrum of users that may attempt to abuse its resources (leakage, modification or destruction of data). These applications can be numerous, and thus implement access control independently in ad hoc ways, making the system more complex and thus less secure.

Moreover, traditional network firewalls (application layer firewalls or packet filters), do not make it possible to define high-level rules (role-based or individual-based rules) that could make the implementation of security policies easier and simpler.

How can we control the hostile actions of users who access our applications? The solution to this problem must resolve the following forces:

- There may be many subjects that need to access an application in different ways; the firewall must accommodate this variety.

- There are many ways to filter application inputs. We need to separate the filtering code from the application code.

- There may be numerous applications that may require different levels of security. We need to define appropriate policies for each application.

- The security policies are constantly changing and need to be constantly updated. It should therefore be easy to change the firewall filtering configuration.

- The number of users and applications may increase significantly. Adding more users or applications should be done transparently and at proper cost.

- Network firewalls cannot understand the semantics of applications and are unable to filter out potentially harmful messages.

- Any type of security policy should be enforceable by the firewall.

- There are many ways to perform authentication. The firewall must support this variety.

Solution

Interpose a firewall that can analyze incoming requests for application services and check them for authorization. A client (user, role) can access a service of an application only if a specific policy authorizes it to do so. Policies for each application are centralized within the APPLICATION FIREWALL, and they are accessed by the firewall through a policy authorization point. Each application is accessed by a client through a policy enforcement point that enforces access control by looking for a matching policy in the policy base (the set of policies). This enforcement may include authenticating the client through its data stored in the identity base (the database of identities).

Structure

Figure 11.2 shows the class diagram for the APPLICATION FIREWALL pattern. The classes `Client` and `Service` have the usual meaning. A `Client` accesses a `Service` provided by an application. The access requests are controlled by authorization rules (denoted here as *policies* to follow the usual industrial notation), and represented by the `Policy` class. Policies are collected in the `PolicyBase` class. `Clients` are denoted as subjects in the authorization rules.

The firewall consists of a `PolicyAuthorizationPoint` which centralizes the definition of the policies and identities throughout the institution, and several `PolicyEnforcementPoints`, which are used to check the accesses to the applications. The data flowing through the firewall is checked by the `ContentInspector`.

The enterprise applications are represented by the class `Application`, which is made up of `Services`. A service is identified by a `serviceId`, which is usually a URI or a URL.

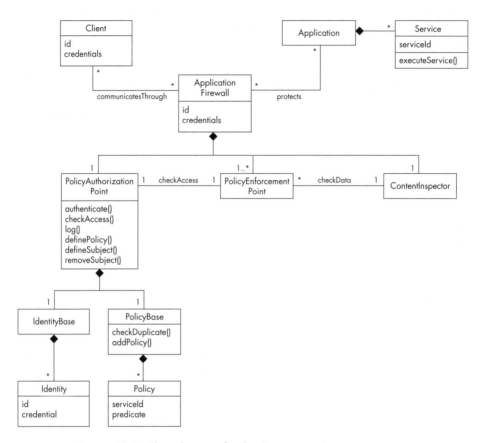

Figure 11.2: Class diagram for the APPLICATION FIREWALL pattern

Dynamics

We describe the dynamic aspects of the APPLICATION FIREWALL pattern using sequence diagrams for two use cases: 'Filter a client's request with user authentication', and 'Add a new policy'.

Use Case: Filter a Client's Request with User Authentication – Figure 11.3

Summary   A `Client` requests access to a service of an `Application` to either input or retrieve information. The access request is made through the `Policy-EnforcementPoint`, which accesses the `PolicyAuthorizationPoint` to determine whether to accept or deny the request (page 238).

Actors   A Client.

Precondition   Existing IdentityBase and PolicyBase classes must be in place in the firewall. The IdentityBase contains the data necessary to authenticate a Client. The PolicyBase contains specific policies defined by the organization.

Description   1 A Client requests access to an Application.

                  2 An ApplicationFirewall, through its PolicyEnforcementPoint, intercepts the request and accesses the PolicyAuthorization-Point.

                  3 The PolicyAuthorizationPoint authenticates the Client through its IdentityBase. This step may be avoided for subsequent requests through the use of a Session class.

                  4 Once the Client is identified and authenticated, the PolicyAuthorizationPoint filters the request according to the PolicyBase. The request is accepted or denied according to the defined policies.

                  5 If the request is accepted, the firewall allows access to the service of the Application and the access is logged by the ApplicationFirewall.

Alternate Flows ■ If the Client is not recognized, or if no policy allows the specific Client to access the specified service, the firewall rejects the access request to the service.

                  ■ If the user has already been authenticated, the Client may not be authenticated again (single sign-on use).

Postcondition   The firewall has provided the access of a Client to a service, based on verifying the identity of the Client and the existence of a matching policy.

Use Case: Add a New Policy – Figure 11.4

Summary   The security administrator intends to add a new policy to the set of policies. Before adding it, the firewall checks that the new policy to be added does not already exist in the policy set (page 239).

Actors   Administrator.

Precondition   The Administrator must have authorization to add rules.

Description   1 After having been authenticated, the Administrator initiates the addition of a new rule.

                  2 If the rule does not already exist in the rule set, then it is added.

                  3 The firewall acknowledges the addition of the new rule.

Alternate Flow The rule is not added because it already exists in the rule set.

Postcondition   A new rule is added to the rule set of the firewall.

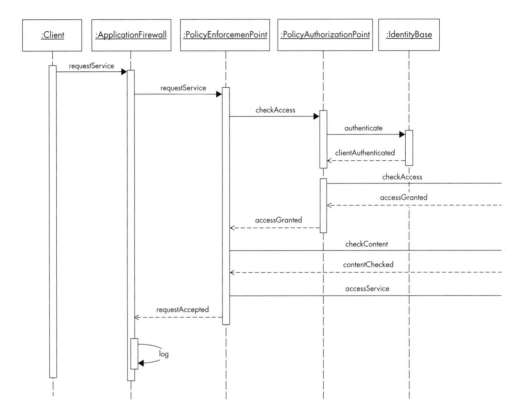

Figure 11.3: Sequence diagram for the use case 'Filter a client's request with user authentication'

Implementation

To implement the APPLICATION FIREWALL the designer needs to understand the semantics of the application. The following tasks need to be performed:

1   Define subjects. These are the active entities, users or roles, who will apply operations to some of the classes in the application model.

2   Define subjects' rights and implement them as policies. Apply a need-to-know policy and give users only the rights they need to perform their functions with respect to the application. For example, a manager needs to have the right to create accounts, but not the right to withdraw money from the accounts they create.

3   Assign individual users to the roles in the application.

4   Add/remove policies when needed. Users come and go, and their association with specific roles needs to be kept up to date.

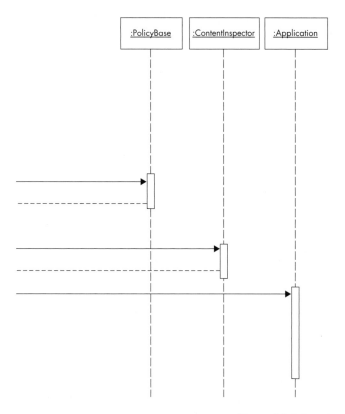

Figure 11.3 (continued)

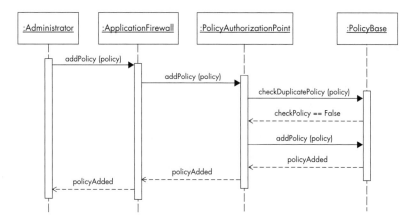

Figure 11.4: Sequence diagram for the use case 'Add a new policy'

5   Define criteria for logging. Some activities, for example performing transactions, need to be recorded for future audit.

Two architectural configurations are possible: reverse proxy and multiple agents.

Reverse Proxy

With the reverse proxy implementation, the input flow is intercepted on a single point (Figure 11.5). There is only one policy enforcement point, and all the flow should go through it [Sch06b].

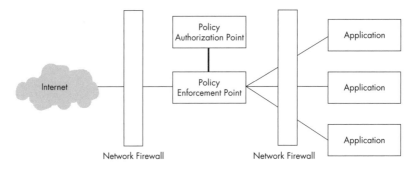

Figure 11.5: Reverse proxy configuration

Multiple Agents

With this implementation, several policy enforcement points are distributed on the network, close to the different applications that have to be controlled (Figure 11.6). These enforcement points together intercept every request to the application. It is also possible to control access for requests coming from internal networks.

Example Resolved

Application firewalls allow separation of the access control code from the application code. This allows reuse of the basic access control code in different applications. For example, in the example discussed at the start of the pattern description, the bulk of the access control code will be common to both medical and scheduling applications.

When application firewalls are used, all accesses to applications (medical or scheduling) have to pass through these firewalls. The application firewall ensures that the users are properly authenticated, and have privileges to the service they are accessing based on configurable policies.

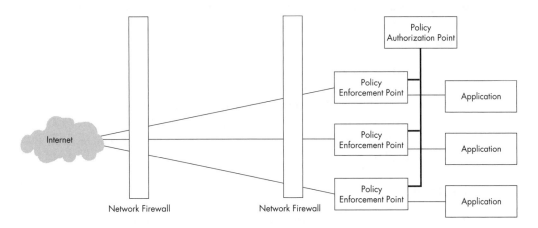

Figure 11.6: Multiple agents configuration

Consequences

The APPLICATION FIREWALL pattern offers the following benefits:

- The institution's policies for controlling access are easily defined and administered, as the policies have centralized administration. This makes the whole system less complex, and thus more secure.

- The pattern could be combined with an intrusion detection system to facilitate the prevention of some attacks.

- The application firewall lends itself to a systematic logging of incoming and outgoing messages.

- As authentication of clients is performed, users can be held responsible for their actions.

- Different types of users or types of access just require specific rules.

- Filtering is separated from application functions. Because of their separation, the application and the filtering policies can evolve independently.

The pattern also has the following potential liabilities:

- The application firewall could affect the performance of the protected system, as it is a bottleneck in the network. This can be improved by considering the firewall a virtual concept and using several physical devices in the implementation.

- The solution is redundant for existing applications that already implement their own access control.

- The application itself must be built in a secure way, or normal service operations could allow attacks through the requests.

- We still need the operating system and the network infrastructure to be secure.

Known Uses

- This pattern is used in several commercial products, such as Cerebit InnerGuard [Cer03] and Netegrity SiteMinder [Net03].

- This model is also used as an underlying architecture for the XML FIREWALL pattern (below).

- There are also products called *application security gateways* that incorporate these functions, plus others.

See Also

- The AUTHORIZATION pattern (page 74) defines the security model for the APPLICATION FIREWALL.

- The ROLE-BASED ACCESS CONTROL pattern (page 78), a specialization of the AUTHORIZATION pattern, is applicable if the business policies are defined in terms of roles and rights [San96].

- The APPLICATION FIREWALL pattern is a special case of the Single Access Point pattern [Yod97].

- The Reverse Proxy pattern [Sch06b] defines a possible architecture for the use of this pattern.

- The policy enforcement point is a special case of a Reference Monitor (page 100).

11.3   XML Firewall

The XML FIREWALL pattern allows filtering of XML messages to/from enterprise applications, based on business access control policies and the contents of the message.

Context

Enterprise applications executing in distributed systems accessed through a local network, from the Internet or from external networks. The applications communicate through XML messages and could be applications using web services. The messages can contain a remote procedure call or a document.

Problem

Some enterprise applications use tunneling into authorized flows (HTTP, SMTP) to communicate with external sites. They use higher-level protocols such as SOAP and communicate through XML documents or XML-wrapped remote procedure calls. The XML content of these messages can contain harmful data and can be used to perform attacks against applications.

Network firewalls provide infrastructure security, but become useless when these high-level protocols and formats are used.

The solution to this problem must resolve the following forces:

- Document or remote procedure call formats are subject to change; some new ones may appear (XML dialects). The firewall must adapt easily to these changes.

- New types of harmful data may be used by attackers; the firewall must adapt easily to these new types of attacks.

- There are many ways to filter; we need to separate the filtering code from the application code.

- There may be numerous applications that may require different levels of security.

- New applications may be integrated into the system after the firewall has been put into operation. This integration should not require significant additional costs.

- Network firewalls cannot understand the contents of XML messages or application semantics, and do not stop potentially harmful messages.

Solution

Use a firewall that intercepts XML messages and can understand their contents. A client can access a service of an application only if a specific policy authorizes it to do so and if the content of the message is considered safe for the application. Policies for each application are centralized in the XML FIREWALL and accessed through a policy authorization point. Each application is accessed by a client through a policy enforcement point that enforces access control for the applications. The authorization decision may include authenticating the client through its identity data stored in the identity base. It also includes looking for a matching policy for the request in the policy base, and checking the contents of the message. First, its structure is validated through a list of valid XML schemas, and the data it conveys is checked through a *harmful data detector*.

Structure

Figure 11.7 shows the class diagram for this pattern. Some of the classes are similar to those of Figure 11.2 (page 236). They include an IdentityBase, a collection of the Client identities registered in the system. A PolicyBase stores authorization policies that define the rights of those users. A PolicyAuthorizationPoint collects both identity and authorization information. A PolicyEnforcementPoint performs access control checks. The new classes include the ContentInspector, which checks the content of the XML messages sent from/to the applications.

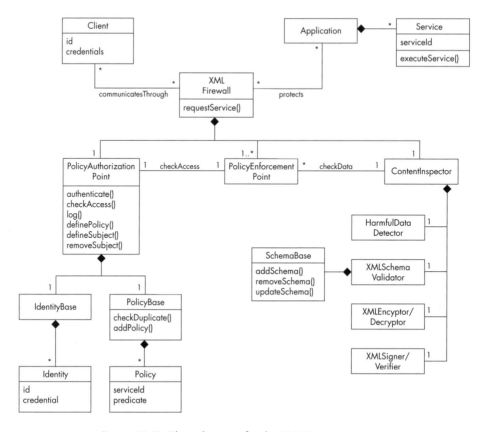

Figure 11.7: Class diagram for the XML FIREWALL pattern

The `ContentInspector` consists of a `HarmfulDataDetector`, an `XMLSchemaValidator`, an `XMLSigner/Verifier` and an `XMLEncryptor/Decryptor`. The `HarmfulDataDetector` perform checks for harmful data embedded in the content of the message. The `XMLSchemaValidator` checks the validity of the XML documents sent to the application. The `XMLSigner/Verifier` and `XMLEncryptor/Decryptor` respectively sign/verify and encrypt/decrypt XML messages that access the firewall, in accordance with the XML Digital Signature [W3C08] and XML Encryption [W3C02] standards proposed by W3C. These mechanisms are used to guarantee confidentiality, data authenticity and integrity of the XML documents, as well as non-repudiation.

Dynamics

Figure 11.8 (page 246) illustrates the dynamic aspects of the XML FIREWALL pattern using a sequence diagram. It corresponds to a use case in which the XML message is encrypted and signed, and whose user needs to be authenticated. A more basic use case would be obtained by removing some of these requests.

Use Case: *Filtering an Encrypted and Signed Client's Request with User Authentication – Figure 11.8*

Summary A `Client` requests access to a service of an application to either transfer or retrieve information via an XML message. First, the content of the message is checked, so that only harmless messages are given access to the applications. Then, the access request goes through the `PolicyEn-forcementPoint`, which accesses the `PolicyAuthorizationPoint` to determines whether to accept or deny the request.

Actors External `Client`.

Precondition Existing `IdentityBase` and `PolicyBase` classes must be in place in the firewall. The `IdentityDatabase` contains the data necessary to authenticate a `Client`. The `PolicyDatabase` contains specific policies defined by the organization.

An existing XML schema database contains the XML schemas trusted by the organization.

Description 1 A `Client` requests access to an `Application`.

2 An `XMLFirewall`, through its `ContentInspector`, checks the validity of the XML message and decrypts it.

3 The `PolicyEnforcementPoint` intercepts the request and relays it to the `PolicyAuthorizationPoint`.

4 The `PolicyAuthorizationPoint` authenticates the `Client` through its `IdentityBase`. This step may be avoided for subsequent requests through the use of a `Session` class.

5 Once the `Client` has been authenticated and identified, the `Policy-AuthorizationPoint` filters the request according to the `PolicyBase`. The request is accepted or denied according to the defined policies.

6 The contents of the message is checked. If the message contains harmful data, it is rejected.

7 The signature of the XML document is verified.

8 The firewall allows access to the service of the application and the access is logged into the `XMLFirewall`.

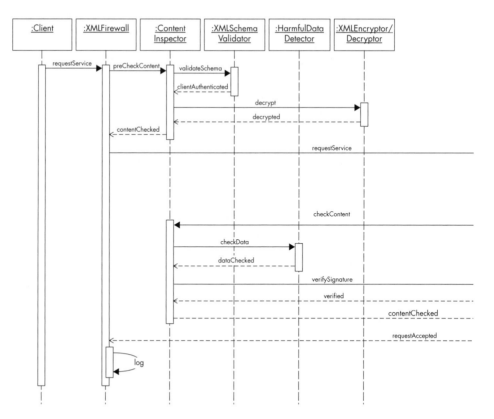

Figure 11.8: Sequence diagram for the use case 'Filtering an encrypted and signed client's request with user authentication'

Alternate Flows ■ If the XML message is invalid, or the XML message contains harmful data, or the Client is not authenticated, or no policy allows the specific Client to access the specified service, the firewall rejects the access request.

■ If the user has already been authenticated, the Client may not be authenticated again (single sign-on use).

■ If the signature is not verified, the request may be relayed, depending on the existing policies.

Postcondition The firewall has filtered the access of a Client to a service, based on the content of the message, the authentication of the Client, and the existence of a matching policy.

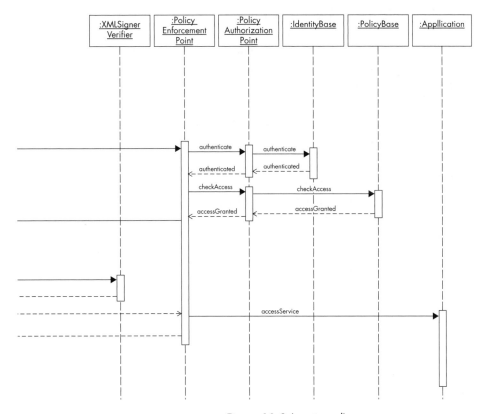

Figure 11.8 (continued)

Implementation

The same architectural structures used for the APPLICATION FIREWALL pattern (page 234) – reverse proxy, multiple agents – can be used to deploy XML FIREWALLs.

Consequences

TheXML FIREWALL pattern has the same benefits as the APPLICATION FIREWALL pattern, and the following additional benefit:

- It provides a higher level of security than the APPLICATION FIREWALL pattern for inputs which are XML documents or requests.

The pattern also has the following potential liabilities:

- The application could affect the performance of the protected system, as it is a bottleneck in the network, and as the XML content checking may create a large overhead. This can be alleviated by using a multiple-agents configuration.

- The solution may be redundant or intrusive for existing applications that already implement their own access control or their own filtering.

- The application firewall needs to manage the corresponding cryptographic keys necessary to encrypt/decrypt data or verify digital signatures.

Known Uses

- This model is used in several commercial products, such as Reactivity's XML Firewall [Rea03], Westbridge's XML Message Server [Wes03], Netegrity's Transaction Minder [Net03], DataPower's Security Gateway [Dat04], Sarvega's XML Security Gateway [Sar04], Xtradyne's WS-DBC [Xtr04] and Forum Systems Xwall [For04a].

- Web application servers such as IBM's WebSphere also include similar devices [WeS].

See Also

- The AUTHORIZATION pattern (page 74) defines the security model for the XML FIREWALL.

- The ROLE-BASED ACCESS CONTROL pattern (page 78), a specialization of the authorization pattern, is applicable if the business policies are defined in terms of roles and rights [San96].

- The XML FIREWALL pattern is a special case of the APPLICATION FIREWALL pattern (page 234).

- The Reverse Proxy pattern [Sch06b] defines a possible architecture for the use of this pattern.

- The policy enforcement point is a special case of a Reference Monitor [Sch06b].

11.4   XACML Authorization

eXtensible Access Control Markup Language (XACML) can be used by an organization to represent authorization rules in a standard manner.

Example

Consider a company that provides financial services to its customers. Their computer systems can be accessed by customers who send orders to the company for buying or selling commodities (stocks, bonds, real estate, art) by e-mail or through their website. Brokers employed by the company can carry out the orders of the customers by sending requests to the systems of various financial markets, or by consulting information from financial news websites. Also, a government auditor visits periodically to check for application of laws and regulations.

All these activities are regulated by policies with various granularities within the company. For example, the billing department can have the rule 'only registered customers whose account status is ok may send orders', the technical department can decide that 'e-mails with attachments bigger than x Mb won't be delivered', the company security policy can state that 'only employees with the 'broker' role can access the financial markets' web services' and that 'only the broker custodian of a customer can access its transaction information', whereas the legal department can issue the rule 'auditors can access all transaction information', and so on.

All these policies are enforced by different components of the company's computer system (e-mail server, file system, web service access control component, financial application). This approach has several problems: the policies are described in possibly different syntaxes, and it is difficult to have a global view of what policies apply to a specific case. Moreover, two policies can be conflicting, with no way to combine them in a clear way. In summary, this approach could be error-prone and complex to manage.

Context

A complex environment such as a large enterprise with many partners, contractors and relations with other enterprises. These various actors access the organization's resources, comprising web services, sensitive documents or system components.

Problem

An organization's resources are usually of various types (XML documents, web services, web components, CORBA services). Access to these resources is controlled by distributed enforcement mechanisms, according to the security policies of the institution. Since the resources are of different types, the enforcement mechanisms come in various forms: they can be part of a web server, an application firewall, and so on. Therefore, policies have to be implemented in many locations, using different syntaxes. It is important to define precisely the policies about accessing these resources.

Moreover, security policies in an organization are typically issued by different actors from its departments (human resources, legal, marketing departments), and the policies they write may concern a wide and overlapping set of resources. Defining these policies in such a way that the correct policies can be applied to each access may be complex, and thus error-prone.

How can we unify the definition of access policies throughout the organization, making the whole system simpler and less error-prone? The solution to this problem must resolve the following forces:

■ The policies are issued by a variety of actors and may be stored in many locations. This means that they may be expressed in different forms.

■ The policies are constantly changing and need to be constantly updated.

■ An active entity accessing a resource can be represented in a variety of ways, including certificates.

■ Some policies can require a set of actions (or *obligations*) to be performed in conjunction with policy enforcement (auditing, notification).

■ The environment in which an access is requested can also affect the access decision. For instance, an access may only be permitted at some hours of the day.

Solution

Write all policies in a common language using a standard format. This format is generic enough to implement some common high-level policies or models (open/closed systems, extended access matrix, RBAC, multilevel). In addition, define a way to compose policies so that when several policies apply to one access, it is possible to render one unique decision: the policies have a combining algorithm.

Structure

Figure 11.9 shows the class diagram of this pattern. A `PolicyAdministrationPoint` is a rule repository that centralizes the definition of policies throughout the organization. The `Subject` intending the access, the `Resource` at which the access is targeted, and the `Environment` of the access are described through their attributes. The `Environment` represents the characteristics of an access that are independent of the `Subject` or `Resource`. It could include the current date, time or other environmental properties.

A `Rule` is a basic unit of policy and has the usual meaning. In the access matrix model, it defines a set of `Subjects`, `Resources` (protection objects) and `Actions` (access types). However, in this pattern, a `Rule` associates not only one, but a set of `Subjects`, with a set of `Resources` and a set of `Actions`. It also includes a set of `Environments` to which the rule is intended to apply, a condition and an effect ('permit' or 'deny' – that is, positive and negative rules). The condition refines the rule by imposing constraints on the `Subjects`, the `Resources` or the `Environment`. The `Target` of the rule is made up of the sets of `Subjects`, `Resources`, `Actions` and `Environments` to which the rule is intended to apply. A `Target` is used for identifying the applicable rules in a given context.

`Policies` are composed of `Rules`. When evaluating a `Policy`, `Rules` are combined according to the `Policy`'s `ruleCombiningAlgorithm` (deny-overrides, permit-overrides, first-applicable, only-one-applicable or a user-defined algorithm).

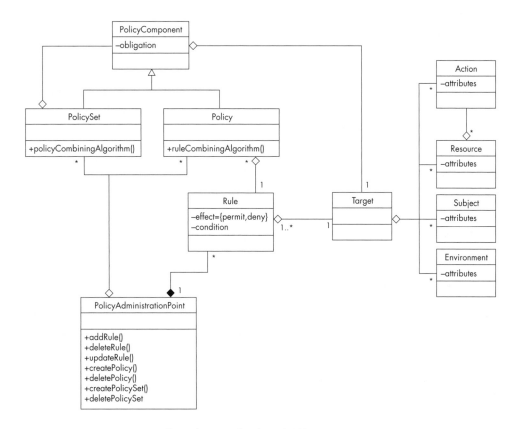

Figure 11.9: Class diagram for the XACML AUTHORIZATION pattern

`Policies` are structured according to a Composite pattern [Gam94], where a `Policy-Set` is the composite element. Similarly, when evaluating a `PolicySet`, `Policies` are combined according to the `PolicySet`'s `policyCombiningAlgorithm`. (We could use a Strategy pattern [Gam94] here to have more than one algorithm.) This indicates that policies have a tree structure. Each `PolicyComponent` may include an obligation that defines an operation that should be performed after enforcing the access decision. For example, an obligation could be an audit operation, or a notification to an external client.

In addition to its rules' `Targets`, each `PolicyComponent` may be associated with a `Target`. A `Target` at this level is either specified by the `Policy` writer, or calculated as the union or the intersection of the `Targets` of the `Rules` comprising this `Policy`.

Dynamics

We describe the dynamic aspects of the XACML AUTHORIZATION pattern using a sequence diagram for the use case 'Create a new policy'.

Use Case: Create a New Policy – Figure 11.10

Summary	A `PolicyWriter` intends to create a new policy component.
Actors	`PolicyWriter`.
Precondition	The `PolicyWriter` must have authorization to create Policies.
Description	1 The `PolicyWriter` creates as many rules as necessary, specifying the target, the effect and possibly a condition for each rule.
	2 The rules are added to the set of existing rules.
	3 The `PolicyWriter` creates a `Policy` by specifying the rules, optionally some obligations and targets, and the `ruleCombiningAlgorithm`.
	4 The `PolicyAdministrationPoint` acknowledges the creation of the new `Policy`.
Postcondition	The new `Policy` is added to the `Policy` set of the `PolicyAdministrationPoint`.

Implementation

The enterprise must have decided to use XACML to provide security for its documents and services. This decision is based on the fact that XACML is a standard and several products support its use. Once this decision is made, we need to:

1 Define semantics for the subject, the resource and the environment's attributes for each intended authorization. These attributes can be from existing standards (LDAP attributes, SAML and so on) and are extensible.

2 Translate existing rules into the XACML format.

3 Define new rules and implement them as XACML rules and policies.

4 Add/remove policies when needed.

For example, we can have rules describing authorization for individual users, roles or any relevant active entity. A complete example of use is given in [Ver04].

Example Resolved

The use of XACML authorization rules makes it possible for the company to centralize a wide range of policies and rules. Those can be easily managed, and the conflicts can be resolved by using algorithms that combine rights when evaluating an access request.

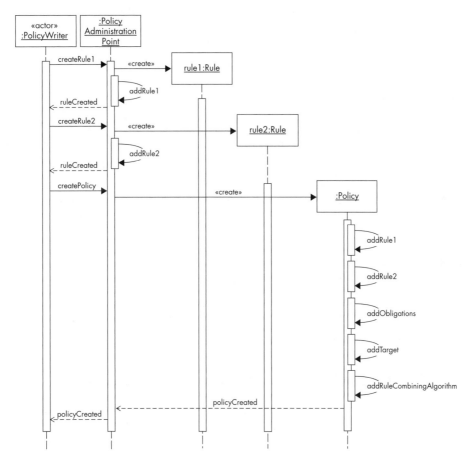

Figure 11.10: Sequence diagram for the use case 'Create a new policy'

Consequences

The XACML AUTHORIZATION pattern offers the following benefits:

■ The organization's policies to control access are easily defined using the constructs of the language. This makes the whole system less complex, and thus more secure.

■ A variety of policy types can be described, as the policy language includes the resource, the subject and the environment's attributes.

■ Similarly, a variety of subject types can be described.

■ Policies and rules can be combined easily.

■ A policy writer can specify complex conditions.

■ The pattern enables logging or other actions by means of obligations.

The pattern also has the following potential liability:

■ The structure of a policy is complex. It is verbose even for simple rules, and may require increased processing time to evaluate a request.

Known Uses

■ This pattern is used in several commercial products, such as Xtradyne's WS-DBC (an XML firewall) [Xtr04] and DataPower's XS40 XML Security Gateway [Dat04].

■ Parthenon Computing produced a suite of policy products based on XACML (Policy Tester, Policy Engine, Policy Server) [Par05].

■ Sun provides an open source implementation written in Java [Sun04b].

See Also

■ The policies are structured according the Composite pattern [Gam94].

■ Rules correspond to a specialization of the AUTHORIZATION pattern (page 74).

■ The Resource Reservation Protocol (RSVP) policy control can be implemented using XACML [Tok04].

■ Our patterns for XACML could also represent the RSVP protocol.

11.5 XACML Access Control Evaluation

The XACML ACCESS CONTROL EVALUATION pattern describes how to decide whether a request is authorized to access a resource according to policies defined by the XACML AUTHORIZATION pattern.

Example

Consider the same financial company as was discussed in the XACML AUTHORIZATION pattern. Its policies and rules are enforced by different components of its computer system: by the e-mail server, file system, web service access control component and financial applications. It requires much time and money to administer access control for those different systems.

Context

A complex environment such as a large enterprise with many partners, contractors and relations with other enterprises. These various actors access the organization's resources, comprising web services, sensitive documents or system components. These accesses are controlled at several enforcement points, according to security policies.

Problem

An organization's resources are usually of various types. Accesses to these resources are controlled by distributed enforcement mechanisms, according to its security policies. Since the resources are of different types, the enforcement mechanisms come in various forms: they can be a part of a web server, an application firewall, and so on. Therefore, the organization has to set up and maintain numerous authorization systems for its networks.

How can we enforce the rules defined in the institution policies? The solution to this problem must resolve the following forces:

- Enforcement points could be implemented in a variety of systems (part of a web server, in a WAN and so on).

- Any type of security policy should be enforceable.

- Enforcement may require reading system or environment variables.

Solution

Protect resources by policy enforcement points. All access requests to a policy enforcement points are evaluated by submitting them to a unique policy decision point in a common format. This policy decision point returns the access decision, based on the applicable policy corresponding to the access context. The policy information point provides attributes from the subject.

Structure

Figure 11.11 shows the class diagram of the XACML ACCESS CONTROL EVALUATION pattern. A `Subject` can access a `Resource` in the current environment only if an `XACMLAccessResponse` authorizes it to do so. The `Subject`, `Resource` and environment are described through their attributes. The specific aspect of this pattern is that an access is realized through three entities, the `Subject`, the `Resource` and the environment, instead of just the `Subject` and the `Resource`. This enables a full description of the characteristics of an access to be evaluated.

The `PolicyEnforcementPoint` requests an access decision from the `PolicyDecisionPoint` through a `ContextHandler`, which is an adapter between any specific enforcement mechanism and the XACML `PolicyDecisionPoint`. The `PolicyDecisionPoint` is responsible for deciding whether or not an access should be permitted, by locating the `ApplicablePolicySet`, the set of policies that is applicable to the particular access attempt applying it to the `XACMLAccessRequest`, and issuing a corresponding `XACMLAccessResponse`.

The `ContextHandler` can also get additional attributes from a `PolicyInformationPoint`, which is responsible for obtaining attributes from the subject.

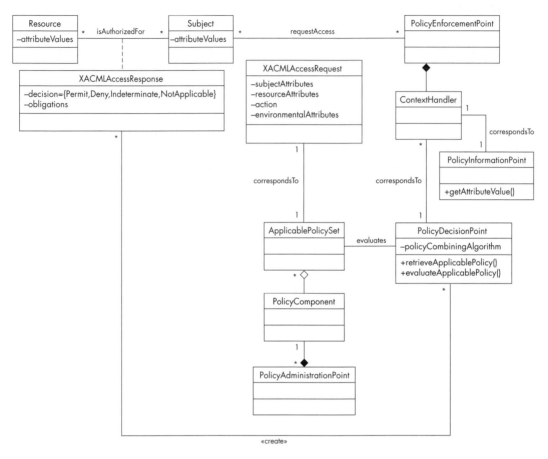

Figure 11.11: Class diagram for the XACML ACCESS CONTROL EVALUATION pattern

Dynamics

We describe the dynamic aspects of the XACML ACCESS CONTROL EVALUATION pattern using a sequence diagram for the use case 'Control an access request to a resource'.

Use Case: Control an Access Request to a Resource – Figure 11.12

Summary   A Subject requests access to a Resource. The access request is made through its PolicyEnforcementPoint, which in turn accesses the PolicyDecisionPoint through its ContextHanlder, in order to determine whether to accept or deny the request (page 258).

Actors   A Subject.

Precondition   An existing `PolicyAdministrationPoint` must be accessible by the `PolicyDecisionPoint`. It contains policies defined by the organization.

Description

1 A `Subject` sends a request for access to a `Resource` to its `PolicyEnforcementPoint`.

2 The `PolicyEnforcementPoint` sends the request to the `ContextHandler` in its native format.

3 The `ContextHandler` sends a corresponding XACML request to the `PolicyDecisionPoint`.

4 The `PolicyDecisionPoint` retrieves the `ApplicablePolicy` for this XACML request from the `PolicyAdministrationPoint`.

5 The `PolicyDecisionPoint` may request additional attributes from the `ContextHandler`.

6 The `ContextHandler` obtains the attributes from a `PolicyInformationPoint` and returns them to the `PolicyDecisionPoint`.

7 The `PolicyDecisionPoint` evaluates the `ApplicablePolicy` corresponding to the XACML request and returns an XACML response to the `ContextHandler`, or sends a request to the `PolicyInforcementPoint` if the attributes are insufficient to make a decision.

8 The `ContextHandler` translates the response into the native response format of the `PolicyEnforcementPoint`.

9 The `PolicyEnforcementPoint` fulfills the obligations contained in the response.

10 If the access is permitted, the `PolicyEnforcementPoint` allows the `Subject` to access the `Resource`.

Alternate Flows
- If the `XACMLAccessResponse`'s decision is 'deny', the `PolicyEnforcementPoint` denies access to the `Resource`.

- If the `XACMLAccessResponse`'s decision is 'indeterminate' or 'not applicable', the decision has to be made by the `PolicyEnforcementPoint`.

Postcondition   Access control to a resource has been realized, based on the `Subject`'s attributes, the `Resource`'s attributes, the environment's attributes and an applicable policy.

Appendix A includes pseudo-code for the functions `retrieveApplicablePolicy()` and `evaluateApplicablePolicy()`.

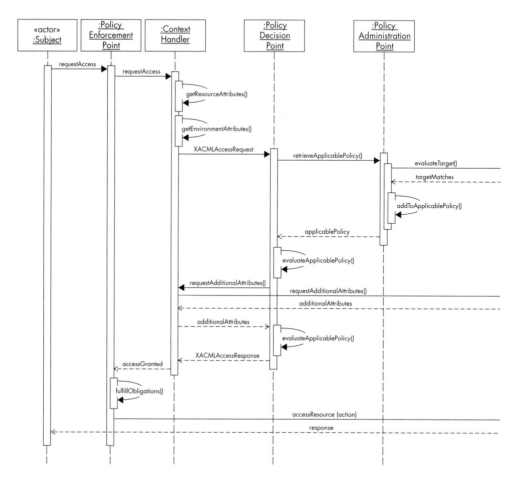

Figure 11.12: Sequence diagram for the use case 'Control an access request to a resource'

Implementation

To implement the XACML ACCESS CONTROL EVALUATION pattern, the following tasks need to be performed:

1 Implement a `ContextHandler` for applications that already have a `PolicyEnforcementPoint` but which use another access decision language.

2 Implement an XACML `PolicyEnforcementPoint` for those applications that do not implement access control.

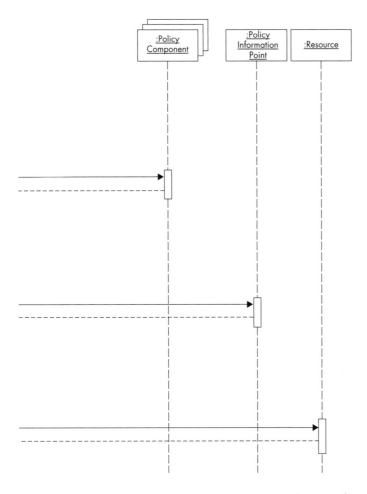

Figure 11.12 (continued)

3   Add the translated existing authorization rules to the `PolicyAdministra-tionPoint`.

4   Add the new authorization rules to the `PolicyAdministrationPoint`.

Example Resolved

The use of the XACML ACCESS CONTROL EVALUATION pattern allows the company to centralize the decisions of accesses to resources in the company. Consequently, applications no longer not need to care about access control decisions. Every access request or response is in the XACML format.

Consequences

The XACML ACCESS CONTROL EVALUATION pattern offers the following benefits:

- Since access decisions are requested in a standard format, an access decision becomes independent of its enforcement. A broad variety of enforcement mechanisms can be supported and can evolve separately from the policy decision point.

- The pattern can support the access matrix, RBAC or multilevel models for access control.

The pattern also has the following potential liabilities:

- It is intrusive for existing applications that already have security, since they require the implementation of a context handler.

- It could affect the performance of the protected system, since XML is a verbose language.

Known Uses

This pattern is used in the commercial products listed on page 254 for the XACML AUTHORIZATION pattern.

See Also

- The Reference Monitor pattern ([Sch06b] and page 100) defines the security model for this pattern. It includes the Metadata-Based Access Control (MBAC) model [Pri04].

- The Application Firewall pattern [Del04] could be implemented according to the XACML patterns – XACML AUTHORIZATION (page 248) and XACML ACCESS CONTROL EVALUATION.

- This pattern uses the MBAC model [Pri04] as a component.

11.6   Web Services Policy Language

The WEB SERVICES POLICY LANGUAGE (WSPL) pattern describes how to represent access control policies for an organization's web services in a standard manner, and to enable a web services consumer to express their requirements in a standard manner.

Example

Our company has a variety of web services for different purposes. Applications incorporate them as part of their structure. Application users pay for the use of these web services. If we want to make any money, we need to control access to them.

Context

Applications that use web services. Providers have security policies to control access to their web services, consumers have requirements for a web service invocation.

Problem

Web services are services that are accessible by means of messages sent using standard web protocols, notations and naming conventions [Pap03]. In addition, they are self-describing through Web Services Description Language (WSDL) and can be discovered (perhaps automatically) using Universal Description, Discovery and Integration (UDDI). Therefore, using different syntaxes for their policy descriptions would reduce the two properties of self-description and discoverability.

Moreover, security policies are typically issued by different actors in different departments, and the policies they write may concern a wide and overlapping set of web services. Applying the right policies to each access to a web service may also be complex, and thus error-prone.

How can we describe policies to control web services invocations? The solution to this problem must resolve the following forces:

- The policies are issued by a variety of actors in an organization and may be stored in many locations.

- Web services consumers can also issue policies (requirements). For example, a consumer could require a service to have a certificate from a well-known certification authority.

- Any type of security policy should be enforceable.

- The policies are constantly changing and need to be constantly updated.

- We have a variety of subjects (roles).

- The environment in which an access is requested can also affect an access decision.

- Some policies can require a set of obligations to be performed in conjunction with policy enforcement (auditing).

Solution

WSPL binds each WSDL web service component to an XACML component. In addition, define combination rules for such policies.

Structure

Figure 11.13 shows the class diagram for this pattern. Each WSDL web service component – Endpoint (port), Message and Operation – involves several Aspects, such as reliable messaging, privacy, authorization, trust, authentication or cryptographic security.

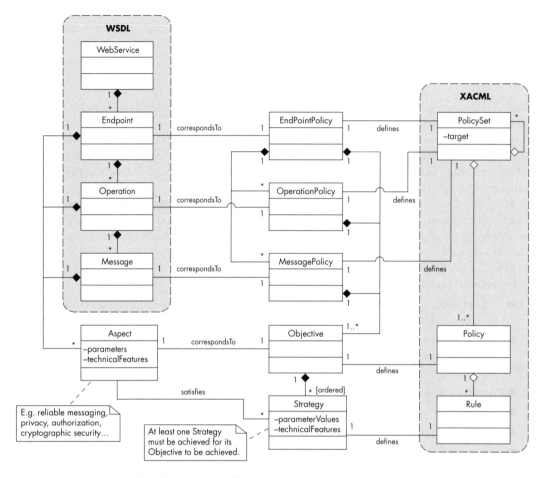

Figure 11.13: Class diagram for the WEB SERVICES POLICY LANGUAGE pattern

Each of the web service components respectively corresponds to an `EndpointPolicy`, `MessagePolicy` and `OperationPolicy` and are described by XACML `PolicySets`.

An `EndpointPolicy`, `MessagePolicy` or `OperationPolicy` consists of `Objectives` that govern an aspect of the web service components. All `Objectives` must be achieved by the service invocation. An `Objective` is defined by an XACML `Policy`.

Each `Objective` consists of a set of ordered `Strategies`. At least one `Strategy` must be achieved for its `Objective` to be achieved. This ordering may enable functions such as policy or trust negotiation. `Strategies` are represented by XACML `Rules`.

An XACML attribute is refined, as an unconstrained attribute can have its value assigned by the policy user, whereas a constrained attribute cannot. An authorized attribute must have its value assigned by an authority.

Implementation

A detailed discussion of some implementation aspects can be found in [And04].

Example Resolved

Using WSPL, we can define precise rules about who can access which resources and in what way. We can then provide security to our users and prevent users who have not paid for using our services from accessing them.

Consequences

In addition to the benefits of the XACML AUTHORIZATION pattern (page 248), the WEB SERVICES POLICY LANGUAGE pattern presents the following benefit:

- Consumers' and providers' policies can be combined to decide how a service invocation should occur.

The pattern also has the following potential liabilities:

- It is intrusive for existing web services that already implement security, since they require the implementation of a context handler.
- It could affect the performance of the protected system, as XML is a verbose language.

Known Uses

OpenWSPL is an open source Java implementation of the Web Service Policy Language [WSPL].

See Also

- WSPL defines a type of Adapter [Gam94] between WSDL and XACML.
- The architecture defined by the XML Firewall pattern [Del04] could be implemented using this pattern.

11.7   WS-Policy

The WS-POLICY pattern describes how to define a base set of assertions that can be used and extended by other web services specifications to describe a broad range of service requirements and capabilities, including security, reliability and others. This pattern also provides a way to check the requests made by requesters in order to verify that they satisfy their assertions and their conditions before interacting with a web service.

Example

Ajiad is a travel agency that intends to provide online services to its customers. Ajiad now offers many of its everyday operations as a web services-based system. In the current situation, some of Ajiad's customers have been accessing web services they are not allowed to access, as some outdated and insecure services do not have systematic guidelines to control their use. Also, some of the services are not available when needed. As a result, Ajiad is losing money because of its reliability and security problems.

Context

Distributed applications need to communicate in a collaborative way to perform work in a web services environment. For this objective, they use the Internet, which is an unreliable and insecure environment.

Problem

In order to assure reliability, availability and security, web services need to apply policies. Without them, they will have no means of specifying what quality factors they enforce and require from their users. This situation would result in all kinds of problems for the institution and its users.

The solution to this problem must resolve the following forces:

- *Data security of web services*. Malicious users may try to read or modify sensitive information stored in a web service. We need to define appropriate policies to protect this information.

- *Guaranteed message exchange*. We need to assure the delivery of messages between partners and give a requester the ability to verify whether the message was delivered.

- *Policy integrity.* Malicious users may try to replace or remove policy assertions for their own benefit. We need to ensure that policy assertions have not been modified.

- *Mutual authentication*. Clients and services must be able to mutually authenticate.

- *Denial of service*. An attacker could try to use malformed assertions to produce a non-terminating loop of policy evaluations.

Solution

Policies can be defined for security, reliability or other business constraints. For example, web services can be protected against unauthorized access by having policies that provide conditions that must be met for the service to be accessible. Requesters wishing to use protected web services are required to comply with these policies. Each policy is defined in terms of nested assertions that describe the restrictions implied by the policy. When the policy is attached to a web service, clients wanting to transact with that web service must comply with its assertions (for example, signing, encryption, timestamp and username) as specified in the policy.

In general, any entity in a web services-based system may expose a policy to convey conditions under which it provides service. Satisfying assertions in the policy usually results in behavior that reflects these conditions. For example, if two entities – requester and provider – expose their policies, a requester might use the policy of the provider to decide whether or not to use the service. A requester may choose either policy – requester or provider, since each is a valid configuration for interaction with the service – but only one of them.

Structure

Figure 11.14 shows the class diagram for this pattern. A `Policy` is a collection of policy alternatives that has its own name, reference (accessed from other subjects) and ID. A policy with zero alternatives contains no choices; a policy with one or more alternatives indicates choice in requirements or capabilities within the policy. A `PolicyAlternative` is a collection of policy assertions. Alternatives and assertions are not necessarily ordered.

A `PolicyAssertion` represents a capability, a constraint or a requirement of the behavior of a web service (for example, a guarantee of message delivery). Or it could be defined as a declaration of facts, such as 'Jad was granted update privileges to database X at time Y'. We can alternatively define a `PolicyAssertion` to be a set of requirements. For example, a `PolicyAssertion` might specify the security token types that are used to digitally sign or encrypt SOAP messages between the client and web service.

A `PolicyAssertion` identifies behaviors that are requirements for an entity (for example human, computer, message, an endpoint, interaction, resource). Satisfying assertions in the policy usually results in behavior that reflects these conditions. A `PolicyAssertion` has two parameters, used to define the behavior indicated by the assertion: `attributes` and `children`. A `PolicyAssertionType` represents a class of policy assertions to indicate domain-specific semantics (for example security, transactions). A `PolicyAssertion` may refer to another policy.

The formal term for a policy is *policy expression*, and we use it to convey a policy in an interoperable form. In other words, a `PolicyExpression` is a set of one or more policy assertions that, combined together, will perform a specific task. It could be interpreted also as a form (document) that is either structured in a normal or a compact form to express a policy.

A `PolicyAttachment` is a mechanism for associating a policy with one or more entities, such as web services. It details how policies are attached to bindings, and is essentially the glue that enforces a web service to adhere to a policy. A `PolicySubject` is an entity with which a policy can be associated, while a `PolicyScope` is composed of a collection of `PolicySubjects` to which a policy applies.

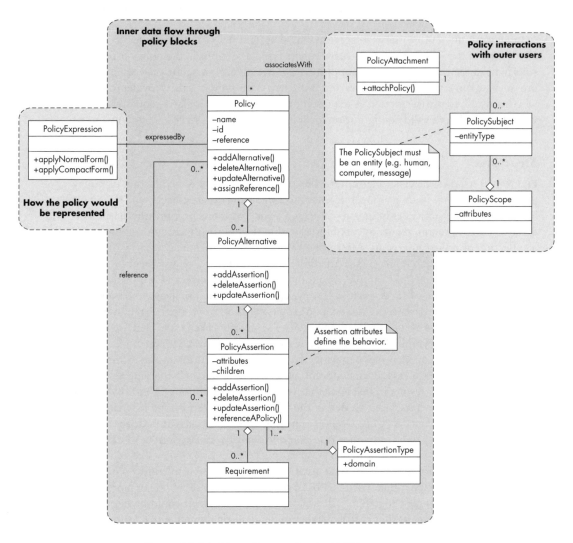

Figure 11.14: Class diagram for the WS-POLICY pattern

Dynamics

We describe two of the most important use cases, 'Create a policy for a web service' and 'Request a service'.

Use Case: Create a Policy for a Web Service – Figure 11.15

Summary   A `Provider` creates a new `Policy` for an existing web service.

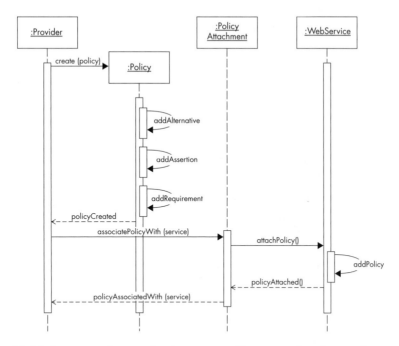

Figure 11.15: Sequence diagram for the use case 'Create a policy for a web service'

Actors Policy `Provider`.

Precondition The `Provider` has already created a `WebService`.

Description 1 The policy `Provider` creates the policy by specifying its required alternatives, assertions and requirements. The `Provider` creates as many assertions as necessary to meet the conditions for the `WebService`.

2 All the alternatives, assertions and requirements are added to the created Policy.

3 The `Provider` sends a request to the `PolicyAttachment` to associate the `Policy` with the end entity (`WebService`).

4 The `PolicyAttachment` attaches the `Policy` to the `WebService`, which in turn updates its content, adds the `Policy` and acknowledges the `PolicyAttachment`.

5 A reply from the `PolicyAttachment` informs the `Provider` that the attachment process is completed.

Postcondition The `Provider` has attached the policy to its designated `WebService`.

Use Case: Request a Service – Figure 11.16

Summary   A `Requester` requests the use of a `WebService` that has an existing policy.

Actors   `Requester`.

Precondition   A `Provider` had already created a `WebService` with a policy that controls its services.

Description   1 The `Requester` sends a request to use the `WebService`.

2 The `WebService` forwards the request to the `PolicyAttachment`.

3 The `WebService` applies its policies for verification of assertions and alternatives.

4 The `WebService` shows its `PolicyAlternatives` to the `Requester`.

5 The `Requester` selects from the alternatives, satisfies the chosen alternative's assertions, and sends a request to be verified against the policy.

6 The `WebService` checks all possibilities that result and approves or denies.

7 The `PolicyAttachment` responds to the `WebService`, which in turn forward it to the `Requester`.

Postcondition   The `Requester` can now use the `WebService` after satisfying its policy conditions.

Implementation

In order to ensure effective implementation, we need to take in consideration the following:

- A policy may or may not reference another policy(ies), depending on the level of authentication that is required.

- A policy alternative may contain multiple assertions of the same type. Policy assertions within a policy alternative are not ordered. However, providers can write assertions that control the order in which behaviors are applied.

- Policy assertions are the main blocks of the policy that specify a particular behavior. For example, the `AsymmetricBinding` assertion is intended to support a specific reliable messaging mechanism, while the `SignedParts` assertion is used to indicate message-level security, and the `EncryptedParts` assertion is used to indicate the parts of a message that require confidentiality.

- A policy expression conveys policy in an interoperable form, either in a normal form, the most straightforward XML representation of the policy data model, or in an equivalent compact form, used to compactly express a policy with more description about definitions and outlines.

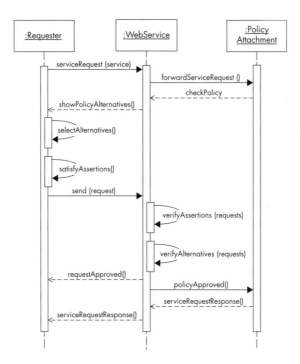

Figure 11.16: Sequence diagram for the use case 'Request a service'

- A `PolicyExpression` should not refer to itself directly or indirectly, because in that case its resolution may be ambiguous.

The example on page 270 defines a policy (starting with a `<wsp:Policy>` tag and ending with a `</wsp:Policy>` tag) for a web service offered by the Ajiad travel agency. This policy will accept X.509 certificates and Keberos tokens, with X.509 certificates preferred. The web service also requires the UTF-8 character encoding, any form of the English language, and specifies the SOAP version. Finally, the policy suggests using the AES algorithm for encryption.

Example Resolved

Ajiad's web-based system has decided to use the WS-POLICY pattern to convey conditions on the interactions between entities (provider, broker, requester and so on). This was supported by the fact that WS-POLICY is a standard and several products support its use.

Ajiad defined systematic rules to specify the way in which its web services should be accessed, in terms of who, when and in what way, as well as conditions. Ajiad's new web-based system now has more control over its services, by applying prerequisite conditions and security constraints through policies. So, in order to use any service, all customers

```
<wsp:Policy xml:base="http://ajiad.com/policies" wsu:Id="AJIADPOLICY">

<!-- This web service has the policy of accepting X.509 certifcates and Kerberos,
with X.509 certificates preferred-->
 <wsp:ExactlyOne>
 <wsse:SecurityToken TokenType="wsse:x509v3"
 wsp:Usage="wsp:Required" wsp:Preference="50">
 </wsse:SecurityToken>

 <wsse:SecurityToken TokenType="wsse:Kerberosv5TGT"
 wsp:Usage="wsp:Required" wsp:Preference="10">
 </wsse:SecurityToken>
 </wsp:ExactlyOne>

<!-- The web service requires the UTF-8 character encoding, any form of the
English language,and SOAP version 1.1 -->
 <wsp:All>
 <wsp:TextEncoding wsp:Usage="wsp:Required" Encoding="utf-8"/>
 <wsp:Language wsp:Usage="wsp:Required" Language="en"/>
 <wsp:SpecVersion wsp:Usage="wsp:Required" URI="http://www.w3.org/TR/2000/
NOTE-SOAP-20000508/" />

<!-- Using AES algorithm is required -->
 <wsse:Integrity wsp:Usage="wsp:Required">
 <wsse:Algorithm Type="wsse:AlgSignature'" URI="http://www.w3.org/2000/09/
xmlenc#aes" />
 </wsse:Integrity>
 </wsp:All>

</wsp:Policy>
```

are required to comply with its policy conditions and satisfy its requirements (for example, by using the required security token types specified by the policy) and agree with its terms before using the web service.

Consequences

The WS-POLICY pattern offers the following benefits:

- *Data security of web services.* It is possible to secure the data of web services, since we can use policies from other web services standards such as WS-Security [IBM04], XML Digital Signature [W3C08] and WS-Metadata Exchange [W3C09].

- *Policy protection.* It is possible to define policies to protect the policies themselves.

- *Guaranteed message exchange.* The pattern offers a way to assure messages exchange between the partners, by giving policy providers the ability to avoid older or weaker policy alternatives, and by giving the requester the ability to verify the policy provider.

- *Policy integrity.* Using the appropriate signing mechanism will protect the policy assertions from tampering: for example, requesters can discard a policy that is not signed by the provider, or when not presented with sufficient credentials.

■ *Availability.* The pattern mitigates the chance of denial of service threats by forcing the policy implementers to use a model with defaults for the policy alternatives, the number of assertions in an alternative and the depth of nested policy expressions.

The pattern also has the following potential liabilities:

■ WS-Policy is an immature specification that is still changing.

■ The WS-Policy standard is a lengthy document with a lot of detail, some of which we left out to avoid making the pattern too complex. For more details, check the WS-Policy Standard web page [W3C07].

Known Uses

■ HP SOA Systinet Standard Edition is a platform for SOA Governance. This SOA architecture tool provides different levels of governance [HP09].

■ The Layer 7 SecureSpan XML Virtual Appliance provides security and threat protection for internal and cloud-based XML and web services applications [VMW09].

■ Xtradyne's WS-DBC is an XML/SOAP firewall that claims to be specifically designed for use in environments that demand performance, scalability, availability and policy management [Pri05].

■ DataPower's XS40 XML Security Gateway is a network appliance that operates as an XML proxy. It provides security functions for XML-based communications [IBM05].

See Also

■ [Ars01] describes the structure of business rules as patterns. Policies are specific types of business rules.

■ [Sch06b] discusses three patterns that correspond to the most common models for security: Authorization, Role-Based Access Control and multilevel Security. Any of these access control models could be implemented through policies.

■ [Del05] presents three architectural patterns for XACML. The XACML AUTHORIZATION pattern (page 248) unifies the definition of authorization rules throughout an organization. WEB SERVICES POLICY LANGUAGE (page 260), a specialization of XACML AUTHORIZATION, describes access control rules for web services. The XACML ACCESS CONTROL EVALUATION pattern (page 254) defines request/response syntax for access control decisions. XACML allows the definition of more complex access control policies.

■ [Del07a] considers patterns for access control in distributed systems. The patterns handle different ways of describing how to decide whether a subject is authorized to access an object, how to implement the access matrix or RBAC models and how to control access to objects.

- [Aja10a] defines a security token service and a trust engine which are used by web services to authenticate other web services. Using the functions defined in WS-TRUST(below), applications can engage in secure communication after establishing trust.

11.8 WS-Trust

The WS-TRUST pattern describes how to define a security token service and a trust engine that are used by web services to authenticate other web services. Using the functions defined in this pattern, applications can engage in secure communication after establishing trust.

Example

The Ajiad travel agency offers its travel services through several different business portals to provide travel tickets, hotel and car rental services to its customers. Ajiad needs to establish trust relationships with its partners through these portals.

Ajiad supports different business relationships and needs to be able to determine which travel services to invoke for which customer. Without a well-defined structure, Ajiad will not be able to know if a partner is trusted or not, or be able to automate the trust relationships quickly and securely with its partners, which may lead to missing a key business goal: offering integrated travel services as a part of the customer's portal environment.

Context

Distributed applications need to establish secure and trusted relationships between themselves to perform work in a web-service environment that may be unreliable and/or insecure, such as the Internet. The concept of 'trusting A' mainly means 'considering true the assertions made by A', which does not necessarily correspond to the intuitive idea of trust in its colloquial use.

Problem

Establishing security relationships is fundamental for the interoperation of distributed systems. Without applying relevant trust relationships expressed in the same way between the involved parties, web services have no means of assuring security and interoperability in their integration. How can we define a means by which the parties are able to trust each other's security credentials?

The solution to this problem must resolve the following forces:

- *Knowledge.* In human relationships, we are concerned with first knowing a person before we trust them. That attitude applies also to web services. We need to have a structure that encapsulates some knowledge about the unit we intend to trust.

- *Policy consideration.* The web service policy contains all the required assertions and conditions that should be met to use that web service. The trust structure should consider this policy for verification purposes.

- *Confidentiality and integrity.* Policies may include sensitive information. Malicious consumers may acquire sensitive information, fingerprint the service and infer service vulnerabilities. This implies that the policy itself should be protected.

- *Message integrity.* The data to be transferred between the partners through messages may be private data that needs to be protected. Attackers may try to modify or replace these messages.

- *Time validity.* For protection purposes, any interactions or means of communications (including the trust relationships) between the web services should have a time limit that determines for how long the trust relationship is valid.

Solution

We define explicitly an artifact (a security token) that implies trust. This artifact implies the kinds of assertions that are required to make trustworthy interactions between the web services involved. We should verify the claims and information sent by the requester in order to obtain the required security token that becomes a proof that is sufficient to establish a trust relationship with its target partners.

Structure

Figure 11.17 shows the class diagram for this pattern. A `Claim` is a statement made about the attributes of a client, service or other resource (for example name, identity, key, group, privilege, capability and so on). `Claims` are assertions, for example 'I am Joman', 'I am an authenticated user and I am authorized to print on printer P'. `Claims` are used to validate the requests made by a sender and need to be verified. A `SecurityToken` is a collection of `Claims`. It is possible to add signatures to tokens. `SecurityToken` also is a generalization of two classes: `SignedSecurityToken`, which is cryptographically endorsed by a specific authority (for example an X.509 certificate or a Kerberos ticket), and `ProofofPossession` (`PoP`), a token that contains a secret data parameter that can be used to prove authorized use of an associated security token, and which provides the function of adding a digital signature. Usually, the proof-of-possession information is encrypted with a key known only to the recipient of the `PoP` token.

The `SecurityTokenService` (`STS`) is a web service that issues security tokens. It makes decisions based on evidence that it trusts. The `STS` is responsible for:

- Generating security tokens.
- Providing challenges for the requester to ensure message freshness (the message has not been replayed and is currently valid).
- Verification of authorized use of a security token.
- Establishing, extending and removing trust in a domain of services.

The STS is the heart of WS-TRUST and forms the basis of trust brokering. The main output of the STS is a trust relationship between the requester and the receiver, expressed as a security token. This represents the characteristic that one entity is willing to rely upon a second entity to execute a set of actions and/or to make set of assertions about a set of subjects and/or scopes in a secure, reliable and time-relevant manner.

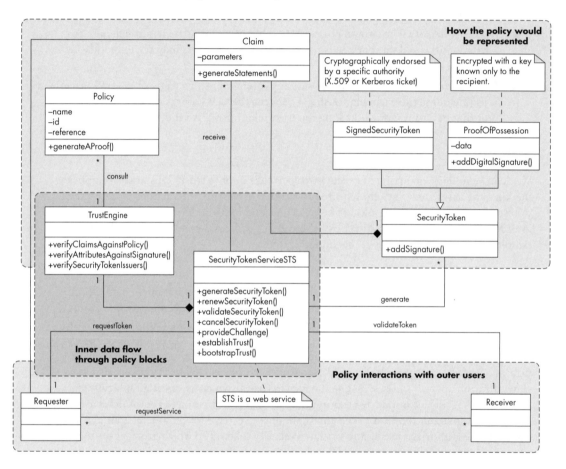

Figure 11.17: Class diagram for the WS-TRUST pattern

Each STS has a TrustEngine that evaluates the security-related aspects of a message using security mechanisms, and includes policies to verify the requester's assertions. The TrustEngine is responsible for verifying security tokens and verifying claims against Policies. A Policy is a collection of policy assertions that have their own name, references and ID. Policies form the basic conditions for establishing a trust relationship. Verifying the requester's claims against policy assertions generates an approval to use the target service. A `Policy` may reference another `Policy` or `Policies` to check the tokens sent by the requester or verified by the `Receiver`.

Dynamics

We describe the dynamic aspects of the WS-TRUST pattern using sequence diagrams for the use cases 'Create security token' and 'Access a resource using a token'.

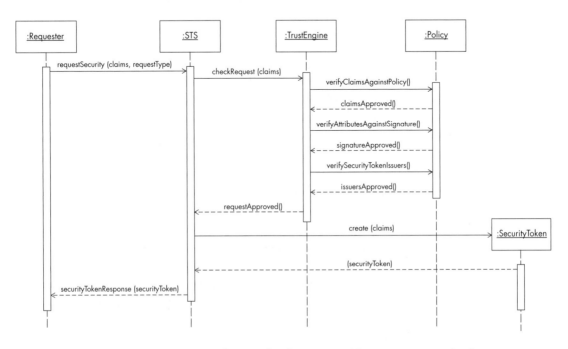

Figure 11.18: Sequence diagram for the use case 'Create a security token'

Use Case: *Create a Security Token – Figure 11.18*

Summary   STS creates a security token using the claims provided by the `Requester`.

Actors   A `Requester`.

Precondition   The `STS` has the required policy to verify the `Requester`'s claims, and the `Requester` provides parameters in the form of claims and `Request-Type` signed by a signature.

Description   1 The `Requester` requests a security token by sending the required claims and `RequestType` signed by a signature to the `STS`. The signature verifies that the request is legitimate.

                 2 The `STS` contacts the `TrustEngine` to check the `Requester`'s claims.

3 The `TrustEngine` contacts the web service's `Policy` to verify the claims, including attributes and security token issuers of the requester.

4 Once approved, the `STS` creates a `SecurityToken` containing the requested claims.

5 The `STS` sends back its `securityTokenResponse` with a `Security-Token` issued for the `Requester`.

Postcondition The `Requester` has a security token that can be used to access resources in a trusted unit.

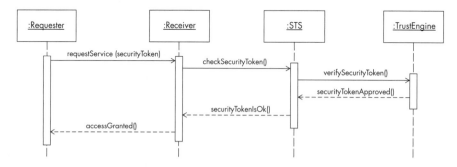

Figure 11.19: Sequence diagram for the use case 'Access a resource using a token'

Use Case: Access a Resource using a Token – Figure 11.19

Summary An `STS` allows the use of resources by establishing trust by verifying `ProofofClaims` sent by the `Requester`.

Actors: A `Requester`.

Precondition The `TrustEngine` has the required `Policy` to verify the `Requester`'s security token.

Description
1 The `Requester` asks for a service access by providing the required security token.

2 The `Receiver` sends the security token to the `STS` for verification.

3 The `STS` use its `TrustEngine` to verify the security token claims.

4 Once approved, the `STS` notifies the `Receiver` that the security token is valid and verified.

5 The `Receiver` gives the `Requester` a token that implies the right to use the service.

Postcondition The `Requester` has a security token that can be used to access services in a `Receiver` web service.

Implementation

In this solution, the concept of trust is realized by obtaining a security token from the web service (the `SecurityTokenService` in Figure 11.17 on page 274) and submitting it to the `Receiver`, which in turn validates the security token through the same web service. Upon approval, the `Receiver` establishes a valid trust relationship with the `Requester` that lasts as long as the security token is valid.

In order to assure effective implementation, we need to take in consideration the following:

- To communicate trust, a service requires proof, such as a signature to prove knowledge of a security token or set of security tokens. A service itself can generate tokens, or it can rely on a separate STS to issue a security token with its own trust statement.

- Although the messages exchanged between the involved entities are protected by WS-SECURITY (page 330), three issues related to security tokens are possible: security token format incompatibility, security token trust and namespace differences. The WS-TRUST pattern addresses these issues by defining a request/response protocol (in which the client sends a `RequestSecurityToken` and receives a `Request-SecurityTokenResponse`) and introducing a `SecurityTokenService` (STS), which is another web service.

- Based on the credential provided by the `Requester`, there are different aspects of requesting a security token, each of which has a unique format that the requester should follow:

  - The issuing process: formed as `RequestSecurityToken` (`RequestType`, `Claims`). This is our use case 'Create a security token' in the Dynamics section.

  - The renewal process: formed as `RequestSecurityToken` (`RequestType`, `RenewTarget`).

  - The cancel process: formed as `RequestSecurityToken` (`RequestType`, `CancelTarget`). The cancelled token is no longer valid for authentication and authorization.

  - The validate process: formed as `RequestSecurityToken` (`RequestType`, `ValidateTarget`).

[Bha04] proves security properties of combinations of WS-TRUST and WS-Secure conversation to implement secure sessions.

The WS-Trust specification was created as part of the Global XML Web Services Architecture (GXA) framework, which is a protocol framework designed to provide a consistent model for building infrastructure-level protocols for web services and applications [Box02]. It was authored by Microsoft, IBM, Verisign and RSA Security, and was approved by OASIS as a standard in March 2007.

Example Resolved

Ajiad now has the ability to automate its trust relationships with its partners, by managing the registration tasks for all its partners and issuing customers a unique ID. In this case, Ajiad acts as a mediator between the customers and its participating partners, playing the role of a negotiator and third-party player who is trying to satisfy both sides.

Ajiad now can offer a security token service for its business partners, who may find useful ways to take advantage of its credit processing and other services, giving Ajiad new business opportunities.

Consequences

The WS-TRUST pattern offers the following benefits:

- *Security.* By extending the WS-SECURITY mechanisms, we can handle security issues such as security tokens (the possibility of a token substitution attack), and signing (where all private elements should be included in the scope of the signature and the signature must include a timestamp).

- *Trust.* With this solution, we have the choice of implementing the WS-Policy framework to support trust partners by expressing and exchanging their statements of trust. The description of this expected behavior within the security space can also be expressed as a trust policy.

- *Confidentiality.* We can achieve confidentiality of users' information. Since policy providers now can use mechanisms provided by other web services specifications such as WS-SECURITY (page 330) [ibm09b] to secure access to the policy, XML Digital Signature [W3C08] to authenticate sensitive information, and WS-Metadata Exchange [W3C09].

- All the security tokens exchanged between the involved parties are signed and stamped with unique keys that are known only to the recipients.

- *Time validity.* We can specify time constraints in the parameters of a security token issued by STS. This constraint will specify for how long that security token is valid. Upon expiring, the security token's holder may renew or cancel it.

The pattern also has the following potential liabilities:

- The efficiency of WS-TRUST may suffer from the repeated round-trips for multiple token requests. We need to make an effort to reduce the number of messages exchanged.

- The WS-Trust Standard is a lengthy document and several details were left out to avoid making the pattern too complex. Interested readers can find more details via the WS-Trust Standard web page [OAS09].

Known Uses

- DataPower's XS40 XML Security Gateway [Dat05] is a device for securing web services that provides web services access control, message filtering and field-level encryption. It centralizes policy enforcement, supporting standards such as WS-Security, WS-Trust, WS-Policy and XACML.

- SecureSpan XML Firewall [lay09] enforces WS* and WS-I standards to centralize security and access requirements in policies that can be run as a shared service in front of applications.

- Vordel Security Token Service [Vor09] is used to issue security tokens and to convert security tokens from one format to another. The security tokens created by an STS are bound to the messages travelling between web services.

- PingTrust, a standalone WS-Trust security token server [pin06] creates and validates security tokens that are bound into SOAP messages according to the Web Services Security (WSS) standard.

See Also

- The Trust analysis pattern [Fay04] has the objective of providing a conceptual model that embodies the abstract aspects of trust to make it applicable to different domains and applications.

- The CREDENTIAL pattern (page 62) addresses the problem of exchanging data between trust boundaries, and how to resolve the problem of authenticating and authorizing a principal's identity over different systems.

- The CIRCLE OF TRUST pattern (page 34) allows the formation of trust relationships among service providers in order for their subjects to access an integrated and more secure environment. The WS-TRUST pattern could be used to establish trust between providers.

- A set of patterns to establish initial trust, based on secret handshakes, are presented in [Lau10].

11.9   SAML Assertion

The SAML ASSERTION pattern describes how to provide a way to communicate security information about a particular subject between different security domains.

Context

One or several security domains in a distributed system, typically using web services. A security domain is a set of resources (web services, applications, CORBA services and so on) in which the administration of security is performed by a unique entity, which typically stores identity information about the subjects of the domain. Those subjects can perform actions inside or outside their security domain.

Problem

A subject may need to access a resource in a domain that does not know about it because the relevant user is from a different security domain. In order to apply access control to the target domain's resources, security information about the subject should be transmitted between those two domains.

How can we communicate this information? The solution to this problem must resolve the following forces:

■ The target security domain may implement different levels of security functionalities (authentication or not, access control or not).

■ The identity management unit of the subject's domain and the target security domain may be implemented using different platforms. We need a platform-independent way of communicating identity information.

■ Different domains may express security constraints or apply authentication in different ways. We need a unifying structure.

Solution

Define an identity management unit in the subject's domain that issues assertions about subjects in that domain. A SAML assertion is a collection of security-related statements about the subject. It is defined in a common XML format, so that the semantics of the assertions can be extended easily. The target security domain uses the security-related information contained in the assertion to make its access control decisions. A trust relationship must have previously been developed between the identity management unit of the subject's domain and the target security domain.

Structure

Figure 11.20 shows a class diagram for this pattern. SAMLAssertions are issued by the identity management entity of the source domain, the SAMLAuthority. The TargetSecurityDomains use the security information in the SAMLAssertions to compute an access decision. The SAMLAssertion consists of Statements about the subject. A Statement is a basic piece of security-related information about the subject, such as an attribute, the fact that they have been authenticated, or a capability. It also comprises the identity of the SAMLAuthority that issued it, and a possible set of conditions, advice and an XML digital signature for integrity and authenticity purposes.

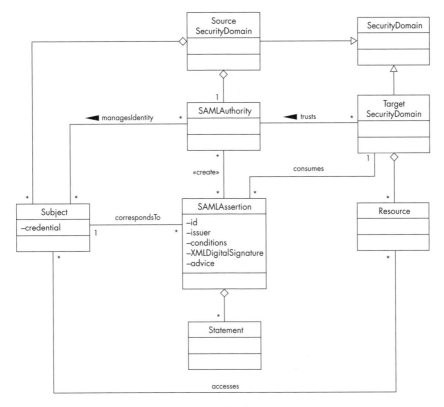

Figure 11.20: Class diagram for the SAML ASSERTION pattern

Dynamics

We describe the dynamic aspects of the SAML ASSERTION pattern using the sequence diagram for the use case 'Subject accesses a resource in the target security domain'.

Use Case:	Subject Accesses a Resource in the Target Security Domain – Figure 11.21
Summary	A Subject requests a SAMLAssertion from a SAMLAuthority and forwards it to the TargetSecurityDomain. The TargetSecurityDomain uses the security information contained in the SAMLAssertion to compute an access decision.
Actors	Subject, SAMLAuthority, TargetSecurityDomain.
Precondition	The Subject has been previously registered with the SAMLAuthority. A trust relationship exists between the SAMLAuthority and the TargetSecurityDomain.

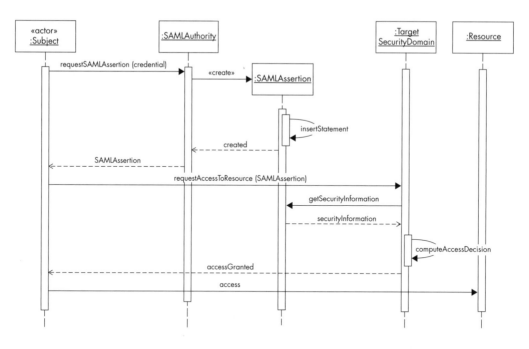

Figure 11.21: Sequence diagram for use case 'Subject accesses a resource in the target security domain'

Description 1 A `Subject` sends a request for a `SAMLAssertion` to the `SAMLAuthority`.

2 The `SAMLAuthority` creates a `SAMLAssertion` based on the `Subject`'s credentials, inserts in it statements about the `Subject`, and sends it to the `Subject`.

3 The `Subject` requests access to a `Resource` and includes the `SAMLAssertion`.

4 The `TargetSecurityDomain` computes an access decision based on the security information contained in the `SAMLAssertion`.

5 If access is granted, the `TargetSecurityDomain` sends back a response corresponding to the request, and the `Subject` accesses the `Resource`.

Postcondition The access to the `TargetSecurityDomain` has been controlled based on the security information contained in the `SAMLAssertion`.

Consequences

The SAML ASSERTION pattern offers the following benefits:

- Identity information can be exchanged between domains implemented on different platforms.
- The target application or domain can implement various levels of security controls.
- The security constraints or authentication methods are expressed using a common language.

The pattern also has the following potential liabilities:

- A prior trust relationship must exist between the SAML authority and the target security domain. This relationship will allow the target security domain to verify the origin and integrity of the assertion.
- Possible identity misuse by the SAML authority.

Variants

This pattern has three variants, depending on the type of statement in the assertion:

- *Attribute-based SAML assertion.* Because the subject and the resource accessed may be from different domains, only a fraction of the identity of the user may be useful to the target domain. This variant provides a common format for communicating attribute-based identity information, such as a role or membership, between different security domains. The SAML assertion states that a subject is associated with a set of pairs of attribute names/attribute values. In that case, the target domain has its own access control functionalities. It should base its authorization decision on the value of these attributes.

  This variant has an additional advantage: the use of attributes provides a way to represent a broad range of identity-related information types.

- *Authentication SAML assertion* provides a common format for communicating authentication information between different security domains. In this case, the target domain has its own access control functionalities. The SAML assertion states that a subject was authenticated by a particular means at a particular time.

- *Authorization SAML assertion* provides a common format for communicating authorization information between different security domains. The target application or target domain may not have its own access control functionalities. The SAML assertion states that a request to allow the subject to access the specified resource has been granted or denied. The target domain just needs to apply the decision contained in the assertion.

This pattern variant offers an additional advantage: the target application does not need to implement access control functionalities. But it has an additional liability: the security of the scheme relies on the trust granted to the identity manager of the source domain.

Known Uses

■ The Liberty Alliance Identity Framework [Libb] uses SAML as a foundation for protecting the security of identity information.

■ Several vendors use SAML in their access management products, for example IONA Orbix E2A XMLBus [ION], Netegrity SiteMinder [Net03], IBM Tivoli Federated Identity Manager [IBMc], Sun Java System Access Manager [SunC] and RSA [Wre04].

See Also

■ The Security Assertion Coordinator pattern [Fer04a] allows seamless exchange of security data in distributed environments while maintaining role-based access controls to resources in organizations using SAML assertions.

■ The Attribute-Based Access Control (ABAC) pattern [Pri04] grants accesses to resources based on the attributes possessed by the subject.

■ The Attribute-Based SAML Assertion variant allows transmission of attribute information about a subject.

Patterns for Web Services Cryptography

He told me that toward 1886 he had devised a new system of enumeration and that in a very few days he had gone slightly over twenty-four thousand. He had not written it down, for what he had thought just once would not be erased. His first stimulus, I believe, had been his discontent with the fact that 'thirty-three Uruguayans' required two symbols and three words, rather than a single word and a single symbol. Later he applied his extravagant principle to the other numbers. In place of seven thousand thirteen, he would say (for example) Máximo Perez; in place of seven thousand fourteen, The Railway; other numbers were Luis Melián Lafinur, Olimar, sulphur, Clubs, The Whale, Gas, The Cauldron, Napoleon, Agustín Vedia. In lieu of five hundred, he would say nine. Each word had a particular sign, a species of mark; the last were very complicated...[1]

Jorge Luis Borges, 'Funes el memorioso', http://www.literatura.us/borges/funes.html

---

[1] My improvements on the translation in http://evans-experientialism.freewebspace.com/borges.htm

12.1   Introduction

Information can be captured and read during its transmission. A message can also be modified or replayed. How can we protect this information from such attacks? Encryption provides message confidentiality by transforming readable data (plain text) into an unreadable format (cipher text) that can be understood only by the intended recipient after decryption, the inverse function that makes the encrypted information readable again. There are two types of encryption: *symmetric* and *asymmetric*. In symmetric encryption a common key is used for both encryption and decryption. In asymmetric encryption a public/private key pair is used for encryption/decryption; the sender encrypts the information using the receiver's public key, while the receiver uses their private key to decrypt the ciphered text.

How can we prove that a message came from a specific user? Digital signatures use public-key cryptography to provide message authentication by proving that a message was sent indeed from a specific sender [dig] [Sta06]. The sender encrypts the message and uses their private key to sign it. In this case, the signature has at least the same length as the message. This works, but it wastes bandwidth and time. Thus, we need to reduce the length of the message before signing it. This can be done by producing a digest through *hashing*. When the receiver gets the signed message, they verify the signature by decrypting it using the sender's public key, thus proving that the message was encrypted by the sender.

Digital signatures can also provide message integrity, by verifying whether a message was modified during its transmission. They can also protect the integrity of and verify the origin of a digital document, for example a certificate, or of programs. Digital signatures finally provide *non-repudiation*: the sender cannot deny having sent the message they signed. In several countries, including the US, digital signatures have legal validity.

Web services that exchange XML messages can be targets of similar attacks. Some security standards have been developed to correctly apply encryption functions and thus reduce security risks. XML Encryption is one of the basic standards in securing web services. It describes how to encrypt/decrypt an entire XML message, part of an XML message, or an external object linked to the message, and how to represent the encrypted content, and information such as the encryption algorithm and key, in XML format.

The XML Signature standard is a joint effort between the World Wide Web Consortium (W3C) and the Internet Engineering Task Force (ITEF). XML Signature describes how to digitally sign an entire XML message, part of an XML message, or an external object. XML Signature also includes hashing, but the pattern name follows the name of the standard. Because XML documents can have the same contents but in different layouts, we need to convert the documents into a canonical form before we apply digital signatures. XML Signature solves the same problem as the DIGITAL SIGNATURE WITH HASHING pattern (page 301), but in a more specialized context.

WS-Security is an OASIS standard that describes how SOAP messages can be secured through message integrity, message authentication and message confidentiality [OAS06b]. WS-Security is a flexible protocol that supports different formats of security tokens, different encryption technologies and different signature formats. WS-Security does not define new security mechanisms, but it leverages existing technologies such as XML Encryption, XML Signature, and security tokens, for example Kerberos tickets and X.509 certificates. We describe this standard in the form of a pattern. It has already been applied in a variety of applications, such as the travel industry [Nak05].

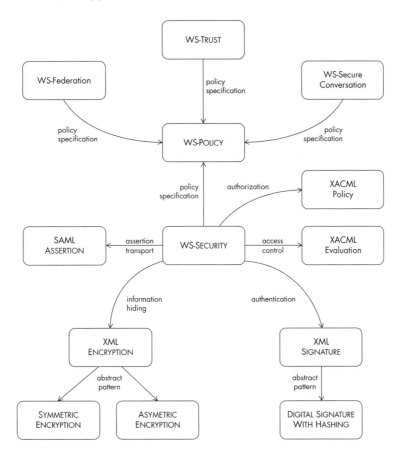

Figure 12.1: Pattern diagram for web services security standards
and abstract cryptographic patterns

We present three abstract cryptographic patterns here:

■ *SYMMETRIC ENCRYPTION* protects message confidentiality by making a message unreadable to those that do not have access to the key. Symmetric encryption uses the same key for encryption and decryption.

■ *ASYMMETRIC ENCRYPTION* provides message confidentiality by keeping information secret in such a way that it can only be understood by intended recipients who have access to the valid key. In asymmetric encryption, a public/private key pair is used for encryption and decryption respectively.

- *DIGITAL SIGNATURE WITH HASHING* allows a principal to prove that a message was originated from it. It also provides message integrity by indicating whether a message was altered during transmission.

We then present patterns for encryption in web services. Figure 12.1 shows how these patterns relate to the patterns of Chapter 11:

- *XML ENCRYPTION* describes a process to apply encryption functions to XML data, keeping a correct XML syntax.

- *XML SIGNATURE* provides a means of identifying the source of the XML message (message authentication), and also provides message integrity.

- *WS-SECURITY* describes how to secure SOAP messages, applying XML security technologies such as XML ENCRYPTION and XML SIGNATURE. It also describes how to embed different security tokens. Security tokens provides authentication by proving one's identity (certificates or SAML assertions are examples).

Figure 12.1 also shows the abstract patterns that provide the basis for the more specialized XML patterns.

Symmetric Encryption and XML Encryption come from [Has09b]. Digital Signature with Hashing and XML Signature appeared in [Has09a]. WS-Security appeared in [Has09c]. All these patterns, as well as Asymmetric Encryption, come from Keiko Hashizume's MS Thesis.

Patterns for WS-Secure Conversation and WS-Federation were produced after we had completed this book: see [Aja13] and [Aja12].

12.2 Symmetric Encryption

Encryption protects message confidentiality by making a message unreadable to those that do not have access to the key. Symmetric encryption uses the same key for encryption and decryption.

Example

Alice in the purchasing department regularly sends purchase orders to Bob in the distribution office. A purchase order contains sensitive data such as credit card numbers and other company information, so it is important to keep it secret. Eve can intercept her messages and may try to read them to get the confidential information. As part of her work Alice needs to communicate with only a few employees in the company.

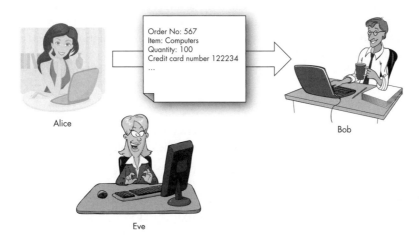

Alice

Bob

Eve

Context

Applications that exchange sensitive information over insecure channels and where the number of users and applications is not very large.

Problem

Applications that communicate with external applications interchange sensitive data that may be read by unauthorized users while they are in transit. Clearly, if we send sensitive information, we are exposing confidential information and we may be risking the privacy of many individuals. How can we protect messages from being read by intruders?

The solution to this problem must resolve the following forces:

■ *Confidentiality.* Messages may be captured while they are in transit, so we need to prevent unauthorized users from reading them by hiding the information in the message.

■ *Convenient reception.* The hidden information should be revealed conveniently to the receiver.

■ *Protocol.* We need to apply the solution properly, or it will not be able to withstand attacks (there are several ways to attack a method of hiding information).

■ *Performance.* The time to hide and recover the message should be acceptable.

■ *Security.* In some cases we need to have a very high level of security.

Solution

We can prevent unauthorized users from reading messages by hiding the information in the message using symmetric cryptographic encryption. Symmetric encryption transforms a message in such a way that it can only be understood by the intended receiver after applying the reverse transformation using a valid key. The transformation process at the sender's end is called *encryption*, while the reverse transformation process at the receiver's end is called *decryption*.

The sender applies an encryption function (E) to the message (M) using a key (k); the output is the cipher text (C):

$$C = Ek\ (M)$$

When the cipher text (C) is delivered, the receiver applies a decryption function (D) to the cipher text using the same key (k) and recovers the message:

$$M = Dk\ (C)$$

Structure

Figure 12.2 shows the class diagram for the SYMMETRIC ENCRYPTION pattern. A `Principal` may be a user or an organization that is responsible for sending or receiving messages. This `Principal` may have the roles of `Sender` or `Receiver`. A `Sender` may send a `Message` and/or an `EncryptedMessage` to a `Receiver` with which it shares a secret `Key`.

The `Encryptor` creates the `EncryptedMessage` that contain the cipher text using the shared `Key` provided by the sender, while the `Decryptor` deciphers the encrypted data into its original form using the same `Key`. Both the `Encryptor` and `Decryptor` use the same `Algorithm` to encipher and decipher a message.

Dynamics

We describe the dynamic aspects of the SYMMETRIC ENCRYPTION pattern using sequence diagrams for the use cases 'Encrypt a message' and 'Decrypt a message'.

Use Case: Encrypt a Message – Figure 12.3

Summary	A `Sender` wants to encrypt a message.
Actors	A `Sender`.
Precondition	Both `Sender` and `Receiver` have a shared key and access to a repository of algorithms. The message has already been created by the `Sender`.
Description	1 A `Sender` sends the message, the shared key, and the algorithm identifier to the `Encryptor`.
	2 The `Encryptor` ciphers the message using the algorithm specified by the `Sender`.
	3 The `Encryptor` creates the `EncryptedMessage` that includes the cipher text.
Postcondition	The message has been encrypted and is ready to send.

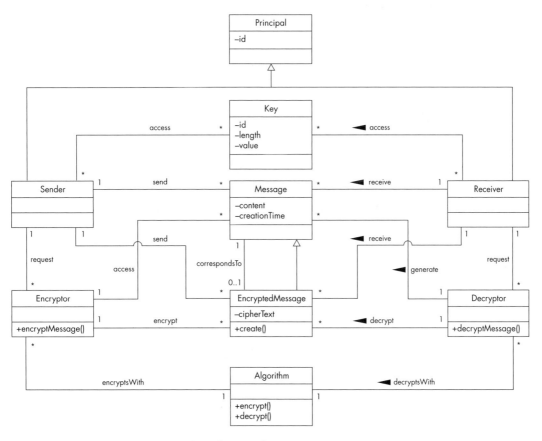

Figure 12.2: Class diagram for SYMMETRIC ENCRYPTION pattern

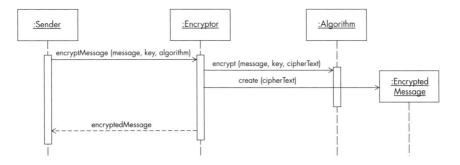

Figure 12.3: Sequence diagram for the use case 'Encrypt a message'

Use Case: Decrypt an Encrypted Message – Figure 12.4

Summary	A `Receiver` wants to decrypt an encrypted message from a `Sender`.
Actors	A `Receiver`.
Precondition	Both the `Sender` and `Receiver` have a shared key and access to a repository of algorithms.
Description	1 A `Receiver` sends the encrypted message and the shared key to the `Decryptor`.
	2 The `Decryptor` deciphers the encrypted message using the shared key.
	3 The `Decryptor` creates the `Message` that contains the plain text obtained from the previous step.
	4 The `Decryptor` sends the plain text `Message` to the receiver.
Alternate Flow	If the key used in step 2 is not the same as the one used for encryption, the decryption process fails.
Postcondition	The encrypted message has been deciphered and delivered to the `Receiver`.

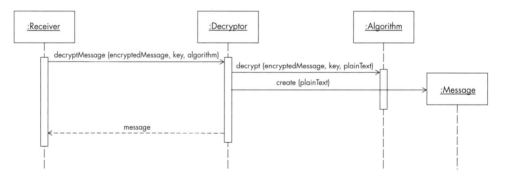

Figure 12.4: Sequence diagram for the use case 'Decrypt an encrypted message'

Implementation

- Use the Strategy pattern [Gam94] to select different encryption algorithms. Selection could be based on speed, computational resources, key length or memory constraints. The selection could happen when instantiating the pattern in an application, or dynamically according to environmental parameters.

- The designer should choose well-known algorithms such as AES (Advanced Encryption Standard) [Fed01] and DES (Data Encryption Standard) [Fed99]. Books such as [Sta06] describe their features and criteria for selection.

- Encryption can be implemented in different applications, such as in e-mail communication, distribution of documents over the Internet, or web services. In these applications we may need to encrypt an entire document or just its body. However, in web services we may want to encrypt specific elements of a message.

- Both the sender and the receiver have to previously agree what cryptographic algorithms they support, and they both must have the same key. This is the *key distribution problem*, which can be handled in several ways.

- A key management strategy is needed, including key generator, storage and distribution. This strategy should generate keys that are as random as possible, or an attacker who captures some messages might be able to deduce the key. The key should be properly protected, or an attacker who penetrates the operating system might be able to get it. Timely and secure key distribution is obviously very important.

- A long encryption key should be used (at least 64 bits). Only brute force is known to work against the DES and AES algorithms, for example: using a short key would let an attacker generate all possible keys. Of course, this might change and the repertoire of algorithms may need to be updated.

Example Resolved

Alice now encrypts the purchase orders she sends to Bob. The purchase order's sensitive data is now unreadable by Eve. Eve can try to apply to it all possible keys, but if the algorithm has been well-chosen and well-implemented, Eve cannot read the confidential information. Since Alice only needs to communicate with a few people within the company, key distribution is rather easy.

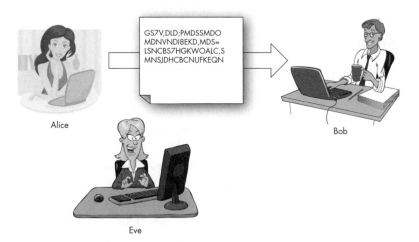

Alice

GS7V,DLD;PMDSSMDO
MDNVNDI8EKD,MDS=
LSNCBS7HGKWOALC,S
MNSJDHCBCNUFKEQN

Bob

Eve

Consequences

The SYMMETRIC ENCRYPTION pattern offers the following benefits:

- Only receivers who possess the shared key can decrypt a message, transforming it into a readable form. A captured message is unreadable to the attacker. This also makes attacks based on modifying a message very hard.

- The strength of a cryptosystem is based on the secrecy of a long key [Sta06]. The cryptographic algorithms are publicly known, so the key should be kept protected from unauthorized users.

- It is possible to select from several encryption algorithms the one suitable for the application's needs.

- Encryption algorithms that take an acceptable time to encrypt messages exist.

The pattern also has the following potential liabilities:

- The pattern assumes that the shared key is distributed in a secure way. This may not be easy for large groups of nodes exchanging messages. Asymmetric cryptography can be used to solve this problem.

- Cryptographic operations are computationally intensive and may affect the performance of the application. This is particularly important for mobile devices.

- Encryption does not provide data integrity. The encrypted data can be modified by an attacker: other means, such as hashing, are needed to verify that the message was not changed.

- Encryption does not prevent a replay attack, because an encrypted message can be captured and resent without being decrypted. It is better to use another security mechanism, such as time stamps or Nonces, to prevent this attack.

Known Uses

SYMMETRIC ENCRYPTION has been widely used in different products.

- GNuPG [Gnu] is free software that secures data from eavesdroppers.

- OpenSSL [Ope1] is an open source toolkit that encrypts and decrypts files.

- Java Cryptographic Extension [SunA] provides a framework and implementations for encryption.

- The .NET framework [Mic07] provides several classes to perform encryption and decryption using symmetric algorithms.

- XML Encryption [W3C02] is one of the foundation web services security standards that defines the structure and process of encryption for XML messages.

- Pretty Good Privacy (PGP), a set of programs used mostly for e-mail security, includes methods for symmetric encryption and decryption [PGP].

See Also

- The Secure Channel Communication pattern [Bra00] supports the encryption/decryption of data. This pattern describes encryption in more general terms: it does not distinguish between asymmetric and symmetric encryption. Another version is given in [Sch06b]. An extension of these patterns is given in [Via05].

- The Strategy pattern [Gam94] describes how to separate the implementation of related algorithms from the selection of one of them. This pattern can be used to select an encryption algorithm dynamically.

- ASYMMETRIC ENCRYPTION is commonly used to distribute keys (see below).

- Patterns for key management are given in [Leh02].

12.3 Asymmetric Encryption

Asymmetric encryption provides message confidentiality by keeping information secret in such a way that it can only be understood by intended recipients who have the access to the valid key. In asymmetric encryption, a public/private key pair is used for encryption and decryption respectively.

Example

Alice wants to send a personal message to Bob. They have not met each other to agree upon a shared key. Alice wants to keep the message secret, since it contains personal information. Eve can intercept Alice's messages, and may try to obtain the confidential information.

Context

Applications that exchange sensitive information over insecure networks.

Problem

Applications that communicate with external applications interchange messages that may contain sensitive information. These messages can be intercepted and read by imposters during transmission. How can we send sensitive information securely over insecure channels?

The solution to this problem must resolve the following forces:

- *Confidentiality.* Messages may be captured while they are in transit, so we need to prevent unauthorized users from reading them by hiding the information the message contains. Hiding information also makes replaying of messages by an attacker harder to perform.

- *Reception.* The hidden information should be revealed conveniently to the receiver.
- *Protocol.* We need to apply the solution properly, or it will not be able to withstand attacks (there are several ways to attack a method of hiding information).
- *Performance.* The time to hide and recover the message should be acceptable.
- *Key distribution.* Two parties may want to communicate to each other, but they have not agreed on a shared key: we need a way to send messages without establishing a common key.

Solution

Apply mathematical functions to a message to make it unreadable to those that do not have a valid key.

This approach uses a key pair: *private* and *public* key. The sender encrypts (E) the message (M) using the receiver's public key (PuK), which is accessible by anyone. The result of this process is cipher text (C):

$$C = E_{PuK} (M)$$

On the other side, the receiver decrypts (D) the cipher text (C) using their private key (PrK) to recover the plain message (M):

$$M = D_{PrK} (C)$$

Structure

Figure 12.5 shows the class diagram for the ASYMMETRIC ENCRYPTION pattern. A `Principal` may be a user or an organization that is responsible for sending or receiving messages. The `Principal` may have the roles of `Sender` or `Receiver`. A `Sender` may send a `Message` and/or an `EncryptedMessage` to a `Receiver` with which it shares a secret key.

A `Principal` has one or more `KeyPairs` that are composed of a private key, kept secret by its owner, and a public key. which is publicly published. `PublicKeyRepository` is a repository that contains a list of public keys where users can register and/or access public keys. These two keys are mathematically related, so while one encrypts, the other decrypts. However, it is not feasible to deduce a private key from its corresponding public key.

The `Encryptor` creates the `EncryptedMessage` that contain the cipher text using the public key of the `Receiver` provided by the sender, while the `Decryptor` deciphers the encrypted data into its original form using its private key. Both the `Encryptor` and `Decryptor` use the same `Algorithm` to encipher and decipher a message.

Dynamics

We describe the dynamic aspects of the ASYMMETRIC ENCRYPTION pattern using sequence diagrams for the following use cases: 'Encrypt a message' and 'Decrypt a message'.

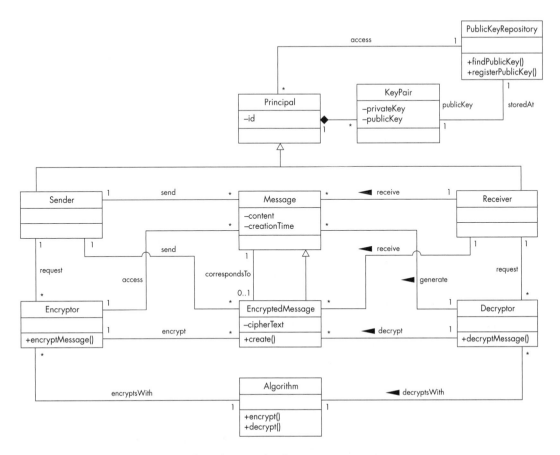

Figure 12.5: Class diagram for the ASYMMETRIC ENCRYPTION pattern

Use Case: *Encrypt a Message – Figure 12.6*

Summary A Sender wants to encrypt a message.

Actors A Sender.

Precondition The Sender has access to the Receiver's public key. Both Sender and Receiver have access to a repository of algorithms. The message has already been created by the Sender.

Description 1 A Sender sends the message, the Receiver's public key, and the algorithm identifier to the Encryptor.

2 The Encryptor ciphers the message using the algorithm specified by the Sender.

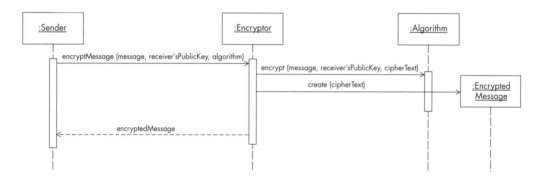

Figure 12.6: Sequence diagram for the use case 'Encrypt a message'

> 3   The `Encryptor` creates the `EncryptedMessage` that includes the cipher text.

Postcondition   The message has been encrypted and sent to the `Sender`.

Use Case: Decrypt an Encrypted Message – Figure 12.7

Summary   A `Receiver` wants to decrypt an encrypted message from a `Sender`.

Actors   A `Receiver`.

Precondition   Both the `Sender` and `Receiver` have access to a repository of algorithms.

Description   1   A `Receiver` sends the encrypted message and their private key to the `Decryptor`.

2   The `Decryptor` deciphers the encrypted message using the `Receiver`'s public key.

3   The `Decryptor` creates the `Message` that contains the plain text obtained from the previous step.

4   The `Decryptor` sends the plain text `Message` to the receiver.

Alternate Flow   If the key used in step 2 is not mathematically related to the key used for encryption, the decryption process fails.

Postcondition   The encrypted message has been deciphered and delivered to the `Receiver`.

Implementation

■   Use the Strategy pattern [Gam94] to select different encryption algorithms.

■   The designer should choose well-known algorithms such as RSA [Riv78].

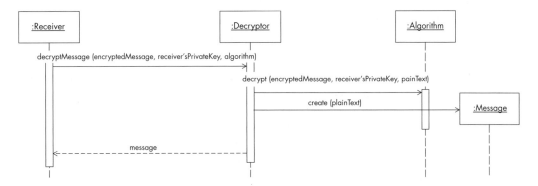

Figure 12.7: Sequence diagram for the use case 'Decrypt an encrypted message'

- Encryption can be implemented in different applications, such as in e-mail communication, distribution of documents over the Internet, or web services. In these applications we are able to encrypt an entire document. However, in web services we can encrypt parts of a message.

- Both the sender and the receiver have to previously agree what cryptographic algorithms they support.

- A good key pair generator is very important. It should generate key pairs for which the private key cannot be deduced from the public key.

Example Resolved

Alice now can look up Bob's public key and encrypt the message using this key. Since Bob keeps his private key secret, he is the only one who can decrypt Alice's message. Eve cannot understand the encrypted data, since Eve does not have access to Bob's private key.

Consequences

The ASYMMETRIC ENCRYPTION pattern offers the following benefits:

- Asymmetric encryption does not require a secret key to be shared among all the participants. Anyone can look up the public key in the repository and send messaged to the owner of the public key.

- Only recipients that possess the corresponding private key can make the encrypted message readable again.

- The strength of a cryptosystem is based on the secrecy of a long key [Sta06]. The cryptographic algorithms are known to the public, so the private key should be kept protected from unauthorized users.

- It is possible to select from several encryption algorithms the one suitable for the application's needs.
- Encryption algorithms that take an acceptable time to encrypt messages exist.

The pattern also has the following potential liabilities:

- Cryptography operations are computationally intensive and may affect the performance of the application. Asymmetric encryption is slower than symmetric encryption. It is best to use a combination of both algorithms: asymmetric encryption for key distribution, and symmetric encryption for message exchange.
- Encryption does not provide data integrity. The encrypted data can be modified by an attacker: other means, such as hashing, are needed to verify that a message has not been changed.
- Encryption does not prevent a replay attack, because an encrypted message can be captured and resent without being decrypted. It is recommended to use another security mechanism, such as timestamps or Nonces, to prevent this attack.
- This pattern assumes that a public key belongs to the person who they claim to be. How can we know that this person is not impersonating another? To confirm that someone is who they say they are, we can use certificates issued by a certification authority (CA). If the CA is not trustworthy, we may lose security.

Known Uses

ASYMMETRIC ENCRYPTION has been widely used in different products.

- GNuPG [Gnu] is free software that secures data from eavesdroppers.
- Java Cryptographic Extension [SunA] supports a variety of algorithms, including asymmetric encryption.
- The .NET framework [Mic07] provides several classes to perform asymmetric encryption and decryption.
- XML Encryption [W3C02] is one of the foundation web services security standards that defines the structure and process of encryption for XML messages. This standard supports both types of encryption: symmetric and asymmetric encryption.
- Pretty Good Privacy (PGP) uses asymmetric encryption and decryption as one of its process to secure e-mail communication [PGP].

See Also

- The Secure Channel Communication pattern [Bra00] supports the encryption/decryption of data. This pattern describes encryption in more general terms: it does not distinguish between asymmetric and symmetric encryption. Another version is given in [Sch06b].

- The Strategy pattern [Gam94] describes how to separate the implementation of related algorithms from the selection of one of them. This pattern can be used to select an encryption algorithm dynamically.

- Predicate-based encryption is a family of public key encryption schemes; patterns for them are described in [Mui12].

12.4   Digital Signature with Hashing

The DIGITAL SIGNATURE WITH HASHING pattern allows a principal to prove that a message was originated from it. It also provides message integrity, by indicating whether a message was altered during transmission.

Example

Alice in the sales department wants to send a product order to Bob in the production department. The product order does not contain sensitive data such as credit card numbers, so it is not important to keep it secret. However, Bob wants to be certain that the message was created by Alice, so he can charge the order to her account. Also, because this order includes the quantity of items to be produced, an unauthorized modification to the order will make Bob manufacture the wrong quantity of items. Eve is a disgruntled employee who can intercept the messages and may want to attempt this kind of modification to hurt the company.

Context

People or systems often need to exchange documents or messages through insecure networks and need to prove their origin and integrity. Stored legal documents need to be kept without modification and with indication of their origin. Software sent by a vendor through the Internet is required to prove its origin.

We assume that those exchanging documents have access to a public key system where a principal possesses a key pair: a private key that is secretly kept by the principal, and a public key that is in a publicly-accessible repository. We assume that there is a mechanism for the generation of these key pairs and for the distribution of public keys; that is, a public key infrastructure (PKI).

Problem

In many applications we need to verify the origin of a message (message authentication). Since an imposter may assume the identity of a principal, how can we verify that a message came from a particular principal? Also, messages that travel through insecure channels can be captured and modified by attackers. How can we know that the message or document that we are receiving has not been modified?

The solution to this problem must resolve the following forces:

■ For legal or business reasons we need to be able to verify who sent a particular message. Otherwise, we may not be sure of its origin, and the sender may deny having sent it (repudiation).

■ Messages may be altered during transmission, so we need to verify that the data is in its original form when it reaches its destination.

■ The length of the signed message should not be significantly larger than the original message, otherwise we would waste time and bandwidth.

■ Producing a signed message should not require large computational power or take a long time.

Solution

Apply properties of public key cryptographic algorithms to messages in order to create a signature that will be unique for each sender [Sta06]. The message is first compressed (hashed) to a smaller size (digest), then encrypted using the sender's private key. When the signed message arrives at its target, the receiver verifies the signature using the sender's public key to decrypt the message. If it produces a readable message, it could only have been sent by this sender. The receiver then generates the hashed digest of the received message and compares it with the received hashed digest: if it matches, the message has not been altered.

This approach uses public key cryptography in which one key is used for encryption and the other for decryption. To produce a digital signature (SIG), we encrypt (E) the *hash value* of a message (H(M)) using the sender's private key (PrK):

$$SIG = E_{PrK} (H(M))$$

We recover the hash value of the message (H(M)) by applying decryption function D to the signature (SIG) using the sender's public key (PuK). If this produces a legible message, we can be confident that the sender created the message, because they are the only one who has access to their private key. Finally, we calculate the hash value of the message as:

$$H(M) = D_{PuK}(SIG)$$

If this value is the same as the message digest obtained when the signature was decrypted, then we know that the message has not been modified.

It is clear that the sender and receiver should agree to use the same encryption and hashing algorithms.

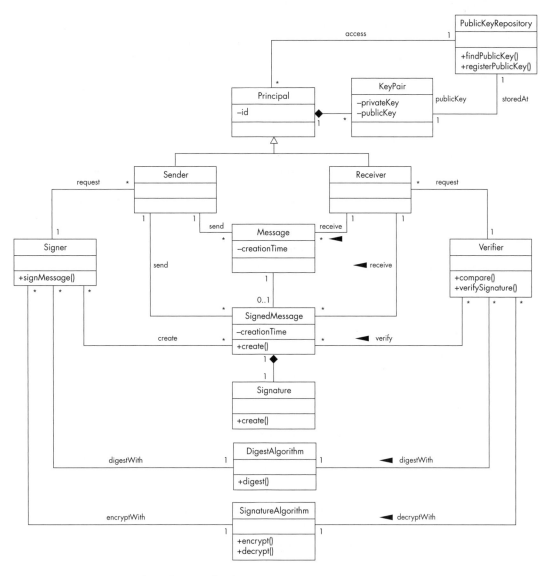

Figure 12.8: Class diagram for the DIGITAL SIGNATURE WITH HASHING pattern

Structure

Figure 12.8 shows the class diagram for the DIGITAL SIGNATURE WITH HASHING pattern. A `Principal` may be a process, a user or an organization that is responsible for sending or receiving messages. This `Principal` may have the roles of `Sender` or `Receiver`. A `Sender` may send a plain `Message` and/or a `SignedMessage` to a receiver.

The `KeyPair` entity contains two keys, public and private, that belong to a `Principal`. The public key is registered and accessed through a repository, while the private key is kept secret by its owner. `PublicKeyRepository` is a repository that contains public keys. The `PublicKeyRepository` may be located in the same local network as the `Principal`, or on an external network.

The `Signer` creates the `SignedMessage` that includes the `Signature` for a specific message. On the other side, the `Verifier` checks that the `Signature` within the `SignedMessage` corresponds to that message. The `Signer` and `Verifier` use the `DigestAlgorithm` and `SignatureAlgorithm` to create and verify a signature respectively. The `DigestAlgorithm` is a hash function that condenses a message to a fixed length called a hash value, or *message digest*. The `SignatureAlgorithm` encrypts and decrypts messages using public/private key pairs.

Dynamics

We describe the dynamic aspects of the DIGITAL SIGNATURE WITH HASHING pattern using sequence diagrams for the use cases 'Sign a message' and 'Verify a signature'.

Use Case: Sign a Message – Figure 12.9

Summary	A `Sender` wants to sign a message before sending it.
Actors	A `Sender`.
Precondition	A `Sender` has a public/private pair key.
Description	1 A `Sender` sends the message and its private key to the `Signer`.
	2 The `Signer` calculates the hash value of the message (digest) and returns it to the `Sender`.
	3 The `Signer` encrypts the hash value using the `Sender`'s private key with the `SignatureAlgorithm`. The output of this calculation is the digital signature value.
	4 The `Signer` creates the `Signature` object that contains the digital signature value.
	5 The `Signer` creates the `SignedMessage` that contains the original message and the `Signature`.
Postcondition	A `SignedMessage` object has been created.

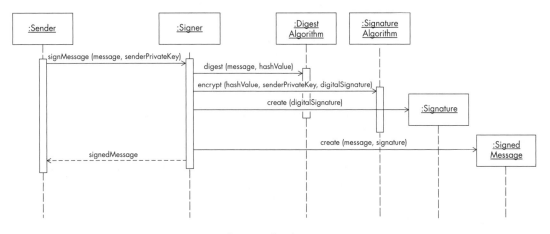

Figure 12.9: Sequence diagram for the use case 'Sign a message'

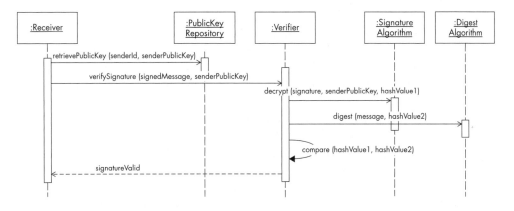

Figure 12.10: Sequence diagram for the use case 'Verify a signature'

Use Case: *Verify a Signature – Figure 12.10*

Summary	A `Receiver` wants to verify that the signature corresponds to the received message.
Actors	A `Receiver`.
Precondition	None.
Description	1 A `Receiver` retrieves the `Sender`'s public key from the `PublicKey-Repository`.

    2   A `Receiver` sends the signed message and the Sender's public key to the `Verifier`.

    3   The `Verifier` decrypts the signature using the `Sender`'s public key with the `SignatureAlgorithm`.

    4   The `Verifier` calculates the digest value of the message.

    5   The `Verifier` compares the outputs from step 3 and 4.

    6   The `Verifier` sends an acknowledgement to the `Receiver` that the signature is valid.

Alternate Flow   The outputs from step 3 and 4 are not the same. In this case, the verifier sends an acknowledgement to the receiver that the signature failed.

Postcondition   The signature has been verified.

Implementation

- Use the Strategy pattern [Gam94] to select different hashing and signature algorithms. The most widely used hashing algorithms are MD5 and SHA1. These and others are discussed in [Sta06].

- A good hashing algorithm produces digests that are very unlikely to be produced by other meaningful messages, meaning that it is very hard for an attacker to create an altered message with the same hash value. The message digest should be encrypted after being signed to avoid man-in-the-middle attacks, where someone who captures a message could reconstruct its hash value.

- Two popular digital signature algorithms are RSA [Riv78] [RSA] and Digital Signature Algorithm (DSA) [Fed00] [Sta06].

- The designer should choose strong and proven algorithms to prevent attackers from breaking them. The cryptographic protocol aspects, for example key generation, are as important as the algorithms used.

- The sender and receiver should have a way of agreeing on the hash and encryption algorithms used for a specific set of messages. (XML documents indicate which algorithms they use, and pre-agreements are not necessary in this case.)

- Access to the sender's public key should be available from a public directory or from certificates presented by the signer.

- Digital signatures can be implemented in different applications, such as in e-mail communication, distribution of documents over the Internet, or web services. For example, it is possible to sign an e-mail's contents, or any other document's content, such as a PDF. In both cases, the signature is appended to the e-mail or document. When digital signatures are applied in web services, they are also embedded within XML messages. However, these signatures are treated as XML elements, and they have additional features, such as signing parts of a message, or external resources, which can be XML or any other data type.

■ When certificates are used to provide the sender's public key, there must be a convenient way to verify that the certificate is still valid [SOA01].

■ There should be a way of authenticating the signer software [dig], as an attacker who gains control of a user's computer could replace the signing software with their own software.

Example Resolved

Alice and Bob agree on the use of a digital signature algorithm, and Bob has access to Alice's public key. Alice can then send a signed message to Bob. When the message is received by Bob, he verifies that the signature is valid using Alice's public key and the agreed signature algorithm. If the signature is valid, Bob can be confident that the message was created by Alice. If the hash value is correct, Bob also knows that Eve has not been able to modify the message.

Consequences

The DIGITAL SIGNATURE WITH HASHING pattern offers the following benefits:

■ Because a principal's private key is used to sign the message, the signature can be validated using its public key, which proves that the sender created and sent the message.

■ When a signature is validated using a principal's public key, the sender cannot deny that they created and sent the message (non-repudiation). If a message is signed using another private key that does not belong to the sender, the validity of the signature fails.

■ If the proper precautions are followed, any change in the original message will produce a digest value that will be different (with a very high probability) from the value obtained after decrypting the signature using the sender's public key.

■ A message is compressed into a fixed length string using the hash algorithm before it is signed. As a result, the process of signing is faster, and the signed message is much shorter.

■ The available algorithms that can be used for digital signatures do not require very large amounts of computational power and do not take large amounts of time.

The pattern also has the following potential liabilities:

■ We need a well-established public key infrastructure that can provide reliable public keys. Certificates issued by a certification authority are the most common way to obtain this [Sta06].

■ Both the sender and the receiver have to previously agree what signature and hashing algorithms they support. (This is not necessary in XML documents, because they are self-describing.)

- Cryptographic algorithms create some overhead (time, memory, computational power), which can be reduced but not eliminated.

- The required storage and computational power may not be available, for example in mobile devices.

- Users must implement the signature protocol properly.

- There may be attacks against specific algorithms or implementations [dig]. These are difficult to use against careful implementations of this pattern.

- This solution only allows one signer for the whole message. A variant or specialization, such as the XML SIGNATURE pattern (page 317), allows multiple signers.

- Digital signatures do not provide message authentication, and replay attacks are possible [SOA01]. Nonces or time stamps could prevent this type of attack.

Known Uses

Digital signatures have been widely used in different products.

- Adobe Reader and Acrobat [Ado] have an extended security feature that allows users to digitally sign PDF documents.

- CoSign [Arx] digitally signs different types of documents, files, forms and other electronic transactions.

- GNuPG [Gnu] digitally signs e-mail messages.

- The Java Cryptographic Architecture [SunB] includes APIs for digital signature.

- Microsoft .NET [Mic07] includes APIs for asymmetric cryptography such as digital signature.

- XML Signature [W3C08] is one of the foundation web services security standards that defines the structure and process of digital signatures in XML messages.

See Also

- Encryption/decryption using public key cryptography [Bra00].

- Generation and distribution of public keys [Leh02].

- Certificates [Mor06a] are issued by a certificate authority (CA) that digitally signs them using its private key. A certificate carries a user's public key and allows anyone who has access to the CA's public key to verify that the certificate was signed by the CA.

- The Strategy pattern [Gam94] describes how to separate the implementation of related algorithms from the selection of one of them.

12.5   XML Encryption

The XML ENCRYPTION pattern provides confidentiality by hiding selected sensitive information in a message using cryptography.

Example

Alice in the purchasing department regularly sends purchase orders in the form of XML documents to Bob, who works in the distribution office. The purchase order contains sensitive data such as credit card numbers and other company information, so it is important to keep it secret. Messages may also contain non-sensitive data. At the receiving end, different people will handle different parts of the order. Eve can intercept these orders and may try to read them to access the confidential information.

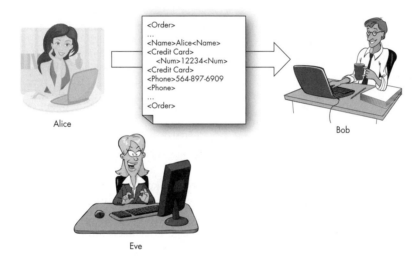

Context

Users of web services sending and receiving XML messages through insecure networks such as the Internet.

Problem

In many applications that communicate with external applications users exchange sensitive data. This data may be read by unauthorized people while the messages are in transit. How can we prevent this?

The solution to this problem must resolve the following forces:

- Messages may be captured while they are in transit, so we need to prevent unauthorized users from reading them by hiding the information the message contains using encryption.

- We need to express encrypted elements in a standardized XML format to allow encrypted data to be nested within an XML message, otherwise different applications cannot interoperate.

- Different parts of a message may be intended for different recipients, and not all the information contained within a message should be available to all the recipients. Thus, recipients should be able to read only those parts of the message that are intended for them.

- For flexibility reasons, both symmetric and asymmetric encryption algorithms should be supported.

- If a secret key is embedded in the message, it should be protected, otherwise an attacker could read some messages.

Solution

Transform an XML message using some encryption algorithm so that it can only be understood by legitimate receivers that possess a valid key.

XML Encryption supports both types of encryption: symmetric and asymmetric. The symmetric encryption algorithm uses a common key for both encryption and decryption. The asymmetric encryption algorithm uses a key pair: a public key and a private key. The sender encrypts a message using the receiver's public key, and the receiver uses their private key to decrypt the encrypted message. Thus, in both types of encryption, only recipients who possess the shared key or the private key that matches the public key used in the encryption process can read the encrypted message after decryption. Different parts of the message may be encrypted with different keys, or not encrypted.

Structure

Figure 12.11 shows the class diagram of the XML ENCRYPTION pattern. The shaded classes correspond to the classes of the XML ENCRYPTION pattern, while the unshaded classes describe the structure of the message and show that encryption can now be applied to specific portions of the message.

A Principal may be a user or an organization that sends and receives XMLMessages and/or EncryptedXMLMessages. This Principal may have the roles of Sender and Receiver. Both an XMLMessage and a EncryptedXMLMessage are composed of XMLElements. Each XMLElement may have many children, and each child also can be composed of other XMLElements, and so on. The XMLEncryptor and the XMLDecryptor encipher a message and decipher an encrypted message respectively.

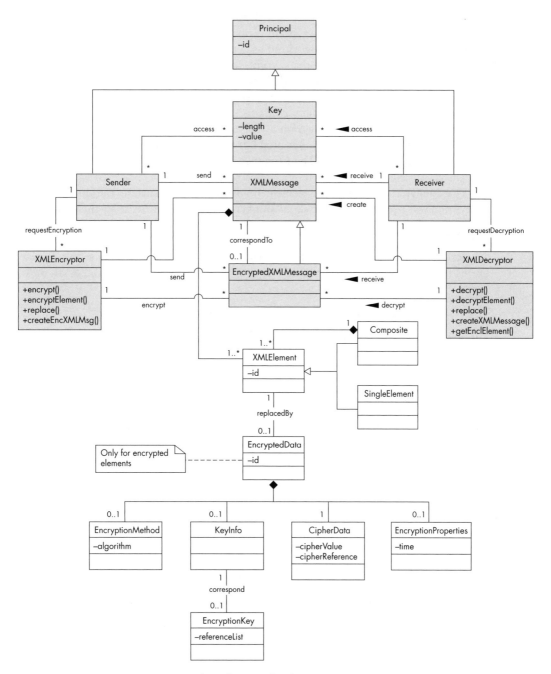

Figure 12.11: Class diagram for the XML ENCRYPTION pattern

The EncryptedData contains other subelements, such as the encryption method, key information, cipher value and encryption properties. The EncryptionMethod is an optional element that specifies the algorithm used to encrypt the data. If this element is not specified, the receiver must know the encryption algorithm. The optional KeyInfo contains the same key information as that described in the XML Signature standard [W3C08]. However, this standard defines two other subelements: EncryptedKey and ReferenceList. The EncryptedKey contains similar elements to the EncryptedData; they are not shown in the class diagram.

The EncryptedKey includes an optional ReferenceList element that points to data or keys encrypted using this key. The CipherData is a mandatory element that stores either the cipher value or a pointer (cipher reference) to where the encrypted data is located. The EncryptionProperties element holds information such as the time that the encryption was performed, or the serial number of the hardware used for the process.

Dynamics

We describe the dynamic aspects of the XML ENCRYPTION pattern using sequence diagrams for the use cases 'Encrypt XML elements' and 'Decrypt an encrypted XML message'.

Use Case: Encrypt XML Elements – Figure 12.12

Summary	A Sender wants to encrypt different elements of an XML message using a shared key.
Actors	A Sender.
Precondition	Both Sender and Receiver have a shared key and a list of encryption algorithms.
Description	1 A Sender requests the Encryptor to encrypt a list of XML elements. This list is represented by an asterisk (*) in the sequence diagram.
	2 The Encryptor creates the EncryptedXMLMessage.
	3 The Encryptor encrypts the XML elements using the shared key and the encryption method provided by the Sender and produces an encrypted value.
	4 The Encryptor creates the EncryptionData element, including the encryptionMethod that holds the encryption algorithm used to encrypt the data, the KeyInfo that contains information about the key and the CipherData obtained from step 3.
	5 The Encryptor replaces the XML element with the encrypted data.
	6 The Encryptor repeats steps 3 to 5 for each XML element to encrypt.
	7 The Encryptor sends the EncryptedXMLMessage to the sender.
Postcondition	The encrypted XML message has been created.

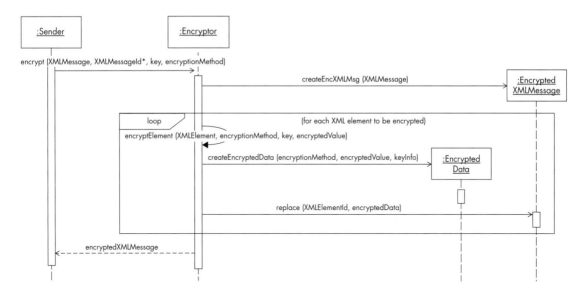

Figure 12.12: Sequence diagram for the use case 'Encrypt XML elements'

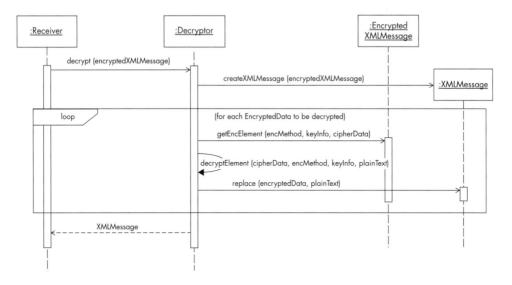

Figure 12.13: Sequence diagram for the use case 'Decrypt an encrypted XML message'

Use Case: *Decrypt an Encrypted XML Message – Figure 12.13*

Summary	A `Receiver` wants to decrypt an encrypted XML message.
Actors	A `Receiver`.
Precondition	Both `Sender` and `Receiver` have a shared key and a list of encryption algorithms.
Description	1 A `Receiver` requests the `Decryptor` to decrypt an encrypted XML message.
	2 The `Decryptor` creates the `XMLMessage` that contains a copy of the `EncryptedXMLMessage`.
	3 The `Decryptor` obtains the elements within the `EncryptedData` element such as the `encryptionMethod`, `KeyInfo`, and the cipher-Value.
	4 The `Decryptor` decrypts the cipher value using the encryption method and the shared key.
	5 The `Decryptor` replaces the encrypted data with the plain text obtained from the previous step.
	6 The `Decryptor` repeats steps 3 to 5 for each XML element to decrypt.
	7 The `Decryptor` sends the decrypted `XMLMessage` to the `Receiver`.
Alternate Flows	If the key used in step 4 is not the same as the one used in the encryption, then the decryption process fails.
Postcondition	The message has been decrypted.

Implementation

- The designer should choose strong encryption algorithms to prevent attackers from breaking them, such as AES (Advanced Encryption Standard) or DES (Data Encryption Standard) for symmetric encryption, and RSA for asymmetric encryption [RSA].

- Asymmetric encryption or public-key encryption is more computationally intensive than symmetric encryption. However, symmetric encryption requires that both sender and receiver share a common key. A better practice is to use asymmetric encryption in combination with symmetric encryption: use symmetric encryption for the message and asymmetric encryption for secure key distribution.

- XML ENCRYPTION supports both symmetric and asymmetric encryption. This provides application flexibility; for example, a session can use symmetric encryption and key distribution can use asymmetric encryption.

- Encryption does not require creation of a new document, as shown in the solution, but could be done in place, replacing the message by an encrypted message.

■ Data is usually serialized before encryption. The serialization process converts the data into octets. This serialized data is then encrypted using the chosen algorithm and the encryption key. The cipher data and the information of the encryption (algorithm, key and other properties) are represented in XML format.

■ The following example illustrates how an encrypted part is embedded within an XML message.

Suppose you want to send a purchase order to the distribution office. This document contains details of the order, such as what item to buy, quantity and credit card information for payment. We want to keep the XML document simple by just focusing on the encryption part.

```
<Order>
<Item> Item X </Item>
<Quantity> 24 </Quantity>
<Payment Info>
<Credit Card>
<Number>1234566 </Number>
<Expiration Date> 12/12/2010</Expiration Date>
</Credit Card>
</Payment Info>
</Order>
```

Because `Payment Info` contains sensitive information, we want to encrypt only this element, so it can only be understood by the intended receiver.

```
<Order>
<Item> Item X </Item>
<Quantity> 24 </Quantity>
<Encrypted Data>
<Encryption Method Algorithm='AlgorithmX'/>
<Cipher Data>
<Cipher Value>ijutfrewsvbnmlkk</Cipher Value>
</Cipher Data>
<Key Info>
<Key Name> KeyA </KeyName>
</Key Info>
</Encrypted Data>
</Order>
```

The `Payment Info` element is replaced by the `Encrypted Data` element that includes all the information needed by the receiver. The `Encryption Method` element includes the algorithm used for the encryption. The `Cipher Value` element contains the actual encrypted data. For this example, the `Key Info` element includes the name that identifies the key.

Example Resolved

Alice now encrypts the purchase orders she sends to Bob, using different keys for the parts that should be read by different people. The purchase order's sensitive data is now unreadable by Eve. Eve can try to apply to it all possible keys, but if the algorithm has been well-chosen and well-implemented, Eve cannot read the confidential information. Non-sensitive information is not encrypted, which saves time and bandwidth.

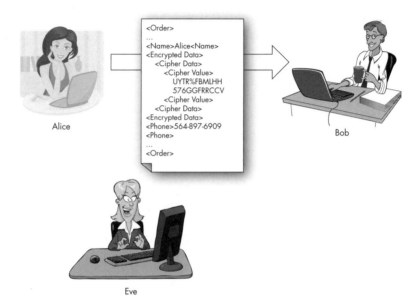

Consequences

The XML ENCRYPTION pattern offers the following benefits:

- Only users that know the key can decrypt and read the message. Each recipient can only decrypt parts of a message that are intended for them, but are unable to decrypt the remainder of the message.

- The Encrypted Data is an XML element that replaces the data to be encrypted. The Encrypted Data, as well as the EncryptedKey, are composed of other subelements such as encryption method, key information and cipher value.

- The entire XML message, or only some parts of it, can be encrypted.

- If both the sender and the receiver have not exchanged the keys previously, the key can be sent in the message, encrypted using a public key system.

The pattern also has the following potential liabilities:

- The general liabilities of symmetric and asymmetric encryption still apply.

- The structure is rather complex and users may be confused.

- Unencrypted portions of the message may help a possible attacker. This might be improved by *superencryption* of the whole message at a lower level, such as using TLS.

Known Uses

Several vendors have developed tools that support XML ENCRYPTION:

- Xtradyne's Web Services Domain Boundary Controller (WS-DBC) [Xtr]. The WS-DBC is an XML firewall that provides protection against malformed messages and malicious content, XML encryption, XML signature, and authentication, authorization and audit.

- IBM DataPower XML Security Gateway XS40 [IBM05] parses, filters, validates schema, decrypts, verifies signatures, signs, and encrypts XML message flows.

- Forum Sentry SOA Gateway [For] conforms to XML Digital Signature, XML Encryption, WS-Trust, WS-Policy and other standards.

- Microsoft .NET [Mic07] includes APIs that support the encryption and decryption of XML data.

See Also

- This pattern includes a specialization of the SYMMETRIC ENCRYPTION pattern (page 288).

- The WS-SECURITY pattern (page 330) is a standard for securing XML messages using XML SIGNATURE, XML ENCRYPTION and security tokens.

- The Strategy pattern [Gam94] describes how to separate the implementation of related algorithms from the selection of one of them.

- The XML Key Management Specification (XKMS) [W3C01] specifies the distribution and registration of public keys, and works together with XML ENCRYPTION.

- The WS-Security Policy [Aja10b] standard describes how to express security policies, such as what algorithms are supported by a web service or what parts of an incoming message need to be signed or encrypted.

12.6 XML Signature

The XML SIGNATURE pattern allows a principal to prove that a message was originated from it. It also provides message integrity by detecting whether a message was altered during transmission. The XML Signature standard [W3C08] describes the syntax and the process of generating and validating digital signatures for authenticating XML documents. XML Signature also provides message integrity, and requires canonicalization before hashing and signing.

Example

Alice in the sales department wants to send product orders to Bob in the production department. The product orders are XML documents and do not contain sensitive data such as credit card numbers, so it is not important to keep them secret. Each order must be signed by Alice's supervisor Susie to indicate approval. Bob wants to be certain that the message was created by Alice so he can charge the order to her account, and also needs to know that the orders are approved. Because the orders include the quantity of items to be produced, an unauthorized modification to an order will make Bob manufacture the wrong quantity of items. Eve can intercept the messages and may want to make this kind of modification.

Context

Users of web services send and receive SOAP messages through insecure networks such as the Internet and need to prove their origin and integrity. During their transmission these messages can be subject to a variety of attacks.

We assume that a principal possesses a key pair: a private key that is secretly kept by the principal, and a public key that is in a publicly-accessible repository. We assume that there is a mechanism for the generation of these key pairs and for the distribution of public keys.

Problem

In many applications we need to verify the origin of a message (message authentication). Since an imposter may assume the identity of a principal, how can we verify that a message came from a particular principal? Also, messages that travel through insecure channels can be captured and modified by attackers. How do we know that the message or document that we are receiving has not been modified?

The solution to this problem must resolve the following forces:

- For legal or business reasons we need to be able to verify who sent a particular message, otherwise we may not be sure of its origin, and the sender may deny having sent it (repudiation). We assume the sender has signed the message to prove they are its author.

- Messages may be altered during transmission, so we need to verify that the data is in its original form when it reaches its destination.

- The length of the signed message should not be significantly greater than the original message, otherwise we would waste time and bandwidth.

- Producing a signed message should not require a lot of computational power or take a long time.

- We need to express a digital signature in a standardized XML format, so interoperability can be ensured between applications.

■ There may be situations in which we want to ensure proper origin or integrity in specific parts of a message. For example, an XML message can travel through many intermediaries that add or subtract information, so if we sign the entire message, the signature would have no meaning. We need to be able to sign portions of a message.

Solution

Apply cryptographic algorithms to messages to create a signature that will be unique for each message. First, the data to be signed may need to be transformed before applying any digest algorithm. The series of XML elements (that includes other subelements) is canonicalized before applying a signature algorithm. Canonicalization is a type of transformational algorithm that converts data into a standard format, to remove differences due to layout formatting. This process is required because XML is a flexible language in which a document can be represented in different ways that are semantically equal. Thus, after calculating the canonical form, both the sender and the receiver will sign and verify the same XML data respectively. After applying a canonicalization algorithm, the result value is digested and then encrypted using the sender's private key. Finally, the signature, in XML form, is embedded in the message.

At the other end, the receiver verifies the signature appended to the signed message. The verification process has two parts: reference verification and signature verification. In the reference verification, the verifier recalculates the digest value of the original data. This value is compared with the digest value included in the signature. If there is any mismatch, the verification fails. In the signature verification, the verifier calculates the canonical form of the signed XML element, then applies the digest algorithm. This digest value is compared against the decrypted value of the signature. The decryption is done using the sender's public key.

There are three types of XML Signature: enveloped, enveloping and detached signature. In an enveloped signature, the signature is a child element of the signed data. For example, when you sign the entire XML message, the signature is embedded within the message. An enveloping signature is a signature where the signed data is a child of the signature. You can sign elements of a signature, such as the `<Object>` or `<KeyInfo>` element. A detached signature is calculated over external network resources or over elements within the message. In the latter case, the signature is neither an enveloped nor an enveloping signature.

Structure

Figure 12.14 shows the class diagram of the XML SIGNATURE pattern. Note that the upper part of this figure is almost the same as Figure 12.8 (page 303). The main difference is that Figure 12.14 adds more details about the structure of the elements of the message so that signatures can be applied more finely.

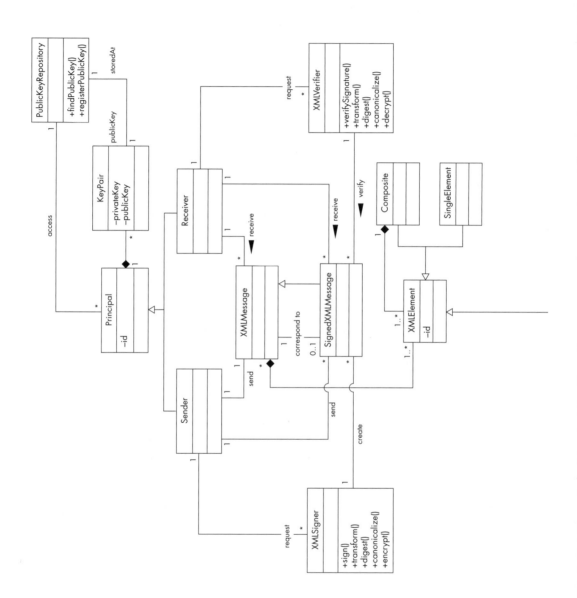

Figure 12.14: Class diagram for the XML SIGNATURE pattern

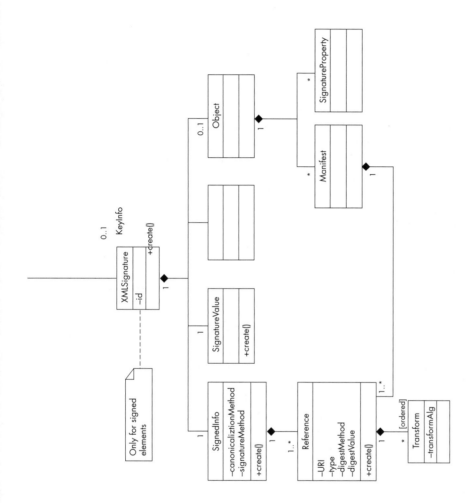

Figure 12.14 (continued)

A `Principal` may be a process, a system, a user, or an organization that sends and receives `XMLMessages` and/or `SignedXMLMessages`. This `Principal` may have the roles of `Sender` and `Receiver`. Both an `XMLMessage` and a `SignedXMLMessage` are composed of `XMLElements`, but this is only shown in the `SignedXMLMessage`. Each `XMLElement` may be a `SingleElement` that does not have any children, or be a `Composite` element which is composed by other `XMLElements`.

The `XMLSigner` and the `XMLVerifier` create and verify a signature respectively. They can select signature and digest algorithms. An `XMLSignature` element is an `XMLElement` that has two required children, `SignedInfo` and `SignatureValue`, and two optional children, `KeyInfo` and `Object`. The `SignedInfo` element is the one that is actually signed. It contains one or more `Reference` elements, the canonicalization algorithm identifier, and the signature algorithm identifier. The canonicalization algorithm is used to convert the `SignedInfo` element into a standard form before it is signed or verified. The signature algorithm also includes a digest algorithm that is applied after calculating the canonical form of the `SignedInfo` in both process creation and verification of XML signatures.

Each `Reference` element includes a URI, a hash value (`digestValue`), the digest algorithm identifier (`digestMethod`) and an optional list of `Transform` elements. The URI is a pointer that identifies the data to be signed. It can point to an element inside an XML message, an element inside the signature element such as `Object` or `KeyInfo`, or resources located on the Internet. The `digestValue` contains a hash value created after applying the digest algorithm to the data pointed to by its URI. If the `Transform` element exists, it includes an ordered list of transform algorithms that are applied to the data before the digest is created. The `SignatureValue` element includes the value of the digital signature.

If the `KeyInfo` element is present, it indicates the information about the sender's public key that will be used to verify the signature. This flexible element may contain certificates, key names and other public keys forms. Additional information about this element can be found in [W3C08]. The optional `Object` element may contain `SignatureProperties` and/or a `Manifest`. The `SignatureProperty` identifies properties of the signature itself, such as the date/time when the signature was created. The `Manifest` element includes one or more `Reference` elements, as for the `Reference` element within the `SignedInfo` element. They are semantically equal; however, each `Reference` in the `SignedInfo` has to be validated in order for the `XMLSignature` to be considered a valid signature. On the other hand, the list of `Reference` elements within the `Manifest` is validated.

The `Sender` and `Receiver` must use the same hash, signature and canonicalization algorithms. XML documents are self-descriptive and indicate this information, so the sender only needs to find the corresponding algorithms.

Dynamics

We describe the dynamic aspects of the XML SIGNATURE pattern using sequence diagrams for the use cases 'Sign different XML elements of an XML message' and 'Verify an XML signature with multiple references'.

Use Case: *Sign Different XML Elements of an XML Message – Figure 12.15*

Summary	A `Sender` wants to sign specified XML elements of an XML message.
Actors	A `Sender`.
Precondition	The `Sender` has a private/public key pair.
Description	

1 A `Sender` requests the `Signer` to sign different XML elements of a message.

2 The `Signer` calculates the digest value over the XML element.

3 The `Signer` creates the `<Reference>` element, including the digest value, and using the digest algorithm.

4 The `Signer` repeats steps 2 and 3 for each XML element to be signed.

5 The `Signer` creates the `<SignedInfo>` element that includes the `<Reference>` elements, the canonicalization algorithm identifier, and the signature algorithm identifier.

6 The `Signer` applies the canonicalization algorithm to the `<SignedInfo>` element.

7 The `Signer` signs the output from step 6. First, it applies the digest algorithm, then it encrypts the digest using the `Sender`'s public key. The output is the signature value.

8 The `Signer` creates the `<SignatureValue>` element that includes the signature value.

9 The `Signer` creates the `<KeyInfo>` element that holds the sender's public key, which will be used to verify the signature.

10 The `Signer` creates the `<Signature>` element that includes the `<SignedInfo>`, the `<SignatureValue>` and the `<KeyInfo>` elements.

11 The `Signer` creates the `SignedXMLMessage` that includes the `Signature` and the `XMLMessage`.

Postcondition The specified elements of the document have been signed.

Use Case: *Verify an XML Signature with Multiple References – Figure 12.16*

Summary	A `Receiver` wants to verify the signature of a received document.
Actors	A `Receiver`.
Precondition	None.
Description	

1 A `Receiver` requests verification of the signature that is included in the `SignedXMLMessage`.

2 The `Verifier` obtains the signature elements, such as `<SignedInfo>`, which includes the `<Reference>` elements, the `<SignatureValue>` and the `<KeyInfo>` elements.

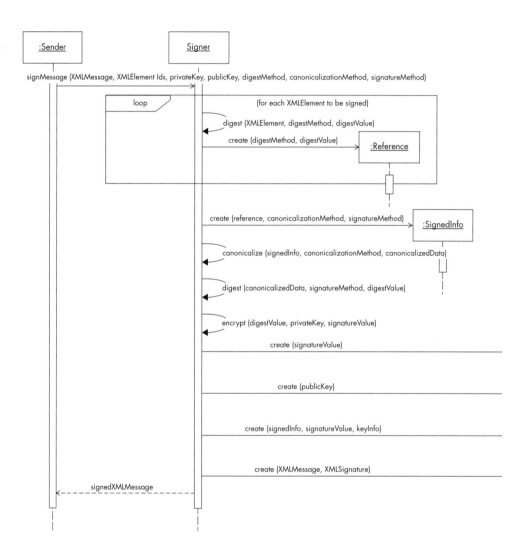

Figure 12.15: Sequence diagram for the use case 'Sign different XML elements of an XML message'

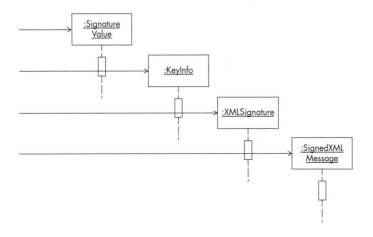

Figure 12.15 (continued)

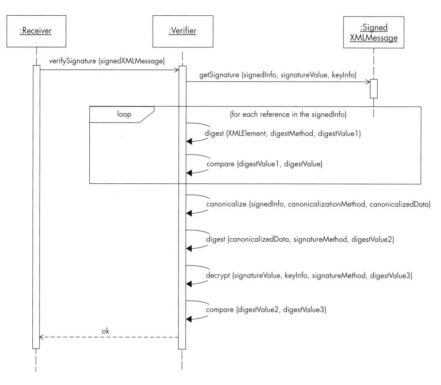

Figure 12.16: Sequence diagram for the use case 'Verify an
XML signature with multiple references'

3   The Verifier calculates the digest value over the XML element that
is pointed to by the URI in the <Reference> element, using the
digest algorithm specified in the <Reference> element as well.

4   The Verifier compares the output from step 3 against the digest
value specified in the Reference element.

5   The Verifier repeats step 3 and 4 for each <Reference> element
included in the <SignedInfo> element.

6   The Verifier canonicalizes the <SignedInfo> element using the
canonicalization method specified in the <SignedInfo> element.

7   The Verifier digests the output from step 6 using the digest
algorithm specified in the signature algorithm.

8   The Verifier decrypts the signature value using the sender's public
key (<KeyInfo>).

9   The Verifier compares the outputs from step 6 and 8.

10 The `Verifier` sends an acknowledgement to the `Receiver` that the signature is valid.

Alternate Flows ■ If the values compared in step 4 are not the same, then the signature is invalid.

■ If the outputs in step 9 are not the same, then the validation fails.

Postcondition: The signature is validated.

Implementation

■ Identifiers of algorithms used to create a signature are attached along with the signature, so they also should be protected from being modified by attackers.

■ XML documents may be parsed by different processors; XML allows some flexibility without changing the semantics of the message. Thus, we need to convert the data to be signed to a standard format.

■ All the signers of a given document should have the same level of trust, to avoid misleading the receivers about the trust level of the whole message. Allowing untrusted signers might give them a better chance of attacking the message.

■ Use the Strategy pattern [Gam94] to select different hashing and signature algorithms. The most widely used hashing algorithms are MD5 and SHA1. Two popular digital signature algorithms are RSA [RSA] and the Digital Signature Algorithm (DSA) [Fed00].

■ The data to be signed may need to be transformed before producing a digest. For instance, if the object to be signed is an image, it needs to be converted into text.

■ The use of certificates issued by a certification authority that are trusted by the sender and the receiver is recommended.

Example Resolved

Alice and Susie sign each production order sent to Bob. Bob has access to Alice's and Susie's public keys. When the message is received by Bob, he verifies whether the signatures are valid using Alice's and Susie's public keys and the signature algorithm specified in the order. If the signature are valid, Bob can be confident that the message was created by Alice and approved by Susie. If the hash value is correct, Bob also knows that Eve has not been able to modify the message.

Consequences

The XML SIGNATURE pattern offers the following benefits:

■ A principal's private key is used to sign the message. The signature is validated using its public key, which proves that the principal created and sent the message.

- When a signature is validated using a principal's public key, the principal (sender) cannot deny that they created and sent the message. If a message is signed using another private key that does not belong to the sender, the validity of the signature fails.

- Any change in the original message will produce a digest value that will be different from the value obtained after decrypting the signature using the sender's public key.

- Before applying any signature algorithm, the data is compressed to a short fixed-length string. In XML SIGNATURE, digest algorithms are used twice: one is used to digest data to be signed indirectly, and the other digest algorithm is used to digest the canonical form of the `SignedInfo` element.

- Any change in the data that was indirectly signed will produce another digest that will invalidate the signature.

- The available algorithms that can be used for digital signatures do not require a lot of computational power and do not take large amounts of time.

- We can sign different parts of a message with different signatures. This allows a set of principals to write portions of one document and sign them individually.

- An XML signature is an XML element that is embedded in the message. The XML signature is composed of several XML elements that include information such as the value of the signature, the key that will be used to verify the signature, and algorithms used to compute the signature. This standard format helps XML parsers to better understand signature elements during the validation process.

- This pattern also supports message authentication codes (MAC). Both signatures and MACs are syntactically identical: the difference between them is that signatures use public key cryptography, while MACs uses a shared common key.

- The data being signed is pointed by its URI, so elements within XML messages and external network resources can be located using their identifiers.

- `SignedInfo` is the element that is actually signed. It includes the references that point the data being signed, along with their digest values and algorithm identifiers. Thus the XML signature also protects the algorithm identifiers from modification.

- XML SIGNATURE uses canonicalization algorithms to ensure that different representations of XML are transformed into a standard format before applying any signature algorithm.

- XML documents are self-describing; the sender and receiver don't need to agree in advance on the algorithms to be used.

The pattern also has the following potential liabilities:

- We need a well-established public key infrastructure that can provide reliable public keys. Certificates issued by a certification authority are the usual way to obtain this [Sta06]. There is a public key standard for XML that should be used.

- Users must properly implement the signature protocol.

- There may be attacks against specific algorithms or implementations [dig]. These are difficult to use against careful implementations of this pattern.

- Even using efficient algorithms, signing and verifying XML messages may create a significant overhead.

The pattern does not describe the complete standard. For example, details of transforms and key values have been left out for simplicity [W3C08].

Known Uses

Several vendors have developed tools that support XML SIGNATURE:

- IBM DataPower XS40 XML Security Gateway [IBM05] parses, filters, validates schema, decrypts, verifies signatures, signs and encrypts XML message flows.

- Xtradyne's WS-DBC [Xtr]. The Web Services Domain Boundary Controller is an XML firewall that provides protection against malformed messages and malicious content, XML encryption, XML signature, as well as authentication, authorization and audit.

- Forum Sentry SOA Gateway [For] conforms to XML Digital Signature, XML Encryption, WS-Trust, WS-Policy and other standards.

- Microsoft .NET [Mic07] includes APIs that support the creation and verification of XML digital signatures.

- Java XML Digital Signature API [Mul07] allows XML signatures to be generated and validated.

See Also

- This pattern is a specialization of the DIGITAL SIGNATURE WITH HASHING pattern (page 301).

- The WS-SECURITY pattern (below) is a standard for securing XML messages using XML SIGNATURE, XML ENCRYPTION and security tokens.

The following specifications are related to XML SIGNATURE, but they have not been expressed as patterns:

- The XML Key Management Specification (XKMS) [W3C01] specifies the distribution and registration of public keys, which works together with XML SIGNATURE.

- The WS-Security Policy [OAS07] standard describes how to express security policies, such as what algorithms are supported by a web service, or what parts of an incoming message need to be signed or encrypted.

12.7 WS-Security

The WS-Security standard [OAS07]describes how to embed existing security mechanisms such as XML Encryption [W3C02], XML Digital Signature [W3C08] and security tokens into SOAP messages in order to provide message confidentiality, integrity, authentication and non-repudiation.

Context

Users of web services sending and receiving SOAP messages through insecure channels such as the Internet.

Problem

Sending messages through insecure channels exposes the messages to a variety of attacks, including illegal reading, modification or replay, and the sender can deny having sent a specific message [Sta06]. We have cryptographic solutions for these problems; however, there are many algorithms and protocols and we need to make a selection self-descriptive.

The solution to this problem must resolve the following forces:

- *Interoperability.* We need a common format in SOAP messages in order to add security features, so both senders and receivers can process messages that contain security features without the need for previous agreements.

- *Fine degree of protection.* SOAP messages may travel through many intermediaries in a network environment, and different users may need access to different parts of them. We may need to protect different parts of a message in different ways.

Solution

Define areas in the message format with parameters that specify security mechanisms such as encryption, digital signatures and security tokens.

A SOAP message is composed of a body and an optional header. Three major elements can be embedded within the header of a message: XML encryption, XML signature and security tokens. If an element within the message is signed, the header can include information about the signature, such as the algorithm, the key and the value of the signature. For XML encryption, the security header can enclose a list of references that point to the parts of the message that have been encrypted, and describe how they were encrypted.

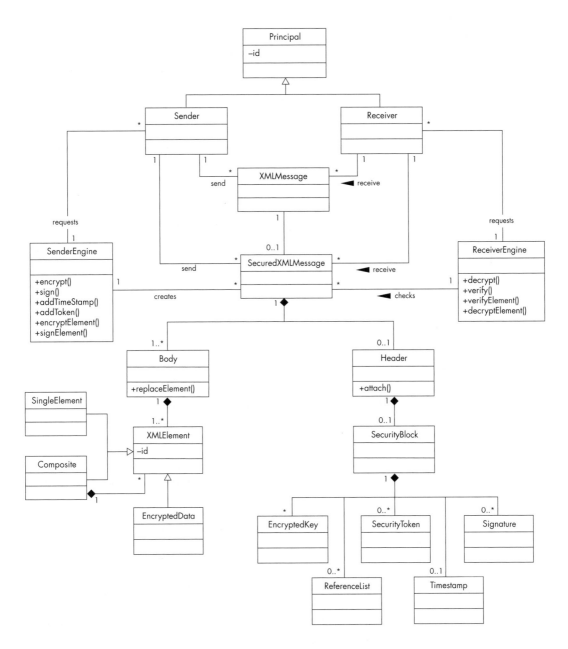

Figure 12.17: Class diagram for the WS-SECURITY pattern

Structure

Figure 12.17 shows the class diagram for this pattern. A `Principal` may be a system, a user or an organization that sends and receives `XMLMessages`. This principal may have the roles of `Sender` and `Receiver`. The `SenderEngine` includes a `Sender` and an `Encryptor`, while the `ReceiverEngine` includes a `Verifier` and a `Decryptor`[1]. `SecurityTokens` such as username/password, X.509 certificates and Kerberos tickets are used for authentication and authorization purposes.

    `XMLMessages` are composed of a `Body` and an optional `Header`. A `Header` may contain a `SecurityBlock`, which may enclose `Timestamp`, `EncryptedKey`, `ReferenceList`, `SignedElement` and `SecurityToken` elements. `Timestamps` provide the time of creation and expiration of a message. `EncryptedKey` element represents the key used to encrypt parts or the entire message, and this key is encrypted according to the XML encryption standard. The `ReferenceList` element points to the parts of the message that are encrypted with XML encryption. The `SignedElement`[2] holds information about the signatures generated according to XML Signature standard. The `Body` is a collection of `XMLElements`, some of which are `EncryptedData` elements. Elements can be structured into Composite pattern hierarchies [Gam94].

Dynamics

We describe the dynamic aspects of the WS-Security standard using sequence diagrams for the use cases 'Encrypt an element using an encrypted key' and 'Sign an element using a security token'.

Use Case: Encrypt an Element using an Encrypted Key – Figure 12.19

Summary	A `Sender` encrypts an element using a symmetric key that is itself encrypted using a security token.
Actors	A `Sender`.
Precondition	The `Sender` has a symmetric key for this communication.
Description	1 A `Sender` requests the `EncryptorEngine` to encrypt an XML element.
	2 The `Encryptor` encrypts the XML element using the symmetric key and the encryption method provided by the `Sender`.
	3 The `Encryptor` creates the `SecureXMLMessage` that will contain the encrypted element.
	4 The `Encryptor` replaces the plain XML element with the output from step 2.
	5 The `Encryptor` sends the `SecuredXMLMessage` to the `Sender`, which can now sent it to some receiver.
Postcondition	The encrypted element is attached to the message.

---

[1] These classes are not shown in Figure 12.17.

[2] Not shown in Figure 12.17.

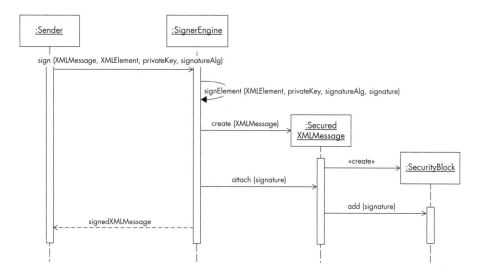

Figure 12.18: Sequence diagram for the use case 'Sign an element using a security token'

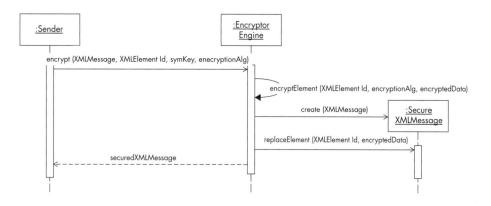

Figure 12.19: Sequence diagram for the use case
'Encrypt an element using an encrypted key'

Use Case: Sign an Element using a Security Token – Figure 12.18

Summary   A Sender signs an element in a message.

Actors   A Sender.

Precondition   The Sender has a private key in some PKI system.

Description   1   A Sender requests the Signer to sign an XML element.

     2 The `Signer` signs the XML element using the `Sender`'s private key and the signature algorithm provided by the `Sender`.

     3 The `Signer` creates the `SecuredXMLMessage` that will contain the digital signature.

     4 The `Signer` attaches the signature to the `SecurityBlock`.

     5 The `Signer` sends the `SecureXMLMessage` to the `Sender`.

Postcondition   The signature has been attached to the header of the message.

Implementation

To implement the WS-Security standard, the following aspects are required:

- Clients need to have knowledge of cryptographic algorithms, such as security token formats, signature formats and encryption technologies.

- A message can have multiple headers if they are targeted for different recipients. In other words, message security information targeted to different recipients must be in different headers.

Consequences

The WS-SECURITY pattern offers the following benefits:

- Using the header of a SOAP message, we can specify the security features of a message, such as XML encryption, XML signatures and security tokens.

- We can specify different parts of a message with different types of encryption, different keys or different signatures.

The pattern also has the following potential liabilities:

- The pattern does not describe details of encryption, digital signatures or security tokens: these require separate standards.

- WS-Security does not tell you whether you should sign or encrypt a whole message, a part of it, or only the header. It is up to the designer to define these aspects.

- WS-Security is an immature specification that is still changing.

Known Uses

Several vendors have developed products that support WS-SECURITY:

- Xtradyne's Web Service Domain Boundary Controller (WS-DBC) [Xtr] is an XML firewall that supports the WS-Security standard and other standards.

- IONA's Artix iSF Security Framework [ION] implements most of the web services standards, including WS-Security.

- Forum Sentry SOA Gateway [For] conforms to XML Digital Signature, XML Encryption, WS-Trust, WS-Policy and other standards.

See Also

- The DIGITAL SIGNATURE WITH HASHING (page 301) and XML ENCRYPTION patterns (page 309) provide message security for the WS-Security standard.
- Secure Channel is a way to transport messages providing message authentication, message confidentiality and message integrity [Bra00], and is the generalization of WS-SECURITY.
- WS-SECURITY uses WS-POLICY (page 263) for policy specification.
- As shown in Figure 12.1 (page 287), WS-Federation, WS-TRUST and WS-Secure Conversation use WS-SECURITY for secure token transport.
- SAML uses WS-SECURITY for security assertion transport.

CHAPTER

13

Patterns for Secure Middleware

Medio tutissimus ibis. (You will be safest in the middle.)

Ovid

The most perfect political community is one in which the middle class is in control, and outnumbers both of the other classes.

Aristotle

13.1   Introduction

Middleware typically includes a set of functions that provide services to applications, including distributed aspects such as brokering, as well as specific services such as blackboards, pipes and filters, adapters and others. Middleware may also include global services such as authentication, authorization and other services. These services can support development of applications or their execution. There is a great deal of pattern-ori-

337

ented advice on how to build distributed systems, for example [Bus96] [Bus07] [Cra95], [Kir04] [Sch00b]. There is also a great deal of experience with securing distributed systems, for example [And08] [Dem04] [Kau02]. However, much of the experience gained in securing distributed systems has not worked its way back into design patterns. In [Fer07b] we showed how to add security to middleware patterns; we describe here specific patterns obtained using this approach.

Figure 13.1 shows the patterns discussed in this chapter. The SECURE THREE-TIER AR-CHITECTURE pattern typically organizes the structure of middleware systems. Three-tier systems frequently implement a SECURE MODEL-VIEW-CONTROLLER pattern. Distribution is organized using a SECURE BROKER, which is implemented as part of a SECURE EN-TERPRISE SERVICE BUS (ESB), and may also use a SECURE DISTRIBUTED PUBLISH/SUBSCRIBE pattern. Other frequently used middleware patterns include SECURE BLACK-BOARD, SECURE PIPES AND FILTERS and SECURE ADAPTER. The objectives of these patterns are:

- *SECURE BROKER* [Mor06b] extends the Broker pattern [Bus96] to provide secure interactions between distributed components.

- *SECURE PIPES AND FILTERS* [Fer09a] provides secure handling of data streams. Each processing step applies some data transformation or filtering. The rights to apply specific transformations to the data can be controlled. The communication of data between stages can be also protected, and the operations applied can be logged.

- *SECURE BLACKBOARD* [Ort08] provides secure handling of data when its blackboard is accessed by a set of knowledge sources. Each knowledge source reads data from the blackboard, applies some processing or data transformation, and updates the blackboard. To prevent violations of integrity and confidentiality, the rights to reading and updating data are controlled according to their predefined rights, and their actions are logged. The sources are authenticated before being allowed to access the blackboard.

- *SECURE ADAPTER* [Fer09b] converts the interface of an existing class into a more convenient interface. Both adapter and adaptee are secured.

- *SECURE THREE-TIER ARCHITECTURE* [Fer08d] extends the Three-Tier Architecture pattern by enforcing a global view of security for all three layers. In the presentation part of the system, security aspects dealing with user interaction are enforced; in the business logic, global security constraints are applied; the data storage applies policies to constrain access of users to data.

- *SECURE ENTERPRISE SERVICE BUS* [Fer11b] provides a convenient infrastructure to integrate a variety of distributed services and related components in a simple and secure way.

- *SECURE DISTRIBUTED PUBLISH/SUBSCRIBE* [Fer12e] decouples the publishers of events from those interested in the events (subscribers). Subscription and publishing are performed securely.

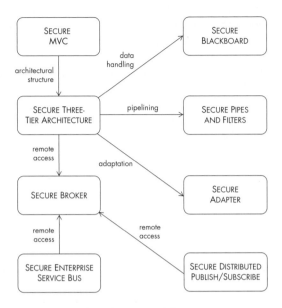

Figure 13.1: Secure middleware patterns

- *SECURE MODEL-VIEW-CONTROLLER* [Del12] adds security to the interactions of users with systems configured using the MVC (Model-View-Controller) pattern.

13.2   Secure Broker

The SECURE BROKER pattern extends the Broker pattern to provide secure interactions between distributed components.

Example

An organization uses an electronic messaging system such as conferencing software, chat or instant messaging. A group within the organization wants to arrange for private communications within the group. Members of the group should be able to exchange messages with each other that are not made known to the organization at large. Members have a variety of devices (laptops, smart phones) that run the organization's messaging client.

Context

Distributed computing systems, homogeneous or heterogeneous, with independent cooperating components that must be secured.

The Broker architectural pattern can be used to structure distributed software systems with decoupled components that interact by remote service invocations. A broker component is responsible for coordinating communication, such as forwarding requests, as well as for transmitting results and exceptions [Bus96].

Proxies insulate their callers, client and server, from the implementation details of communications. The Bridge class implements a similar concept for communications between brokers. There are two basic use cases for Broker, illustrating its role in structuring transparent communications between clients and servers: server registration and client requests service; see [Bus96] for details.

Problem

In addition to the liabilities of the broker [Bus96], security threats add a new set of problems. How can we secure the broker's activities?

The threats affecting the pattern include:

- *Illegal access*. Clients' access to servers may need to be restricted, and servers' access to clients may need to be restricted, for compliance and application semantics purposes.

- *Message interception or replaying*. An attacker may intercept the messages from client to server and read or modify them. Message replaying is another possibility.

- *Spoofing (forgery)*. If a rogue server can portray itself as valid to the broker, it can appear to service client requests while also compromising client data, or perform a wide variety of other attacks on unsuspecting clients. Likewise, if a rogue broker can portray itself as valid to servers and clients, it can do harm by recording traffic between clients and servers, substituting other clients and servers for valid ones, and so on. And if a client can forge its identity to a broker, it can access services for which it does not have rights. There are a wide variety of attacks based on forgery: redirection of traffic from official sites to forged sites; spamming while masking the source's destination; cache poisoning, in which invalid entries are stored in the broker's repository; and routing attacks, in which traffic intended for one destination is sent to another [NTC01].

- *Denial of service*. Valid entries in the repository could be removed, and they will not be accessible. And with access to the broker's server repository, DoS attacks can be launched against member servers. By limiting the server's abilities to respond to requests, clients can be disabled [Kau02].

Solution

In addition to the Broker pattern's role in decoupling communications from applications, a secure broker must introduce mutual authentication between servers and clients. It must also provide authorization and a reference monitor to control access to resources, and cryptographic controls to prevent message attacks.

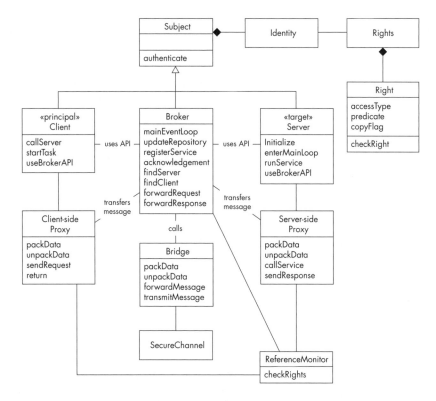

Figure 13.2: Class diagram for the SECURE BROKER pattern

Structure

Figure 13.2 shows the class diagram for the SECURE BROKER pattern. Subject is a role that can be taken by the Broker, Client (a principal), and Server. Its function is to provide identity to components participating in communication, and to allow components to authenticate each other. Identity management and creation is beyond the scope of this description, but it must be sufficient to uniquely identify components in the universe of possible interactions.

The ReferenceMonitor authorizes participant requests. It is responsible for allowing and denying service requests based on the identity of the requester and the prevailing set of rights. Rights structure and configuration are discussed in Chapter 6.

SecureChannel is responsible for encrypting traffic between components that may travel over secure links that are not limited to trusted components.

Dynamics

A secure broker implements or supports the use cases 'Subject creation', 'Registration' and 'Secure service request'. Each client and server wishing to participate in secured communications must be assigned identity and rights.

- *Subject creation.* In contrast to the Broker pattern, where it is assumed that the broker can be trusted, servers, clients and brokers, in their roles as principals, must be assigned identities and credentials in order to safeguard access. Therefore, we need a preliminary use case for each principal (subject), 'Subject creation', incorporating identity and rights assignment. This use case is straightforward and requires a security administrator to assign rights to a new subject according to predefined policies (see Chapter 6).

- *Secure registration.* Registration is similar to the standard sequences in [Bus96], except that mutual authentication must be done before registration.

Use Case: Secure Service Request – Figure 13.3

Given that the participating `Client`, `Server` and `Broker` have been previously authenticated and assigned credentials, service requests flow as indicated in the sequence diagram of Figure 13.3.

A `Client` makes a request indicating its ID and its rights. The `Client-SideProxy` marshals and forwards the request to the `Broker`. The `Broker` checks the rights of the `Client` to perform this operation on the servant object[1], finds the `Server`, and routes the request to the `Server-SideProxy`. The proxy unpacks the data, may check rights (in addition or instead of the `Broker`) and performs the service. The response is sent as in a standard Broker implementation. (The figure does not show the encryption operations.)

Implementation

CORBA

In order to show a specific set of defenses, we choose an example Broker implementation, the Common Object Request Broker (CORBA), to see how transactions are secured. To do this requires some introduction to CORBA's security architecture.

CORBA security explicitly defines the threats it is designed to address:

Threat 1 An authorized user of the system gaining access to information that should be hidden from them.

Threat 2 A user masquerading as someone else, directly or through delegation.

Threat 3 Security controls being bypassed.

Threat 4 Eavesdropping on a communication line.

Threat 5 Tampering with communication.

Threat 6 Lack of accountability, due, for example, to inadequate identification of users [NTC01].

---

[1] The object within the Server that provides the specific service requested.

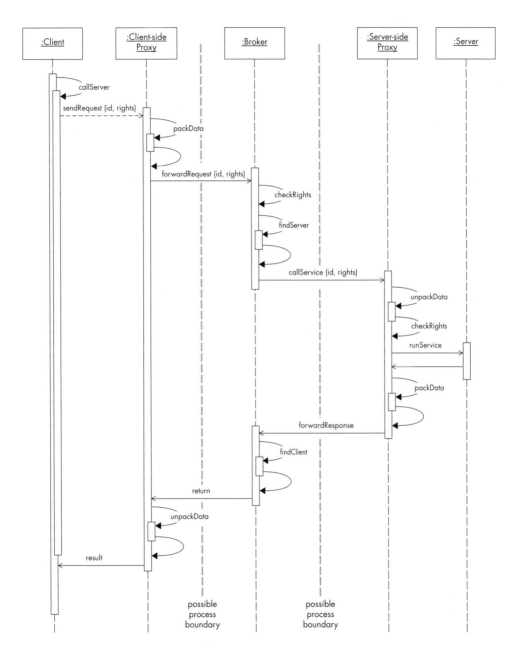

Figure 13.3: Sequence diagram for the use case 'Secure service request'

This architecture can be mapped to Broker's defenses in the following way:

- *Threats 1, 2, 3.* Protect clients from illegitimate servers and brokers.
- *Threats 1, 2, 3.* Protect servers from illegitimate clients and brokers.
- *Threats 1, 2, 3.* Protect brokers from illegitimate clients and servers.
- *Threats 4 and 5.* Allow for securing communications between clients and servers.

CORBA, in its Security Service, approaches securing transactions by treating clients, servers and Brokers as *principals*, which are 'a human user or system entity that is registered in and authenticated to the system' [NTC01]. The distinguishing characteristic of a principal is its identity. There are several consequences of identity: it makes the principal accountable for its actions; it identifies the originator of a message; it identifies whom to charge for use of a system; and it allows access control/rights management to be defined. Principals may be granted *security attributes* (rights). These attributes are used to determine access control for objects within the system. An object's collection of security attributes is known as its *credentials* (see Chapter 5). Authorization is implemented between principals and objects through *security context* objects, which carry the identity and credential information necessary to determine the calling principal's rights for the called object.

The *principal authenticator* interface provides facilities for generating sets of credentials and for generating security contexts, given a principal, an object and an access request. An object implementing the principal authenticator (called 'vault' in the CORBA architecture) accepts a principal's identity as an argument and authenticates that principal, returning its set of credentials (Figure 13.4). Access decision objects are responsible for binary (yes/no) access decisions, based on the applicable principal, object and security context. When a client makes a request of a server, both client and server proxies submit the request for evaluation according to security policies through these access decision objects (Figure 13.5). Note that no checking is done by the CORBA Broker; CORBA assumes that the proxies can be trusted.

.NET Remoting

.NET Remoting implements HTTP and TCP transport mechanisms ('channels'). The .NET Remoting security architecture does not enumerate specific threats; rather, it provides a generic set of tools for authentication, authorization and confidentiality that must be adapted in an application's context. These tools, implemented through the GSS-API, include credentials to identify clients and servers, contexts in which these credentials are valid, and provisions for encrypted transport [MS04A].

Microsoft has illustrated how to use .NET Remoting to implement the Broker pattern [MS03A]. In considering .NET Remoting security, and how to apply it to the SECURE BROKER pattern, we look to the GSS-API [RFC2743] for guidance.

Follow the steps for Broker [Bus96], but amend them in the following ways:

1   Include identity and rights in the object model. Ensure that all participants are assigned identity, that they are authenticated in order to participate, and that rights are checked before requests are granted.

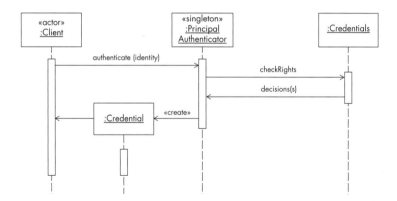

Figure 13.4: Subject authentication in CORBA

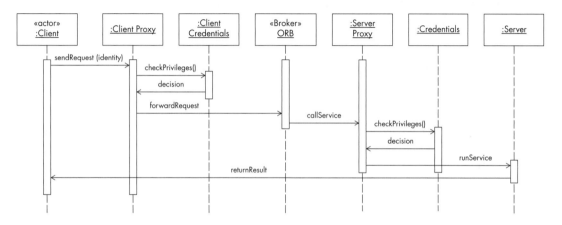

Figure 13.5: Secure object invocation in CORBA

2   Implement a reference monitor to check authorization.

3   Implement the Secure Channel pattern [Bra00] to protect message traffic.

Therefore, in addition to the broker role in decoupling communications from applications, a SECURE BROKER must:

■   Protect clients from illegitimate servers and brokers.

■   Protect servers from illegitimate clients and brokers.

■   Protect brokers from illegitimate clients and servers.

■   Allow for securing communications between its clients and servers.

Example Resolved

In the messaging example, each group member participating in the conversation is issued an identity for the system, together with rights to chat with other members of the group. The messaging server is also assigned an identity, together with rights permitting each member of the group to send messages to other members of the group. As client proxies send messages to the server, each message is checked by the server's reference monitor (and possibly the server-proxy's reference monitor, depending on the configuration and security requirements). Eligible messages from authenticated participants are relayed. As some of the group members communicate over public lines, Secure Channel [Bra00] is set in operation for these links, to ensure message confidentiality.

Consequences

The SECURE BROKER pattern offers the following benefits:

- *Illegal access.* Based on authentication, access control can be implemented, enabling restrictions on the use of privileged information and functionality.

- *Message interception.* Encryption can handle all these problems (see Chapter 12).

- *Forgery.* By requiring authentication of each broker, client and server, trust can be established between transaction participants.

- *Denial of service.* Authentication and access control prevent removal of valid entries. With control of access to the broker's server repository, DoS attacks cannot be launched against member servers.

The pattern also has the following potential liabilities:

- Extra overhead.

- Added complexity.

Known Uses

The CORBA Security Service, Microsoft .NET Remoting and the World Wide Web implement at least some aspects of the pattern described here.

See Also

- [Bus96] defined the Broker pattern. [Fer01a] provides a language that addresses the relationship between authentication and rights management. [Fer03c] shows authentication and rights management in a distributed context.

- AUTHENTICATOR (page 52), AUTHORIZATION (page 74).

- A revised version of Broker, Broker Revisited, is described in [Kir04]. Our security extensions apply also to this pattern.

- The Secure Channel pattern provides cryptographically-protected communications [Bra00].

13.3 Secure Pipes and Filters

The SECURE PIPES AND FILTERS pattern describes how to provide secure handling of data streams. Each processing step applies some data transformation or filtering. The rights to apply specific transformations to the data can be controlled. The communication of data between stages can be also protected. The operations applied can be logged.

Example

ArtisticRenderings is a company that prepares brochures and reports for marketing real estate, stocks and all kind of products. To prepare each brochure needs a product specialist, a graphic designer and an artist. To insert information from databases, for example sales statistics, we need some IT people. The whole process is under the control of a supervisor. Each person has their own interface, and once they complete their jobs, their inputs will be applied in sequence to the stream of documents. However, some documents are sensitive and we need to control who makes the changes, or a disgruntled employee might introduce incorrect contents.

Context

Consider Pipes and Filters software or other processing systems which are used to process data streams. Some of them may be parallel, attempting to improve the process performance. The execution platform for this kind of system is frequently a distributed one, whose components may require a certain level of security for processing the stream of data. *Parallel* here means that several components (whether human or automatic) act simultaneously. Even a human Pipes and Filters pattern aims to improve performance. In this case we don't have significant performance improvements, but this architecture may be valuable for flexibility reasons, or to have a systematic, well-structured process.

Problem

The essence of the Pipes and Filters pattern is that every time data reaches a different stage, different functions are applied on it, and in a secure version these actions should be controlled. In this kind of system, we may also need the flexibility to reorder the steps of the process or change the processing steps. In the example above, a new person may be assigned to the workflow to perform additional functions on the documents, which may require adding an extra step. How can we control the actions to be performed in a data pipeline and provide security for the pipeline activities? Additionally, the data may be moved along the pipeline using insecure channels, and the users defining the data transformations may be remote.

The solution to this problem must resolve the following forces:

- *Stage control*. The system may need to control, at each stage of processing, who can do what (what operations can be applied) with the data in the pipeline. This may be necessary in both automatic and interactive pipelines, otherwise employees might introduce illegal content or filter out wanted information.

- *Authenticity*. We might require the data or the message carrying it to be authenticated before it is accepted by the next or the previous stage, otherwise an imposter might send data to be processed.

- *Message protection*. Before sending data in the pipes we may need to hide it to prevent eavesdropping. We may also need to verify the authenticity of messages.

- *Reconfiguration control*. Due to regulatory constraints, work changes, or efficiency, some documents may need extra stages, or to skip stages. We need to be able to reconfigure the number or order of the steps. This reconfiguration should be controlled, or a user might skip necessary stages or add unintended stages.

- *Recording*. We should keep track of any actions applied to the data in cases where legal documents or regulatory compliance is involved.

- *Transparency*. The security controls should be transparent to the users of the pipeline.

- *Overhead*. The security controls should not affect performance significantly.

Solution

The SECURE PIPES AND FILTERS pattern provides a secure way to process data in different stages or steps, by adding basic security mechanisms (as instances of security patterns) to each of them to provide authentication, authorization, information hiding and logging. Because the functions to be performed at each stage depend on people doing specific tasks, we use a Role-Based Access Control (RBAC) model [Fer01a] to describe their required rights. An RBAC model assigns rights to roles to access data or resources in specific ways. Individual users may belong to one or more roles.

Structure

We apply an RBAC pattern to control access to stages. In this model, users are members of `Roles` and `Rights` are assigned to roles. A `Right` defines the access type that can be applied by a `Role` to a protection object. Pattern instances corresponding to security mechanisms have been added to the Pipes and Filters pattern in Figure 13.6. Since we are considering a set of stages the pattern is made clearer by showing an object diagram (describing three typical stages) rather than a class diagram. The subsystems named `Authenticator` are instances of the AUTHENTICATOR pattern, and allow each `Filter` to authenticate the sender of the data it is receiving. `Log` indicates instances of the SECURITY LOGGER AND AUDITOR pattern, used to keep track of any accesses to the data.

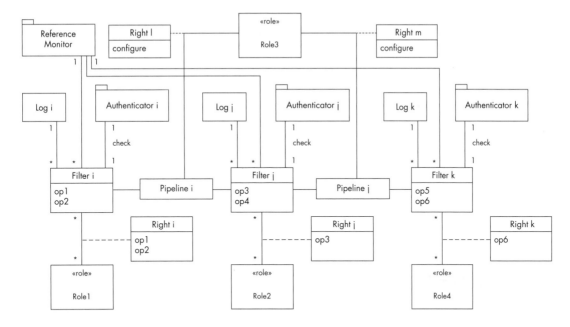

Figure 13.6: Object diagram for the SECURE PIPES AND FILTERS pattern

Objects with the stereotype <<role>> and `Right` are instances of the ROLE-BASED AC-CESS CONTROL pattern. For example, `Role1` has the right to apply operations `op1` and `op2` to the data in `Filter i`. The ReferenceMonitor subsystem indicates the enforcement of the authorization rights defined by the RBAC instances. We show the `ReferenceMonitor` as a shared resource and the `Authenticators` as individual for each stage; their actual distribution depends on the distribution architecture of the complete system. In order to control the reconfiguration of the stages, the ROLE-BASED ACCESS CONTROL pattern is also applied to the pipeline structure, so that only someone with an administrator role (`Role3`) can perform any changes to it.

Dynamics

Figure 13.7 shows the use case in which a subject with a specific role tries to execute an operation, op3, on a document. The `ReferenceMonitor` checks whether its role allows the operation, and if true, reads data from the input pipe, `Pipe i`, to the filter where op3 is applied. After the operation the data is moved to the next pipe, `Pipe j`.

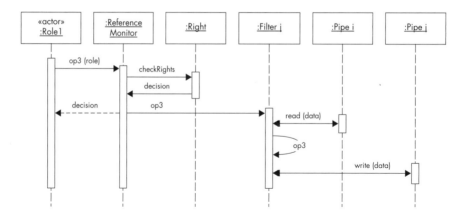

Figure 13.7: Sequence diagram for the use case 'Apply an operation on a data stream'

Implementation

We follow the steps suggested in [Bus96] and indicate where security is needed:

1 *Divide the application into a sequence of stages.* Who should have access to which operations or results from each stage should be defined in the conceptual model. When the application is divided into stages we need to define how the rights in the complete model are reflected in each stage.

2 *Define the data format to be passed along each pipe.* This aspect has no effect on security.

3 *Perform threat enumeration (see Chapter 3) and risk analysis.* This is necessary to decide about what security mechanisms to add in each stage.

4 *Decide how to implement each pipe connection.* Aspects such as active or passive components, or push or pull movement of data are defined at this point. We have to decide whether to use authentication between filters, and if we do, what type of authentication. For communications within the same physical building, filter authentication may not be required, although user authentication to the system is always needed.

5 *Design and implement the filters.* Each filter enforces the rights defined in the first implementation step, and must have a reference monitor and a means to access the authorization rules. In distributed systems one needs to decide where these rules should be stored. Filters also implement logging, as well as encryption and decryption.

6 *Design error handling.* From the security side this implies handling security violations. This handling is application-dependent and no general policy is possible.

7 *Set up the processing pipeline.* The initial configuration, as well as changes to the configuration, must be restricted only to administrators.

We can apply the principle of *defense in depth*, defining a coherent set of security mechanisms that provide a secure core for this application. In some cases, specific mechanisms can be left out, being careful about security consistency; for example, authorization requires authentication. In other cases, more security controls may be needed to prevent, for example, conflicts of interest.

The ROLE-BASED ACCESS CONTROL pattern (page 78) provides the option of abstracting different roles within the data flow. It may be that we need to work with individual subjects instead of roles; in this case implementing the AUTHORIZATION pattern (page 74) should be a better approach. The link between stages could be subject to attacks, and optional operations of encryption and decryption could be implemented in each filter, as well as digital signatures in each data message (not shown in Figure 13.6).

Example Resolved

We implemented the ROLE-BASED ACCESS CONTROL pattern in the pipes and filters of the example. Now people making changes to documents need to be authorized before they can do so. The operations they can apply depend on their roles with respect to the application. Logging protects the company in case they need to show that they comply with regulations, and they can track who made a specific change to a given document. Authentication is needed to apply authorization, and maybe also between stages if necessary.

Consequences

The SECURE PIPES AND FILTERS pattern offers the following benefits:

■ *Access control.* We can assign privileges according to the functions needed at each stage of processing and the roles of those performing the functions. The use of operations over the data can be restricted according to the rules of either role-based access control or access matrix models.

■ *Authenticity.* Each filter stage can authenticate its users before they are authorized to perform specific functions, and can authenticate the filter sending data to it. Authentication is necessary if we apply authorization at each filter.

■ *Message protection.* The use of encryption between stages is possible, adding the possibilities of secure messages (preventing eavesdropping) and digital signatures (to confirm the origin of a message).

■ *Controlled reconfiguration.* The administrator role can control the reconfiguration of stages to accommodate changes in the process.

■ *Recording.* Logging can be performed at each stage to keep track of any accesses and changes to the data. This allows us to prove that we have followed any regulations: we can prosecute illegal actions, and we can improve the system if it failed to prevent an attack.

■ *Transparency.* The security restrictions are transparent to the users provided that they do not attempt illegal actions.

The pattern also has the following potential liabilities:

■ The general performance of the system worsens due to the overhead of the security checks. With careful implementations of these functions, the loss in performance should be small. For example, encryption/decryption takes time and should be used only when needed; access control to the filters happens only when a new type of data is being analyzed. In parallel pipelines the performance loss can be further reduced by performing some security functions in parallel with normal functions.

■ The system is more complex, due to the extra services that have been added.

Known Uses

■ Microsoft's BizTalk Server 2004 [Biz04] can implement the Pipes and Filters pattern. In addition to security features that are provided by the transport, such as encryption when using HTTPS, BizTalk Server 2004 provides security at the message level. It can receive decrypted messages and validate digital signatures that are attached to these messages. Similarly, it can encrypt messages and attach digital signatures to messages before sending them.

■ Apache Cocoon [Coc07] is a web development framework using components. It can be used to build XML pipelines in which security restrictions can be added.

■ The tax offices of some countries implement a human pipeline to process tax returns. Workers may check different aspects of a tax return either manually or using computers, and need to be authorized to do this.

■ [Ten05] discusses the use of XML pipelines for document preparation, including stages for adding content, formatting and personalization. What is done at each stage can be controlled.

■ Pipelines are common for data reduction when large volumes of data must be handled. [Sco05] discusses a data reduction pipeline for spectroscopic data, in which different transformations by different researchers are applied at each stage. What is done at each stage is controlled according to the functions of the researchers.

■ A cloud-based secure pipeline for document processing and management is discussed in [Joo11].

See Also

■ [Bus96] and [Mica] present the basic Pipes and Filters pattern, without security controls.

- The AUTHORIZATION (page 74), ROLE-BASED ACCESS CONTROL (page 78) and AUTHENTICATOR (page 52) patterns can be used to secure the stages.
- The Secure Channel pattern can be used to secure the communications channels ([Bra00] and Chapter 12).
- The SECURITY LOGGER AND AUDITOR pattern is described on page 111.

13.4 Secure Blackboard

The SECURE BLACKBOARD pattern describes how to provide secure handling of data when its blackboard is accessed by knowledge sources. Each knowledge source reads data from the blackboard, applies some processing or data transformation, and updates the blackboard. In order to prevent violations of integrity and confidentiality, the rights to reading and updating data are controlled according to their predefined rights, and their actions are logged. The sources are authenticated before being allowed to access the blackboard.

Example

Suppose we are developing an application for a law firm [Fer07c]. The conduction of a case requires inputs from many data sources: lawyers, witnesses, defendants and so on. Court appearances are scheduled according to court and lawyer availability. All this makes the sequence of actions unpredictable. A blackboard is used to conduct a case, where immediate results of court appearances and case strategy are kept for analysis and updating by lawyers. The data handled is very sensitive and access to it needs to be controlled. If we are not careful, we might end up with invalid data, or data will leak to our opponent, which will damage our chances of winning the case.

Context

A blackboard system is used to receive and modify information about a problem in progress from several data sources. The execution platform for this kind of system is normally distributed, with knowledge sources possibly remote. The data is exchanged between blackboard and knowledge sources in a client/server fashion.

This pattern useful for problems for which no deterministic solution is known. In the Blackboard pattern several specialized subsystems assemble their knowledge to build a possibly partial or approximate solution [Bus96].

The organization of this process has been well defined and converted into patterns: the Blackboard pattern (Figure 13.8), and its parallel counterpart, the Shared Resource pattern [Ort03]. The descriptions provided for these patterns take into consideration only functional properties, such as their potential for improving performance. These patterns have been proposed assuming that all components (blackboard, control, and knowledge sources) 'implicitly trust' each other, and there is no concern about unwanted activity among them. However, many distributed applications (such as those mentioned earlier) require taking security into consideration, since data sources may handle sensitive or valuable data such as personal or business information.

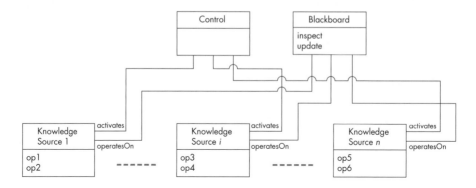

Figure 13.8: Object diagram of the Blackboard pattern

Problem

Usually we want a variety of knowledge sources to solve a difficult problem or conduct a process. Nevertheless, how can we control the actions to be performed in the blackboard so that we provide the required level of security for the system?

The solution to this problem must resolve the following forces:

- *Nondeterminism.* The sequence of activities or operations over data is usually unpredictable. Also, the number of knowledge sources might be hard to predict.

- *Access control.* Blackboard data should only be read or modified by authorized knowledge sources, otherwise users may see or override important information.

- *Authenticity.* It might be necessary to verify that the knowledge sources are authentic, otherwise we might receive false information, or our information could be leaked outside our system. The channels they use must be secure.

- *Controlled reconfiguration.* Due to regulatory constraints, work changes or efficiency, we need to be able to reconfigure the number of knowledge sources or their order of operation. This reconfiguration must be controlled. A faulty reconfiguration could lead to incorrect conclusions, or to the inclusion of inconsistent or erroneous information.

- *Records.* For billing and security purposes, logging the actions at each update of the blackboard may be necessary. This information can be audited later.

- *Transparency.* The security controls should be transparent to the users of the system, or they might not use them.

- *Overhead.* The security controls should not impose a significant overhead on the functions of the system.

Solution

Add security mechanisms to control the threats. The SECURE BLACKBOARD pattern provides a way to access blackboard data from a variety of knowledge sources in a secure way, by adding some basic security mechanisms to the control component (as instances of security patterns), providing authentication (AUTHENTICATOR, page 52), authorization (ROLE-BASED ACCESS CONTROL, page 78) and logging (SECURITY LOGGER AND AUDITOR, page 111) in each access operation.

Structure

Figure 13.9 shows a class diagram of the SECURE BLACKBOARD pattern, in which security pattern instances have been added to the components of the original Blackboard pattern. SecurityLogger indicates an instance of the SECURITY LOGGER AND AUDITOR pattern [Fer11d]. The Reference Monitor associated with the control indicates the enforcement of authorization (page 100). KnowledgeSources can be humans, not just software components. Nevertheless, either automated or human knowledge sources require that their access is authenticated by the Authenticator (page 52) to verify their origin. The sources belong to Roles, according to their functions, and their Rights depend on these Roles.

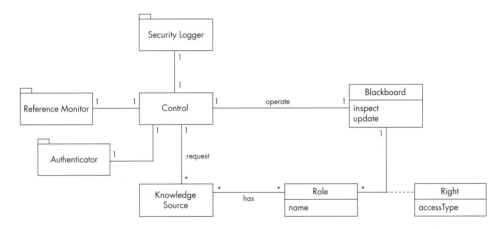

Figure 13.9: Class diagram for the SECURE BLACKBOARD pattern

Dynamics

Figure 13.10 shows a sequence diagram in which a KnowledgeSource (with a specific role) requests an operation on the Blackboard. The Control receives the request and invokes the Authenticator to validate that it originates from a legitimate source. After source validation, the ReferenceMonitor checks whether its role is allowed to use the operation and, if true, it performs the operation on the Blackboard. A SecurityLogger record is created after the operation is performed.

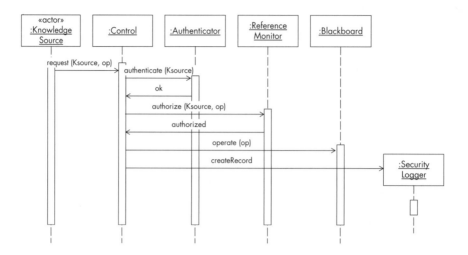

Figure 13.10: Sequence diagram for the use case 'Apply an operation to the Blackboard'

Implementation

[Bus96] list several general implementation aspects. From a security point of view we need to consider the following points:

- The authentication system should be appropriate to the value of the information handled; passwords are enough for most cases.

- Instead of Role-Base Access Control, we could use an access matrix (page 74) or even a multilevel access control model [Gol06], depending on the environment.

- Since the repository and its control are centralized, applying the proposed security functions is relatively simple. Knowledge sources could be remote, and they could require digital signatures in addition to device authentication.

Example Resolved

The law firm now uses a SECURE BLACKBOARD structure to conduct its cases. The case blackboard receives changes for the case documents, which are stored in specific classes. The blackboard can be protected from unauthorized access.

Consequences

The SECURE BLACKBOARD pattern shares the same general benefits of the original Blackboard pattern [Bus96], but adds the following:

- *Nondeterminism*. Knowledge sources can be added or removed dynamically.

- *Access control.* We can define precise role rights; for example, an expert can only add to the information, not change it; a lawyer can decide on the next step, bring new witnesses, but cannot change depositions, and so on. The access control mechanism in the blackboard enforces controlled access to the information.

- *Authenticity.* Authentication services can validate the fact that the data sources are legitimate. The channels can be encrypted.

- *Controlled reconfiguration.* We can control who can reconfigure the knowledge sources

- *Records.* We can log accesses to the blackboard for future auditing.

- *Transparency.* The specific security controls used are transparent to the users of the system.

- *Overhead.* The security controls should not impose a significant overhead on the functions of the system. Blackboard systems are not real-time systems, so the added overhead is easy to accept.

The SECURE BLACKBOARD pattern shares the same liabilities as the original Blackboard pattern [Bus96], and also:

- Even though the implementation of the Blackboard pattern normally requires developing the blackboard, the control and the knowledge sources as simple, loosely connected components, when adding security capabilities a more complex implementation is required. Several software components, such as the reference monitor, the authenticator, the logger, and authorization components should be taken into consideration in order to build the correct functionality.

- The three security mechanisms incorporated in this pattern are not enough to control all possible security threats, and must be complemented with additional mechanisms according to the needs of the application.

Known Uses

- The software system used by many news agencies (such as AP, AFP or Reuters) has a structure similar to the SECURE BLACKBOARD pattern. All information retrieved by reporters and correspondents (articles, editorials, notes, photographs and so on) is gathered into a single blackboard, which at the same time is read by many other news and media enterprises (newspapers, television, radio and so on), who distribute the information. Nevertheless, all the information written to or read from the blackboard should be secure. This means that nobody should be allowed to modify or read the blackboard unless authentication and authorization are applied.

- A Wiki web is also an example of the use of the SECURE BLACKBOARD pattern. In this case the knowledge sources are humans, whose role within the Wiki could be 'reader', 'editor', 'administrator' and so on. The Wiki should function like a blackboard, whose secure use requires that users are always authenticated, and access is controlled according to their roles within the Wiki system.

- Designs for applications that may use this pattern include a travel booking system [Tem], a law firm [Fer07c] and a Java-based knowledge processing and agent programming software framework [Tar02].

- The Reflective Blackboard pattern [Sil02] includes security services.

See Also

- The Blackboard pattern [Bus96] is the basis for this pattern.

- Assignment of knowledge sources can use the Resource Assignment pattern [Fer05h].

- The rights structure can follow an RBAC pattern [Sch06b].

- Authentication is performed by means of instances of the AUTHENTICATOR pattern (page 52).

- Logging can be done using a SECURITY LOGGER AND AUDITOR (page 111) [Fer11d].

13.5 Secure Adapter

Also known as Secure Wrapper

The SECURE ADAPTER pattern describes how to convert the interface of an existing class into a more convenient interface, while preserving the security of the adapted entity.

Example

We have a text message system that sends, receives and manipulates text messages. We want to convert our text messages into XML messages so that we can handle more complex transactions. We purchased an off-the-shelf tool, XmlMessage, which manipulates XML messages. The problem is that these two interfaces are incompatible: XmlMessage expects an XML message, while our text message system does not know how to create an XML message. Our messages are sensitive and we don't want unauthorized people to read or change the adapted data.

Context

A computational environment in which users or processes need to use a class that has an interface that is incompatible with the current class. The old class may have sensitive data.

Problem

The `Adapter` converts the interface of an existing class into a more convenient interface, but its original description does not take in consideration security issues.

To illustrate and identify some possible attacks, consider the following example: we have an interface, `RequestServices`, which is used to request services from various servers. We want to be able to send requests to a JDBC API; however, our interface is incompatible with the JDBC API. We create a `RequestServicesAdapter` that adapts requests to JDBC. For example, a client sends a request for a database connection. The `Request-ServicesAdapter` converts the request to a JDBC request, which in turn returns a response containing the requested data items.

We can identify the following threats in this case:

Threat 1 The database accessed through the JDBC interface could be an imposter, and we could be sending or receiving data from a malicious database.

Threat 2 The client may be an imposter, trying to access the data of an authorized user.

Threat 3 The client making the request may not have permission to send such a request; that is, the client may try to access data to which it is not authorized.

Threat 4 If the client is remote, the data sent and received may be intercepted by intruders.

Solution

After we identify the possible threats to the adapter, we need to define policies and their corresponding mechanisms to stop them:

Threat 1 Authenticate the database.

Threat 2 Authenticate the client.

Threat 3 Control access to the adaptee functions through the adapter.

Threat 4 Add a secure channel between the client and the adapter.

Structure

Figure 13.11 shows a class diagram for the SECURE ADAPTER pattern. We add role-based access control for the clients and a corresponding set of authorization rules. Requests made to the `Adapter` have to be authorized, ensuring that the client has permission to send such requests. The `Adapter` also checks responses returned by the `Adaptee`. For example, when a client requests a database connection, the `Adapter` authenticates the database identity returned in the response from the `Adaptee`. (The secure channel is not shown in the figure.)

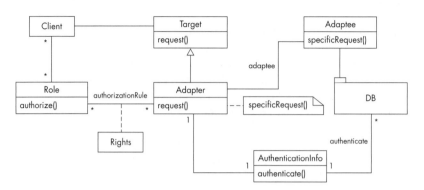

Figure 13.11: Class diagram of the SECURE ADAPTER pattern

Dynamics

Figure 13.12 shows a sequence diagram for the use case 'Request data via the secure adapter'. The client sends a request to the `Target`. The request is captured by the `Adapter`, which is responsible for authorizing the `Client`. Once the `Client`'s permission is verified, the `Adapter` converts the request to a specific request. The `Adaptee` fulfills the request and sends a response back to the `Adapter`. At this point the `Adapter` needs to make sure that the identity of the subject in the response is not an imposter. After authenticating the response subject, the `Adapter` sends the response to the `Client`.

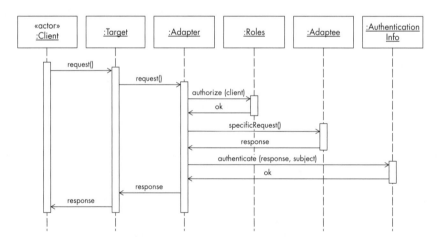

Figure 13.12: Sequence diagram for the use case 'Request data via the Secure Adapter'

Example Resolved

We can create an adapter class, `Message`, which receives all requests to create XML messages and returns XML messages. The text message is structured in a certain format; for example, sender's ID, location, name, message and so forth. We use this format to create the XML message.

Consequences

We can stop the threats identified on page 359 as follows:

■ *Threat 1.* The database can be authenticated.
■ *Threat 2.* The client can be authenticated.
■ *Threat 3.* We can apply authorization to user requests.
■ *Threat 4.* We can use cryptography to avoid attacks to the messages used in these interactions.

Known Uses

■ CORBA-based systems use adaptors to adapt a remote request to the servant object [Sch00b]. The adaptor also applies authorization constraints.
■ Microkernels use adaptors to adapt process requests that might have different formats [Bus96]. This makes the microkernel more reusable. In some implementations the adaptor applies authorization restrictions.

See Also

■ ROLE-BASED ACCESS CONTROL (page 78). This pattern assigns rights to people based on their functions or tasks by assigning people to roles and giving rights to these roles.
■ AUTHENTICATOR (page 52). This pattern allows us to verify that a subject is who they say they are, by using a single point of access to receive the interactions of a subject with the system and applying a protocol to verify the identity of the subject.
■ SECURITY LOGGER AND AUDITOR (page 111). This pattern allows us to capture application-specific events and exceptions in a secure and reliable manner, to support security auditing.
■ Secure Channel [Bra00]. This pattern defines a secure communication channel between two remote processes.
■ Microkernel [Bus96]. Microkernels use adapters to adapt to different types of client requests.

13.6 Secure Three-Tier Architecture

The Three-Tier Architecture pattern provides a means of structuring and decomposing applications into tiers or layers in which each tier provides a different level of responsibility. One tier deals with the presentation part of the system (user and system interfaces), another handles the business logic – the core of the system – and the last tier handles the data storage.

The SECURE THREE-TIER ARCHITECTURE pattern extends the Three-tier Architecture pattern by enforcing a global view of security for all three layers. In the presentation part of the system, security aspects dealing with user interaction are enforced; in the business logic, global security constraints are applied, while the data storage applies policies to constrain access of users to data.

Context

The SECURE THREE-TIER ARCHITECTURE pattern is applicable to distributed systems and systems executing complex and heterogeneous applications, involving databases, with data and documents that contain sensitive information.

Problem

Systems that contain sensitive and valuable data will attract attackers. How can we provide security in the presence of internal and external threats?

The solution to this problem must resolve the following forces:

- *Completeness.* We need to secure all the tiers of the system. Leaving any layer unprotected will allow some attacks to succeed.

- *Threats.* Attacks may come from legitimate users, using the resources available to them, while other attacks may come from external users through Internet vulnerabilities. Possible misuses of the system include illegal reading or modification of information. These actions may have serious negative effects on the institution that owns the information, and so cannot be tolerated. We need to stop or mitigate these attacks.

- *Availability and recovery.* We need to provide availability through service continuity and robust recovery in case of disaster, otherwise economic losses might result.

- *Transparency.* The security system should be mostly transparent to the users. If the users need to perform special actions for security, they may just skip them.

- *Accountability.* A user may deny having carried out some action. We need to be able to show that they actually performed the action.

- *Policies.* We should be able to apply institution policies to control the use of the information.

Solution

Apply appropriate security services to each layer. The presentation layer requires authentication and authorization of users. Secure the communication channel between the users and the system and enforce encryption of the data sent between the user and the system. The business tier defines a unified access control model for the complete system, while the presentation layer shows subsets of this model to the users and controls their interactions. The storage layer may have additional constraints based on the sensitivity of the data; for example, some parts may be encrypted.

Structure

The main architectural view of the SECURE THREE-TIER ARCHITECTURE pattern is shown in Figure 13.13. The `PresentationTier` includes user and system interfaces; the `PresentationSecurityServices` include authentication and authorization. The `BusinessTier` includes a unified model of the enterprise data and provides global authorization rules and their reference monitor. Its `BusinessSecurityServices` include global authorization rules, and must be coordinated with a SECURE BROKER (not shown), which may introduce additional restrictions. The `DataTier` defines authorization to access stored data items and mechanisms for encryption. The specific services used depend on the application, but to support a variety of applications we need a complete set of services.

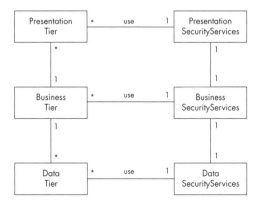

Figure 13.13: Class diagram for the SECURE THREE-TIER ARCHITECTURE pattern

Dynamics

The dynamic behavior of the SECURE THREE-TIER ARCHITECTURE pattern is illustrated by the sequence diagram of Figure 13.14, which shows the use case 'Process a database request'.

A request is issued by a `Client`, which goes to the `Presentation` layer for processing. This layer cannot satisfy the request by itself, so it calls the next layer, the `Business` (logical) layer, for more support with the request. As with the `Presentation` layer, part of the request can be handled here, but there are some parts which need support from the `Data` layer, so this is finally called. Here, at the last level, the subtask specific to this layer is performed and the results are sent back to the `Business` layer, which aggregates its results with what was received and returns them to the `Presentation` layer. The `Presentation`, `Business` and the `Data` layers may apply access and authorization constraints.

The `Business` layer will typically include a global enterprise model and will centralize authorization rules, but these may be applied at other layers. Each layer protects the layer below. For example, the `Presentation` layer may protect the `Business` layers from a denial of service attack. Communication between `Clients` and the `Presentation` layer may require authentication, as part of the first phase shown in Figure 13.14. Processing in the `Data` layer may require authorization from the requesting business component, or directly from the client – that is, through an authorization granted on the `Presentation` layer.

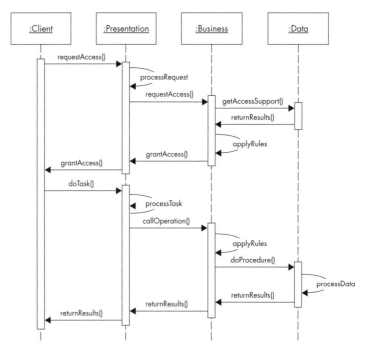

Figure 13.14: Sequence diagram for the use case 'Process a database request'

Implementation

The following steps are needed to implement this pattern:

1   Define a global authorization model for the enterprise, unifying the possible variety of authorization models used by the databases. Typically, ROLE-BASED ACCESS CONTROL (page 78) is used.

2   Select authentication approaches based on the needs of the applications. For example, remote user interfaces may need to be authenticated. The type of authentication depends on the sensitivity of the data.

3   Select an approach for encrypting messages and for digital signatures. Languages such as Java and C# include cryptographic libraries with different algorithms.

Consequences

The SECURE THREE-TIER ARCHITECTURE pattern offers the following benefits:

- *Centralized security.* Authorization constraints, authentication information and logging repositories can be associated with the Business layer.

- *Coverage.* All layers may apply security restrictions, tailored to the needs of the applications.

- *Unified security.* The pattern achieves this by the use of a global business model with its corresponding authorization structure. We can enforce any semantic constraints on access.

- *Transparency.* The application of security controls is transparent to the users.

- *Availability.* Because this is a distributed architecture, we can introduce some redundancy and improve availability.

- *Non-repudiation.* The user interfaces can apply digital signatures for specific interactions.

The pattern also has the following potential liabilities:

- *Security overhead.* Security actions imply some overhead.

- *Extra complexity.* The addition of security functions makes the system more complex; for example, it may not be clear where to apply specific security constraints.

Known Uses

- A three-tier security dashboard for cloud computing is presented in [Joo11].

- Sun One Application Server offers services to clients [SunD], protected using certificates, SSL/TLS encryption, authentication and auditing.

- IBM WebSphere's architecture can be mapped into three-tier architecture, and users can enable security by making use of the LTPA mechanism [IBMd]. Security mechanisms such as authentication, certificates, SSL, and PKI can be configured to provide security.

- The BEA Web Logic Server architecture is built using three layers [BEA]. Certificates and different encryption mechanisms can be used to provide security.

See Also

- AUTHORIZATION (page 74)) and ROLE-BASED ACCESS CONTROL (page 78) patterns define the models used in the unified security model of the business tier.
- AUTHENTICATOR (page 52) defines an abstract authentication process.
- Several papers have presented patterns for three-tier architectures [Aar96] [Jos01] [Mah] [Ren]. They are important to the study of other aspects of this architecture.
- The Business layer requires a Broker [Bus96] or web services for distribution.
- [Bou11] use security patterns for component-based design that could be used to implement the business tier.
- Patterns to build components for the business layer can be found in [Voe02].

13.7 Secure Enterprise Service Bus

The SECURE ENTERPRISE SERVICE BUS pattern describes how to provide a convenient infrastructure to integrate a variety of distributed services and related components in a simple and secure way.

Example

A travel agency interacts with many services to make flight reservations, check hotel availability, check customer credit and others. This interaction is currently done by direct interaction, which results in many ad hoc interfaces and requires many format conversions. The system is not scalable and it is hard to support standards. It is also insecure.

Context

Distributed applications using web services, as well as related services such as directories, databases, security and monitoring, or other types of components (J2EE, .NET). There may be different standards applying to specific components, as well as components that do not follow any standards.

Problem

When an organization has many scattered services, how can we aggregate them so they can be used together to assemble applications, at the same time keeping the architectural structure as simple as possible, and apply uniform standards?

The solution to this problem must resolve the following forces:

- *Interoperability*. It is fundamental for a business unit in an institution to be able to interact with a variety of services, internal or external.

- *Simplicity of structure*. We want a simple way to interconnect services; this simplifies the work of the integrators.

- *Scalability*. We need to have the ability to expand the number of interconnected services without making changes to the basic architecture.

- *Message flexibility*. We need to provide a variety of message invocation styles (synchronous and asynchronous) and formatting. We can thus accommodate all service needs.

- *Simplicity of management*. We need to monitor and manage many services, performing load balancing, logging, routing, format conversion and filtering.

- *Flexibility*. New types of services should be accommodated easily.

- *Transparency*. We should be able to find services without needing to know their locations.

- *Quality of service*. We may need to provide different degrees of security, reliability, availability or performance.

- *Use of policies*. We need a policy-based configuration and management. This allows convenient governance and systematic changes. Policies are high-level guidelines about architectural or institutional aspects, and are important in any system that supports systematic governance, as well as security and compliance [Sch06b].

- *Standard interfaces*. We need explicit and formal interface contracts.

- *Recording*. We need to record sensitive transactions.

- *Security*. We can enumerate threats and add defenses.

Solution

Introduce a common bus structure that provides basic brokerage functions as well as a set of other appropriate services. Figure 13.15 shows a typical structure. One can think of this bus as an intermediate layer of processing that can include services to handle problems associated with reliability, scalability, security and communications disparity. An ESB is typically part of a Service-Oriented Architecture (SOA) implementation framework, which includes the infrastructure needed to implement a SOA system. This infrastructure may also include support for stateful services.

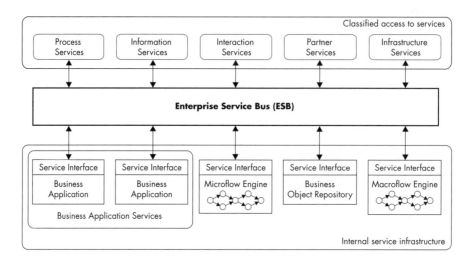

Figure 13.15: An Enterprise Service Bus (from [Zdu06])

Structure

Figure 13.16 shows the class diagram of the SECURE ENTERPRISE SERVICE BUS pattern. The ESB connects business services with each other, providing support for the needs of these services through a service that can be made up of `Business Application Servic-es` (BASs), which in turn use `Internal Services` to perform their functions. BASs are accessed through `Service Interfaces` (SIs).

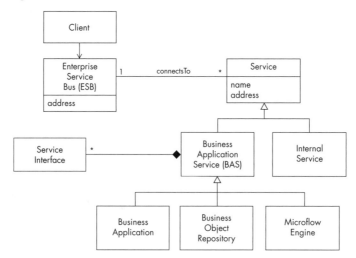

Figure 13.16: Class diagram for the SECURE ENTERPRISE SERVICE BUS pattern

Dynamics

Figure 13.17 shows the sequence diagram for the use case 'Access a service'. A `Client` sends a request for a BAS through the ESB, which finds the corresponding service interface.

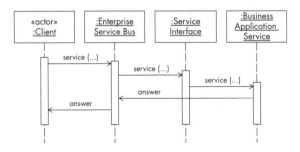

Figure 13.17: Sequence diagram for the use case 'Access a service'

Implementation

The SECURE ENTERPRISE SERVICE BUS itself is an example of a SOA architecture, since it performs its functions using internal services.

An important implementation decision is whether stateful services should be supported or not. Stateless services are easier to design and manage, but there are some applications that require stateful execution.

Consequences

The SECURE ENTERPRISE SERVICE BUS pattern offers the following benefits:

- *Interoperability*. The SESB, through its architecture and use of adapters, provides a way to interact with a variety of services, internal or external.
- *Simplicity of structure*. The pattern is much simpler – has fewer interconnections – than point-to-point or any other interconnection structure.
- *Scalability*. The number of interconnected services can be increased easily.
- *Message flexibility*. We can provide a variety of message invocation styles (synchronous and asynchronous) by using different message patterns.
- *Flexibility*. New types of services can be accommodated easily, since they only need to conform to the interface standards.
- *Simplicity of management*. We can centralize the functions of monitoring and management of services, as well as any other required functions.
- *Transparency*. We can find services conveniently by providing lookup services.
- *Quality of service*. By using appropriate associated services we can provide different degrees of security, reliability, availability or performance.

- *Use of policies.* We can use institution policies for configuration and management. This allows convenient governance and systematic changes. Security policies can define rights for the users with respect to the services.

- *Standard interfaces.* We can define explicit and formal interface contracts that must be followed by all aggregated functions.

- *Recording.* We can add a SECURITY LOGGER AND AUDITOR (page 111) to record sensitive transactions.

- *Security.* We can enumerate threats and add defenses. Specifically, we could add a SECURE BROKER (page 339), SECURE ADAPTERS (page 358), SECURE MODEL-VIEW-CONTROLLER (page 375) and others.

The pattern also has the following potential liabilities:

- Extra overhead compared to point-to-point, because of the indirection involved and the overhead of the ESB itself.

- The bus is a single point of failure, but this can be overcome using redundancy.

- A common interface standard may not be the most convenient for some services. Some applications may need more functions or parameters to interact than those defined in the common interfaces. Designing such a common interface may not be easy either.

- The bus may hide component dependencies.

Variants

- According to [Fer], the ESB will evolve into an *Internet bus*.
- The Secure Broker pattern has access control for web services, secure channels and logging [Mor06b].

Known Uses

- BEA AquaLogic Service Bus, now Oracle Service Bus, has operational service-management. It allows interaction between services, routing relationships, transformations and policies [BEA] [BEA11].

- WebSphere Application Server [Sph]. IBM's Business Integration Reference Architecture consists of products from the WebSphere family.

- The Service Provider Delivery Environment (SPDE) architecture is an implementation of this reference architecture for the Telecommunications industry [WSE].

- Microsoft BizTalk Server [Biz09] also uses ESBs and SESBs.

- Mule ESB Enterprise is a supported version of the open source product Mule ESB [Mul]. [Swa08] shows its use to integrate web services written in Java and Ada using SOAP and REST protocols with an Ada web server.

See Also

- The ESB is a type of Message Channel and is closely related to the Message Bus pattern, both described in [Hop04]. Because of its role as a communicator, the ESB is related to a variety of patterns that provide communication or adaptation. The ESB can be seen also as a microkernel, in that it forwards client requests to a set of services [Bus96].

- The Enterprise Service Bus can be considered a composite pattern comprised of the following patterns [Erl09]:

  - The (Service) Broker pattern, which itself is a composite pattern that consists of a set of integration-centric patterns used to translate between incompatible data models, data formats and communication protocols [Bus96].

  - The Asynchronous Queuing pattern, which establishes an intermediate queuing mechanism that enables asynchronous message exchanges and increases the reliability of message transmissions when service availability is uncertain [Sch00b].

  - The Intermediate Routing pattern, which provides intelligent agent-based routing options to facilitate various runtime conditions [IRP].

- Adapters are necessary to connect some services to the bus, because their interfaces may not follow the standard interface defined in the bus architecture. Database systems will typically need an Adapter [Gam94] or SECURE ADAPTER (page 358).

- A repository for web services and objects is usually attached to and used by the ESB [Gar10].

- Microflows and macroflows can be realized using a Process Manager [Hop04].

- A Lookup pattern may be used to find a specific service, or a service of some given type [Kir04].

- The Mediator pattern encapsulates how a set of objects interacts [Gam94].

- The SECURITY LOGGER AND AUDITOR pattern (page 111) is intended to keep track of security-sensitive actions [Fer11d].

- [Chat04] considers several channel patterns, including point–to-point, but not bus channels.

- [Erl09] considers Asynchronous Queuing, Event-Driven Messaging and other patterns.

- The Publish/Subscribe pattern can perform its communication functions using an ESB. Conversely, the SECURE DISTRIBUTED PUBLISH/SUBSCRIBE pattern (below) adds a way for the ESB to communicate events to its services.

  Figure 13.18 shows how some of these patterns are related.

- A use of an ESB to provide Security as a Service is described in [Hut05].

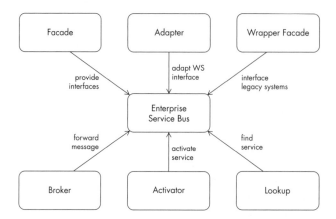

Figure 13.18: Some of the related patterns of the ESB

13.8   Secure Distributed Publish/Subscribe

The SECURE DISTRIBUTED PUBLISH/SUBSCRIBE pattern describes how to decouple the publishers of events from those interested in the events (subscribers) in a distributed system. Subscription and publishing are performed securely.

Context

Distributed applications using web services, as well as related services such as directories, databases, security and monitoring. There may be also other types of components (J2EE, .NET). Different standards may apply to specific components, and there may be components that do not follow any standards.

Problem

Subscribers register and receive messages in which they are interested. How can we organize publishers and subscribers such that their interactions are secure?

We relate threats to use cases as goals of the attacker [Fer06b]:

- *Subscription*
    - S1: An imposter subscribes to receive information.
    - S2: The publisher is an imposter and collects information (and maybe money) from potential subscribers.
    - S3: The subscription messages are intercepted and read or modified by an attacker.

- *Unsubscription*
  - U1: An imposter removes a subscriber.
- *Publish*
  - P1: An imposter receives information illegally.
  - P2: An imposter publishes illegal information.
  - P3: An attacker reads or modifies intercepted information.

Solution

Use a secure event channel by which publishers send their events and interested subscribers can receive the events. Subscribers register for the events in which they are interested.

Defenses

- S1, S2, U1, P1: Mutual authentication
- S3, P3: Message encryption
- P2: Digital signature
- P4: Authorization

Structure

Figure 13.19 shows the class diagram for this pattern. Subscribers can register to receive specific events. Their conditions are described in the class `Subscription`. The `Channel` represents different ways of publishing events.

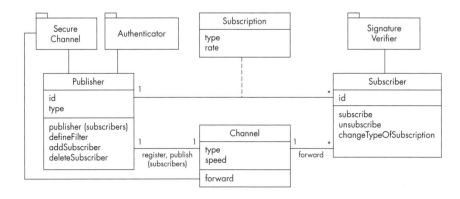

Figure 13.19: Class diagram for the SECURE DISTRIBUTED PUBLISH/SUBSCRIBE pattern

Dynamics

Figure 13.20 shows a sequence diagram for the use case 'Publish event'. Other use cases include 'Register subscriber' and 'Remove subscriber'.

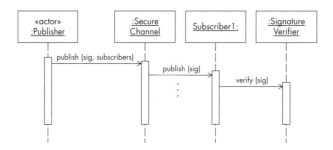

Figure 13.20: Sequence diagram for the use case 'Publish event'

Consequences

The SECURE DISTRIBUTED PUBLISH/SUBSCRIBE pattern offers the following benefits:

- *Loose coupling.* Publishers can work without knowledge of their subscriber details, and vice versa. This fact protects the subscribers if the publisher is compromised.

- *Location transparency.* Neither subscribers nor publishers need to know each other's locations; a lookup service can find their locations. This aspect protects both publishers and subscribers.

- *Threats.* If events are sensitive we can encrypt the event channel. We can also use digital signatures for authenticity.

The pattern also has the following potential liabilities:

- *Overhead.* There is some overhead in the event structure; tight coupling of subscribers to their publishers would have better performance at the cost of flexibility.

- *Excessive interoperability.* Because of its decoupling effect, this pattern allows the interaction of any type of publishers and subscribers, and hence is liable to attackers gaining easier access (the extended version of the pattern in the Variants section can mitigate this).

- A distributed system may also suffer denial of service attacks which cannot be controlled at the middleware level (a network problem).

Variants

- The Secure Distributed Publish/Subscribe with Access Control pattern extends the basic pattern presented here by adding authorization and a reference monitor (see the Secure Facade pattern, [Fer12e]) to control the publish and subscribe functions.

- An example that uses an instance of this variant can be found in [Bac08], which describes a Hermes-based secure publish/subscribe middleware using role-based access control for controlling access.

- Other authorization patterns such as Attribute-Based Access Control (ABAC) [Pri04] could be useful to determine whether subscription is allowed based on subject attributes.

Known Uses

- [Won08] describes an architecture for secure content-based publish/subscribe networks.

- [Sse10] describes an e-commerce network using secure publish/subscribe units.

- [Sri05] presents a security architecture of a publish/subscribe system (including a consideration of possible attacks) based on event guards.

See Also

- A Broker can be used as the distribution channel. It typically includes a look-up service and can distribute events to subscribers in a transparent way. A broker may include further security services; see SECURE BROKER (page 339).

- The Secure Channel pattern [Bra00] supports the encryption/decryption of data. This pattern describes encryption in general terms.

- In publish/subscribe middleware communication may be based on group broadcast, which would require secure group communication protocols. There are currently no security patterns for this.

- An Enterprise Service Bus (ESB) includes all the services needed for the publish/subscribe functions and uses the publish/subscribe functions for its own functions. An ESB may include its own security services; see SECURE ENTERPRISE SERVICE BUS (page 366).

- AUTHENTICATOR (page 52).

- DIGITAL SIGNATURE WITH HASHING (page 301).

- Although clearly different, this pattern is sometimes confused with the Observer pattern [Gam94].

13.9   Secure Model-View-Controller

The SECURE MODEL-VIEW-CONTROLLER pattern describes how to add security to the interactions of users with systems configured using the Model-View-Controller pattern.

Example

eLeague is a company that provides tournament management applications to a variety of sport leagues. The company develops service-based mobile applications allowing sport administrators, athletes and coaches to view and/or maintain their teams, schedules and scores from any location. The user interface of the application is susceptible to frequent change, as it has to adapt to new generations of mobile devices, whereas the structure of a tournament's information changes less often. In addition, tournament information is sensitive and should be modified only by authorized users.

Context

The Model-View-Controller (MVC) pattern [Bus96] provides a way to add modularity to an application by separating its functionalities into three loosely-coupled components, the Model, the View and the Controller, thus rendering the entire application more maintainable. This pattern has long been applied to both standalone applications and distributed systems. The MVC pattern is now widely used in web applications, ranging from service-based applications to mobile web applications. Figure 13.21 shows the class diagram of the structure of the MVC pattern.

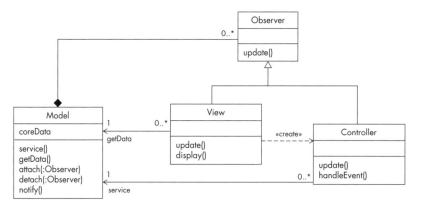

Figure 13.21: Class diagram of the structure of the MVC pattern (adapted from [Bus96])

Systems applying the MVC pattern are typically multi-user systems, and their model should be accessible and/or modifiable only by certain categories of users. At the same time, the use of the web as a transport layer has brought some new threats that must be mitigated: eavesdropping, impersonation via session hijacking, unauthorized modification via such attacks as SQL injection, or cross-site scripting.

Problem

How can we maintain an acceptable level of security between the model, the view and the controller in the presence of possible attacks?

The solution to this problem must resolve the following forces:

- *Authenticity.* We need to be sure that users who interact with our system are legitimate. Remote users will want to be sure that our system is authentic.

- *Confidentiality.* We may need to restrict access to the model's information to some users or roles. Also some portions of the data in transit from the model to the view must be protected against eavesdropping.

- *Integrity.* We may want to allow only some users or roles to make changes to the model, and only authorized changes.

- *Records.* The model may contain sensitive information and we want to have a record of all accesses to it.

Solution

The SECURE MODEL-VIEW-CONTROLLER pattern allows users to securely access and/or modify sensitive information located in the Model component. Basic security patterns are applied to provide authentication, authorization, secure communications and logging. In addition, it might be necessary to sanitize incoming and/or outgoing data, to prevent malicious payload attacks such as SQL injection or cross-site scripting attacks.

Access control can be added at the Model level and/or at the Controller and View levels. Adding access control at the Controller and View levels is less intrusive for the model; however, it is coarse-grained. Access control at the Model level can be finer-grained and could be based on specific attributes of the Model.

Structure

Security is added to the MVC pattern by applying several security patterns (Figure 13.22). An `Authenticator` identifies and authenticates the `User` requesting access to the `Model` and/or to the `Controller` through the `View`. We apply the ROLE-BASED ACCESS CONTROL (RBAC) pattern to the MVC pattern. `Users` are members of `Roles`, and `Rights` are assigned to `Roles`. A `Right` defines the access type that can be applied by a `Role` to the `Model`, to the `Controller` or to the `View`. A `ReferenceMonitor` enforces the access control rights defined in the RBAC pattern. A `SecureChannel` is responsible for securing traffic between the elements of the MVC pattern. A `SecureLogger` records all security-sensitive actions on the model. Finally, incoming data and outgoing data must be filtered by an `DataSanitizer` to prevent malicious payloads embedded into otherwise authorized requests from accessing the model.

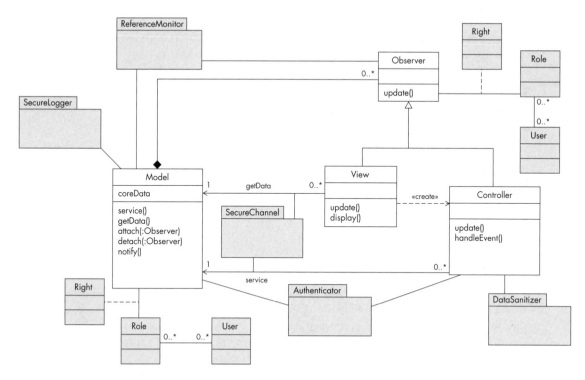

Figure 13.22: Structure of the SECURE MODEL-VIEW-CONTROLLER pattern

Dynamics

Figure 13.23 (page 380) shows a sequence diagram in which an authenticated user enters some input through the currently displayed View. The data embedded in the request sent to the Controller is first inspected by the DataSanitizer, then the request is intercepted by the ReferenceMonitor, and if a Right exists for the requested operation on the Controller, it can accept the user input.

The Controller handles a user event by updating the Model and selecting another View. The request for updating the Model can also be intercepted by the ReferenceMonitor for finer access control. The access control decision is recorded by the Security-Logger. Finally the selected View gets data from the Model. The request is again intercepted by the ReferenceMonitor.

Implementation

In order for the View to obtain data updates from the Model, it is possible to use a push or pull strategy. In an asymmetric context such as the web, the View has no choice but to constantly poll the Model. In [Str11], a method called *long poll* is used. In standalone applications, the Observer pattern can be applied [Gam94].

[Gal10] indicates how to avoid open redirection attacks in ASP MVC. An open redirection attack is performed by a tampered-with web application that redirects a request to a URL to an external, malicious URL.

Example Resolved

eLeague can apply the SECURE MODEL-VIEW-CONTROLLER pattern. The following roles are defined: administrator, coach, athlete. Each individual user is asked to register with the system so that they can be authenticated whenever they need to access it. Each operation of the controller can be mapped to a set of authorized roles; for accessing sensitive data, it can be modified to use a secure transport protocol.

Consequences

The SECURE MODEL-VIEW-CONTROLLER pattern offers the following benefits:

- *Authenticity.* An authentication system may confirm to the users that they are talking to the right model. Conversely, authentication indicates that the users accessing the model are legitimate.
- *Confidentiality and integrity.* An authorization system can enforce confidentiality and integrity. A secure communication protocol ensures that data in transit remains confidential. The integrity of the system is also guaranteed by the data sanitizer, which eliminates attacks from malicious embedded payloads.
- *Records.* A security logger (page 111) can record all security-sensitive actions.

The pattern also has the following potential liabilities:

- The security controls introduce some overhead.
- The security controls add complexity to the architecture.

Known Uses

- The ASP .NET MVC framework [Mic11] provides authentication and authorization functionalities at the Controller's method level. In addition, AntiXSSLibrary and HtmlSanitizationLibrary are two libraries that can be used for protecting against XSS (cross-site scripting) attacks as well as CSRF or XSRF (cross-site request forgery) attacks.

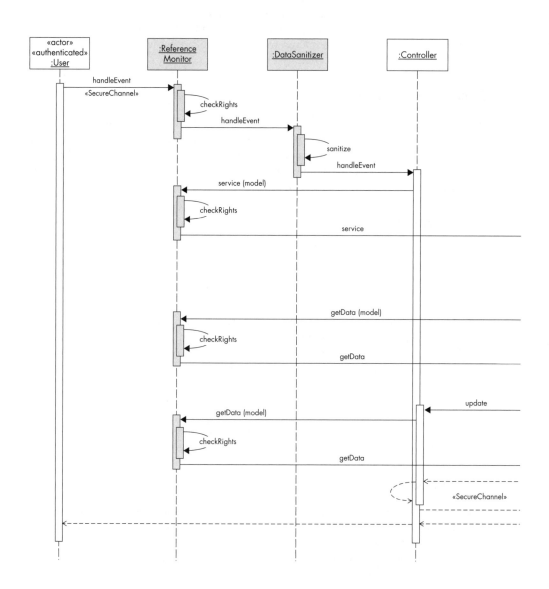

Figure 13.23: Sequence diagram for the use case 'Propagation of a change to the model'

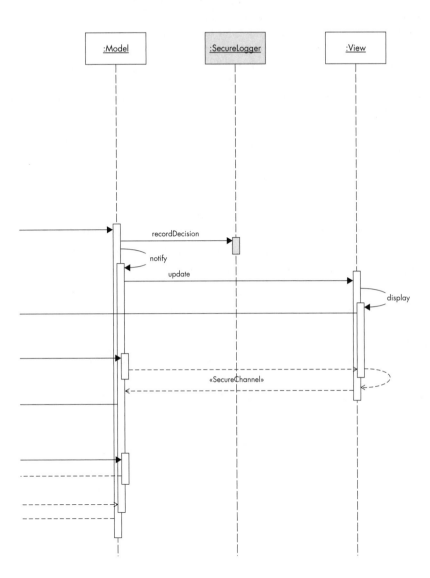

Figure 13.23 (continued)

- The Struts web framework [The12] provides a validation framework, which is the primary method of validating a Struts-based application. Output sanitization is the process of ensuring that your output does not contain HTML- or XML-specific characters. In addition, roles can be mapped to *action mapping* objects, a Controller component, and authentication attributes can be specified. The framework supports multiple authentication schemes, such as password authentication, FORM-based authentication, authentication using encrypted passwords, and authentication using client-side digital certificates. SSL can be enabled as a secure transport layer.

- The Spring Web MVC framework [Spr12] offers similar security features.

See Also

- Authorization is enforced by a REIFIED REFERENCE MONITOR (page 100).

- The rights structure can follow a ROLE-BASED ACCESS CONTROL (page 78) model.

- Authentication is performed by means of the AUTHENTICATOR pattern (page 52).

- Logging can be done using a SECURITY LOGGER AND AUDITOR (page 111).

- The Secure Channel pattern is used to secure the communications channels [Bra00]. It supports the encryption/decryption of data. Another version is given in [Sch06b].

- The relationship between Views and the Model can use the SECURE DISTRIBUTED PUBLISH/SUBSCRIBE pattern (page 372). Views could subscribe to updates from the Model.

- The MVC pattern can be structure according to the SECURE THREE-TIER ARCHITECTURE (page 362).

- The Input Validator pattern sanitizes inputs to a system [Net06].

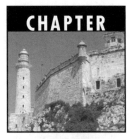

CHAPTER 14

Misuse Patterns

That some good can be derived from every event is a better proposition than that everything happens for the best, which it assuredly does not.

James Kern Feibleman, philosopher and psychiatrist (1904–1987)

The study of error is not only in the highest degree prophylactic, but it serves as a stimulating introduction to the study of truth.

Walter Lippmann, journalist (1889–1974)

14.1 Introduction

To design a secure system, we first need to understand the possible threats to the system. We have proposed a systematic approach to threat identification, starting from the analysis of the activities in the use cases of the system, and postulating possible threats [Fer06a]. This method identifies high-level threats such as 'the customer can be an imposter', but once the system is designed we need to see how the chosen components could be used by the attacker to reach their objectives. A misuse is an unauthorized use (read, modify, deny use) of information, and our emphasis is in how the misuse is performed. A *misuse pattern* describes, from the point of view of the attacker, how a type of attack is performed (what units it uses and how), analyzes the ways of stopping the attack by enumerating possible security patterns that can be applied for this purpose, and describes how to trace the attack once it has happened by appropriate collection and observation of forensics data. It also describes precisely the context in which the attack may occur.

Figure 14.1 presents a UML model that describes the sections of a misuse pattern [Fer09d]. The components of the pattern correspond to sections of the template used to describe it in words. Below, we describe each section in detail.

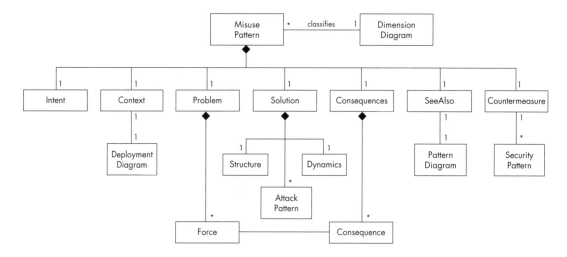

Figure 14.1: UML class model for misuse patterns

An important value of the proposed approach is that the misuse, described dynamically in a sequence or collaboration diagram, makes direct reference to the components of the system, described in turn by the class diagram of the system. The sequence or collaboration diagram uses objects from classes in the class diagram, and we can then relate messages to the components where they are sent (classes represent the components of the system). The parameters in these messages consist of data that can be found in the corresponding component. In other words, the combination of sequence and class diagrams tells us what information we can find in a component after an attack.

Figure 14.2 (a composition of three UML diagrams) shows a global view of a misuse pattern. Objects O1 and O2 are communicating with object O3, as shown in the deployment part of the diagram. Dotted lines show their correspondence with system classes; for example, O1 and O2 belong to A. The collaboration part of the diagram in Figure 14.2 indicates the sequence of messages needed for an attack and the patterns sp1, sp2, sp3 show security patterns that can stop or mitigate the attack. This diagram emphasizes the fact that to stop specific attacks more than one pattern may be needed.

In [Was09] we introduced the concept of a *dimension graph* to classify patterns. However, the dimensions needed to classify misuse patterns are different from those used to classify security patterns. Misuse patterns describe specific attacks in a particular environment, such as VoIP, web services and so on. This means that the two main dimensions are the type of generic attack or misuse – for example, denial of service – and the environment where the attack is possible. An additional dimension is the set of attack actions or patterns that are necessary to perform the misuse (An attack pattern is an action leading to a misuse, for example a buffer overflow).

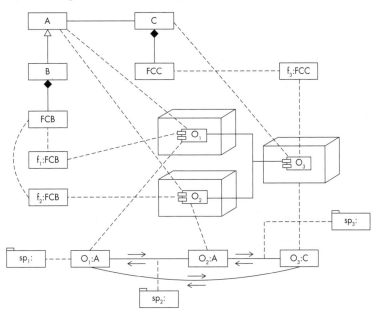

Figure 14.2: A misuse pattern

Finally, a solution dimension includes the security patterns needed to stop or mitigate the misuse. As an example, Figure 14.3 shows a pattern for a denial of service attack in VoIP [Pel09]. This pattern describes a generic denial of service attack, and its environment is VoIP networks. To perform it, a hacker first needs to install their malware in unprotected systems (zombies), followed by activation of these systems to make them flood the target with requests. To mitigate this attack we need to filter traffic from specific address ranges using Packet Filter Firewall and Proxy Firewall patterns [Sch06b] and an IDS to detect the attack (see Chapter 10).

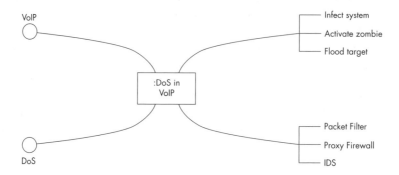

Figure 14.3: Classifying the DENIAL-OF-SERVICE IN VOIP misuse pattern

We now enumerate each section of the template of Figure 14.1 and characterize them using graph representations.

Name

The name of the pattern should correspond to the generic name given to the specific type of misuse in standard attack/misuse repositories such as CERT [Cer06] or Symantec [Sym].

Thumbnail Description

A short description of the intended purpose of the pattern (which problem it solves for an attacker).

Context

The context describes the generic environment, including the conditions under which the misuse may occur. This may include minimal defenses present in the system, as well as typical vulnerabilities of the system. The context is specified using a deployment diagram of the relevant portions of the system, as well as sequence or collaboration diagrams that show the normal use of the system. Figure 14.2 shows an example, where two client objects communicate with a server. A class diagram may show the relevant system structure.

We can list specific preconditions for an attack to happen, as well as other patterns necessary to apply this pattern, such as preparatory actions. The context of the misuse pattern may be defined by a partial dimension graph, describing the classification of the pattern according to the dimensions above except for the solution section. (In the complete pattern description we show the complete dimension graph.)

Pattern hierarchies are important to precisely characterize the architectural environment. For example, Figure 14.4 shows a hierarchy for VoIP misuses. Misuses that apply to distributed or real-time systems may also apply to VoIP systems, because they belong to these two categories. On the other hand, the misuse can only apply to environments that use the SIP protocol.

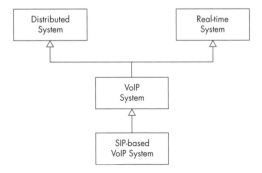

Figure 14.4: A hierarchy of architectural contexts

Problem

From a hacker's perspective, the problem is how to find a way to attack the system. An additional problem occurs whenever a system is protected by defense mechanisms. The forces indicate what factors may be required in order to accomplish the attack and in what way; for example, which vulnerabilities can be exploited. They also include which factors may obstruct or delay accomplishing the attack.

Solution

This section describes the solution of the hacker's problem – that is, how the misuse can be accomplished and the expected results of the attack. UML class diagrams show the system under attack. Sequence or collaboration diagrams show the exchange of messages needed to accomplish the attack. State or activity diagrams may add further detail. Attack patterns that are necessary for the misuse are also listed here. For example, to perform DoS in VoIp, we need to infect zombies (Figure 14.3).

The UML class model should not be a comprehensive representation of all components and relationships involved in an attack. Rather, the pattern solution should represent all components that are important to perform or prevent the attack and are essential to the forensics examination. This can be represented by a class diagram that is a subset or superset of the architectural class diagram of the context.

In cases in which primary sources of forensic data (firewalls, IDSs and network forensic analysis tools) don't contain enough evidence, investigators need to look for secondary sources. The most obvious and common secondary sources of data are terminal devices, servers and network storage devices. Many wireless devices may also contain forensic data. This may require refining the class diagrams to show more details of the system structure.

The section may include a diagram with only the selected classes and associations relevant to the forensic examination (Figure 14.5). Forensic information can be collected into *forensic objects*, f1 to f4 in the diagram. All forensic objects that collect information from different objects of the same class are collected into *forensic classes*; f2, f3, and f4 are part of forensic class forB. A collaboration diagram shows which objects interact during the misuse; this can be obtained directly from the sequence diagram of the misuse.

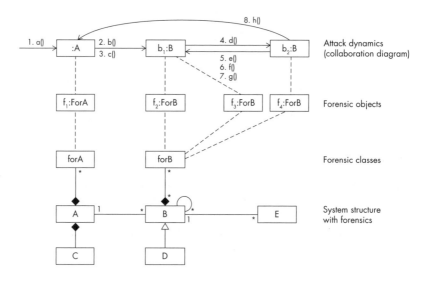

Figure 14.5: Forensic objects and classes

Consequences

This section discusses the benefits and drawbacks of a misuse pattern from the attacker's viewpoint. Is the effort and cost of the attack commensurate with the results obtained? This is an evaluation that must be made by the attacker when deciding to perform the attack; the designers should evaluate their assets using some risk analysis approach. The enumeration includes good and bad aspects and should match the forces, but there may be consequences that do not correspond to any forces.

Countermeasures and Forensics

This section describes the security measures necessary to stop, mitigate or trace this type of attack. This implies an enumeration of which security patterns are effective against the attack. From a forensic viewpoint, it describes what information can be obtained at each stage of tracing back the attack and what can be deduced from this data in order to identify this specific attack. Finally, it may indicate what additional information should be collected at the system components through which the attack was propagated to improve forensic analysis, using the model of Figure 14.5 as a reference. Each pattern may also carry information about the time it takes to apply its solution [Yos04].

Known Uses

This section describes specific incidents when the attack has been used. For new vulnerabilities, where an attack has not yet occurred, specific contexts where the potential attack may occur are enough.

See Also

This section discusses other misuse patterns with different objectives but performed in a similar way, or with similar objectives but performed in a different way. It also considers patterns of complementary misuses or patterns of attacks that support the misuse. These patterns can be related using a misuse pattern diagram, analogous to the pattern diagrams used in [Bus96] and many pattern papers.

We have applied this approach to the construction of a small catalog of the most typical attack patterns in VoIP [Pel09]. We are also integrating this method with our methodologies to build secure systems [Fer06b]. We need to expand this catalog to make it of more practical value. Note that as usual, patterns provide only guidelines, not plug-in solutions; that is, for each new application, the patterns provide guidelines about what to expect, where to look and how to start, but their solutions must be tailored to the specific environment.

A catalog of misuse patterns can be organized using contexts as the main classification dimension; for example, misuse patterns for VoIP, for client/server architectures, for component structures and so on. More detailed patterns are possible depending on finer architectural aspects, for example DoS in VoIP in a SIP environment. While security patterns have been used in many practical projects, there is no practical experience with misuse patterns; we will have to wait until they are used to get a realistic appraisal of their value.

The misuse patterns described above are used to describe attacks against an existing system. Misuse patterns can also be defined in the analysis stage of a new system. As we have shown in [Fer06c], we can enumerate threats from activity diagrams for use cases or sequences of use cases. Using the classes in the conceptual model, we can describe misuse patterns as part of the lifecycle of systems under development.

We show here three misuse patterns:

■ A *WORM* pattern [Fer10c]. Malicious software propagates itself to as many places as possible (or to specific systems), usually indicating its presence, and maybe performing some damage.

- *DENIAL-OF-SERVICE IN VOIP* [Pel09]. A VoIP DoS attack overwhelms limited resources in order to disrupt VoIP operations, typically through a flood of messages. This leads to degradation of response time, preventing subscribers from effectively using the service.

- *SPOOFING WEB SERVICES* [Mun11]. A web service spoofing misuse tries to impersonate the identity of a user by stealing their credentials, and then makes requests in their name with these credentials, with the intention of accessing a victim's web service.

More VoIP misuse patterns can be found in [Pel09]. A misuse pattern for stealing data through SQL injection is shown in [Fer12f]. Failure patterns, their counterpart for dependability, were defined in [Buc12].

14.2 Worm

The WORM pattern describes how a worm can propagate itself to as many places as possible (or to specific systems), usually indicating its presence, and maybe performing some damage.

Context

Sites connected through the Internet or another type of network. The Internet provides a variety of services such as e-mail, file transfer and web services. Any of these services can be used for propagation. Both fixed and wireless networks can be used by a worm. Portable storage devices such as memory sticks can also propagate worms.

Problem

A worm tries to take advantage of any input to invade a system. Users might open attachments carrying worms and some ports of a system may be unprotected or have vulnerabilities; all of these give the worm a chance to invade. Mail systems and file transfer systems for example, include lists of addresses that can be used by the worm to find places to which to propagate. Many systems do not control access to their system directories and do not restrict Internet traffic, which facilitates a worm invasion.

The solution to this problem must resolve the following forces:

- *Objectives*. A worm's objectives may be political, monetary or vandalism. A political or terrorist worm typically tries to produce damage to an antagonist; a monetary worm tries to reach many places to collect information or drop spyware; a vandal worm tries to destroy or damage information.

- *Reach*. To try to reach as many places as possible or to specific sites. For most worms, reaching many places is a basic objective.

- *Presence manifestation.* To try to show its presence in the system, so that victims know about it. Exceptions to this are cases in which the objective is to drop spyware.

- *Credit.* To embed an identification or mark so that the worm's creator can take credit for it.

- *Misuse.* Perform some destruction and/or other misuses (confidentiality, integrity, or availability). The misuse may be delayed (time bomb).

- *Obfuscation.* To try to hide its structure to make its detection and removal harder.

- *Collateral damage.* In addition to specific misuses, the worm may require costly operations for its removal, stopping or disrupting business activities. Its propagation may affect the normal traffic in the network.

- *Latency.* A worm's propagation must be as fast as possible to avoid detection and countermeasures.

- *Activation.* This can be done by enticing offers which may tempt users to open e-mail attachments or download procedures (social engineering). Other possibilities are invading through unprotected ports or taking advantage of vulnerabilities.

Solution

Attach a core portion of the worm to e-mail messages or to files. When the user opens the message attachments or executes the file, the core of the worm starts executing. Alternatively, invade through an unprotected or flawed port. Download remaining portions from complementary network sites. Use some procedure to hide the structure of the worm. Perform its mission and propagate. Figure 14.6 shows the propagation of a typical worm; speed comes from a tree-like propagation.

Structure

Figure 14.7 shows a class diagram of the units involved. Node represents any node in the network, defined by its address (URL on the Internet). Any node can be the origin of a worm and any node can be its target (and be invaded). Some nodes are complementary sites from which commands or other parts of the worm may be retrieved. The class Worm represents the worm itself, including procedures for initial setup, to bring complementary parts, to hide the worm, to perform its mission and to propagate.

Dynamics

Use cases for a worm may include 'Create a worm', 'Remove a worm', and 'Activate a worm'. Create and remove are specific to the type of worm (see Variants). We describe the use case 'Activate a worm' here because it is the most important for defenders. Its scenario (Figure 14.8) includes:

- *Triggering.* After the attacker (Hacker) sends a message, a Target (user) may activate an executable procedure with a core part of the worm.

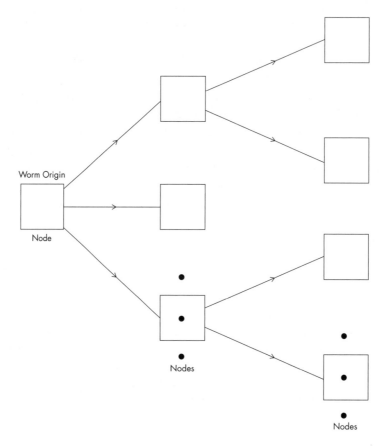

Figure 14.6: Worm propagation

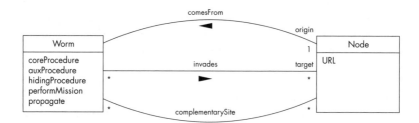

Figure 14.7: Class diagram for the WORM pattern

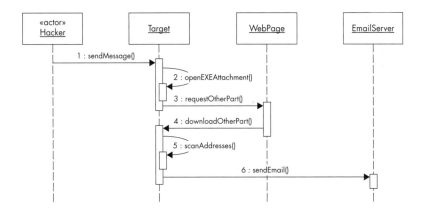

Figure 14.8: Sequence diagram for the use case 'Activate a worm'

- *Assembly.* The core of the worm downloads its remaining parts via the Internet (optional).

- *Obfuscation.* The worm uses some procedure to hide parts of itself, for example encryption or dispersion.

- *Address search.* The worm finds destination addresses as new targets for propagation. Addresses may also be generated randomly.

- *Manifestation.* The worm displays some messages (optional).

- *Propagation.* The worm sends its core via the connection to another node in the address list. This operation is repeated for all the addresses found or generated.

Implementation

We show a typical implementation of the Bagle worm. It follows the sequence diagram of Figure 14.8 very closely. A typical scenario in a Microsoft environment would follow this sequence:

1 A user invokes executable code by opening an infected Microsoft Word file, which starts execution of a VBA macro.

2 The VBA macro downloads its remaining parts from a web server via the Internet.

3 The worm finds target addresses in the Microsoft Office address book using VBA code and an SMTP server name extracted from Outlook settings.

4 The worm displays some messages using a VBA function.

5 The worm opens an SMTP connection to mail its core to the next target. This operation is repeated for all addresses found.

Active worms take advantage of vulnerabilities such as buffer overflows and can get in through port 80, or through other, unprotected ports. In the case of worms such as Code Red the core of the worm was sent to the input buffer of port 80 in Microsoft's IIS server [Ber01]. A virus or worm may send a web address link as an instant message to all the contacts of the invaded site, and if the recipients answer, they bring the virus to their sites.

Consequences

The WORM pattern offers the following benefits for the attacker:

- *Objectives*. Its economic objectives can be achieved if the worm has a long 'reach' and clever social engineering. Its political objectives can be achieved if the worm reaches its intended audience and manifests its presence and reasons. Its vandalism objectives can be achieved if the worm does considerable damage.
- *Reach*. If the system has easily accessible address lists, the worm can find many new targets. Random address generation is not so effective.
- *Manifestation of its presence*. A good procedure for display can make its presence well noticed. This may intimidate its victims, which brings satisfaction to the attacker.
- *Credit*. The worm may include a distinctive tag or icon which should not identify the attacker. The creator can get recognition for their efforts.
- *Misuse*. A worm can perform destruction and/or other misuses (confidentiality, integrity, denial of service, dropping spyware or spam).
- *Obfuscation*. Encryption and dispersion can make its detection and removal harder. Some worms mutate, that is, they change their structure when they propagate.
- *Side effects*. A fast-propagating worm can produce a lot of traffic and, if it is hard to detect, its cost increases.
- *Latency*. A fast-propagating worm can do much damage before being stopped.
- *Activation*. Good ways to activate the worm are necessary, since all its objectives depend on this step.

A worm can also have some liabilities for the attacker:

- A worm can be used to detect infected nodes or to destroy viruses or other worms.

Countermeasures

The following policies and their corresponding mechanisms (realized as patterns), can stop or mitigate the worm:

- *Policy about attachments*. Users should be trained to recognize trustable attachments and should be forbidden from opening unknown or suspicious attachments.

- *Need-to-know policy.* This should be established to define access by system processes to resources. For example, address lists should use authorization to control access to their contents.

- *Control of network communications.* Connections should be established only with trusted addresses (control through the firewalls). This policy may avoid downloads from complementary sites.

- *Intrusion detection.* An intrusion detection system can detect some attacks in real time and alert the firewall to stop them.

- *Use of antivirus software.* This can help detect and clean worms after an attack.

- *Backups.* Checkpointing files and keeping backup images of them is a fundamental precaution against data destruction or unauthorized modification.

- *Specialized hardware.* Process communication controls in the operating system can be enforced through specialized hardware [Shi00]. It is possible to define partitions in the operating system that can be enforced by hardware that will prevent a worm from performing its actions.

Forensics

The pieces of the worm may be scattered across different components within a site. The specific places to look for worm components depend on the specific variant or type of worm. The places where worms normally penetrate include e-mail attachments, files and unprotected ports, and these must be inspected. One should also look for the specific parts of the worm, such as core procedure, obfuscation procedure and so on.

Web logs can help in finding worm parts that might have been downloaded. GUIs may have log records of the use of procedures to display the worm's announcements. Units that contain addresses may contain indications of search.

Variants

- A *passive worm* requires a user to activate an executable program, and usually propagates through e-mail. Melissa, ILOVEYOU, Anna Kournikova, and Bagle are examples of this type of worm.

- An *active worm* takes advantage of some system flaw to provoke a buffer overflow or another attack to get access to a system through some port. It may scan ports looking for unprotected ones. Code Red is an active worm; Storm can be active or passive [Smi08].

- A *virus* attaches itself to a program (infects an executable file) and, when the user executes the program, is activated. Jerusalem, Christmas and Chernobyl are examples of viruses.

- Some worms have several versions with different purposes; for example, Storm has variants that perform different types of misuses, including targeted spam and DDoS (distributed denial-of-service) attacks [Smi08].

- Some worms are *multimode* (multivector) worms, which can use a variety of methods to invade their targets; for example, Storm infects computers using multiple payloads [Smi08].

Known Uses

Typical examples of worms include:

- *ILOVEYOU* [ILO] [wor09]. An e-mail attachment worm that appeared in 2000. It relied on social engineering to entice users to open the attachment. It also used specific weaknesses of Microsoft Windows. It propagated using the addresses in the address book of the e-mail system.

- *Bagle.* A mass-mailing worm written in assembly language [bag] and affecting all versions of Windows. After activation, it copied itself to the Windows system directory and downloaded an SMTP engine to e-mail its core to other nodes as an attachment (see the Implementation section for its typical behavior).

- *Code Red* [Ber01]. This worm appeared in July 2001. It propagated through port 80, indicated its presence by defacing web pages, propagated using a random IP address generator, and later activated a denial of service attack from infected sites.

- *Nimda* [Nima]. Nimda is a multivector worm that can use several methods to propagate: e-mail, visiting an infected site, seeking out vulnerable servers to upload files, or through the network.

- *Slapper* [Arc03]. This worm can launch denial of service attacks. It propagates by finding addresses in files. The nodes invaded by the worm communicate using a P2P protocol to collaborate in their misuses.

- *Conficker* [Conb] [wor09]. This is a multivector worm with an auto-update facility (signed updates) and encrypted communications. It downloads parts of itself from some Internet sites.

These worms are really worm types, from which many variants can be derived. It is possible to define separate patterns for each type of the generic WORM pattern. For example, the Slapper worm and the Apache Scalper operate in a similar way, while Conficker is really a series of worms [wor09].

See Also

- *Authorization and Reference Monitor.* These patterns together can prevent access to address lists, stopping the worm propagation [Sch06b].

- *Firewall.* A firewall can filter attempts to download further pieces of the worm [Sch06b].

■ *Intrusion detection.* An intrusion detection system can detect a worm invasion in real time and collaborate with the firewall to block its traffic [Fer05d].

14.3   Denial-of-Service in VoIP

A VoIP DoS attack overwhelms limited resources in order to disrupt VoIP operations, typically through a flood of messages. This leads to degradation of response time, preventing subscribers from effectively using the service.

Context

There are two targets for DoS attacks: those in which end systems are targets, and those that target gateways or gatekeepers. In the former, subscribers try to establish a call over a VoIP channel (VoIP services should be available to subscribers when requested). In the latter, some VoIP systems use control protocols (for example MGCP and Megaco/H.248) and security mechanisms to manage the Media gateways deployed across the infrastructure. In general, the VoIP system should have adequate capacity (bandwidth) to meet the peak communication load. The system may have a minimum set of perimeter defenses, such as firewalls. More complex VoIP implementations may have an intrusion detection system (IDS) and firewall on the phone itself to check the media packet flow, or perform authentication. All Internet building blocks – and thus VoIP – are vulnerable to DoS attacks, which have not previously been a security issue with circuit-switched telephony systems because of their inherent bandwidth limitations. In particular, this pattern assumes the use of the H.323 protocol.

Problem

How can we trigger a DoS attack on a VoIP system? IP telephony subscribers need to be blocked from using VoIP services. The attack can be carried out by taking advantage of the following conditions:

■ VoIP security is in an incipient phase at the moment: there is lack of expertise and security standards. Users might inadvertently expose the system. While some basic countermeasures exist, such as IDSs and firewalls, administrators may not configure them appropriately due to a lack of training and time.

■ Until now VoIP has been developed and deployed focusing on functionality with less thought for security [Wie06b]. That means that the defenses that are in place are not very advanced. For example, strong authentication is not common in VoIP.

■ With the rush to implement new VoIP systems, features and standards, implementation flaws are common. IP PBXs include many layers of software that may contain vulnerabilities. Programming mistakes, such as not properly checking the size of the parameters of a protocol request, when exploited, can result in the following issues:

- *Remote access.* An attacker obtaining remote (often administrator level) access.

- *Malformed request DoS.* A carefully crafted protocol request (a packet) exploiting a vulnerability that results in a partial or complete loss of function (in this case a single malformed packet may lead to a DoS).

- *Load-based DoS.* A flood of legitimate requests overwhelming a system [Col04].

- As with any network-based service, enterprise VoIP must communicate with other components on a LAN and possibly over an untrusted network such as the Internet, where packets are easy to intercept.

- Because RTP (real-time transport protocol) carries media that must be delivered in real time to be usable for an acceptable conversation, VoIP is vulnerable to DoS attacks that impact the quality delivery of audio, such as those that affect jitter and delay.

- VoIP traffic can offer very good cover for DoS attacks, because VoIP runs continuous media over IP packets [CRN06].

Solution

One method to launch a DoS attack is to flood a VoIP server (for example Gatekeeper) with repeated requests for legitimate service in an attempt to overload it. This may cause severe degradation or complete unavailability of the voice service. A flooding attack can also be launched against IP phones, Gateways or any VoIP network components that accept signaling. With this form of DoS attack, the target system is so busy processing packets from the attack that it will be unable to process legitimate packets, which will either be ignored or processed so slowly that the VoIP service is unusable. Attackers can also use the TCP SYN flood attack (also known as resource starvation attack) to obtain similar results. This attack floods the port with synchronization packets, which are normally used to start a connection.

In a distributed denial-of-service (DDoS) attack, multiple systems are used to generate a massive flood of packets. To launch a massive DDoS attack, the hacker previously installs malicious software on compromised terminal devices (infected with a Trojan) that can be triggered at a later time ('zombies') to send fake traffic to targeted VoIP components. Targeted DoS attacks are also possible, in which the attacker disrupts specific connections.

The class diagram of Figure 14.9 shows the structure for a DDoS attack in an H.323 architecture where any VoIP component can be a target for DoS. Classes `AttackControlMechanism` and `Zombie` represent the software introduced by the attacker. Note that the zombie is just a terminal device in a different role.

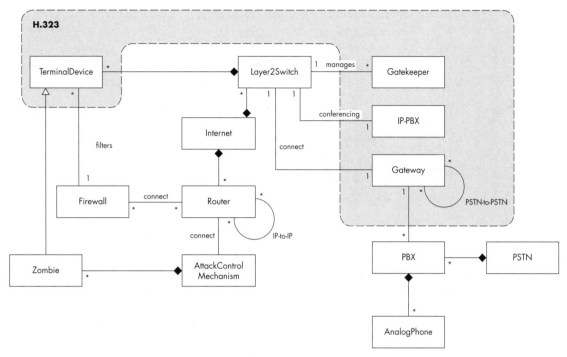

Figure 14.9: Class diagram for DoS attacks in H323

The sequence diagram of Figure 14.10 shows the sequence of steps necessary to perform an instance of an end-system DoS attack. An attacker (internal or remote), with knowledge of a valid user name on a VoIP system could generate enough call requests to overwhelm the IP-PBX server. An attacker may disrupt a subscriber's call attempt by sending specially crafted messages to their ISP server or IP PBX component, causing it to over-allocate resources, so that the caller receives a 'service not available' (busy tone) message. This is an example of a targeted attack.

Similarly, out-of-sequence voice packets (such as receiving media packets before a session is accepted) or a very large phone number could open the way to application layer attacks (aka 'attacks against network services'). Buffer overflow attacks might paralyze a VoIP number using repeated calling. For example, an attacker intermittently sends garbage (that is, both the header and the payload are filled with random bytes, corrupting the callee's jitter buffer voice packets) to the callee's phone between those of the caller's voice packets. The callee's phone is then so busy trying to process the increased packet flow that the jitter (delay variation) causes any conversation to be incomprehensible [Anw06].

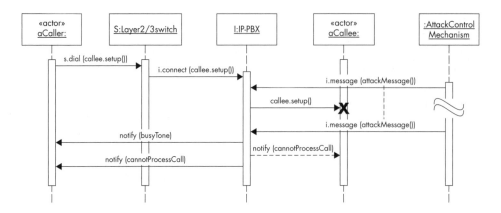

Figure 14.10: Sequence diagram for DoS attacks in H323

DoS attacks against gateways are analyzed from the supporting Megaco/H.248 protocol viewpoint. Figure 14.11 shows the class diagram of the media gateway control protocol structure. Megaco/H.248 is a master-slave, transaction-oriented protocol in which media gateway controllers (MGC) control the operation of MediaGateways (MG) [Ell03]. VoIP media gateways are vulnerable to DoS attack because they accept signaling messages.

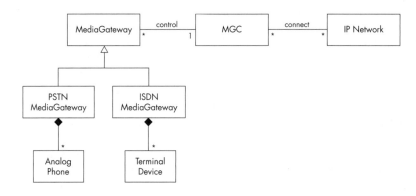

Figure 14.11: Class diagram for a Megaco/H.248 environment

In this setting, a DoS attack would occur at an MGC when the attacker sends a large volume of UDP packets to the protocol's default port 2944 or 2945, which keeps the MGC busy handling illegal messages, and finally blocks the normal service. An attacker can keep sending 'service change' or 'audit capabilities' commands to an MG, and thereby bring down the MediaGateway [Vuo04]. Therefore, VoIP gateways will not be able to initiate calls or maintain a voice call during a DoS attack. The audio quality will be affected as well. An alternative way to launch DoS attacks happens when an attacker redirects media sessions to a media gateway: the attack will overwhelm this voice component and prevent it from processing legitimate requests.

Signaling DoS attacks on media gateways can consume all available TDM channels, preventing other outbound and inbound calls and affecting other sites that use TDM. On the other hand, since VoIP media sessions are very sensitive to latency and jitter, DoS on media is a serious problem. VoIP media, which is normally carried with RTP, is vulnerable to any attack that congests the network or slows the ability of an end device (phone or gateway) to process the packets in real time. An attacker with access to the portion of the network where media is present simply needs to inject large numbers of either RTP packets or high QoS packets, which will contend with the legitimate RTP packets [Col04].

Consequences

The DENIAL-OF-SERVICE IN VOIP misuse pattern has the following benefits for the attacker:

- DoS can be especially damaging if key resources are targeted (for example media gateways), which may lead to cascading effects if a server is impacted.
- Flooding of the firewall can prevent it from properly managing ports for legitimate calls.
- VoIP QoS can be degraded by jitter and delay and may become totally unusable.
- The zombies in the targeted network can also be used as DoS launching points to perform attacks on another network.

It can also have some liabilities for the attacker:

- Some defenses can stop this attack – see the next section.

Countermeasures and Forensics

The attack can be stopped or mitigated by the following countermeasures:

- DoS is mitigated by disabling and removing unnecessary network services, reinforcing the operating system, and using host-based intrusion detection systems (the IDS pattern [Fer05d]). This makes it harder to introduce Trojan horses that may make terminal devices become zombies.
- IDSs and firewalls can ensure that packets with very large sequence numbers and garbage packets are discarded. Again, the IDS pattern is relevant, as well as the Firewall patterns [Sch06b].
- Use of Proxy and Stateful Firewalls [Sch06b], which can look inside the voice packet and analyze its contents, as well as the headers, to decide if the information is safe or not.

- Use of the Authenticated Call pattern [Fer07a], which performs both device and user authentication before allowing access to VoIP services. Although this takes longer, it can protect against targeted attacks from devices that do not possess authentication tokens.

Likewise, the following *network forensics mechanisms* can be used to collect evidence of the attack:

- Logs in the terminal devices not only provide VoIP-specific details (for example, start/end times and dates of each call), but they can also reveal the presence of malware. As we indicated, some attacks come from compromised devices that become zombies.

- Network analysis procedures such as the examination of router logs (for example denied connection attempts, connectionless packets) and firewall logs, provide information about the location (that is, where the attack entered the network) and the way that attackers performed their exploits.

- Selective use of events sent to the ISP or IP PBX has been shown to produce another range of attacks. Those could be traced through logs on these devices.

- Network forensic analysis techniques such as IP traceback and packet marking are useful for attack attribution. During a denial of service attack the victim will receive sufficient traceback packets to reconstruct the attack path [Sha03]. Locating attackers with IP traceback technology is also a potential security mechanism to counter DoS attacks. The deployment of a traceback mechanism on a single router would provide minimal benefit: this process requires the cooperation of all network operators along the attack path in order to trace it back to the source. IP traceback works even when criminals conceal their geographic locations by spoofing source addresses.

- Comparing traffic patterns against predefined signatures (as is done by some IDSs) is an effective method of detecting DDoS attacks. Such a method can produce an alert, helping network examiners to detect malicious traffic (for example observing congestion in a router's buffer) from entering or leaving their networks.

- Event logging allows network administrators to collect important information (for example date, time and result of each action) during the set up and execution of the attack. For example, logs may identify the type of DDoS attack used against a targeted system.

- The use of 'honeypots' placed on selected VoIP components (see Figure 14.9) and other network forensics tools can help in the event of a successful attack. Honeypots can attract attackers and provide investigators with useful information about new types of intrusions.

- In VoIP, the attack pattern technique may be complemented with the use of a network forensics analysis tool to offer a better view (interpretation) of the collected voice packets.

Where to Look for Evidence

Based on Figure 14.2 (page 385), the following may be considered secondary sources of forensic information in a VoIP environment:

- Terminal devices (softphones, hardphones and wireless VoIP phones)
- Gatekeepers
- Gateways
- IP-PBXs

Known Uses

DoS attacks are performed on different systems in the Internet every day on all protocol layers. Some of those attacks affect VoIP systems.

See Also

Several security patterns for defending against these (and related) attacks are listed in [Anw06] [Fer07a]. Some general security patterns such as firewalls [Sch06b], IDSs [Fer05d] and authentication [Sch06b] can be used to control these attacks, as discussed earlier. A misuse pattern can be developed to describe similar attacks on SIP networks.

14.4   Spoofing Web Services

Also known as Principal Spoofing in Web Services

A web service spoofing misuse tries to impersonate the identity of a user by stealing their credentials, then makes requests in their name with these credentials with the intention of accessing a victim's web service.

Context

Enterprises can exchange data through the use of web services. In order to let other entities access the web service, they publish a WSDL (Web Services Description Language) file with functionalities and security policies.

The client must create a request which should adapt its methods and policies to those of the web service provider. Security can be implemented at the level of messages: each user is given credentials to access services and the responsibility of protecting their messages from other users. The web service can be protected using standards such as WS-Security [Aja10a] to protect messages and WS-Policy [Bar07] to verify the security requirements of the web service.

Problem

How we can effectively perform a principal spoofing attack against web services so that we can access the information of another user?

The attack can take advantage of the following vulnerabilities:

- Currently there is no method of verifying identity unequivocally.
- When a WSDL file is published, the interfaces of the web service are exposed, and thus its entry points.
- The source address of the request can be altered.
- There is a tendency to trust presented credentials without a more thorough check.
- Once the authentication stage is passed, other attacks can be generated more easily: for example, DDoS attacks
- Maybe the interchanged data items are not encrypted, and it may be possible to steal the credentials using special software.
- The resulting damage depends on the privileges of the credentials submitted.

Solution

Security standards such as WS-SECURITY (page 330) use the credentials of the user to protect communication between web services by signing and encrypting messages. If an attacker manages to obtain valid credentials, they can communicate with other web services. This type of vulnerability is mentioned in [Mor06a] and is termed *principal spoofing*. In this attack, the user does not know that their credentials have been stolen until the damage is done (such as alteration of information, access to their resources, alteration of privilege, even attaching malicious code that could be harmful to the server).

When the attacker has the credentials, they can use the WSDL file to discover the security policies of the web services and create a valid message. This situation is conditional on the attacker obtaining a user's credentials, the valid user not knowing of the theft and not having reported the theft.

The attack can be carried out by taking advantage of the following vulnerabilities:

- If communications between web services are not protected, sniffer software such as WireShark or WebScarab could intercept packages while they travel in the network and obtain the credentials carried in the messages.
- Using social engineering to obtain the credentials of the user.
- Inadequate security policies used by the system; it is possible to cheat the system in this way.
- The system not verifying the origin of the request.

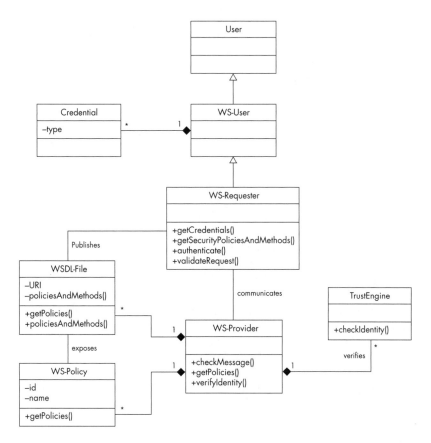

Figure 14.12: Class diagram for the SPOOFING WEB SERVICES pattern

The class diagram of Figure 14.12 shows the typical relationships between web services. The `WS-User` has `Credentials` to communicate with other web services. The `WS-Requester` can be a `WS-User` on another kind of web service. The `WS-Provider` has several `WS-Policies`, stored in the `WSDL-File`. In this way, a `WS-Requester` can be created based on the `WS-Policies` shown in the `WSDL-File`. When the `WS-Requester` tries to communicate with the `WS-Provider`, the `WS-Provider` checks the request with its `TrustEngine`, which checks the requester's credentials.

To make this attack possible, the user must have the user's credentials, as shown in Figure 14.13. This diagram shows the structure of a *principal spoofing attack*, the classes `WS-Attacker` and `Attacker` being the new elements introduced by the attacker.

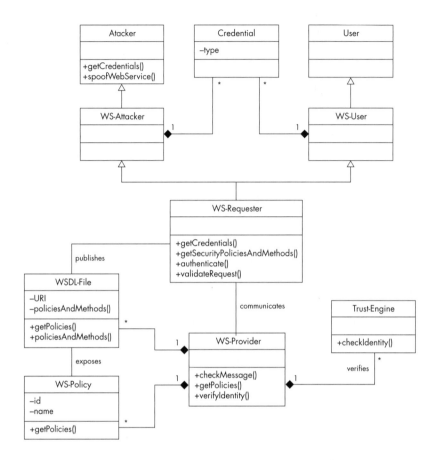

Figure 14.13: Misuse pattern: principal spoofing

The sequence diagram of Figure 14.14 shows the sequence of steps to perform a principal spoofing attack. An Attacker can obtain credentials of a valid User. When the attacker has the credentials, they can access the WSDL-File of the WS-Provider, where the WS-Policies and methods to access the web service are published. The WSDL-File can be found through the UDDI service, or it can be accessed through techniques such as 'crawling'. With the information obtained from the WSDL-File and the credentials of the User, the Attacker can create a web service.

When the Attacker has the web service, they can make a request to the WS-Provider using the credentials of the user. The WS-Provider receives the request and checks the message against the policies of the web service. If the message is correct, the WS-Provider sends the credentials to the TrustEngine to check the identity of the user. Because the credentials are valid, the request will be authenticated. When security policies are known, the Attacker will be able to develop another web service with a different behavior, according to their intentions. User credentials will be used as identification to access the system's functionality.

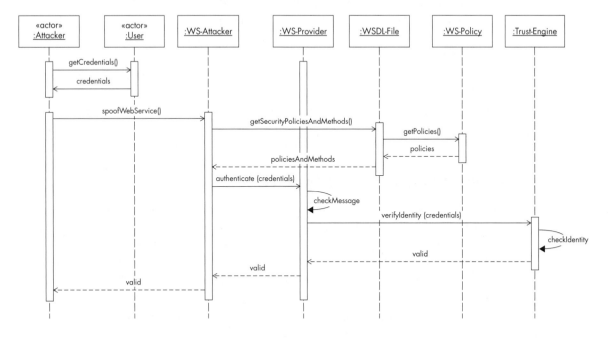

Figure 14.14: Sequence diagram for principal spoofing

Consequences

The SPOOFING WEB SERVICES misuse pattern has the following benefits for the attacker:

■ The attacker can access the sensitive information from a valid user.

■ Malicious code can be attached to the messages to make further attacks on the user or their associates.

■ The attacker can read or modify information or make transactions in the name of the valid user.

It can also have some liabilities for the attacker:

■ Knowing the attacker's behavior, forensics proofs could be shown in order to verify that the attack was carried out, and by whom.

■ If an attacker does not know about the forensics evidence that they would generate, they might be identified.

■ Some defences, described below, can stop this attack.

Affected Components

When the attack is over several components will be affected:

- *WSDL-File.* This file will no longer be trustable, because it was used by the attacker, and the file may contain vulnerabilities that would allow further attacks to the web service.

- *User credentials.* The user's credentials are compromised, so they are no longer useful and should be revoked.

- *User trust.* The user's trust in the authentication method will be compromised.

- *WS-Requester.* When the attack is over, the requests from the authorized web service should be viewed with suspicion.

Countermeasures and Forensics

Human behavior cannot be controlled, so we cannot prevent people from be deceived into releasing their credentials. Also, a victim could be robbed of their credentials.

This attack can be mitigated through the following countermeasures:

- Encrypting communications between web services. Encryption can be performed by following security standards such as XML Encryption and WS-Security.

- For each of the web services that are developed:

  - Generating an internal credential, which can be an ID or some kind of token. This credential will be embedded in the code.

  - The web service provider publishing a policy about credential requests for each transaction.

  - If the communication is done using a PKI infrastructure, the credential being sent encrypted using the public key provided by the web services provider. With this countermeasure the attacker will not be able to access the content of the message even if the message is intercepted by sniffer software.

The following forensic evidences are possible:

- We can identify which user was affected and the actions performed using logs from the web service provider.

- We can check the origin from the attack (IP address) – although the attacker can spoof its IP address.

Known Uses

- *Scenario I.* Hole [Hol06] describes some online banking security issues identified over a period of two years. During this period, several attacks were identified against a bank system by combining simple brute-force attacks with distributed-denial-of-service (DDoS) attacks that exploited the bank's login procedure. In the bank, the authentication procedure was based on a web service, which was the only point for access to users' information at which requests were authenticated.

A web service could be deployed in the bank or externally. This web service was attacked using IP spoofing and became a victim of a DDoS attack because it was not well configured; all the requests that it received were sent to the main server, skipping authentication in the web service from the bank. With this attack, the bandwidth and the resources of the bank were affected; in the worst case, the system could go down. This could be achieved if the attacker had the credentials of a user from the bank.

■ *Scenario II*. In this case a web service from an information service provided information only to authorized personnel. Every user had credentials to use the web service, which were needed because of the sensitive information being handled. The attacker obtained credentials from users and built another web service to try to access the information.

The attacker was also able to make several requests to the web service target, using the credentials from a valid user, the requests being generated from several parts of the network. The attacker used techniques from IP spoofing to hide their position. The web service target could first verify the identity from the sender of the message, or check the structure of the message, and finally check the identity of the requester. With this scenario, several attacks could be realized [Jen07]. All of these were DDoS attacks.

■ *Scenario III*. In October 2010 a Firefox plugin, 'Firesheep', was delivered. Through this plugin, an attacker without much technical knowledge could access the information of other users on the same wireless network. In this way, the attacker could see the information exchanged by other sites in their browser, such as Facebook, Twitter or Google. With a small modification to this plugin, it is possible to build a sniffer. When a session was captured, the credentials of the users could be captured without their knowledge.

The first of these attacks uses *resource exhaustion*. This type of attack attempts to compromise a web service's availability by exhausting the resources of the service's host system, such as memory, processing resources or network bandwidth. The attack can be performed using a large SOAP message document, a technique called *oversize payload*.

Another attack type, *attack obfuscation,* is made using the WS-Security standard. By providing confidentiality to sensitive data, XML encryption can hide the contents of messages. The encrypted message can contain an intended attack, such as oversize payload or XML injection. The advantage of this method is that the defender must decrypt the message to be able to analyze it.

The attacks described above are based on the trust that the system may have for its users, because an important step in the attack is the verification of the identity of the requester.

See Also

- *WS-TRUST.* This pattern helps to establish the relationships that should arise between web services in order to share their credentials (page 272 and [Aja10a]).

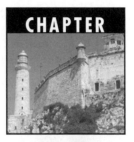

CHAPTER

15

Patterns for Cloud Computing Architecture

There are no rules of architecture for a castle in the clouds.

G K Chesterton

15.1   Introduction

Cloud computing is a new paradigm that improves the utilization of resources and decreases the power consumption of hardware. Cloud computing allows users to have access to resources, software and information using any device that has access to the Internet. The users consume these resources and pay only for the resources they use.

A cloud model provides three types of services: infrastructure-as-a-service (IaaS), platform-as-a-service (PaaS), and software-as-a-service (SaaS). IaaS provides processing, storage, networks and other fundamental computing resources on which the consumer is able to deploy and run arbitrary software, which can include operating systems and applications. PaaS offers platform layer resources, including operating system support and software development frameworks to build, deploy and deliver applications into the

411

cloud. SaaS provides end-user applications that are running on a cloud infrastructure. The applications are accessible from various client devices through a thin client interface such as a web browser (for example web-based e-mail).

We present here patterns for the three service levels of clouds:

- *Infrastructure-as-a-service* [Has12a] describes the infrastructure to allow the sharing of distributed virtualized computational resources, such as servers, storage and networks.

- *Platform-as-a-service* [Has12a] provides virtual environments for developing, deploying, monitoring and managing applications online without the cost of buying and managing the corresponding software tools or hardware.

- *Software-as-a-service* [Has12d] provides a set of software applications available in a cloud system that can be accessed by client devices through the Internet.

These are not strictly speaking security patterns, although they include security aspects in their definition. Our view is that to understand the security issues of clouds we need to look at their complete architecture. A fair amount of work has been done on specific aspects of the security of clouds, but we know of no effort to define a holistic view of their security. In a conceptual architecture we can apply the methodology we saw in Chapter 3 and which is illustrated with several examples in Chapter 16. We have not done this here, leaving it as an exercise for the reader, our point being that it should be fairly easy to apply this (or another) methodology to protect the cloud system.

Our methodology requires a systematic enumeration of threats, which we have already done [Has12c]. The next step is to consider each use cases and analyze the threats to its activities [Has12e]. We have also defined misuse patterns that describe how an attack (misuse of information) is performed from the point of view of the attacker ([Has12b], Chapter 14). This approach represents a variation of the methodology of Chapter 3 in that, instead of building a specific application, for example a financial application, we are building a distributed platform on which applications may execute. The security level of this platform contributes to the security level of the application, so an evaluation of the security of the platform must be combined with a security evaluation of the application.

Using the Patterns for Securing Clouds

Chapter 14 showed some misuse patterns. By defining precisely the units of a cloud architecture, we can observe the progression of an attack through them and define ways to stop its advance. We have started building a catalog of cloud misuse patterns; with a complete catalog we can apply them systematically and use a reference architecture [Has13] to find where we should add corresponding security patterns to stop them. This work also implies developing some new security patterns for this purpose.

The reference architecture should also support the standards that apply to each service level. There are still no accepted standards for clouds, but NIST is leading some work in this direction [Hog11]. Some of the cloud services are XML web services and they should follow their security standards (Chapter 11 and Chapter 12). The increasing use of *repre-*

sentational state transfer (REST) services, for which there is no security standard, implies that they will be handled in a mostly ad hoc fashion [Rod08]. The reference architecture and its security patterns should be valuable in providing designers with a systematic approach to handling both XML and REST-based types of web service.

Another use of the architecture is to provide a reference for security certification of services. Knowing the misuse patterns that affect a particular service, a provider can show that their service can handle the corresponding threats by incorporating appropriate security patterns, which would increase customer trust in their use.

Finally, patterns provide a way to evaluate the security of complete systems, by finding a matching security pattern to defend against each threat [Fer10a]. We can apply them to evaluate the security of cloud systems.

15.2   Infrastructure-as-a-Service

The INFRASTRUCTURE-AS-A-SERVICE pattern describes the infrastructure to allow the sharing of distributed virtualized computational resources, such as servers, storage and networks.

Context

Distributed systems in which we want to improve the utilization of resources and provide convenient access to all users.

Problem

Some organizations do not have the resources to invest in the infrastructure, middleware or applications that are needed to run their businesses. Also, they may not be able to handle increases in demand, or cannot afford to maintain and store unused resources. How can we provide these users with quality access to computational resources?

The solution to this problem must resolve the following forces:

- *Transparency.* The underlying architecture should be transparent to its users. Users should be able to use the provider's services without understanding its infrastructure.
- *Flexibility.* Different infrastructure configurations and resource volumes can be demanded by users.
- *Elasticity.* Users should be able to expand or reduce resources in order to meet the different needs of their applications.
- *Pay-per-use.* Users should only pay for the resources they consume.
- *On-demand-service.* Services should be provided on demand.
- *Manageability.* In order to manage a large volume of service requests, cloud resources must be easy to deploy and manage.

- *Accessibility.* Users should be able to access resources from anywhere at any time.
- *Testability.* We intend to develop system programs in this environment and we need to test them conveniently.
- *Shared resources.* Many users should be able to share resources in order to increase the volume of resource utilization and thus reduce costs.
- *Isolation.* Different user execution instances should be isolated from each other.
- *Shared non-functional requirements provision* (NFRs). Sharing of the costs of providing NFRs is necessary to allow providers to offer a higher level of NFRs.
- *Security.* The IaaS level is the basis for execution of the complete cloud system and its degree of security will affect all the applications running on it. We should provide a convenient and measurable structure to define security requirements.

Solution

The solution to this problem is a structure that is composed of many servers, storage and a network, which can be shared by multiple users and is accessible through the Internet. These resources are provided to the users in the form of infrastructure-as-a-service (IaaS). IaaS is based on virtualization technology, which creates unified resources that can be shared by different applications. This foundation layer – IaaS – can be used as a reference for non-functional requirements.

Structure

Figure 15.1 shows a class diagram for the cloud-based INFRASTRUCTURE-AS-A-SERVICE pattern. The `CloudController` is the main component, which processes requests from a `Party`. A `Party` can be an institution or a user (customers and administrators). A `Party` can have one or more `Accounts`. The `CloudController` coordinates a collection of services such as virtual machine (VM) scheduling, authentication, VM monitoring and management. When a `CloudController` receives a request from the `Party` to create a VM, it requests its corresponding `ClusterControllers` to provide a list of their free resources. With this information, the `CloudController` can choose which cluster will host the requested VM.

A `ClusterController` is composed of a collection of `NodeControllers`, which consist of a pool of `Servers` that host VM instances. The `ClusterController` handles the state information of its `NodeControllers`, and schedules incoming requests to run instances.

A `NodeController` controls the execution, monitoring, and termination of the VMs through a virtual machine monitor (VMM), which is responsible for running VM instances. The `CloudController` retrieves and stores user data and `VMImages`. The `VMImageRepository` contains a collection of `VMImages` that are used to instantiate a VM. The DHCP server assigns a MAC/IP (media access control/internet protocol) pair address for each VM through the `CloudController`, and requests the DNS server to translate domain names into IP addresses in order to locate cloud resources.

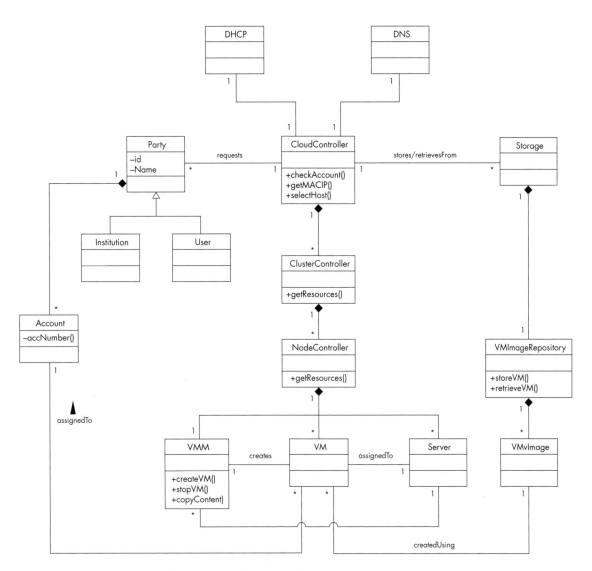

Figure 15.1: Class diagram for a cloud-based INFRASTRUCTURE-AS-A-SERVICE pattern

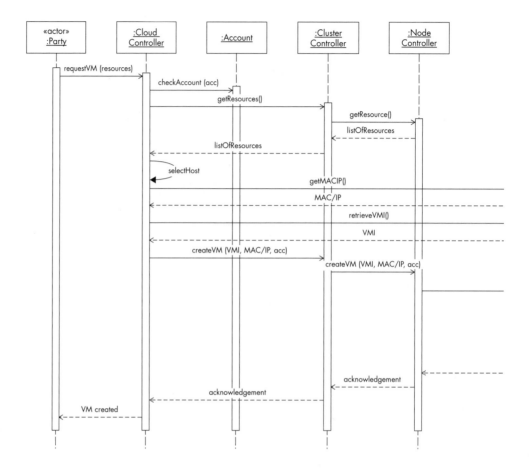

Figure 15.2: Sequence diagram for the use case 'Create a virtual machine'

Dynamics

Use cases include [Nis]:

- Open/close an account (actor: user)
- Copy data objects into/out of a cloud (actor: administrator)
- Erase data objects in a cloud (actor: administrator)
- Store/remove virtual machine images (actors: administrator, user)
- Create a virtual machine (actor: user)
- Migrate a virtual machine (actors: administrator, user)

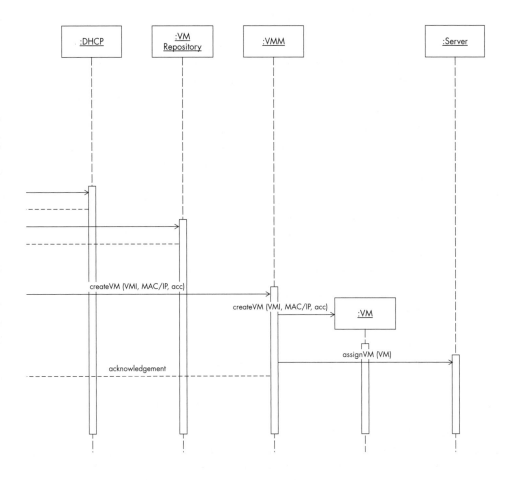

Figure 15.2 (continued)

We show two use cases below, 'Create a virtual machine' and 'Migrate a virtual machine'.

Use Case: Create a Virtual Machine – Figure 15.2

Summary	Create a virtual machine for a party, assign to it the required resources and assign it to a server.
Actor	Party.
Precondition	The Party has a valid account.
Description	1 A Party requests a VM with some computational resources from the CloudController.

2 The `CloudController` verifies whether the requester has a valid account.

3 The `CloudController` requests the available resources from the `ClusterController` closest to the location of the `Party`. In turn, the `ClusterController` queries its `NodeControllers` about their available resources. (In the sequence diagram, there is only one `ClusterController` and one `NodeController` to keep the diagram simple, but there can be more cluster and node controllers.)

4 The `NodeController` sends the list of its available resources to the `ClusterController`, and the `ClusterController` sends it back to the `CloudController`.

5 The `CloudController` chooses the first `ClusterController` that can support the computational resource requirements.

6 The `CloudController` requests a MAC/IP pair address from the `DHCP` server for the new `VM`.

7 The `CloudController` retrieves a `VM` image from the `VMRepository`.

8 The `CloudController` sends a request to the `ClusterController` to instantiate a `VM`.

9 The `ClusterController` forwards the request to the `NodeController`, which forwards it to the `VMM` (virtual machine monitor).

10 The `VMM` creates a `VM` with the requested resources.

11 The `VMM` assigns the `VM` to one of the servers.

Postcondition A virtual machine is created and assigned to an account and a server.

Use Case: Migrate a Virtual Machine – Figure 15.3

The administrator can migrate a VM to a specific node controller that can be located in the same or in a different cluster controller. The administrator can also migrate a VM to a specific location, or to the first node that has the available resources. For the scenario below, we assume that the administrator will move a VM to the first available node controller within the same cluster controller. However, the migration process can be automatic, for example due to load balancing.

Summary A virtual machine is migrated from one node controller to another.

Actor `Administrator`.

Precondition A `VM` resides on some `NodeController`.

Description 1 The `Administrator` requests the `CloudController` to migrate a `VM`.

2 The `CloudController` sends a request to the `ClusterController` to start the migration of the `VM`.

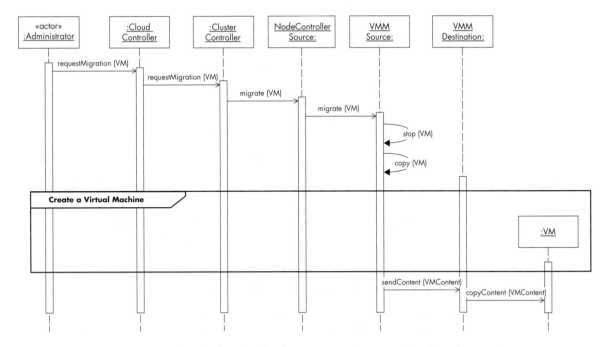

Figure 15.3: Sequence diagram for the use case 'Migrate a virtual machine'

3   The ClusterController requests the NodeControllerSource to stop the VM. The NodeControllerSource forwards this request to the VMMSource.

4   The VMMSource stops the VM and copies the content of the VM.

5   All the steps of the use case Create a Virtual Machine – Figure 15.2 are carried out.

6   The VMMSource sends the content of the VM to the VMMDestination.

7   The VMMDestination copies the content into the new VM.

Postcondition   The virtual machine has migrated to another host.

Implementation

As an example, we show the implementation of one of the known uses of this pattern. There are many ways to implement our conceptual models; this is just one possible way to do it. Eucalyptus [Euc] is open source software that allows IaaS to be implemented in order to run and control virtual machine instances via Xen and KVM. Eucalyptus consists of five main components that are described in Figure 15.4 [Bau09].

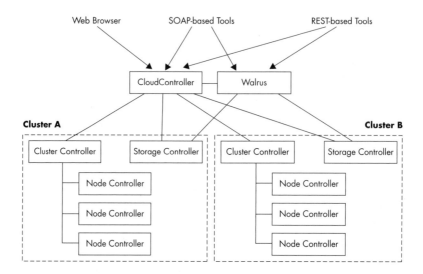

Figure 15.4: Eucalyptus' main components

The two higher-level components are the Cloud Controller and Walrus. The Cloud Controller is a Java program that offers EC2-compatible [Ama] SOAP and web interfaces. Walrus is a data storage system where users can store and access virtual machine images and their data. Walrus can be accessed through S3-compatible SOAP and REST interfaces. Top-level components can aggregate resources from several clusters.

Each cluster needs a Cluster Controller, which is typically deployed on the head node of a cluster. Each node will also need a Node Controller for controlling the VMM. Cluster Controller and Node Controllers are deployed as web services, and communications between them takes place over SOAP with WS-Security [Has09c].

A cloud can be set up as a single cluster in which the Cloud Controller and the Cluster Controller are located on the same machine, which are referred to as 'front-end'. All other machines running the Node Controllers are referred to as 'back-end'. However, a more advanced configuration is possible, comprising several Cluster Controller or Walrus' deployed on different machines.

A typical configuration around 2012 includes [Ubu]:

■ One cloud controller (CPU 1GHz, memory 512MB, disk 5400rpm IDE, disk space 40GB)

■ One Walrus controller (CPU 1GHz, memory 512MB, disk 5400rpm IDE, disk space 40GB)

■ One cluster controller plus storage Controller (CPU 1GHz, memory 512MB, disk-5400rpm IDE, disk space 40GB)

- Nodes (virtualization technology extensions, memory 1GB, disk 5400rpm IDE, disk space 40GB)

Consequences

The INFRASTRUCTURE-AS-A-SERVICE pattern offers the following benefits:

- *Transparency.* Cloud users are usually not aware of where their virtual machines are running or where their data is stored. However, in some cases users can request a general location zone for virtual machines or data.

- *Flexibility.* Cloud users can request different types of computational and storage resources. For instance, Amazon's EC2 [Ama] provides a variety of instance types and operating systems.

- *Elasticity.* Resources provided to users can be scaled up or down depending on their needs. Multiple virtual machines can be initiated and stopped to handle increased or decreased workloads.

- *Pay-per-use.* Cloud users can save on hardware investment because they do not need to purchase more servers; they just need to pay for the services that they use. Cloud services are usually charged using a fee-for-service billing model [Cen10]. For example, users might pay for the storage, bandwidth or computing resources they consume per month.

- *On-demand-services.* IaaS providers deliver computational resources, storage and network as services at users' request.

- *Manageability.* Users place their requests with the cloud administrator, who allocates, migrates and monitors VMs.

- *Accessibility.* Cloud services are delivered using user-centric interfaces via the Internet [Wan08] from anywhere and at any time.

- *Testability.* Having an environment isolated in a virtual machine allows the testing of system programs without affecting the execution of other virtual machines.

- *Shared resources.* Virtualization enables sharing a pool of resources such as processing capacity, storage and networks to be shared, so that a higher utilization rate can be achieved [Amr].

- *Isolation.* A VMM provides strong isolation between different virtual machines, whose guest operating systems are then protected from one another [Kar08].

- *Shared non-functional requirements (NFRs) provision.* Some IaaS providers offer security features such as authentication and authorization to customers, which can be added as part of the service. Sharing allows the provider to offer a higher degree of NFRs at a reasonable cost.

- *Security.* Security defenses can be defined with respect to the architecture. For example, connection of users to the cloud controller may be mutually authenticated to avoid imposters from either side.

The pattern also has the following potential liabilities:

- Cloud computing is dependent on network connections. While using cloud services, users must be connected to the Internet, although a limited amount of work can be done offline.

- The cloud may bring security risks associated with privacy and confidentiality, since users do not have control of the underlying infrastructure.

- The isolation between VMs may not be strong [Has12a].

- Virtualization introduces some performance overhead.

Known Uses

- Eucalyptus [Euc] is an open source framework used for hybrid and private cloud computing.

- OpenNebula [Ope2] is an open source toolkit for building clouds.

- Nimbus [Nimb] is an open source set of tools that offers IaaS capabilities to the scientific community.

- Amazon's EC2 [Ama] provides computing capacity though web services.

- HP Cloud Services [Hp] is a public cloud solution that provides scalable virtual servers on demand.

- IBM SmartCloud Foundation [IBMa] offers servers, storage and virtualization components for building private, public and hybrid clouds.

See Also

- The VIRTUAL MACHINE OPERATING SYSTEM ARCHITECTURE pattern ([Fer05c] and page 179) describes the VMM and its created VMs from the point of view of an operating system architecture.

- The Grid architectural pattern [Cam06] allows the sharing of distributed and heterogeneous computational resources such as CPU, memory and disk storage for a grid environment.

- Misuse patterns in [Has12a] describe possible attacks to cloud infrastructures.

- The PLATFORM-AS-A-SERVICE (PaaS) pattern (page 423) describes development platforms that provide virtual environments for developing applications in the cloud.

- The Party pattern [Fow97] indicates that users can be individuals or institutions.

- Several of the patterns shown earlier in this book can be used to protect different aspects of the cloud system.

15.3   Platform-as-a-Service

The PLATFORM-AS-A-SERVICE pattern describes how to provide virtual environments for developing, deploying, monitoring and managing applications online without the cost of buying and managing the corresponding software tools or hardware.

Context

PaaS services are built on top of the cloud's infrastructure-as-a-service (IaaS) features, which provides the underlying infrastructure.

Problem

Organizations may want to develop their own custom applications without buying and maintaining the developing tools, databases, operating systems and infrastructure underlying them. Also, when a team is spread across several locations, it is necessary to have a convenient way to coordinate their work. How can we provide secure PaaS functions?

The solution to this problem must resolve the following forces:

- *Collaboration.* Sometimes teams of developers are located in different geographic locations. When working on a project, they all should have access to the development tools, code and data.

- *Coordination.* When many developers work on a complex project, they need to coordinate their work.

- *Elasticity.* There should be a way to increase or decrease resources for more compute-intense development and deployment tasks.

- *Pay-per-use.* Parties should only pay for the resources that they use.

- *Transparency.* Developers should not have to be concerned about the underlying infrastructure, including hardware and operating systems, and its configuration for development and deployment.

- *On-demand services.* Developers should be able to request an application tool and start using it.

- *Accessibility.* Developers should be able to access tools via standard networks, from anywhere at any time.

- *Testability.* We intend to develop application programs in this environment and we need to test them conveniently.

- *Versatility.* The platform should be able to be used to build applications for any domain or type of application. Different options for developing tools should be offered to the users.

- *Simplification.* Developers should be able to build applications without installing any tool or specialized software on their computers.

■ *Security.* The platform should offer facilities for developing secure programs, and should itself be protected from attacks.

Solution

PaaS offers virtual execution environments with shared tools and libraries for application development and deployment into the cloud. PaaS uses IaaS as a foundation layer (servers, storage and network), and hides the complexity of managing the infrastructure underneath.

Structure

Figure 15.5 shows a class diagram for a cloud-based platform-as-a-service. The `PaaSProvider` processes requests from `Parties`. A `Party` can be an institution or a user (developers, administrators). The `Party` will choose the development tools from the `SoftwareRepository`, which contains a list of available tools. The `PaaSProvider` offers `VirtualEnvironments` such as `DevelopmentEnvironment` and `DeploymentEnvironment`. The `DevelopmentEnvironment` is composed of `DevelopmentTools`, `Libraries`, `Databases`. The `VirtualEnvironments` are built on the IaaS features, which provide the underlying hardware. The same `PaaSProvider` can manage the IaaS, or it can be managed by a third-party service provider.

Dynamics

Use cases include the following [Dod10]:

■ Open/close an account

■ Request a virtual environment

■ Use a virtual environment

■ Install development software

■ Deploy an application

■ Undo deploying an application

■ Consume development software – Figure 15.6, below

Use Case: Consume Development Software – Figure 15.6

Summary	A party requests to the use of a development application for the first time.
Actor	`Party`.
Precondition	The `Party` has an account.
Description	1 The `Party` requests the use of specific development software.
	2 The `PaaSProvider` checks whether the `Party` has a valid account.
	3 The `Party` downloads the client applications onto its machine.
Postcondition	The client application is downloaded on the party's machine.

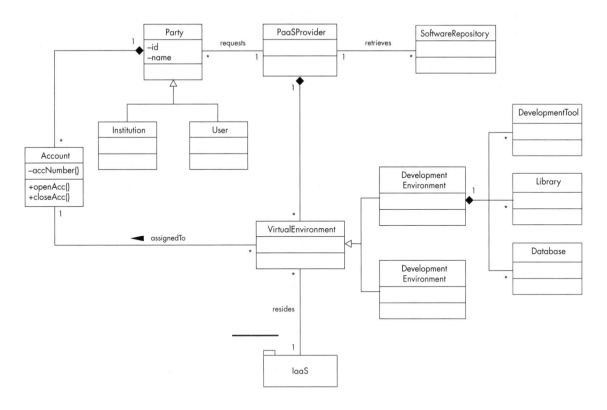

Figure 15.5: Class diagram for the PLATFORM-AS-A-SERVICE pattern

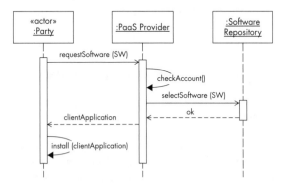

Figure 15.6: Sequence diagram for the use case 'Consume development software'

Use Case: Deploy an Application – Figure 15.7

Summary	A party requests deployment of an application into the cloud, so that the application can be accessed by end-users from anywhere at any time.
Actor	Party (developer).
Precondition	The Party has an account.
Description	1 A Party asks to deploy their application into the cloud.
	2 The PaaSProvider checks whether the Party has a valid account.
	3 The PaaSProvider calculates the computational resources needed for the deployment, such as the number of virtual machines.
	4 The PaaSProvider asks the IaaS to create a set of virtual machines (VEs).
	5 The PaaSProvider installs and runs the code.
Postcondition	The application is running and ready to be accessed by the end users.

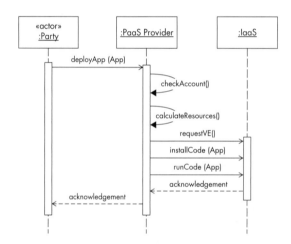

Figure 15.7: Sequence diagram for the use case 'Deploy an application'

Implementation

As an example of the implementation of a typical PaaS approach, we describe the approach used by Force.com [Sal]. Force.com is a cloud platform-as-a-service system from Salesforce.com. Force.com's platform provides PaaS services as a stack of technologies and services covering infrastructure, database as a service, integration as a service, logic as a service, user interface as a service, development as a service, and AppExchange [Sal2], to enable the creation of business applications.

Figure 15.8 shows the stack of Force.com's technologies and services, which includes:

- *Infrastructure.* The foundation of the Force.com platform is the infrastructure that supports the other layers. Force.com uses three geographically dispersed data centers and a production-class development laboratory which use replication to mirror the data at each location.

- *Database as a service.* Customers can create customized data objects, such as relational tables, and use metadata to describes those objects. Force.com provides data security by offering features such as user authentication, administrative permissions, object-level permissions and field-level permissions.

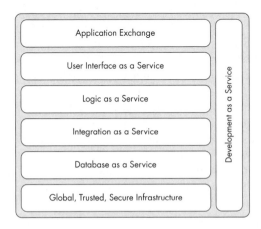

Figure 15.8: The Force.com stack and services (from [Sal2])

- *Integration as a service.* Force.com provides integration technologies that are compliant with open web services and service-oriented architecture (SOA) standards, including SOAP, WSDL and WS-I Basic Profile [Fer10b]. Force.com offers different prepackaged integration solutions, such as Web Services API, Web Services Apex, callouts and mashups, and outbound messaging.

- *Logic as a service.* Force.com provides three options for implementing an application's business processing logic: declarative logic (unique fields, audit history tracking, history tracking and approval processes), formula-based logic (formula fields, data validation rules, workflow rules and approval processes), and procedural logic (Apex triggers and classes).

- *User interface as a service.* Force.com provides two types of tools for creating the user interface of applications built on the platform applications: Force.com's Builder and Visualforce. Builder creates metadata, which Force.com uses to generate a default user interface for each database object, with its corresponding methods such as create, edit and delete. With Visualforce, developers can use standard web development technologies such as HTML, Ajax and Adobe Flex to create user interfaces for their cloud applications.

- *Development as a service.* Force.com offers some features to create cloud applications: Metadata API, Integrated Development Environment (IDE), Force.com Sandbox and Code Share. Metadata API allows modification of the XML files that control an organization's metadata. The IDE provides a code editor for adding, modifying and testing Apex applications. Apex is the Force.com proprietary programming language. Multiple developers can share a code source repository using the synchronization features of the IDE. Force.com Sandbox provides a separate cloud-based application environment for development, quality assurance and training. Force.com Code Share allows developers from different organizations to collaborate on the development, testing and deployment of cloud applications.

Force.com IDE [Sal3] is a client application for creating, modifying, and deploying applications. Once the user downloads the IDE to their local machine, they can start coding. The IDE is in communication with the Force.com platform servers. There are two types of operations: online and offline. For example, in the online mode, when a class is saved, the IDE sends the class to the Force.com servers that compile the class and return any result (error message). In the offline mode, all changes are performed on a local machine, and once connected to Force.com gain, the changes are submitted and committed. Force.com provides built-in support for automated testing. Once an application is developed in the development environment, it may be migrated to another environment, such as testing, or production.

- *Application exchange.* AppExchange is a cloud application marketplace where users can find applications that are delivered by partners or third-party developers.

Force.com offers environments [Sal4] where users can start developing, testing and deploying cloud computing applications. There are different types of environments, such as production, development and test environments. The production environment stores live data, while the development environment stores test data and is used for developing and testing applications. The development environment has two types: Developer Edition and Sandbox. Sandbox is a copy of the production environment that can include data, configurations, or both. A Developer Edition environment [Sal5] includes the following developer technologies: Apex programming language, Visualforce for building custom user interface and controllers, the Integration APIs, and more. Figure 15.9 shows the platform for the Developer Edition environment. The Force.com's virtual environments run on Salesforce's infrastructure.

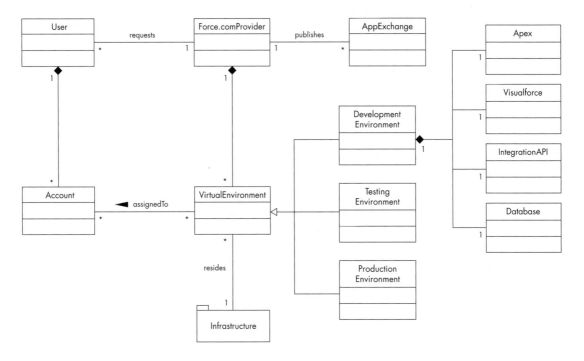

Figure 15.9: Class diagram of Force.com's PaaS architecture

Force.com uses various security techniques to defend its platform from different types of threats [Sal6]:

■ User authentication: most users are authenticated on the login page, but there are also other forms of user authentication, such as delegated authentication and Security Assertion Markup Language (SAML).

■ An authenticated session needs to be established before accessing the Force.com SOAP API and Metadata API.

■ Force.com secures its network using various mechanisms, such as stateful packet inspection (SPI), *bastion hosts*, two-factor authentication processes and end-to-end TLS/SSL cryptographic protocols.

■ For sensitive data such as customer passwords, Force.com applies an MD5 one-way cryptographic hash function, and supports encryption of field data.

■ At an infrastructure and network level, Salesforce.com applies rigorous security standards, such as SysTrust SAS 70 Type II.

- Salesforce.com implements industry best practices to harden the host computers. For example, all hosts use Linux or Solaris distribution with non-default configurations and minimal processes, user accounts and network protocols.

Consequences

The PLATFORM-AS-A-SERVICE pattern offers the following benefits:

- *Collaboration*. Geographically dispersed developers can collaborate on the same project because the code is managed online [Law08].
- *Coordination*. A project can be conveniently administered from a central point.
- *Elasticity*. The resources (storage, networking resources and servers) needed to develop and deploy an application can grow or shrink to accommodate varying workload volumes. Scaling application deployments horizontally by replicating application components such as application servers and data stores is also possible.
- *Pay-per-use*. Users only pay for the services they consume, and do not need to buy any development tools or full year licenses.
- *Transparency*. The PaaS provider manages upgrades, patches and other maintenance, as well as the infrastructure. Users do not need to worry about compatibility issues between the server configurations and the development software.
- *On-demand services*. PaaS providers offer software development tools that can be used by developers when needed.
- *Accessibility*. PaaS services are accessed through the Internet via web browsers from anywhere at any time.
- *Testability*. The variety of tools available makes testing application programs more convenient in this environment.
- *Versatility*. PaaS offers various programming languages and databases. For example, with Microsoft Azure you can build applications using .NET, Java, PHP and others.
- *Simplification*. Developers do not need to buy or install any development tools, or to keep the servers updated. The development tools are managed and maintained by the PaaS providers.
- *Security*. The development tools offered should include tools to develop, test and deploy secure applications, supporting some secure methodology [Uzu12c]. The platform itself should have protection against its identified threats.

The pattern also has the following potential liabilities:

- PaaS providers usually offer their own proprietary development software, which makes it hard to migrate an application from one PaaS vendor to another. Also, APIs from different providers vary, which raises portability issues.

- The availability of the PaaS products depends mostly on the Internet. Thus, the services are available only as long there are network connections.

- A PaaS provider can either own or subcontract the underlying infrastructure from an IaaS provider. In either case, the security or availability of PaaS services may not be assured.

- Unscheduled upgrades of cloud-based software can be disruptive.

Known Uses

- Google App Engine [Goo2] provides an environment for building and hosting web applications on Google's infrastructure. Google App Engine supports two application environments: Java and Python.

- Microsoft Azure [Micb] provides a platform to build, deploy and manage applications. It provides various programming languages, such as .NET, Java, PHP and others, to build applications.

- Salesforce [Sal] offers a development platform for building custom applications. (See the Implementation section above)

- IBM SmartCloud Applications Services [Dod10] delivers a collaborative environment that supports the full lifecycle for software development, deployment and delivery.

See Also

- The INFRASTRUCTURE-AS-A-SERVICE pattern (page 413) describes the infrastructure to allow sharing of distributed virtualized computational resources.

- Misuse Patterns in [Has12a] describe possible attacks to cloud environments, which may affect the security of PaaS.

- The Cloud Computing: Platform as a Service (PaaS) pattern [Nex10] describes execution environments for PaaS applications.

- The Party pattern [Fow97] indicates that users can be individuals or institutions.

- Several of the patterns presented earlier can be used to protect the platform. The catalog of patterns in Chapter 17 can be used to provide guidance about what to include in a development tool.

15.4 Software-as-a-Service

The SOFTWARE-AS-A-SERVICE pattern describes how to provide a set of software applications available in a cloud system that can be accessed by client devices through the Internet.

Example

Bob has a small business that sells services. Currently, he has three salespeople who are offering the services and meeting potential customers. He is thinking of expanding his company and hiring more salespeople, which will make it more difficult to track the sales and potential customer's information.

Context

SaaS applications are hosted by a provider and accessed through the Internet via user interfaces or APIs.

Problem

Customers may need to use software products that do not require local installation and maintenance of the software. How can software be delivered over the network?

The solution to this problem must resolve the following forces:

- *Pay-per-use*. Customers should be charged on a per-use basis, like utility services.

- *Transparency*. Customers should not be concerned about maintenance or updates to the software.

- *On-demand services*. Customers should have the ability to start using an application when they need to.

- *Accessibility*. Customers should be able to access the software applications at any time and anywhere.

- *Flexibility*. Customers should be able to configure the software application to their needs, such as currency or date formats.

- *Elasticity*. Applications should be able to scale down or up depending on the customers' needs [Ju10]. For example, it should be possible to increase or decrease the number of users using the application.

- *Simplification*. Customers should not need to install any special software on their local machine.

- *Security*. The software offered to users must be secure: it should be built following a secure methodology [Uzu12c].

Solution

SaaS applications are delivered as a service to users typically thorough the Internet via web browsers or APIs. SaaS based in the cloud enables users to access applications on demand, in which both computation and storage are hosted in the cloud without installing any software on their local machines. SaaS can be developed and deployed using underlying platform-as-a-service (PaaS) or infrastructure-as-a-service (IaaS) offerings.

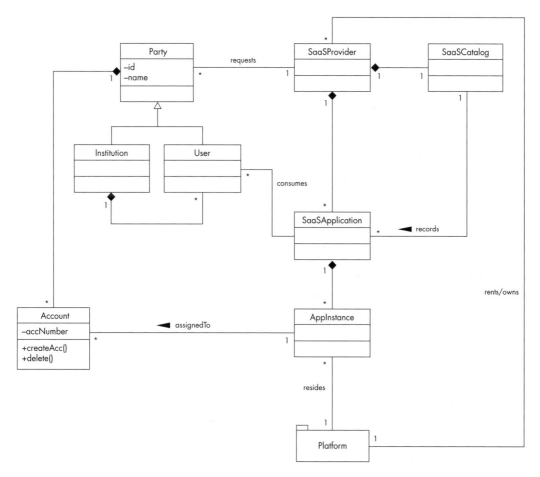

Figure 15.10: Class diagram for the SOFTWARE-AS-A-SERVICE pattern

Structure

Figure 15.10 shows the class diagram for software-as-a-service. A `SaaSProvider` processes requests from `Parties`. A `Party` can be either a `User` or a group of users (an `Institution`). A `Party` can have one or more `Accounts`. A `SaaSProvider` offers a set of `SaaSApplications`. The `SaaSCatalog` contains the list of `SaaSApplications` that are offered to the users. There can be a single `AppInstance` of the application that is shared by different users, or a single instance per user. The `SaaSApplications` resides on a `Platform`. `SaaSApplications` can be deployed using underlying platform-as-a-service or infrastructure-as-a-service offerings. The platform can be owned or rented to a third-party provider.

Dynamics

The set of use cases includes the following [Spe09]:

- Open/close an account (actor: party)
- Set up an application (actor: SaaS provider)
- Meter usage (actor: SaaS provider)
- Subscribe to an application (actor: SaaS provider)
- Consume an application (actor: party)

We show the last two of these use cases in detail below.

Use Case: Subscribe to an Application – Figure 15.11

Summary	A user asks to buy a subscription in order to access an application from the SaaS provider
Actor	User.
Precondition	The User has a valid account.
Description	1 A User asks to subscribe to an application.
	2 The SaaSProvider checks whether the User has a valid account.
	3 The SaaSProvider creates an instance of the software application. In this case we assume that each application instance serves one party.
	4 The SaaSProvider acknowledges the User that his subscription to the application is complete.
Postcondition	The user can start using the application.

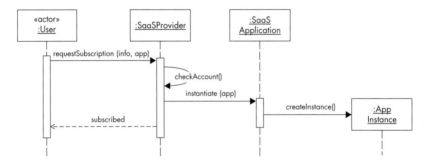

Figure 15.11: Sequence diagram for the use case 'Subscribe to an application'

Use Case: Consume an Application – Figure 15.12

Summary	A user asks to use an application for which they are already subscribed.
Actor	User.

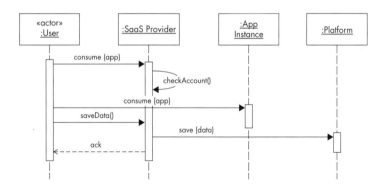

Figure 15.12: Sequence diagram for the use case 'Consume an application'

Precondition   The User has an account and they have subscribed to the application.

Description   1   A User asks to consume an application to which they are subscribed.

2   The SaaSProvider checks whether the user has a valid account.

3   The User starts consuming the application.

4   The User asks for their data to be saved.

Postcondition   The User's data is stored in the cloud.

Implementation

SaaS can be categorized into four distinct levels [Per10]. The first-level services are *ad hoc/ custom*, in which each customer has their own customized version of the hosted application. For the second-level services, *configurable*, the SaaS provider's servers host a separate instance of the application for each customer, similarly to the previous level. However, the instances are not customized for each customer, but provide some configuration options.

The third-level services are *configurable, multi-tenant efficient*, in which a single instance of the software serves all customers, with configurable metadata. At the fourth level, *scalable, configurable, multi-tenant-efficient*, multiple identical instances are controlled by the load balancer.

In order to manage multi-tenant data, there are three approaches for databases [Liu10]. The simplest approach is to store data in different databases for each customer. For the second approach, the same database hosts multiple customers' data, where each customer has their own tables and schema. In the third approach, customers' data is stored in the same database and set of tables.

In Salesforce's model, a single instance of an application is shared among many customers, and customers' data is stored in a shared database. For customization purpose, metadata can be used to configure the way in which an application appears and behaves, such as appearance of the screen and data fields.

Example Resolved

Bob has two options:

- Bob has to make an initial investment in infrastructure, such as the hardware, middleware and software needed for an application that can track sales, customer's information, potential customers and reports. He has also to be in charge of the maintenance of the equipment and the necessary software to run the application. The problem with this option is that if demand decreases, there are still operational costs for unused resources. The benefit of this option is that he can have control over the underlying infrastructure as well as his data.

- Bob can subscribe to SaaS application hosted by a cloud provider. The cloud provider takes control of the software application. The SaaS provider may rent the infrastructure to a third-party provider, which makes the process of compliance more complicated. The location where the data is processed or stored may be uncertain, which may raise data privacy issues. Since SaaS solutions are web-hosted, they have to be accessed by an Internet connection, which can be insecure. Sensitive data has to be stored online on provider's servers. If the provider goes into bankruptcy, lock-in can be a possible issue.

Consequences

The SOFTWARE-AS-A-SERVICE pattern offers the following benefits:

- *Pay-per-use*. SaaS providers often charge for their applications based on some parameters such as number of users. For example, Salesforce's Enterprise CRM costs $125 per user per month. Google Apps for business costs $5 per user per month, but it is free for individuals and small teams.

- *Transparency*. SaaS applications are deployed, supported, maintained and upgraded by the provider. Due to the fact that SaaS applications are hosted in the cloud, updates and upgrades are available immediately to the users [Ju10]. Users typically do not need to install or set up any application on their local machines. Also, SaaS applications can be used from any operating system.

- *On-demand services*. SaaS applications can be used as soon as they are needed. For example, to get access to Google Gmail, a user just opens a browser, logs into their account, and starts using the application.

- *Accessibility*. SaaS applications can be accessed across the Internet by a user at any time.

- *Flexibility.* SaaS applications can be customized to some degree, depending on how they were designed. Not all providers offer customization. For example, a customer may be able to modify a page layout.

- *Elasticity.* SaaS applications are hosted in the cloud, so users do not need to install them on their local machines.

- *Simplification.* Typically SaaS applications are accessed through web browsers or APIs, which do not require specific software on the client.

- *Security.* It is possible to deploy secure applications if they have been built using a secure development methodology [Uzu12c].

The pattern also has the following potential liabilities:

- There are some applications that demand high user interaction; in such cases the SaaS model may not be suitable because of the network latency.

- Since customers' data is stored on the vendor's servers, or even on a third-party's servers, data security becomes an issue.

- The network used to accessed SaaS applications, such as the Internet, can be insecure. This can raise security issues such as integrity and confidentiality.

- SaaS applications typically are unique to each provider, which makes it harder for users to switch to a different vendor.

- SaaS applications may be updated frequently by their providers, which may make it difficult for users to manage the integration of SaaS applications with their business processes.

- Unplanned upgrades can be a disadvantage, especially if they impose an unscheduled training requirement on the customer.

- Cloud applications may introduce compliance issues because the users' data is stored and managed by the provider.

- If the provider goes into bankruptcy, lock-in can be a possible issue.

Known Uses

- Salesforce.com's CRM (Customer Relationship Management) [Sal] is online web-based software that records, tracks, manages and analyzes sales data.

- Google applications such as Gmail, Google Calendar and Google Docs [Goo1] are web-based applications that can be accessed through different thin clients with Internet connection.

- Freshbooks.com [Freb] is an online invoicing service intended mainly to serve small businesses.

- IBM SmartCloud Solutions [IBMa] provides a set of software and business processes delivered by IBM as a service, including Business Analytics and Optimization, Social Business, Smarter Commerce and Smarter Cities.

See Also

- The INFRASTRUCTURE-AS-A-SERVICE pattern (page 413) describes the infrastructure to allow sharing of distributed virtualized computational resources [Has12a].

- The PLATFORM-AS-A-SERVICE pattern (page 423) describes virtual environments for developing, deploying, testing, and managing applications online [Has12a].

- The Misuse patterns in [Has12b] describe possible attacks to cloud environments.

- The Party pattern [Fow97] indicates that users can be individuals or institutions.

- The patterns in this book and our secure methodology (Chapter 3) can offer an effective way to make SaaS secure.

Part III

Use of the Patterns

Part III

Use of the Proteins

CHAPTER

16

Building Secure Architectures

Design in art, is a recognition of the relation between various things, various elements in the creative flux. You can't invent a design. You recognize it, in the fourth dimension. That is, with your blood and your bones, as well as with your eyes.

D H Lawrence

We present now some examples of how the patterns we have described in this book can be used to build secure architectures. We use the methodology we presented in Chapter 3, although other methodologies are also possible. It is even possible not to use any methodology, but in this case the application of the patterns depends entirely on the experience and knowledge of the designer. We first expand some aspects of our methodology, then show four examples taken from different types of applications, from financial [Bra08a], control [Fer10d], legal [Fer07c] and medical domains[Fer05g] [Fer12b] [Sor04] [Sor05].

The examples show the use of the patterns in the following stages of the application lifecycle:

- *Requirements stage*. Use cases define the required interactions with the system. We study each action within a use case and see which attacks are possible. We then determine which policies would stop these attacks. From the use cases we can also determine the required rights for each actor, and thus apply a *need-to-know* policy.

- *Analysis stage*. Analysis patterns, and in particular semantic analysis patterns, are used to build conceptual application models. Security patterns are superimposed to apply security mechanisms. We build a conceptual model in which repeated applications of a security pattern realizes the rights determined from use cases.

- *Design stage*. We map the abstract security patterns identified in the analysis stage to design artifacts: interfaces, components, distribution and networking. Design mechanisms are selected to stop these attacks. User interfaces should correspond to use cases and may be used to enforce the authorizations defined in the analysis stage. Components can be secured by using authorization rules.

- *Implementation stage*. This stage requires reflecting the security rules defined at the design stage in the code. Because these rules are expressed as classes, associations and constraints, they can be implemented as classes in object-oriented languages. At this stage we can also select specific security packages or COTS components.

We do not show examples of the deployment and maintenance stages.

16.1   Enumerating Threats

An important aspect of security requirements is a systematic and accurate listing of the potential attacks (threats) to the system. With this listing we can decide what specific defense mechanisms to use. There have been several attempts to consider attacks to define the system security requirements, for example [Hal08b]. In our approach we consider each action in each use case and see how it can be subverted by an internal or external attacker [Bra08a] [Fer06c]. For those actions which use (read/write) or produce data, we can see how this data can be misused by the attacker, which results in a very complete (and possibly exhaustive) list of threats. From this list we can deduce what policies are necessary to prevent or mitigate the attacks. The idea is that all the use cases of an application define all the possible interactions of actors with the application. It is in these interactions where attackers could try to misuse the system.

Other approaches to enumerating threats based on attack trees are shown in [Sch99b] and [Ste02].

Use cases are not atomic, but imply a set of actions [Lar05]. For example, in a use case of borrowing a book from the library, one must check whether the user has a valid account, they are not overdue and so on. Consider a financial company that provides investment services to its customers. Customers hold accounts and send orders to the company for buying or selling commodities (stocks, bonds, real estate, art). Each customer account is in the charge of a custodian (a broker), who carries out the orders of the customer. Customers send orders to their brokers by e-mail or by phone. Brokers advise their customers about investments. A government auditor visits periodically to check for application of laws and regulations.

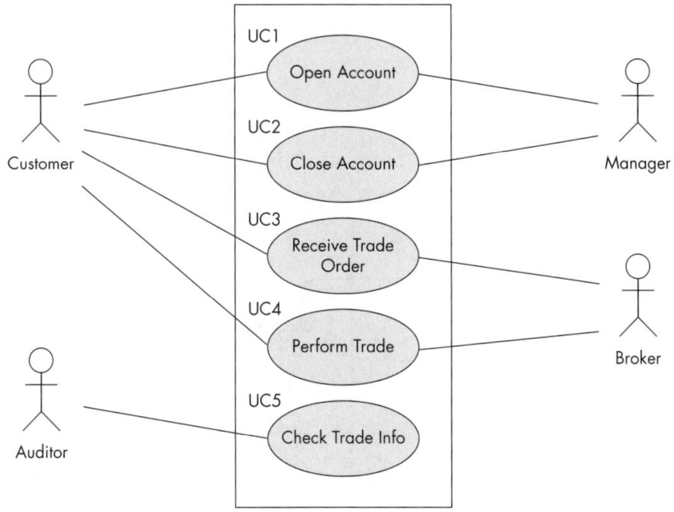

Figure 16.1: Use cases for a financial institution

Figure 16.1 shows the use case diagram for this institution. Figure 16.2 shows the activity diagram for the use case 'Open an account'. Potentially each action (activity) is susceptible to attack, although not necessarily through the computer system. For each potential attack (threat) we can attach a possible goal. For this use case we could have the following potential threats:

Threat 1 The customer is an imposter and opens a spurious account to transfer money at a later time.

Threat 2 The customer provides false information and opens an account with this false information.

Threat 3 The manager is an imposter and collects user information.

Threat 4 The (legitimate) manager collects customer information to sell or use illegally.

Threat 5 The manager creates a spurious account with the customer's information.

Threat 6 The manager creates a spurious bank card to access the account.

Threat 7 An attacker prevents the customers from accessing their accounts.

Threat 8 An attacker tries to move money from an account to their own (legitimate) account.

Relating threats to use cases provides a systematic and relatively complete list of possible threats. Each threat identified can be analyzed to see how it can be accomplished in the specific environment. The list can then be used to guide the design and to select security products. It can also be used to evaluate the final design by analyzing whether the system's defenses can stop all these attacks. Since use cases define all the interactions with the system, we can find from them the rights needed by these roles to perform their work (the *need-to-know* principle).

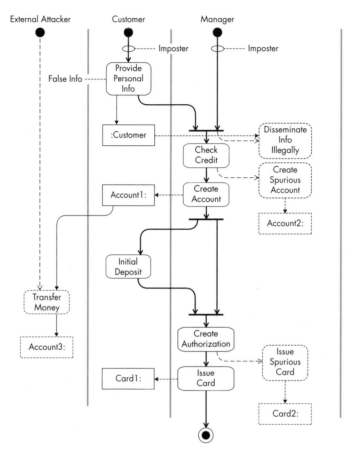

Figure 16.2: Activity diagram for the use case 'Open an account'

In the activity diagram in Figure 16.2 the threats are shown as misuse actions. Undesired consequences in the form of additional or alternative artifacts created have also been added. With these annotations, the attacks and vulnerabilities presented by the use case become part of our understanding of the use case and are explicit in its analysis.

From our analysis we can now find out what policies are needed to stop these attacks. For this we can select from the typical policies used in secure systems [Fer13]. This should result in a minimum set of mechanisms, instead of an approach in which mechanisms are piled up because they might be useful. For example, to avoid imposters we can have a policy of identification and authentication (I&A) for every subject participating in a use case.

To stop the threats in the example on page 443, we need the following policies:

- *Threat 1, 3*. Mutual authentication. Every interaction across system nodes is authenticated.

- *Threat 2*. Verify source of information.

- *Threat 4*. Logging. Since the manager is using his legitimate rights, we can only log his actions for auditing at a later time.

- *Threats 5, 6*. Separation of administration from the use of data. For example, a manager can create accounts, but should have no rights to withdraw from or deposit in the account.

- *Threat 7*. Protection against denial of service. We need some redundancy in the system to increase its availability.

- *Threat 8*. Authorization. If the user is not explicitly authorized, they should not be able to move money from any account.

We made this approach more systematic in [Bra08a]. We believe that this approach can produce all the attacks that can be defined at the application level. There is a trade-off between cost, usability and acceptable level of risk. Finding the right mix for your application involves a risk analysis. In our use case approach, we identify risks as an integral part of the use case's definitions. Vulnerabilities are combined with specific actors and their motivations. In the analysis phase we match security breaches with defense strategies using patterns. Because the vulnerabilities, and corresponding defenses, are an integral part of both structural and functional views, the consequences of specific security failures can be analyzed in the appropriate context. Risk analysis is better supported than in methodologies that lacks these views.

16.2 The Analysis Stage

We proposed a new type of analysis pattern, called a *semantic analysis pattern* (SAP) [Fer00]. A semantic analysis pattern is a pattern that describes a small set of coherent use cases that together describe a basic generic application. The use cases are selected in such a way that the application can fit a variety of situations. Using SAPs we developed a methodology to build the conceptual model systematically. To use the methodology, it is necessary to first have a collection of patterns, such as those in this book. We have developed several analysis patterns, for example [Fer99a] [Sor04] [Sor05] [Yua03], and others exist in the literature, for example [Fow97] [Ham04].

We can use SAPs as part of our secure system development methodology. We extend the SAP to consider possible attacks to the fundamental use cases that define it, and we define policies to prevent the attacks. This is the application of an idea proposed in [Fer06c] which emphasizes that the secure design of a system should be based on its expected types of attacks. Since the SAPs are used to build the conceptual model of an application, we have now a portion of a conceptual model in which functional and security aspects are integrated from the start. We call this a *secure semantic analysis pattern* (SSAP). As an example, Section 16.4 (page 451) describes a SSAP to handle legal cases. SSAPs follow the current tendency in security research of integrating business functions with security aspects from the beginning of the development lifecycle [Nag05] [Sch06a].

It is possible to superimpose in the SAPs the authorizations that are required to apply a *least privilege* policy. The use cases define all the ways to use the system, and we need to give the actors involved the rights they need to perform their interactions [Fer97]. We will illustrate these concepts using a medical application (another medical application is described later in this chapter).

Figure 16.3 shows a sequence diagram that implements the use case 'Admit a new patient' when a medical center gets a new patient. The 'Admit a new patient' use case is an interaction with a medical system in the PATIENT TREATMENT RECORDS pattern described on page 468. An administrative clerk needs rights to define a guardian and to create a patient record, patient information, a medical history and a treatment instance. We can add authorization rules to perform these functions to the PATIENT TREATMENT RECORDS pattern by adding instances of some security policy.

One of the most basic security policies is that defined by the ROLE-BASED ACCESS CONTROL (RBAC) pattern (page 78). In this model users join roles according to their tasks or jobs, and rights are assigned to the roles. In this way a need-to-know policy can be applied, in which roles get only the rights they need to perform their tasks (see Chapter 6).

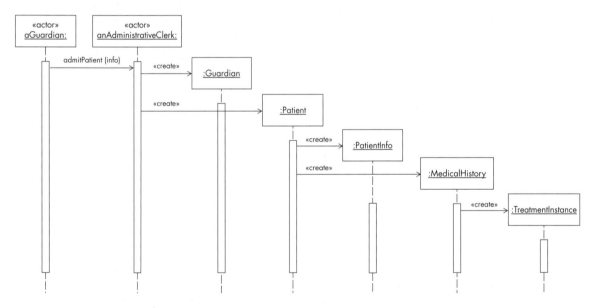

Figure 16.3: Sequence diagram for the use case 'Admit a new patient'

As an example of our approach, we add RBAC constraints to the SAP mentioned earlier. The PATIENT TREATMENT RECORDS pattern describes the treatment or stay instance of a patient in a hospital [Sor04]. The hospital may be a member of a medical group. Each patient has a primary physician, an employee of the hospital. Upon admission the patient record is created, or information is updated from previous visit(s). Inpatients are assigned a location, nurse team and consulting doctors. This pattern realizes use cases 'Admit a new patient', 'Discharge patient', 'Assign assets to an inpatient', and 'Assign nurse to a location'. Assets of the medical group are assigned to a patient through associations. Figure 16.4 shows associations between the classes `Doctor`, `Nurse` and `Location` and the class `Patient`, which describe the corresponding assignments. In particular, all patients are assigned a primary doctor, while inpatients may also be assigned consulting doctors. `Locations` include the room assigned to an inpatient, or other places for specific treatments.

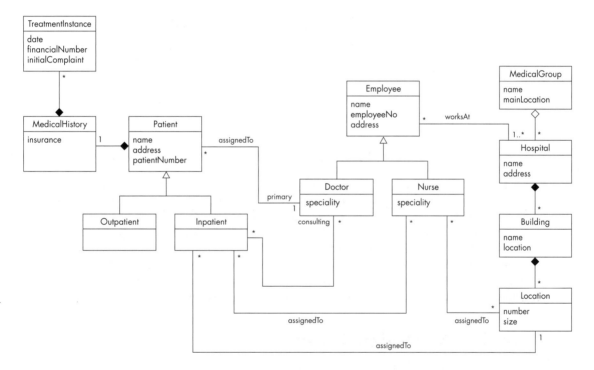

Figure 16.4: Class diagram for the PATIENT TREATMENT RECORDS pattern

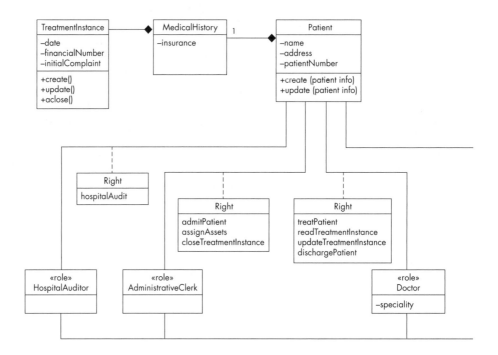

Figure 16.5: PATIENT TREATMENT RECORDS pattern with RBAC authorizations

The assets of the medical group are organized in a hierarchical arrangement that describes their physical or administrative structure. Specifically, `MedicalGroup` includes some `Hospitals`, and in turn each `Hospital` includes some `Buildings` (we assume that hospitals do not share buildings). Each treatment `Location` is part of a `Building`. The class `Employee` classifies the types of personnel that are assigned to patients. Figure 16.5 superimposes RBAC rights on some of the classes of Figure 16.4, indicating rights for several roles. We have now an SSAP that, in addition to being a unit for building a conceptual model, also indicates the typical roles that would perform its use cases, and their rights.

16.3   The Design Stage

We can now carry over the security architecture of the analysis stage to the design stage. One approach to enforcing security constraints is to use a Model-View-Controller (MVC) pattern [Bus96]. Each View corresponds to an interface for a use case, and we can enforce role rights at these interfaces. Figure 16.6 (page 450) implements the use case 'Admit a new patient' and shows the `AdministrativeClerk` role to be the only role with the ability to admit patients and perform the required actions.

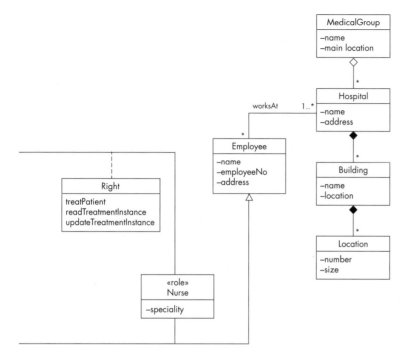

Figure 16.5 (continued)

A design model can be made more specific by specializing it for a particular language. For example, it could be tailored for Java and J2EE components by using the classes `Observable` (instead of `Model`), `Observer` and `Controller` from the Java libraries. It is also possible to define rights in J2EE components. This security is specified in the deployment descriptor that is written in XML [Kov01]. Security in J2EE is based on roles and matches the model we are using well. For example, if the `Patient` class is implemented as a component, its descriptor may specify that `TreatmentInstance` can only be modified by doctors. This rule is at a lower level than interface rules and could not be overridden – that is, no rule in the `AdmitPatientView` can give somebody who is not a doctor the right to modify patient treatment instances. This approach adds a second line of defense against administrator errors (the *defense in depth* principle). Similarly, components can access persistent data in relational databases using JDBC. These relations could include further authorizations to provide another line of defense. When we do this, it is necessary to make sure that the rights defined in the views, components and database items do not conflict with each other. To determine possible conflicts, we need to map security constraints across architectural levels [Fer99b].

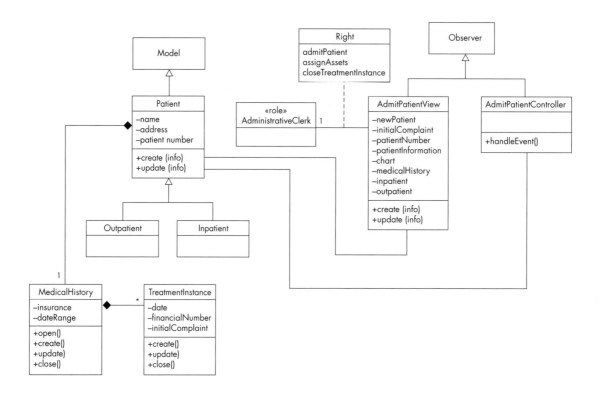

Figure 16.6: Adding security enforcement through interfaces

Distribution provides another place to perform access control and it needs again to be coordinated with the other authorizations. Distribution is usually performed through three basic approaches:

- Distribution of objects using an Object Request Broker, such as CORBA, DCOM or .NET Remoting. We can add security rules to the Broker pattern to control access to remote objects.

- Distribution of component and interfaces, for example web services. We can control access to web services using an access control standard such as WSPL (page 260) and enforce it using an XML FIREWALL (page 242) [Del04].

- Cloud computing. Services are provided by the three major layers of a cloud system [Zha10].

Experience has shown that a good way to build dependable systems is to structure them into a set of hierarchical layers. Some important issues for hierarchies are what functions to include in each layer, and how much security is needed in each layer to accomplish an intended level of security for the whole system. Not all layers need be equally secure; the lower levels are more critical and need stronger protection. Security and other non-functional requirements affect all the architectural levels of a system. The Layers architectural pattern [Bus96] [Fer02] is therefore a good starting point to apply these requirements. Using layers we can define patterns at all levels that together implement a secure or reliable system. The main idea of the Layers pattern is the decomposition of a system into hierarchical layers of abstraction, in which the higher levels use the services of the lower levels. Earlier we discussed why all these levels must be coordinated to assure security [Fer99b] and how the definition of non-functional specifications should be done at a specific level [Fer95].

The conceptual enterprise models, both static and dynamic, are defined at the application level. It is here where the security (and other types of) policies of the institution should be applied. At this level the semantics of the application are well understood and roles can be used to apply the need-to-know policy; that is, we can define the required rights according to the functions of each role. Other non-functional aspects are also specified here, such as the required degree of reliability. The lower levels enforce the restrictions defined at the higher levels. Each level has its own security mechanism and should participate in enforcing the security constraints. For example, a DBMS enforces the authorizations in the application by restricting access to database items; this restriction is propagated down to control access to the files where the data resides.

16.4   Secure Handling of Legal Cases

This is an example of an SSAP which shows an application of the patterns in building a secure semantic unit that includes a set of basic functions from the same application domain. The SSAP describes the handling of legal cases in which a client is either suing another party (a plaintiff) or is being defended from a suit (a defendant) using a legal firm. The pattern includes the necessary policies (in the form of security patterns) to stop or mitigate attacks.

Example

The SueThem law firm is having trouble staying in business. It keeps some documents in electronic form and others on paper. Documents are hard to find and can easily be accessed by unauthorized people. It is hard for the company to keep track of their clients and to know how much it should charge them. The conduction of cases is disorganized, which leads to lost cases because of lack of preparation.

Context

A legal firm sues parties (people, organizations or groups) on behalf of their clients; it can also defend their clients when they are sued. We call a *legal case* the sequence of actions (process) needed to pursue a suit until its completion. The standard legal system of most countries allows parties to sue other parties. There are different types of lawsuits, but they are not of interest here. Interactions between the people involved can be in person, by telephone, by regular mail or by e-mail. Law firms are commercial entities and must compete with other law firms for clients.

Problem

A law suit or defense implies a sequence of actions and generates many documents, of several types. If the firm doesn't organize these actions and the corresponding documents properly, it will have problems in conducting the suit or defense, which will result in unnecessary expenses and a higher possibility of losing the case. Because the information handed in a case is very sensitive, there is motivation to misuse it.

We need to consider possible attacks and take measures to avoid them. We consider here the main use cases in this process: 'Handle legal case' (for a plaintiff), 'Handle legal case (for a defendant)', and its auxiliary use cases 'Keep track of costs', 'Research case', and 'Bill Client'. Figure 16.7 shows the actors involved in these use cases. 'Other' here represents people involved in the case, such as witnesses or experts. There are other related use cases, such as the writing of Wills, or divorce cases, which are left out for simplicity and to make the pattern more reusable.

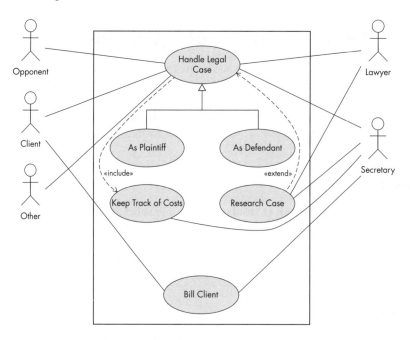

Figure 16.7: Use cases for handling legal cases

How can we model this system to consider all these factors in a balanced way? The solution to this problem must resolve the following forces:

- *Unpredictability of activities.* The sequence of activities in a case is usually unpredictable. Depositions, witness court appearances and lawyers' briefs to the court might be required in any sequence, depending on the course of the case.

- *Unpredictability of people.* Complex cases may require several lawyers with the assistance of some secretaries. The actual number of these people might be hard to predict. In addition to the defendant and the plaintiff (and their respective opponents), we may need witnesses, experts and others. Who they are and when they are needed depends on the case.

- *Logistics.* The total effort and duration of a case is variable, and we need to keep track of expenses, time used, supplies and so on, so that we can bill our clients.

- *Precedent searching.* Handling cases requires searching for precedents (similar cases). To do research for cases, lawyers and secretaries make use of libraries and the Internet and may download many documents.

- *Access control to information.* The information about customers, billing, assignment of lawyers and other aspects related to a current case must be accessible only to authorized people.

- *Control of documents.* Legal documents can only be created by authorized people, and their use (reading or modification) should also be controlled.

- *Confidentiality.* Communications between lawyers and clients must be confidential.

- *Auditability.* Government regulations apply to law firms and their information must be easily auditable.

Possible Attacks

Figure 16.8 shows an activity diagram of the sequence for handling a case, followed by billing, tracking of costs and related case research. Following the approach of [Fer06c], in order to analyze the possible attacks (threats) we consider each activity in the activity diagram and see how it can be subverted by the attacker. In this diagram External People indicates either the opponent or other people involved in the case. The possible threats are then:

Threat 1 In the 'Start Case' activity, the client or the responsible lawyer might be imposters.

Threat 2 A lawyer might create a false contract.

Threat 3 The client or the external people might give a false deposition.

Threat 4 A lawyer might change a deposition.

Threat 5 A lawyer or a secretary might produce intentionally incorrect precedents, briefs or costs.

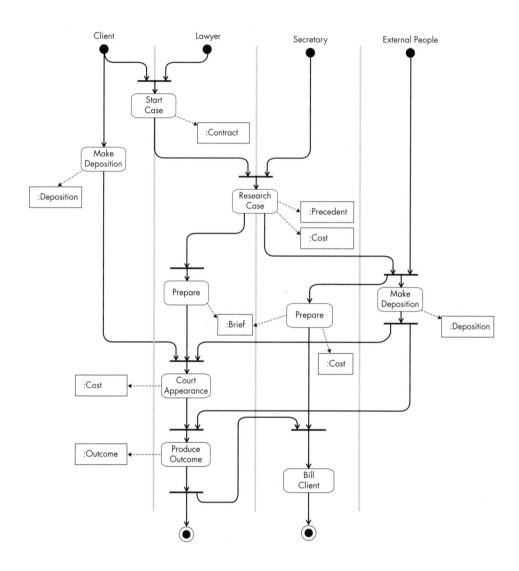

Figure 16.8: Activity diagram of case handling

Threat 6 A secretary might produce an increased or decreased bill.

Threat 7 A lawyer might change some aspects of the outcome to collect a higher fee.

Threat 8 A lawyer can disseminate client or case information for monetary gain.

Threat 9 An external attacker might read/change case information or access client/ lawyer communications.

Solution

Because the handling of cases is unpredictable and we use a variety of knowledge experts in its handling, this problem can be conveniently modeled as a Blackboard pattern [Bus96]. The case itself becomes a blackboard and the experts providing knowledge to the case are the lawyers, witnesses or experts. The control is based on the status of the case and is embodied in the scheduling of activities.

Structure

Figure 16.9 shows a class diagram of the conceptual model for the functional aspects of this pattern. The class `Case` represent the case itself (in the role of blackboard), and includes as components the classes `Cost` (describes accrued costs), `CaseDoc`, `Outcome` (the result of the case) and `Scheduling` (the control role of the blackboard). A `Client` is responsible for a case, and with each case there are some associated `ExternalPeople` (opponents, witnesses, experts). A `CaseDoc` can be a `Contract`, a `Precedent`, a `Brief` or a `Deposition`. `Lawyers` and `Secretaries` are `Employees` of the `LawFirm` and can be assigned to `Cases` (we assume this assignment has been done beforehand). A `Secretary` in the `Case` keeps track of `Costs`. A `Lawyer` in the case is responsible for the general conduction of the case, including `Scheduling`.

Dynamics

Figure 16.10 shows a sequence diagram describing some typical steps for the use cases 'Handle legal case (for a plaintiff) and 'Handle legal case (for a defendant)'. The `Client` starts the case with the `responsibleLawyer`. This lawyer creates an instance of a `Case` and later does some research for it. He assigns an assistant lawyer (`lawyer2`) to prepare a `Brief` for the court and schedules the client to make a `Deposition`.

The other use cases are simpler and are not shown for conciseness.

Secure Structure

The threats identified on page 453 mean that we need the following policies to avoid or mitigate them:

Threat 1 Mutual authentication, to avoid imposters.

Threat 2 Authorization to restrict lawyers to the creation of contracts, and logging to record possible illegal actions by a lawyer.

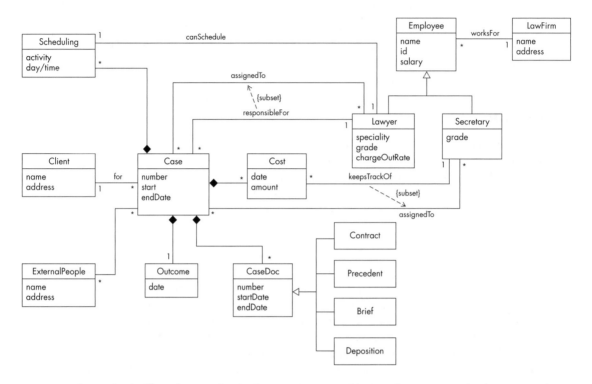

Figure 16.9: Class diagram for the SECURE HANDLING OF LEGAL CASES pattern (without security)

Threat 3 Logging, to keep records for future auditing that could detect false depositions.

Threat 4 Authorization and document protection against change.

Threat 5 Authorization and logging, to restrict who can perform these actions, and to keep records for future auditing.

Threat 6 Logging, to record suspicious actions by a secretary.

Threat 7 Separation of duty: two lawyers must concur on the fees to be charged.

Threat 8 Logging, to record possible illegal actions by lawyers.

Threat 9 Authorization and access control, to stop external attacks, and cryptography, to protect communications.

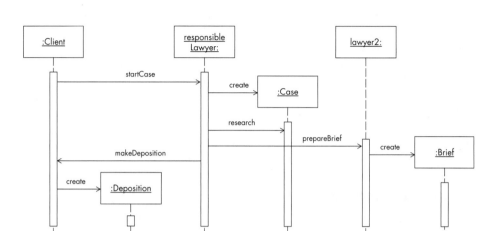

Figure 16.10: Sequence diagram for the use case 'Handle case (etc.)'

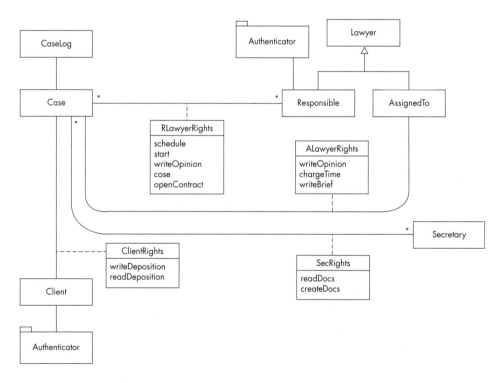

Figure 16.11: Security additions to the class diagram

From these policies we can define abstract security mechanisms to stop or mitigate the identified attack threats. Figure 16.11 shows the relevant part of the conceptual model of Figure 16.9, with the addition of instances of authentication, authorization and logging patterns to realize the identified policies. We assume that the authorization policies follow an RBAC model (see page 78) and the diagram defines the rights for each role. Both the responsible lawyer (who interacts with the client), and the client must have information to authenticate each other, requiring two instances of the AUTHENTICATOR pattern (page 52). The `CaseLog` (an instance of the SECURITY LOGGER AND AUDITOR pattern, page 111) records accesses to the case data. We also need an instance of the REIFIED REFERENCE MONITOR (page 100), not shown here for simplicity.

Example Resolved

The SueThem law firm now has a systematic structure to conduct its cases. All its documents are reflected in the conceptual model and can be easily retrieved and audited. The company can now keep track of the costs associated with a case. Documents and other case information can be protected from illegal access.

Consequences

The SECURE HANDLING OF LEGAL CASES pattern offers the following benefits:

- The Blackboard structure accommodates unpredictable sequences of activities well.
- We can assign lawyers and secretaries dynamically, depending on the course taken by the case.
- The model includes knowledge sources that can be the client, the opponent, witnesses, expert witnesses and other people.
- It is possible to track the current costs of the case.
- Applying legal regulations to the company is easy, because all documents are described by classes with controlled access, and we keep a log of accesses.
- Searching for precedents (similar cases) can be done as part of case handling. We can store this information for future use, and we can associate it with the different stages of the case.

The pattern also has the following potential liabilities:

- The order in which some activities are performed has an effect in the outcome, but the lawyers must decide on the scheduling: the pattern does not help here.
- We might not be able to predict all possible attacks, which could allow some attacks to still happen.

- The pattern's implementation might allow new types of attacks. For example, code flaws might allow an attacker to get control of the operating system, and thus to the case data.

Application of this pattern has the following effects on security:

- We can define precise role rights. For example, an expert can only add to case information, not change it, a lawyer can decide on the next step, bring new witnesses, but cannot change depositions, and so on.

- A designer building a system of this type can produce software that performs its functions and is at the same time reasonably secure, in that it can control all predicted threats.

- The ROLE-BASED ACCESS CONTROL structure (page 78) enforces authorized access to the information, and employees can make sure that they are communicating with the person they intend to.

- Cryptographic methods such as hashing [Gol06] can be added to prevent document modification.

Known Uses

Many large law firms follow a similar structure for their case handling.

See Also

- The SECURE BLACKBOARD pattern (page 353) is the basis for the central function of the case.

- The client and external people can be described by a Party pattern to indicate that they can be individuals or organizations [Fow97].

- Assignment of lawyers and secretaries uses the Resource Assignment pattern [Fer05h].

- The rights structure follows an ROLE-BASED ACCESS CONTROL pattern (page 78).

- Authentication is performed by means of instances of the AUTHENTICATOR pattern (page 52).

16.5 SCADA Systems

Infrastructure systems are needed to sustain civilized life. These include transportation, finance and banking, government, chemical, energy, oil and gas production and distribution, health services, information management, water (for drinking and irrigation), emergency services (fire, police), garbage collection and others. All these infrastructure functions are controlled by systems that are complex and becoming increasingly interdependent: each system typically depends on one or more other systems. Some are mutually dependent; for example, electric power generation may require oil, and oil production will require electricity.

Modern industrial facilities such as water supply systems, electric power generation plants and oil refineries often involve components that are geographically distributed. To continuously monitor and control the different sections of the plant in order to ensure its appropriate operation leads to the use of Supervisory Control and Data Acquisition (SCADA) systems. These systems were designed to meet the basic requirements of process-control systems for which security issues were not a concern. However, the growing demands for increased connectivity between a SCADA system and other network components, such as the corporate network and the Internet, expose the critical parts of a SCADA system to the public, so security issues can no longer be ignored. In fact, some attacks have already been detected [Bra08b] [Byr04]. Here we consider the use of security patterns to define, in a systematic way, the defenses that we need in order to secure such a system. While many approaches to secure SCADA systems exist, for example [Bra08b] [Goe05] [Igu06] [Mil05] [Nae07], none of them make use of security patterns.

Basically, a SCADA system consists of field units, a central controller, and communication networks that connect these components. A field unit consists of field devices and a local programmable logic controller (PLC). Field devices, such as actuators and sensors, are monitored and controlled by a local PLC. The central controller is generally geographically separated from these field units and typically has advanced computation facilities. A typical central controller may be equipped with data servers, human-machine interface (HMI) stations, and other servers with advanced computation capabilities to aid the operators in managing the entire plant.

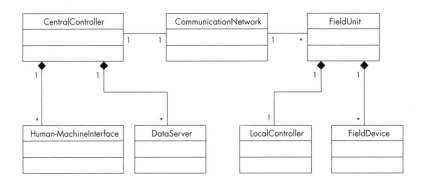

Figure 16.12: Class diagram for a generic SCADA system

Figure 16.12 is a class diagram for a basic SCADA architecture. The functions of the central controller include sending settings and commands to field units and receiving status information from them. The functions of the field units include monitoring the environment, taking actions on the environment and sending status information and/or alarms to the central controller if necessary. The functions of the communication networks include forwarding data and commands in both directions.

Modern SCADA systems are normally connected to the corporate networks and/or the Internet through specialized gateways. The gateway is used to provide protocol conversion between two different networks when they use different protocols. The MODBUS protocol is currently one of the most popular and widely-used protocols with SCADA systems [Goe05], but other protocols are used for specialized applications. Since SCADA systems have a standard structure, we devised a specific pattern to define and model them. Figure 16.12 describes the static structure of this pattern.

Securing a SCADA System

We propose a method to analyze, build and evaluate secure SCADA systems using security patterns. Intuitively, we use security patterns to stop and/or prevent attacks, and we list these attacks first. The result of our solution is a security pattern itself (an SSAP) the SECURE SCADA pattern, which can be used as a guideline for building secure SCADA systems. All the required patterns were described in Chapter 5, Chapter 6 and Chapter 10.

Attacks Against SCADA Systems

Until recently SCADA systems were electronically isolated from all other networks, and hence not likely to be accessible by outside attackers [Bra08b]. As a result, the security issues of a SCADA system focused on physical security, such as physical access control. However, the growing demands of the industry for increased connectivity between SCADA system and the corporate network (and/or the Internet) has resulted in an increase in security threats and vulnerabilities that are not limited to physical attacks [Gor09]. A recent study shows that prior to 2000, almost 70% of the reported incidents with SCADA systems were either due to accidents or to disgruntled employees acting maliciously. Since 2001, apart from an increase in the total number of reported incidents, almost 70% of the incidents have been due to attacks originating from outside [Byr04].

We can systematically enumerate the threats against a system by considering its use cases and activities, and analyzing possible ways of subverting them. A simplified version of our approach is to look at possible attacks against each unit of the system, providing that its platform structure is predefined. This is a preliminary enumeration of threats, which can be expanded at a later stage of design. Note that these threats include external and internal attacks.

Recalling Figure 16.12, a generic SCADA system is mainly composed of a central controller, communication networks and field units, so we can categorize threats corresponding to these three components. Attacks against/through the central controller include:

Threat 1 Physical attacks.

Threat 2 Malicious settings of the field units.

Threat 3 Wrong commands sent to the field units.

Threat 4 Malicious alteration of the runtime parameters of the central controller.

Threat 5 Denial of service attacks.

Attacks against/through the field units include:

Threat 6 Physical attacks.

Threat 7 Malicious alteration of the runtime parameters of the field units.

Threat 8 Incorrect commands sent to the field units.

Threat 9 Malicious alarms sent to the central controller.

Threat 10 Denial of service.

Attacks against/through the communication networks include:

Threat 11 Sniffing.

Threat 12 Spoofing.

Threat 13 Denial of service.

Attacks against the central controller and the network are more harmful, since they may disable the whole system, whereas attacks against field units only affect specific units. For simplicity we are leaving out attacks due to malware, which can be handled using conventional approaches.

Countermeasures

Central Controller

■ To stop Threat 1, we use security patterns for physical access control such as the ROLE-BASED ACCESS CONTROL pattern (page 78) combined with the AUTHENTICATOR pattern (page 52) and the SECURITY LOGGER AND AUDITOR pattern (page 111).

■ To stop Threats 2, 3 and 4, we use the AUTHORIZATION pattern (page 74) together with the AUTHENTICATOR pattern and the SECURITY LOGGER AND AUDITOR pattern. The AUTHENTICATOR restricts access to the system to registered employees, while the AUTHORIZATION pattern controls the actions that the employees can perform on the controller. The SECURITY LOGGER AND AUDITOR pattern is useful for those cases in which a legitimate employee is trying to perform sabotage (we cannot stop the attack, but we have a record of who did it).

■ To stop Threat 5, we use the Firewall pattern [Sch06b] together with an Intrusion Detection System (IDS) pattern (Chapter 10). The IDS detects the attack and instructs the firewall to block traffic from the attacking addresses. Note that the Firewall and the IDS patterns can be deployed at different layers of a system (for example the application layer and the network layers). Figure 16.13 shows the class diagram for the secure central controller after the necessary security patterns have been applied. Note that the users' actions are controlled at the HMI, which acts as a Concrete Reference Monitor [Sch06b] for user interactions: it can apply authorization controls based on user roles.

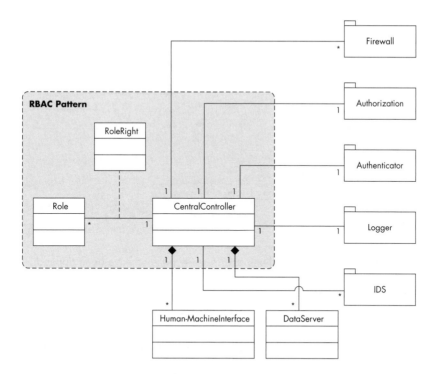

Figure 16.13: Secure central controller where security patterns are applied

Field Units

- To stop Threat 6, we use the ROLE-BASED ACCESS CONTROL pattern (page 78) combined with the AUTHENTICATOR pattern (page 52) and the SECURITY LOGGER AND AUDITOR pattern (page 111).

- We use the AUTHORIZATION pattern (page 74) together with the AUTHENTICATOR pattern and the SECURITY LOGGER AND AUDITOR pattern to stop Threats 7, 8 and 9.

- By applying the Firewall pattern together with the IDS pattern, we can stop Threat 10.

Figure 16.14 shows the class diagram for the secure field unit after necessary security patterns have been applied.

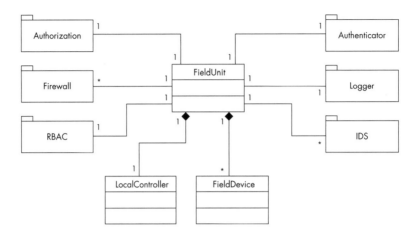

Figure 16.14: Secure field unit after security patterns have been applied

Communication Networks

- To stop Threat 11, we use cryptography-based methods such as secure channels [Bra00].

- To stop Threat 12, we use the AUTHENTICATOR pattern (page 52) to prove the origin of a message. In practice, we can implement the above mechanisms using virtual private networks (VPN).

- Stopping Threat 13 is out of the scope of this pattern: see Chapter 10.

  Figure 16.15 shows the class diagram for the secure communication networks where necessary security patterns are used.

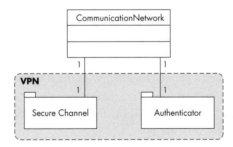

Figure 16.15: Secure communication networks after security patterns have been applied

Secure SCADA

Note that the structure of the class diagram in Figure 16.13 is similar to that in Figure 16.14. This is due to the fact that the central controller and the field units are exposed to similar attacks. As a result, we can produce the SECURE SCADA pattern, which combines these figures, as shown in Figure 16.16.

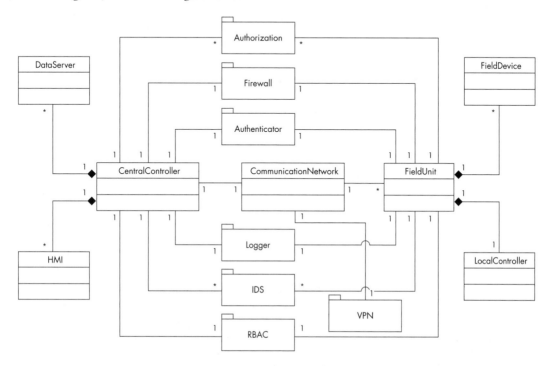

Figure 16.16: Class diagram for the SECURE SCADA pattern

An important aspect in the protection of SCADA systems is controlling access to their physical structures, for example the transformer yard in an electric plant. The recently increased need to protect against terrorism has brought added interest in control of access to buildings and other physical structures. The need to protect assets in buildings and to control access to restricted areas such as airports, naval ports, government agencies and nuclear plants has created a great business opportunity for the physical access control industry, and much interest in the research community. One of the results of this interest has been the recognition that access control to information and access control to physical locations have many common aspects.

The most basic model of access control uses a tuple: subject, object and access type (Chapter 6), or 'S', 'O' and 'T'. If we interpret S as a person (instead of a subject), O as a physical structure (instead of a computational resource), and T as a physical access type (instead of resource access), we can make an analogy where we can apply known results or approaches from information access control. One way to achieve this unification is to use a conceptual abstraction for the definition of security requirements. We have combined analysis and security patterns for this purpose [Fer05g]. Standards and products that deal with physical units use a set of common concepts that may appear different due to a different notation; patterns make this commonality apparent. Examining existing systems, industry standards and government regulations, we have described, in the form of patterns, the relationship and definition of a core set of features that a physical access control system should have [Fer07f].

16.6   Medical Applications

The Internet, wireless systems and RFID sensors are opening a new era in medical care. Most activities in medical care can be integrated and performed remotely and pervasively. This change promises to improve medical care and reduce costs. However, if these systems are not secure, users will lose confidence in them and some of their advances will not be realized. We discuss here some relevant issues, and emphasize again that to have secure systems we must consider security from the beginning, in all phases, and in the whole system. (Another medical application using patterns is shown in [Paz04].)

The so-called *telehealth* applications include assisted living, pervasive healthcare, patient monitoring, distance surgery, remote diagnosis, ambulance and others; they all typically rely on wireless networks. Because of their need to be established over long distances and to often operate without supervision, these networks are exposed to a variety of attacks. We look at some medical applications and the corresponding network security issues. In particular, we consider here aspects of *mHealth* (also written as *m-health*, or sometimes *mobile health*), a recent term for medical and public health practice supported by mobile devices such as cellular phones, patient monitoring devices, PDAs and other wireless devices [Jur08]. Applications of mHealth include the use of mobile devices for collecting clinical data, delivery of healthcare information to practitioners, researchers, and patients, real-time monitoring of patients' vital signs and direct provision of care (via telehealth). We consider mHealth not to be a set of independent systems, but merely a complementary part of the complete medical system.

Most discussions of the security of wireless networks for health applications consider only the communication aspects of the networks, for example [Gia08] [Zen08]. However, a health network is part of a complete health application, and we need to relate its communication aspects to its medical aspects. We need to understand first what information is needed for medical purposes and how this information is used. Once we define what information we need, we present a pattern for patient records management. Then we show a case study, ambient assisted living, followed by an analysis of the threats and defenses in a wireless network such as the ones used in medical applications.

Medical Records and their Regulations

The *electronic healthcare record (EHR)* is a lifetime record of an individual that has the purpose of supporting continuity of care and related education and research. It typically includes information about encounters (visits), lab tests, diagnostics, observations, medications, imaging reports, treatments, allergies and therapies, as well as patient-identifying information and legal permissions [Eic05].

Medical information is very sensitive and must be protected. Most countries have severe restrictions in the use of this information. There are several regulations in the US about the handling of health information, the best known being the Health Insurance Portability and Accountability Act (HIPAA) [HIP] [Hip]. Title II of the HIPAA, known as the Administrative Simplification (AS) provisions, requires the establishment of national standards for electronic health care transactions and national identifiers for providers, health insurance plans and employers. The AS provisions also address the security and privacy of health data. The standards are meant to improve the efficiency and effectiveness of the nation's health care system by encouraging the widespread use of electronic data interchange.

Five rules define Administrative Simplification:

- The *Privacy Rule* regulates the use and disclosure of specific information held by covered entities (healthcare providers, health care clearing-houses, employer sponsored health plans and health insurers) and their business associates (lawyers, accountants, IT consultants). It establishes regulations for the use and disclosure of protected health information (PHI).

- The *Transactions and Code Sets Rule* defines specific transaction types. For example, the EDI Health Care Claim Transaction set (837) is used to submit health care claim billing information, encounter information, or both (except for retail pharmacy claims). It can be sent from providers of health care services to payers, either directly or via intermediary billers and claims clearing-houses.

- The *Security Rule* complements the Privacy Rule. While the Privacy Rule pertains to all PHI, including paper and electronic media, the Security Rule deals specifically with electronic protected health information (EPHI). It lays out three types of security safeguards required for compliance: administrative, physical and technical.

- The *Unique Identifiers Rule* establishes that providers must use only the National Provider Identifier (NPI) to identify themselves in standard transactions. The NPI is a unique 10-digit identification number provided by the US Government.

- The *Enforcement Rule* sets civil financial penalties for violating HIPAA rules and establishes procedures for investigations and hearings for violations. It seems to be rarely applied, however.

Privacy is the right of individuals or groups to keep their personal information away from public knowledge, or their ability to control personal information flow. In the electronic or the real world, people seek privacy, so they can perform their actions without others monitoring them. Individuals should be able to live without being disturbed, and users interact with the web navigate without being identified. People providing information to medical institutions or storing their personal records with commercial companies should know what to expect about the privacy of their information. This right is recognized by all civilized societies and is considered a fundamental human right. The first national privacy protection law was the Swedish Data Act of 1973. This was followed by the US Privacy Act of 1974. The intent of this act was to protect individuals against invasion of privacy by the Federal Government. This law is complemented by the Computer Security Act of 1987, which defines requirements for federal agencies concerning the security of their information. In general, privacy laws are more developed in Europe than in the US.

Patient Treatment Records

We present a pattern to describe some of the basic functions involved in maintaining and using patient records in a hospital, the Patient Treatment Records pattern [Sor04]. A medical record can be thought of as a series of dated treatment instances, or encounters. Each patient encounter is documented on a patient chart and contains dated notes written by physicians, as well as laboratory reports and letters from consulting physicians. In addition, a patient chart will have vital sign documentation from nurses, imaging reports, specific treatment plans, treatments performed, medications given, assessments of patient condition and so on.

The PATIENT TREATMENT RECORDS pattern focuses on the private and sensitive nature of medical information and the need for maintaining accurate and organized records. A patient is admitted to a healthcare facility, where all pertinent information is recorded. A physician and other facility assets are assigned to the patient. Following treatment the patient is discharged. This pattern describes only some of the aspects of patient treatment, which include the creation and maintenance of the patient record and the assignment of the assets for use by the patient. This pattern describes a general non-emergency treatment situation and does not consider the details of patient diagnosis and treatment.

The pattern describes the handling of records during the treatment or stay instance of a patient in a hospital. The hospital may be a member of a medical group. Each patient has a primary physician, an employee of the hospital. Upon admission the patient record is created or information is updated from previous visit(s). Inpatients are assigned a location, nurse team and consulting doctors.

The PATIENT TREATMENT RECORDS pattern is another example of a *semantic analysis pattern* (SAP). In the next section we describe one of its two component patterns, the PATIENT RECORD. The other two component patterns can be found in [Sor04], and a more detailed model for medical records in [Sor05]. Figure 16.17 shows a use case diagram that corresponds to some of the typical needs of patient treatment which define the structure of the PATIENT TREATMENT RECORDS pattern. There are other use cases, such as 'Diagnose', 'Perform patient treatment', and 'Billing', which have been omitted for simplicity.

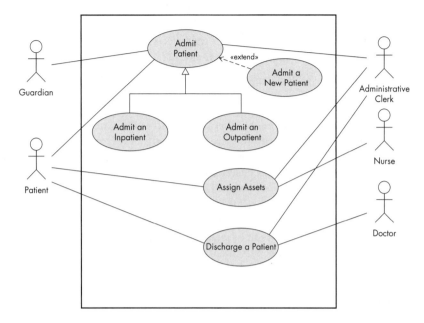

Figure 16.17: Diagram of the use case 'Patient treatment'

Patient Record

Describes the structure of patient records and the process of creating and maintaining them for a stay or treatment in a hospital.

Problem

Maintaining accurate records is crucial for patient treatment. A poor record may result in erroneous treatments, loss of insurance or other problems for the patient or the hospital. How can we keep an accurate picture of what happens during the stay of a patient in a hospital?

The solution to this problem must resolve the following forces:

■ Patient characteristics, for example age, gender, occupation, ethnic or racial origin, weight and others, may have an effect on the diagnosis and treatment of the patient, and it is important to keep this information accurate.

■ We need a detailed record of what has been done to a patient during a specific stay at the hospital. This is necessary for medical, billing and legal reasons.

■ Patients may return to the hospital, so we need to be able to relate new treatments to past treatments.

- We may need to classify different types of patients, otherwise the patients or the hospital might incur unnecessary expenses.

- Patients might not be responsible for their decisions or their expenses, so we may need somebody responsible for the patient.

- The information is sensitive and we need to add security measures.

Solution

Maintain a medical history for each patient. This medical history typically contains insurance information and a record of all treatments within the medical group. If the patient is new to the medical group a patient record and medical history will be created upon admission. If the patient has been treated in any facility within the medical group there will be an existing patient record and a medical history, which may need to be updated. A treatment instance is created for all patients admitted and updated throughout the patient's stay. The treatment instance will subsequently be added to the patient's medical record upon discharge. A person or guardian is responsible for each patient. We classify patients into inpatients and outpatients. Use cases realized by this pattern include 'Assign a guardian', 'Modify medical history' and 'Admit a new patient' (Figure 16.3, page 446).

Figure 16.18 shows the class diagram for this pattern. A unique stay or `TreatmentInstance` for every `Patient` is created upon admission to the hospital. The `Patient` may be admitted to the hospital as an `Inpatient` to stay in the hospital, or they may be admitted as an `Outpatient`, in which case they will receive treatment but will not stay at the hospital. The treatment instances are collected into the `MedicalHistory`. A `Guardian` is responsible for each patient. The `Guardian` can be seen as a role, in that a `Patient` may be their own guardian. Additional relevant patient information is recorded into `PatientInfo`.

We can model other aspects of patient treatment similarly. The remainder of this pattern and the two companion patterns can be found in [Sor04]. These use cases don't specify design aspects: some of them, for example, 'Discharge patient', could be performed from wireless devices. Security can be added similarly, as shown in the next section for ambient assisted living.

Ambient Assisted Living

Ambient assisted living (AAL) defines architectures for home environments which have devices such as sensors and cameras to support and monitor people with impaired functions or disabilities. Assisted living requires a secure infrastructure of services to be in place at the patient's home or place of care. Many of these services are also valuable for family living and the corresponding architectures differ mostly in the specific types of services they provide [Suo08].

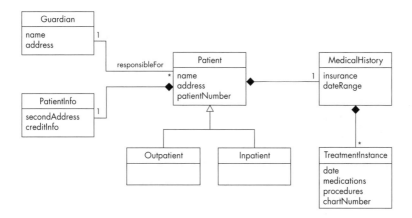

Figure 16.18: Class diagram for the PATIENT RECORD pattern

An assisted living system has the following requirements [Wan06]:

■ *Dependability.* Critical services should be delivered in spite of failure of useful but non-critical services. Moreover, the system as a whole should have high availability and robustness.

■ *Low cost and flexibility.* The general infrastructure should be open with well-defined interfaces, machine-checkable QoS assumptions, and support the use of low-cost third-party devices.

■ *Security and privacy.* Medical and personal data should be protected with different rights for different roles (health care providers, medical team, relatives and assisted people). The complete network architecture must be secure.

■ *Quality-of-service provisioning.* Quality of service (QoS) should be provided at different levels, depending on the level's criticality requirements.

■ *Open standards.* Any brand or type of device should be able to interoperate with any devices and operating systems.

■ *Lightweight, easy-to-use HCIs.* The user interfaces should be easy to use, safe, tolerant of user mistakes, and provide different control levels of information disclosure.

■ *Flexibility.* Hardware architectures and software should be adaptable and extensible.

■ *Interoperability.* Compatibility with electronic healthcare records (EHR) is needed, so that the same concepts appear in the information stored and propagated by the devices.

Some possible use cases are listed below [Wan06]. We are converting these into patterns, and we show some UML models for them.

Use Case: Remind of Activity – Figure 16.19, Figure 16.20

The health provider obtains updated prescription and appointment records of the assisted person (AP) from a dedicated server (to which health care providers have access) through secure channels. When it is time for the AP to carry out their time-driven routines, such as taking medicine or monitoring vital signs, the health provider locates active wireless-enabled devices (for example televisions, cellphones, wearable headsets or active badges) within range, and sends reminder messages to one or more devices that are in the proximity of the AP. (The AP can also prioritize the order in which devices will be used.)

For example, if the AP is watching television at the time when the reminder message is scheduled, the TV will be switched to an information channel (with the use of infrared remote control) and a reminder message will be displayed. In this manner, the AP can be reminded of their time-driven routines. Whether or not these routines are followed as advised is detected in a non-intrusive manner by exploiting sensor localization technologies such as RFID: prescription bottles can have RFID tags with unique barcodes, and one or more RFID readers in the environment can be activated (by the health provider) to track location changes (if any) of these bottles. Each RFID tag costs approximately 40 cents today, and the cost is expected to further decrease in the future.

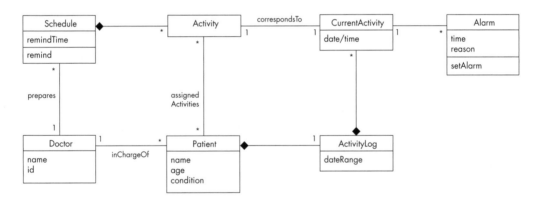

Figure 16.19: Class diagram for the AMBIENT ASSISTED LIVING pattern

Figure 16.19 shows a class diagram for this pattern, while Figure 16.20 shows a corresponding activity diagram.

Use Case: Vital Sign Measurement

In the current practice of glucose monitoring for diabetic patients, a patient measures their glucose level on a daily basis and brings the measuring device to their monthly clinic visits, where the measurements are retrieved and interpreted by health care providers.

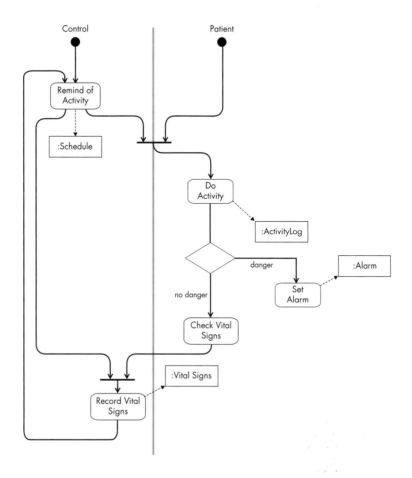

Figure 16.20: Activity diagram for the use case 'Remind of activity'

With the proposed environment in place, vital signs can be measured and transmitted by Bluetooth-enabled meters to the server. In this fashion, healthcare providers can monitor various vital signs at a convenient time granularity. Should the readings suggest any abnormal health situations, medical instructions can be given before the situation deteriorates.

Use Case: Personal Belonging Localization

Personal belongings such as eyeglasses, hearing aids and key chains can be attached with tags and located through the use of RFID readers. When someone cannot find their belongings (because of forgetfulness), they can issue a simple vocal command (through, for example, a lightweight Bluetooth-enabled headset) to the health provider, which then schedules the RFID readers to scan the environment and help locate the object.

Use Case: Personal Behavior Profiling

With the same set of sensor localization techniques, the assisted living environment can profile the movement of APs in a privacy-preserving manner (for example without the use of surveillance cameras) and detect early warning signs of depression (no longer taking medicine regularly, giving up routine activities, or staying in bed for long periods of time) and/or other chronic diseases such as Parkinson's and Alzheimer's. The AP wears an RFID tag or an active badge, which can be disguised as an item of clothing or jewelry.

Use Case: Emergency Detection

In case of the need for emergency attention (for example, dangerously high or low blood pressure or blood sugar levels), or the AP has been detected via localization techniques to be immobile on the floor for an unreasonably long time, real-time communication channels can be established to notify on-site caregivers (in the case of assisted living), health care providers (in the case of clinical use), or designated relatives, and facilitate transmission of electrocardiogram (EKG) data and other measures in real time.

All these approaches require networks, so we next discuss some aspects of network security. Later we'll discuss the security of sensor networks. These systems are also *cyber-physical systems* and we should study them as such.

Wireless Network Security

We consider some aspects of the security of the wireless networks that support these health applications.

Wireless Devices

When compared to wired networks, there are four generic limitations of all wireless devices:

- Limited power
- Limited communications bandwidth
- Limited processing power
- Relatively unreliable network connection

The bandwidth available to wireless systems is usually an order of magnitude (or even more) less than that available to a wired device. Their processing power is limited, due to limits to space and cost in the case of fixed wireless devices typically used for wi-fi networks, and is further limited due to power constraints in other wireless devices. In general, wireless networks are not very reliable. Protocols have been designed to take this lack of reliability into account and to try to improve it. However, in designing these protocols choices have to be made about the size of the packets and frames to be used. Such decisions can have a profound impact on the effectiveness and efficiency of cryptographic protocols.

To this we must add that security needs for wireless devices are greater than those of regular wired-network devices. This is due to the very nature of their use; they are mobile, they are on the edge of the network, their connections are unreliable, and they tend to get destroyed accidentally or maliciously. They can also be stolen, lost or forgotten. Thus, we need more security processing, but security processing can easily overwhelm the processors in wireless devices. This challenge, which is unique to wireless devices, is sometimes referred to as the 'security-processing gap'. Non-fixed wireless devices such as cellular handsets and ad hoc network devices such as sensors are also severely handicapped due to their very low battery power. Even though significant advances are expected in computation and communication speed over the next decade, it is still expected that they will lag behind the power available to fixed computers, due to the need for miniaturization.

To make things worse, battery power is only expected to make modest improvements. The battery limitation in mobile wireless devices is sometimes called the 'battery gap', and refers to the growing disparity between increasing energy requirements for high-end operations needed on such devices and slow improvements in battery technology. To this we add the fact that there is a large variety of devices using different architectures, several operating systems and diverse functionality. With increase in functions, the typical problems of larger systems are also appearing in portable devices.

Threats to Wireless Devices

The analysis of secure systems should start from their possible threats. We can apply our methodology to enumerate the threats to the activities shown in Figure 16.20. We show the threats for two activities; other activities can be analyzed similarly. We then identify policies to stop or mitigate the threats.

These policies can be realized by security patterns, which define the system security requirements and can then be converted into design artifacts, such as secure interfaces. Here the threats appear as attacker goals. When the details of the design start emerging, we can convert these abstract threats into specific threats to the implementation of the components of the system, such as threats to the user interfaces or to the wireless network. This may require adding more security patterns to stop the emergent threats. (A similar analysis is given in [EVI10].)

Activity 1: Remind of activity/task	*Activity 2*: Do activity
T11: Control site or patient site is an imposter	T21: Unauthorized reading of activity log
T12: Unauthorized reading of schedule	
T13: Unauthorized writing of schedule	T22: Unauthorized writing of activity log
T14: Denial of service	

Policies to stop these threats include:

P11: Mutual authentication

P12: Authorization/access control

P12: Authorization/access control

P12: Cell phone backup

P21: Authorization/access control

P22: Authorization/access control

General Wi-Fi Threats

The attacks described above and for other applications can be realized through other parts of the application, but the wireless network is a source for many of them.

- *Attacks related to access points* (APs)

  - *Detection of access points.* This is really attack preparation. Tools exist for this purpose, such as Netstumbler. These tools can detect, for each, AP, its MAC address, its location, the transmission channels it uses and the type of encryption it uses.

  - *Unauthorized (rogue) APs.* An attacker sets up their own AP (*malicious association*). Once the thief has gained access, they can steal passwords, launch attacks on the wired network or plant malware. Fraudulent APs can easily advertise the same network name (SSID) as a legitimate AP, causing nearby wi-fi clients to connect to them. One type of man-in-the-middle attack is a *de-authentication attack*. This attack forces AP-connected computers to drop their connections and reconnect to the fake AP.

  - *Accidental association.* When a user connects to a wireless access point from a neighboring company's overlapping network, it is a security breach, in that proprietary company information may be exposed, allowing a possible link from one company to the other.

  - *Direct endpoint attacks.* These take advantage of flaws in wi-fi drivers, using buffer overflows to escalate privilege.

- *Denial of service.* This is a common attack in wireless networks because of their frequency sharing with other networks, and can be accidental. A reason for performing an intentional DoS attack is to observe the recovery of the wireless network, during which all of the initial authentication information is resent by all devices, providing an opportunity for the attacker to collect this information.

- *Network injection.* The attacker may inject network configuration commands that affect routers and switches.

- *Cryptographic attacks based on message interception.* Data sent over wi-fi networks, including wireless printer traffic, can be easily captured by eavesdroppers. Weaknesses in encryption protocols such as WEP can let an attacker read messages.

- *Operating system attacks through the network.* Operating systems for wireless devices are becoming more and more complex and attackers can exploit code flaws in them to access their files.

General Wi-Fi Defenses

We have discussed earlier how to stop attacks such as the ones enumerated for the ambient assisted living application above. We consider here general approaches to stop attacks on wireless networks. First, a few security principles that also apply to wireless networks:

- For new systems, use a global-level design, starting from requirements. Define policies, analyze threats and select defense mechanisms. A methodology like ours is appropriate. Threats can be enumerated. Security must be applied throughout the whole lifecycle and on all architectural levels of the system.

- Medical records should be integrated with other parts of the hospital, such as lab, pharmacy and so on. A global conceptual model should include all entities relevant to patient care.

- Due to the sensitivity of data, the system should be a closed system, in which everything is forbidden unless explicitly authorized.

- System-critical and life-critical functions must have backups.

- Every access to resources, coming from fixed or mobile devices, should be mediated and checked for validity. There should be no direct access to any data or other resource.

- For existing systems, perform security auditing.

In particular, for the wireless network, we should apply these principles:

- The wireless network should be an integrated unit of the whole medical system, not separate units designed or bought independently. All the policies and models that apply to medical records and related information should also apply to the data handled by the wireless network and its devices.

- The models of all wireless devices should be integrated in a system-wide structure. There should be no outsiders (people, systems) that can access health data.

- Wireless device usage policies must be consistent with the total system policies.

Specific policies for wireless access should at least include:

- List those devices authorized to access the wireless network.

- List the personnel that can access the network.

- Define rules for setting up wireless routers or APs.

- Define rules for the use of wi-fi APs, or about connecting to home networks with company devices.

- Mechanisms such as network access control can be useful to enforce all of the above.

■ Track AP vulnerabilities. It is important to track wi-fi endpoint vulnerabilities and keep the wi-fi drivers up to date.

16.7   Conclusions

We can build patterns for sets of related use cases and add security patterns to them to define a secure unit that can be used by an inexperienced developer to build secure applications. To define the security architecture of the network, we need an analysis of the possible threats; security patterns can then be introduced to stop or mitigate them. In this way we can build, for example, secure health systems in an integrated way, including health records, pharmacy records, and other related information, not just isolated wireless networks; the same is true for financial, SCADA, or other types of applications. We have also designed secure architectures for electronic voting [Fer12d] and for homes.

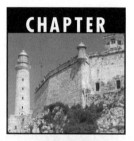

CHAPTER

17

Summary and the Future of Security Patterns

The part can never be well unless the whole is well.

Plato

We complete our book with tables of patterns, a list of research directions, some principles for security and a look at the future.

17.1 Summary of Patterns

This section offers a table that summarizes all the patterns in this book. For each pattern we have listed its classification using four of the dimensions described in Chapter 2. The *Intent* indicates what problem is solved by the pattern, the *concern* is its basic type of intended function, the *context* describes the environment where it can be applied or the prerequisites for its use, and *lifecycle* indicates in what stage of the development lifecycle the pattern is useful. Other dimensions could be added, but they would clutter this table. Ideally, a complete description of each pattern should be implemented in a tool that could present the designer with the relevant patterns according to the step of the design.

We first list the security patterns presented in this book, then (page 489) the misuse patterns in the book. We have written several other security patterns, described on page 490. Finally, we security patterns under development (page 493).

Security Patterns Described in this Book

NAME	INTENT	CONCERN	CONTEXT	LIFECYCLE
ABSTRACT IDS (page 214)	Monitor all traffic as it passes through a network, analyze it to detect possible attacks and trigger an appropriate response.	Traffic monitoring for attack detection	Networks	Design
ABSTRACT VIRTUAL PRIVATE NETWORK (page 195)	Set up a channel between two endpoints using cryptographic tunneling, with authentication at each endpoint.	Secure communication	Networks	Design
ACCESS CONTROL LIST (page 91)	Control access to objects by indicating which subjects can access an object and in what way.	Access control	A computing environment in which we have resources that have value for its users or their institution.	Analysis, design
ADMINISTRATOR HIERARCHY (page 184)	Limit the power of administrators by defining a hierarchy of system administrators, with rights controlled using a Role-Based Access Control (RBAC) model.	Security administration	Operating systems	Design
APPLICATION FIREWALL (page 234)	Filter traffic to/from enterprise applications, based on institution access-control policies.	Access control	Applications	Analysis, design
ASYMMETRIC ENCRYPTION (page 295)	Provide message confidentiality by keeping information secret in such a way that it can only be understood by intended recipients who have the access to the valid key. A public/ private key pair is used for encryption and decryption.	Information hiding, key distribution	Networks	Design

NAME	INTENT	CONCERN	CONTEXT	LIFECYCLE
AUTHENTICATOR (page 52)	Verify that the subject intending to access the system is who they claim to be.	User or system authentication	A computing environment in which we have resources that have value for its users or their institution.	Analysis, design
AUTHORIZATION (page 74)	Describe who is authorized to access specific resources in a system and in what way.	Access control	A computing environment in which we have resources that have value for its users or their institution.	Analysis, design
BEHAVIOR-BASED IDS (page 224)	Check traffic against previous patterns of network traffic to detect possible deviations from normal behavior (anomaly) which may indicate an attack, and trigger appropriate responses.	Attack detection	Networks	Design
CAPABILITY (page 96)	Control access to objects by providing a credential or ticket to be given to a subject for accessing an object in a specific way.	Access control	A computing environment in which we have resources that have value for its users or their institution.	Analysis, design
CIRCLE OF TRUST (page 34)	Define trust relationships among service providers in order for their subjects to access an integrated and more secure environment.	Identity and resource management	Service providers of services to consumers over large distributed systems such as the Internet.	Design

NAME	INTENT	CONCERN	CONTEXT	LIFECYCLE
CONTROLLED ACCESS SESSION (page 104)	Provide a context in which a subject (user, system) can access resources with different rights and without the need to reauthenticate when they access a new resource.	Authentication	Any environment in which we need to control access to computing resources.	Design
CONTROLLED EXECUTION DOMAIN (page 151)	Control access to operating system resources by processes, based on user, group or role authorizations.	Access control	A computing system in which we need to execute processes with different degrees of trust.	Design
CONTROLLED-OBJECT FACTORY (page 129)	Specify rights of processes with respect to a new object.	Rights assignment for access control	A computing system that needs to control access to its created objects because of their different degrees of sensitivity.	Design
CONTROLLED-OBJECT MONITOR (page 132)	Control access by a subject to an object.	Access control	A computing system in which we need to execute processes with different degrees of trust.	Design
CONTROLLED-PROCESS CREATOR (page 126)	Define the rights to be given to a new process.	Rights assignment for access control	Executing processes in operating systems.	Design
CREDENTIAL (page 62)	Provide secure means of recording authentication and authorization information.	Authentication and authorization	Distributed systems	Design

NAME	INTENT	CONCERN	CONTEXT	LIFECYCLE
DIGITAL SIGNATURE WITH HASHING (page 301)	Help a principal prove that a message was originated from it. Provides message integrity by indicating whether a message was altered during transmission.	Message authenticity	Networks	Design
EXECUTION DOMAIN (page 149)	Define an execution environment for processes, indicating explicitly the resources that a process can use during its execution.	Access control	A computing system in which we need to execute processes with different degrees of trust.	Design
FILE ACCESS CONTROL (page 187)	Control access to files in an operating system.	Access control	Operating systems	Design
IDENTITY PROVIDER (page 36)	Centralization of the administration of subjects' identity information for a security domain.	Identity management	Distributed systems	Design
IDENTITY FEDERATION (page 38)	Dynamically create identities within a federation consisting of several service providers.	Identity management	Security domains in a distributed environment which trust each other.	Design
INFRASTRUCTURE-AS-A-SERVICE (page 413)	Describe the infrastructure to allow the sharing of distributed virtualized computational resources such as servers, storage and networks.	Systems architecture	Cloud computing	Design
IPSEC VPN (page 200)	Set up a secure channel between two endpoints using cryptographic tunneling through the IP layer, with authentication at each endpoint.	Secure channel	Networks	Design
LAYERED OPERATING SYSTEM ARCHITECTURE (page 169)	Decompose the overall features and functionality of the OS, assign them to hierarchical layers and define their rights.	Access control	Computer systems with a variety of executing processes.	Design

NAME	INTENT	CONCERN	CONTEXT	LIFECYCLE
LIBERTY ALLIANCE IDENTITY FEDERATION (page 44)	Merging of identities across multiple organizations under a federated identity.	Identity management	Distributed systems	Design
MICROKERNEL OPERATING SYSTEM ARCHITECTURE (page 174)	Move as much of the OS functionality from the kernel and put it in specialized servers, coordinated by a microkernel with a restricted set of functions.	Access control, coordination	Operating systems with a variety of services that may change frequently.	Design
MODULAR OPERATING SYSTEM ARCHITECTURE (page 165)	Separate OS services into modules, each representing a basic function.	Access control, coordination	Operating systems	Design
MULTILEVEL SECURITY (page 81)	Categorize sensitive information and prevent its disclosure.	Access control	Environments in which data and documents may have critical value.	Analysis, design
PATIENT RECORD (page 469)	Describe the structure of patient records and the process of creating and maintaining them for a stay or treatment in a hospital.	Health applications	Applications	Analysis
PATIENT TREATMENT RECORDS (page 468)	Describe the handling of records during the treatment or stay instance of a patient in a hospital.	Health applications	Application	Analysis
PLATFORM-AS-A-SERVICE (page 423)	Provide virtual environments for developing, deploying, monitoring and managing applications online.	Systems architecture	Cloud computing	Design
PROTECTION RINGS (page 139)	Assign processes to a set of hierarchical rings that control how processes call other processes and how they access data.	Process isolation	Processor and OS architecture	Design
ROLE-BASED ACCESS CONTROL (page 78)	Decide whether a subject is authorized to access an object according to policies defined in a central policy repository.	Access control	Centralized or distributed systems with a large number of resources.	Analysis, design

NAME	INTENT	CONCERN	CONTEXT	LIFECYCLE
PROTECTED ENTRY POINTS (page 136)	Force a call from a one process to another to go through only pre-specified entry points where the correctness of the call is checked and other access restrictions may be applied.	Access control	Execution of collaborating processes in a computing system.	Design
REIFIED REFERENCE MONITOR (page 100)	Enforce authorization and define Decision as a separate class.	Access control	Any environment in which we need to control access to computing resources.	Analysis, design
REMOTE AUTHENTICATOR/ AUTHORIZER (page 56)	Provide facilities for authentication and authorization when accessing shared resources.	Authentication and access control	Distributed systems	Design
ROLE-BASED ACCESS CONTROL (page 78)	Describe how to assign rights based on the functions or tasks of people in an environment in which control of access to computing resources is required.	Access control	An environment in which we need to control access to computing resources and where there is a large number of users, information types, or a large variety of resources.	Analysis, design
SAML ASSERTION (page 279)	Provide a way to communicate security information about a particular subject between different security domains.	Security policy	Web services	Design
SECURE ADAPTER (page 358)	Convert the interface of an existing class into a more convenient but secure interface.	Heterogeneous systems	Middleware	Design
SECURE BLACKBOARD (page 353)	Provide secure handling of data when its blackboard is accessed by a set of knowledge sources.	Secure shared data	Middleware	Analysis, design

NAME	INTENT	CONCERN	CONTEXT	LIFECYCLE
SECURE BROKER (page 339)	Extend Broker to provide secure interactions between distributed components.	Secure access to remote objects	Distributed systems middleware	Design
SECURE DISTRIBUTED PUBLISH/ SUBSCRIBE (page 372)	Decouple the publishers of events securely from those interested in the events (subscribers).	Event and message distribution	Distributed systems middleware	Design
SECURE ENTERPRISE SERVICE BUS (page 366)	Provide a convenient infrastructure to integrate a variety of distributed services and related components in a simple and secure way.	Secure systems integration	Middleware, web-based systems	Design
SECURE HANDLING OF LEGAL CASES (page 451)	Describe the handling of legal cases in which a client is either suing another party (a plaintiff) or is being defended from a suit (a defendant) using a legal firm. The pattern includes the necessary policies (in the form of security patterns) to stop or mitigate the expected attacks.	Handling of legal cases using a blackboard	Application	Analysis
SECURE MODEL-VIEW-CONTROLLER (page 375)	Add security to the interactions of users with systems configured using the MVC pattern.	System interaction	Middleware	Design
SECURE PIPES AND FILTERS (page 347)	Provide secure handling of data streams. Each processing step applies some data transformation or filtering. The rights to apply specific transformations to the data can be controlled. The communication of data between stages can be also protected.	Data stream security	Middleware, operating systems	Design

NAME	INTENT	CONCERN	CONTEXT	LIFECYCLE
SECURE PROCESS/ THREAD (page 120)	Ensure that a process or thread does not interfere with other processes or misuse shared resources.	Process isolation and containment	Operating systems supporting a multi-programming environment with several user-defined and system processes active at a given time.	Design
SECURE THREE-TIER ARCHITECTURE (page 362)	Extend the Three-Tier Architecture pattern by enforcing a global view of security for all three layers.	Architectural style	Computer systems executing processes that need to be persistent and interact with users.	Design
SECURITY LOGGER AND AUDITOR (page 111)	Log all security-sensitive actions performed by users and provide controlled access to records for audit purposes.	Auditing	Any system that handles sensitive data, in which it is necessary to keep a record of access to data.	Design
SESSION-BASED ROLE-BASED ACCESS CONTROL (page 107)	Allow access to resources based on the role of the subject, and limit the rights that can be applied at a given time based on the contexts (roles) defined by the access session.	Access control	Operating systems, middleware	Design
SIGNATURE-BASED IDS (page 219)	Check every request for access to the network against a set of existing attack signatures, to detect possible attacks and trigger an appropriate response.	Attack detection	Networks	Design
SOFTWARE-AS-A-SERVICE (page 431)	Provide a set of secure software applications available in a cloud system that can be accessed by client devices through the Internet.	Systems architecture	Cloud computing	Design

NAME	INTENT	CONCERN	CONTEXT	LIFECYCLE
SYMMETRIC ENCRYPTION (page 288)	Protect message confidentiality by making a message unreadable to those that do not have access to the key. Symmetric encryption uses the same key for encryption and decryption.	Information hiding	Networks and databases	Design
TRANSPORT LAYER SECURITY (page 205)	Provide a secure channel between a client and a server where application messages are being communicated over the Transport layer of the Internet.	Secure communication	Networks	Design
TLS VIRTUAL PRIVATE NETWORK (page 202)	Set up a secure channel between two endpoints using cryptographic tunneling through the Transport layer, with authentication and access control at each endpoint.	Secure communication	Networks	Design
VIRTUAL ADDRESS SPACE ACCESS CONTROL (page 146)	Control access by processes to specific areas of their virtual address space (VAS) according to a set of predefined access types.	Access control	Operating systems	Design
VIRTUAL ADDRESS SPACE STRUCTURE SELECTION (page 156)	Select the virtual address space for OSs that have special security needs.	Security architecture	Operating systems	Design
VIRTUAL MACHINE OPERATING SYSTEM ARCHITECTURE (page 179)	Provide a set of replicas of the hardware architecture (virtual machines), that can be used to execute (potentially different) operating systems.	Security architecture	Operating systems	Design
WEB SERVICES POLICY LANGUAGE (page 260)	Enable an organization to represent access control policies for its web services in a standard manner.	Access control	Application	Design
WS-POLICY (page 263)	Define a base set of assertions that can be used and extended by other web services specifications to describe a range of service requirements and capabilities.	Access control, reliability	Web services	Design

NAME	INTENT	CONCERN	CONTEXT	LIFECYCLE
WS-SECURITY (page 330)	Define how to secure SOAP messages applying XML security technologies.	Secure communication	Networks	Design
WS-TRUST (page 272)	Define a security token service and a trust engine that are used by web services to authenticate other web services.	Secure communication	Web services	Design
XACML ACCESS CONTROL EVALUATION (page 254)	Decide whether a request is authorized to access a resource according to policies defined by the XACML AUTHORIZATION pattern.	Access control	Application	Design
XACML AUTHORIZATION (page 248)	XACML enables an organization to represent authorization rules in a standard manner.	Access control	Application	Design
XML ENCRYPTION (page 309)	Describe a process to apply encryption functions to XML data, keeping correct XML syntax.	Information hiding	Databases and networks	Design
XML FIREWALL (page 242)	Filter XML messages to/from enterprise applications, based on business access control policies and the content of the message.	Access control	Applications	Design
XML SIGNATURE (page 317)	Provide a means to identify the source of an XML message.	Message authentication and message integrity.	Networks	Design

Misuse Patterns Described in this Book

NAME	INTENT	CONCERN	CONTEXT	LIFECYCLE
WORM (page 390)	Propagate to as many places as possible (or to specific systems), usually indicating its presence, and maybe performing some damage.	Propagation and optionally destruction of information or DoS.	Networked systems, especially web based systems.	Application
DENIAL-OF-SERVICE IN VOIP (page 397)	Overwhelm limited resources in order to disrupt VoIP operations, typically through a flood of messages.	DoS	VoIP networks	Design

NAME	INTENT	CONCERN	CONTEXT	LIFECYCLE
SPOOFING WEB SERVICES (page 403)	Impersonate the identity of a user by stealing their credentials and making requests in their name with these credentials.	Impersonation	Web services	Application

Security Patterns Described Elsewhere

NAME	INTENT	CONCERN	CONTEXT	LIFECYCLE
Attribute Based (Metadata-based) Access Control (ABAC/MBAC) [Pri04]	Extend the Access Matrix model by adding the concept of metadata or attributes for subjects and/or objects.	Access control	Distributed systems	Analysis, design
Call Hijacking in VoIP [Pel09]	Direct a participant of a VoIP call to a terminal device other than the intended recipient.	Misuse pattern	VoIP networks	Design
Call Interception in VoIP [Pel09]	Provide a way of monitoring voice packets, RTCP transmissions or control channel information.	Misuse pattern	VoIP networks	Design
Data Filter Architecture [Fla99]	Filter unwanted information from a data stream according to a set of predefined policies.	Filtering	Applications	Analysis, design
Distributed Authenticator [Bro99]	Extend the GoF [Gam94] Abstract Factory pattern with generic authentication functionality.	Authentication	Application-level, distributed object-based systems	Design
e-commerce secure patterns [Yua11]	Add security to shopping carts, catalogs and orders.	Authorization	Application	Analysis
Least Privilege [Fer11e]	Assign to subjects only the rights they need to perform their duties.	Access control	Computer systems containing sensitive information	Analysis, design, implementation
Malicious Virtual Machine Creation [Has12b]	Create a virtual machine image that contains malicious code so that it can infect other users when they create their virtual machines.	Misuse pattern	Cloud computing	Design

NAME	INTENT	CONCERN	CONTEXT	LIFECYCLE
Malicious Virtual Machine Migration [Has12b]	When a virtual machine is transferred from one server to another, monitor the network and obtain some confidential information or manipulate the VM content while it is in transit.	Misuse pattern	Cloud computing	Design
Network Segmentation [Fer07d]	Perform separation of the voice and data services to counter possible attacks against the voice VLAN by an attacker in the data VLAN.	Secure communication	VoIP networks	Design
Object Filter and Access Control Framework [Hay00]	Apply AUTHENTICATOR and Data Filtering for traffic control.	Traffic filtering, access control	Networks	Design
Packet Filter Firewall [Sch06b]	Filter incoming and outgoing network traffic in a computer system based on packet inspection at the IP level.	Traffic filtering	Networks	Design
Patterns for Physical Access Control Systems [Fer07f]	Control access to buildings by using RBAC and authentication.	Physical access control	Physical systems	Analysis
Privacy-Aware Network Client [Sad05]	Provide a way to make a user of a network site aware of the privacy policies followed by that site.	Privacy pattern	Web sites, e-commerce	Design
Privacy Policies [Lob09]	Development of privacy policies to be used on web sites.	Privacy patterns	Web sites, e-commerce	Analysis
Proxy-Based Firewall [Sch06b]	Inspect and filter incoming and outgoing network traffic based on the type of application service to be accessed or doing the access.	Traffic filtering	Networks	Design
Reliable Security [Buc11]	Add reliability to security mechanisms.	Reliability	Operating system, networks	Design
Retrieving Data from a Database using SQL Injection [Fer12f]	Insertion of arbitrary code into a SQL query by the client in order to alter its intended function.	Misuse pattern	Database systems with web interfaces	Design

NAME	INTENT	CONCERN	CONTEXT	LIFECYCLE
Role Rights Definition [Sch06b]	Define role rights for access to resources.	Access control	Applications	Design
Secure Facade [Fer12e]	Hide the internal structure of a subsystem, providing only an interface with those functions we want to show and whose access can be controlled.	Access control	Operating systems, middleware	Design
Secure Location-Based Service for Social Networks [Mar11]	Show or hide a user's location on request.	Privacy pattern	Applications	Analysis
Secure Operating System Shell [Kai12]	Create encrypted channel to operating system.	Secure communication	Operating system, networks	Design
Secure Reliability [Buc11]	Add security to reliable systems.	Systems security	Operating system, networks	Design
Secure VoIP Call [Fer07d]	Hide the meaning of messages by performing encryption of calls in a VoIP environment.	Secure communication	VoIP networks	Design
Session-Based Attribute-Based Authorization [Fer06e]	Allow access to resources based on the attributes of the subjects and the properties of the objects. Limit the rights that can be applied at a given time based on the context defined by the access session.	Access control	Applications	Analysis, design
Signed Authenticated Call [Fer07d]	Perform both device and user authentication before deciding access to VoIP services.	Secure communication	VoIP networks	Design
Stateful Firewall [Sch06b]	Filter incoming and outgoing network traffic in a computer system based on state information derived from past communications.	Traffic filtering	Networks	Design
Social networks security [Fer10e]	Add controls to social networks.	Authentication, access control	Social networks	Analysis

NAME	INTENT	CONCERN	CONTEXT	LIFECYCLE
Theft of Service in VoIP [Pel09]	Gain access to the VoIP network by imitating subscribers and/or seizing control of terminal devices to perform free calls.	Misuse pattern	VoIP networks	Design
Traffic Monitoring Inference in Cloud Computing [Has12b]	Place a virtual machine in the same hardware as the victim's virtual machine to obtain some information, such as estimated traffic rates, or to detect cache activity spikes.	Misuse pattern	Cloud computing	Design
Usability of Security [Mun11]	Add visual feedback to security features.	Usability patterns	Computer systems	Application
VoIP Evidence Analyzer [Pel10]	Define a structure and process to analyze the collected forensic data packets. Also presents a method of investigating an alleged IP attack scene and tracing back attackers.	Attack forensics	VoIP networks	Design
VoIP Evidence Collector [Pel10]	Define a structure and process to collect attack packets on the basis of adaptively setting filtering rules for real-time collection.	Attack forensics	VoIP Networks	Design
WiMax [Fer08e]	Establish a secure environment for the users of the wireless network and for the messages exchanged in it.	Secure communications	Wireless networks	Design

Security Patterns under Development

NAME	INTENT	CONCERN	CONTEXT	LIFECYCLE
Software Defined Networking (SDN) Security [Car12]	SDN provides an architectural framework for abstracting the functions associated with controlling the flow of packets within the network.	Message security	Networks	Design
Whitelisting Firewall [Bon12]	Define a list of sites with which we want to communicate.	Traffic filtering	Networks	Design

NAME	INTENT	CONCERN	CONTEXT	LIFECYCLE
WS-Federation [Aja12]	Describe a standard to securely share a principal's identity information across trust boundaries.	Identity	Web services	Design
WS-Secure Conversation [Aja13]	Describe a standard to allow security context establishment and use through the lifetime of a communication session between web services.	Secure communication	Web services	Design
XSS (Cross-Site Scripting) [Pei12]	Leverage vulnerabilities in the code of a web application to execute commands in a user's browser to insert unintended content.	Misuse pattern	Web applications	Design

17.2   Future Research Directions for Security Patterns

This list is not complete, but indicates some interesting possibilities for future work.

- *More security patterns.* Important areas without patterns include database systems. Database views and query intersection are good candidates. Patterns that map OO models to relational databases could also be extended to map the security constraints defined in the OO model to the corresponding relational tables.

  Patterns for administration is another area missing in patterns; we only showed one of this type, ADMINISTRATOR HIERARCHY (page 184). Also, we have only shown prevention patterns, but we need patterns for recovery from attacks, security planning and so on. Some planning patterns were presented in [Sch06b], but more are needed.

- *Catalog of misuse patterns.* We have written only a few misuse patterns (Chapter 14). We need more of them before they can be useful to evaluate systems (see Chapter 2). An appropriate classification of threats is an initial start in this direction [Uzu12d]. An enumeration of threats, for example for cloud systems, can identify required misuse patterns for this specific environment [Has12b].

- *Improvements and extensions to the methodology.* Secure methodologies usually don't pay attention to process aspects; other work studies software processes, but does not consider security. We need to build flexible processes for secure systems development [Uzu12b].

- *Security evaluation.* As discussed in Chapter 3, we have proposed an evaluation method based on enumeration of threats. Methods based on formal models can prove specific parts of a system to be secure, and can be combined with other methods. Argument-based evaluation of systems is another possibility. We believe that a combination of these methods is very promising.

- *Tools.* The general guidance provided to the designer by a methodology can be complemented by tools. For example, in the analysis stage we could only show to the designer security patterns that apply to that stage. Pattern diagrams can help selection between similar patterns. A *design assistant* is needed. In fact, we see the lack of tools for building complete secure systems as a problem: most (all?) of the tools we know of only consider one part of the system. For example, the Samoa tools help in the design of secure web services in a Microsoft environment [MSR08]. Apparently one of them, the WSE Policy Advisor, uses security patterns. Other partial tools include support for pattern builders [Sch03] and support for threat enumeration [Bra09]. Another tool tries to help with the selection of patterns [Shi10].

- *Analysis of the effect of changes.* It is important to study the effect of changes in a system after it is built and put into operation. Changes occur for several reasons: new or changed requirements, performance improvement, expansion of the system to accommodate more users, technological advances in the platform devices and others. Often, the changes are not reflected in the original architecture model. From the architecture point of view, this is called 'architecture erosion'. From a security point of view, we need to evaluate the effect of changes; very little work has been done on this aspect [Fer94b] [Oku11].

- *Traceability.* This is a necessary complement to the previous item; we need to know what components in the architecture are affected when a change is made. Tactics have been used for this purpose, but we believe that patterns are more suitable [Fer12d].

- *Specialized applications.* Some applications have unique requirements, and building them using a general approach may not result in the most secure system. Typical applications that require their own models include financial, medical, transportation and smart grid applications.

- *Specialized environments.* Some types of environments have a large effect on the applications running on them, and methodologies must be modified to consider that effect. Typical cases are systems built using web services [Fer12b], or cloud systems. Specialized patterns for those environments are also needed.

- *Reliability, availability and safety requirements.* We need to develop a process in which security and other nonfunctional aspects can be developed concurrently. These are areas that complement security, and we often need to define trade-offs between them and security. Sometimes we want to combine them with security, as we did in [Buc11], where we describe a fault-tolerant security pattern and a secure fault-tolerance pattern.

- *Mapping across levels.* Security constraints must be defined at the highest levels, where their semantics are clear. They must then be mapped to lower levels, where they are enforced by corresponding concrete mechanisms. We need precise ways to perform this mapping by taking advantage of the fact that the same type of patterns can be used at all levels [Fer99b].

■ *Integration of mobile systems into IT systems.* 'Bring your own device' (BYOD) is the latest paradigm used in many institutions. The approach implies handling a variety of heterogeneous devices, with different capabilities, using different operating systems, different protocols and with their own variety of security systems. We discussed some of this in Chapter 16. We believe that patterns allow a convenient unification and integration of mobile devices with the rest of the information structure.

■ *Compliance with a variety of standards and regulations.* Systems handling medical, financial or government records must comply with appropriate regulations. In addition, institutions have their own policies, which must be followed by all of their applications. It is possible to build patterns to satisfy any regulation or policy, and if we instantiate them in domain models, all applications derived from the domain model will automatically comply with the regulations [Fer11c]. We need patterns to express the policies of diverse regulations.

In summary, there are many possibilities for work on security patterns.

17.3 Security Principles

Building secure systems requires careful application of some principles. In my opinion, the most important principles are:

■ *Holistic approach.* Cover all architectural levels and all units: we cannot have secure systems that are built piece-wise.

■ *Highest level.* Security constraints must be defined where their semantics are clear, and propagated down the architectural levels of the system.

■ *Full mediation.* Every request for resources must be evaluated and fulfilled only if authorized.

■ *Defense in depth.* We need to have more than one line of defense.

■ *Closed system.* Everything is forbidden unless explicitly authorized.

■ *Need-to-know.* Assign only the necessary rights to perform functions.

Well-built patterns implicitly apply some of these principles, and our methodology helps in this respect.

17.4   The Future

Security patterns are still not as used as they should be. Once people know more about their effectiveness in building secure applications, they will be more used. To increase their use we need to:

- *Improve the training of software developers.* While large companies do some patterns training, smaller companies do not. To be able to apply security patterns, a designer first needs to be acquainted with patterns; in turn, to be proficient in the use of patterns, a designer needs to understand OO design and UML. We must convince them that they need to consider security as a fundamental design objective.

- *Increase the technical level of security developers.* Software development is still a pseudo-profession, in which people who do not have the proper background are assigned to the construction of critical software. The technical papers (white papers, development notes) of most companies in the US, and in some other countries, are written in a colloquial style, avoiding any formalism. Even UML diagrams are rarely shown, the idea being that only words and code are understandable to developers.

We believe that through the use of security patterns it is possible to write applications which are considerably more secure than current applications without experiencing serious development delays. Patterns emphasize holistic thinking, which is fundamental to producing secure systems. The current emphasis in industry in building fast and dirty code has resulted in a paradise for hackers; most of the attacks that have happened recently could have been avoided with a minimum set of defenses.

An interesting approach to producing secure architectures is the use of the 'clean slate' approach, which does not try to be compatible with existing architectures. Groups of researchers, sponsored by DARPA, are building this type of architecture. While we see our patterns of most value in designing and evaluating current systems, the collection of security ideas and principles embodied by these patterns can certainly be of value for this project.

Peter Neumann talks of cherry-picking the best ideas for building the systems of the future [Mar12]. A good collection of patterns can provide the ideas that have worked in the past.

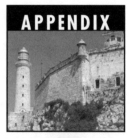
Pseudocode for XACML Access Control Evaluation

A.1   Pseudocode for retrieveApplicablePolicy()

```
retrieveApplicablePolicy(XACMLAccessRequest){
FOR EACH PolicyComponent ∏ PolicyAdministrationPoint
    evaluateTarget(XACMLAccessRequest, PolicyComponent)
    IF targetMatches
    THEN add PolicyComponent to ApplicablePolicy
}


evaluateTarget(XACMLAccessRequest, PolicyComponent){
    IF SubjectsMatch() AND
       ResourcesMatch() AND
       ActionsMatch() AND
       EnvironmentMatch()
    THEN
        targetMatches
}
```

```
SubjectsMatch(XACMLAccessRequest, PolicyComponent){//at least one
    //subject matches
    FOR EACH SubjectDescriptor ∏ PolicyComponent.Target.SubjectDescriptors
        IF SubjectMatches() RETURN true
    RETURN false
}

SubjectMatches(XACMLAccessRequest, PolicyComponent){//all qualifiers
    //match
    FOR EACH SubjectAttributeQualifier ∏ SubjectDescriptor
      IF ! SubjectAttributeQualifier.operator(SubjectAttributeQualifier.value,
XACMLAccessRequest.SubjectAttributeValue)
            RETURN false
    RETURN true
}
```

A.2   Pseudocode for evaluateApplicablePolicy()

```
evaluateApplicablePolicy(ApplicablePolicy, XACMLAccessRequest){
    FOR EACH PolicyComponent p ∏ ApplicablePolicy
        DepthFirstSearch(p)
RETURN PolicyDecisionPoint.policyCombiningAlgorithm()
}


depthFirstSearch(PolicyComponent p){
    FOR EACH PolicyComponent or Rule x ∏ p
        IF x is a Rule
            evaluateRule(x)
        ELSE
            depthFirstSearch(x)
            p.result = p.combiningAlgorithm()
}


evaluateRule(Rule x){
    IF evaluate(Rule.condition)
        RETURN x.result = x.effect
    ELSE RETURN x.result = NotDeterminate
}
```

Glossary

A & A	Authorization and access control. Authorization defines permitted access to resources depending on the accessor (user, executing process), the resource being accessed and the intended use of the resource. Access control defines a mechanism to enforce authorization.
AAL	Ambient assisted living. Architectures for home environments which have devices such as sensors and cameras to support and monitor people with impaired functions or disabilities.
Access matrix	An authorization model which indicates, for each active entity (a subject) which resources it can access (objects or protection objects), and how (access type).
ACL	Access control list. Associated with an object to indicate which subjects can access it and in what way.
Analysis stage	The stage of the software lifecycle at which requirements are made precise.
Antipattern	A pattern that illustrates practices that should be avoided.
API	Application programming interface. Defines a protocol that processes should use to access services or to communicate with each other.
Authentication	Proof to the system that the subject intending to access the system is who or what it says it is. See *I&A*.
Authorization	See *A&A*.
Bastion host	A special-purpose computer on a network point of access designed to withstand attacks.

Brief	A formal document that sets forth the main contentions with supporting statements or evidence.
Class diagram	A type of UML diagram that shows static relationships between entities (represented by classes).
Clearance	A level in a hierarchy that allows individual access to some type of information.
Cloud computing	'A model for enabling convenient, on-demand network access to a shared pool of configurable computing resources (e.g. networks, servers, storage, applications and services) that can be rapidly provisioned and released with minimal management effort or service provider interaction'. (NIST definition)
Collaboration diagram	A diagram that illustrates messages being sent between classes and objects (instances). Complements or replaces sequence diagrams.
Compartment	Divisions of the hierarchies in a multilevel security model.
Confidentiality	Prevention of unauthorized data disclosure. Also called *secrecy.*
Contract	A binding, legally enforceable agreement between two or more parties.
Credential	A document that can be used to prove identity, and which may describe some attributes of the authenticated entity.
CSA	Cloud Security Alliance. A nonprofit organization that promotes research into best practices for securing cloud computing.
Cyberphysical system	A system in which some of its physical properties can be controlled through information.
DDoS	Distributed denial of service. Usually performed by sending a flood of messages to a web site.
Defendant	A person required to make answer in a legal action or suit.
Deployment diagram (UML)	A diagram that shows the distribution of software components into the physical units of the system.
Deposition	A testimony taken down in writing under oath.
Descriptor	Words that typically indicate the location and mode of access of the parts of the *virtual access space* (VAS) of a process.
Diagram	A representation of some model or view of a system.

Digital signature	A cryptographic proof that a message or document comes from a specific user.
Domain	An area of knowledge, a space for the execution of a process (execution domain), an area of control for an administrative entity (administration domain).
DoS	Denial of Service. An attack on the availability of a system, in which users or other systems may prevent the legitimate users from using their system.
EHR	Electronic healthcare record. A lifetime record of an individual with the purpose of supporting continuity of care and related education and research.
ESB	Enterprise service bus. A common bus structure that provides basic brokerage functions as well as a set of other appropriate services in a web services environment.
Execution domain	The set of rights that a process can use during its execution. Also called *execution context* and *sandbox*.
Expert	A person having or displaying special skill or knowledge derived from training or experience.
Federation	A set of autonomous administrative domains which agree on recognizing identities or sharing rights.
Firewall	A security mechanism to filter traffic according to some criteria.
Gatekeeper	A component of the H323 VoIP protocol used for admission control and other functions.
Gateway	A network node that interfaces with other networks that may use different protocols.
HIPAA	Health Insurance Portability and Accountability Act. In the US, defines privacy and security rules for the handling of patient information.
Hypervisor	A layer of software or firmware in direct contact with the hardware which creates and manages virtual machines that can share the hardware.
I&A	Identification and Authentication. Identification implies a user or system providing an identity to access a system. Authentication implies providing some proof that a user or system is the one they or it claims to be.
IAM	Identity and access management. Used by some vendors to indicate the combination of identity management and system access control.

Identity	Representation of a set of claims made by a digital subject about itself or another digital subject.
Identity base	Database containing the set of identities used for authentication.
IDS	Intrusion detection system. A subsystem that alerts the system in real time when an intruder is trying to attack it.
Information hiding	To hide information in order to protect it. Usually performed by the use of cryptography, but steganography is another option.
Integrity	Prevention of unauthorized data modification or destruction.
IP	Internet protocol, used as one layer of network communications.
IPSec	A protocol which provides cryptographic functions at the IP layer.
ITG	IT governance is the processes that ensure the effective and efficient use of IT in enabling an organization to achieve its goals.
Layer	Separation of organization as defined by the three-tier model. Also denoted as *tier*.
Liberty Alliance Identity Federation	A standard allowing services to federate into identity federations.
Logging and auditing	Functions that keep records (log) of actions that may be relevant for security or other purposes, for later analysis (auditing).
MAC	Message authentication code. A part of a message that provides integrity assurance. Also…
MAC	A sublayer of the data link layer (layer 2). Provides addressing and channel access control.
MDD or MDE	Model-driven development or Model-driven engineering. A software development approach that, starting from a domain model, produces conceptual application models that are transformed during the lifecycle stages.
Metamodel	Sets of related concepts that form a prototype to instantiate models as part of a methodology or procedure for designing a system.
Microkernel	An operating system model that puts all or a large part of the OS functionality in specialized servers and coordinates access to them.

Model	Represents some conceptual entity, behavior or structure. A diagram is part of a model or a pattern and represents some aspect of it.
NAS	Network-attached storage. Data storage attached to a network, acting as a file server.
NIST	(US) National Institute of Standards and Technology.
Non-repudiation	The principle that dictates that users should be responsible for their actions and should not be able to deny what they have done.
Nonce	An arbitrary number used only once in a cryptographic communication.
Opponent	A person who takes an opposite position (as in a debate, contest, or conflict).
OWASP	Open Web Application Security Project. An organization focused on improving the security of software.
PAP	Policy administration point. The storage of authorization and authentication rules in a system.
PBX	Private branch exchange, a private telephone network used within an institution.
PCI DSS	Payment Card Industry Data Security Standard.
PDP	Policy decision point. The point in a system at which access decisions are made.
PEP	Policy enforcement point. The point in a system at which access requests are intercepted and enforced. Realized through some type of Reference Monitor.
Plaintiff	A person who brings a legal action.
Policy	A high-level institution guideline; more specifically, a rule about authorization, authentication or access constraints.
Policy base	Set of policies (authorization rules or other type of rules).
Precedent	Something done or said that may serve as an example or rule to authorize or justify a subsequent act of the same or an analogous kind.
Principal	A *subject* responsible for an action in a system.
Process	A program in execution; a *secure process* is also a unit of execution isolation as well as a holder of rights to access resources.

Protected entry point	Prespecified entry points in a program where the correctness of the calls is checked and where other access restrictions may be applied.
Protection ring	A structure to control how processes call other processes and how they access data.
Pull mode	A communication mode in which processes are notified and they must get the new data.
Push mode	A communication mode in which new data is sent to processes without their needing to request it.
RBAC	Role-based access control. A model in which access rights are assigned to roles and roles are assigned to users.
Reference architecture	A high-level software architecture that defines fundamental components of a system and the interaction among these units.
Refinement	The addition of more detail to a design.
Reify	To convert an event into an object in order to manipulate it.
Replay attack	An attack that can happen when somebody captures a message and then resends it.
REST	Representational state transfer, a style of software architecture for distributed hypermedia.
RFID	Radio frequency identifier, used to transfer data from a tag attached to an object.
RTP	Real-time transport protocol defines a standardized packet format for delivering audio and video over the IP layer.
SaaS	Software as a service, a set of software applications available in a cloud system that can be accessed by client devices through the Internet.
Sandbox	See *execution domain*.
SAP	Semantic analysis pattern. A pattern that describes a small set of coherent use cases that together describe a basic generic application.
SCADA	Supervisory control and data acquisition system, the architecture of process control systems.
Secrecy	A synonym of *confidentiality*.
Sensor	A device that measures a physical quantity and converts it into an electric signal.

Separation of duty	A security policy in which some action can only be performed if two subjects agree.
Sequence diagram	A type of UML diagram that describes the interactions between objects over time.
Service provider	Some institution or company that provides web-based services, usually for a fee.
SIEM	Security information and event management. Provides real-time analysis of security alerts generated by network hardware and applications.
Signature	The name and parameters needed for a procedure call or a remote procedure call.
SIP	Session initiation protocol, an IETF signaling protocol used for controlling voice and video calls over IP.
SOA	Service-oriented architecture, an architectural style in which clients request services from providers according to some protocol.
SOX	The Sarbanes–Oxley Act of 2002 is a US federal law that regulates public companies, management and public accounting firms.
Spoofing attack	A situation in which one person or program masquerades as another by falsifying some information. Also known as *forgery.*
SSO	Single sign on, implies the use of only one item of authentication information, for example passwords, to gain access to a variety of related systems.
Subject	An active system component able to request resources.
Suit	An action or process in a court for the recovery of a right or claim.
Superencryption	Encrypting information that has already been encrypted.
TDM	Time-division multiplexing, a type of digital multiplexing in which two or more signals share a channel along time.
Thread	A lightweight process.
Threat enumeration	Systematic listing of system threats based on some methodology
Threat modeling	Synonym for *threat enumeration.*
Tier	Synonym for *layer.*

TLS	Transport layer security, a cryptographic protocol based on SSL (Secure Sockets Layer).
VAS	Virtual address space, the address (memory) space of a program, variables, and data used by a process.
VE	Virtual environment, the virtualization structure available for developing programs in cloud computing.
Virtual machine	A unit of virtual execution, including appropriate resources.
Virtual machine monitor	Synonym for *hypervisor*.
VoIP	Voice over IP, the delivery of voice and multimedia over the IP protocol.
VPN	Virtual private network. A network model that protects communications by establishing a cryptographic tunnel between endpoints at one of the layers of the communication protocol.
Vulnerability	A flaw in a system that allows a security attack.
Web service	A type of XML-based component that is available on the web and can be incorporated in applications or used as a standalone service
Wi-Fi	Wireless protocol defined by the Wi-Fi Alliance.
Witness	A person who testifies in a cause or before a judicial tribunal.
WS-Federation	A proposed standard allowing web services to federate their identities.
WSDL	An XML format for describing web services as a set of endpoints operating on messages containing either document-oriented or procedure-oriented information.
X.509	A standard for a public-key infrastructure (PKI) and privilege management infrastructure (PMI). Defines formats for certificates and other functions.
XACML	eXtensible Access Control Markup Language. The standard defines a declarative access control policy language implemented in XML, and a processing model describing how to evaluate authorization requests according to the rules defined in policies.
XML	Extensible modeling language. Defines a set of rules for encoding documents in a format readable by humans and machines.

References

I have always imagined that Paradise will be a kind of library.

Jorge Luis Borges

[Aar96]   A. Aarsten, D. Brugali, G. Menga, K. Brown and R. Hirschfeld, 'Patterns of three-tier client server architectures', *Proceedings of the 1996 Pattern Languages of Programs (PLoP) Conference*, Monticello, IL, September 1996, http://members.aol.com/kgb1001001/Articles/threetier/threetier.htm

[ACS]   ActivCard Synchronous Authentication http://www.activcard.com/activ/services/library/synchronous_authentication.pdf

[Ado]   Adobe System Incorporated, Digital Signatures, http://www.adobe.com/security/digsig.html

[Air]   Airtight Networks: WLAN Intrusion Prevention, http://www.airtightnetworks.com/home/solutions/wireless-intrusion-prevention.html

[aix10]   AIX System Security Auditing, http://www.aixmind.com/?p=1019

[Aja10a]   O. Ajaj and E. B. Fernandez, 'A pattern for the WS-Trust standard of Web Services', *Proceedings of the 1st Asian Conference on Pattern Languages of Programs (AsianPLoP 2010)*, Tokyo, Japan, March 16–17, 2010, http://patterns-wg.fuka.info.waseda.ac.jp/asianplop/

[Aja10b]   O. Ajaj and E. B. Fernandez, 'A pattern for the WS-Policy standard'. In *Proceedings of the 8th Latin American Conference on Pattern Languages of Programs (SugarLoafPLoP 2010)*, Salvador, Bahia, Brazil, Sept 23–26, 2010

[Aja12]   O. Ajaj and E. B. Fernandez, 'A pattern for the WS-SecureConversation standard for web services', *19th International Conference on Pattern Languages of Programs (PLoP2012)*

[Aja13]   O. Ajaj and E. B. Fernandez, 'A pattern for the WS-Federation standard for web services', in preparation

[Ama]   Amazon Web Services LLC, 'Amazon Elastic Compute Cloud (Amazon EC2),
             http://aws.amazon.com/ec2/

[Amo96]   Amoeba Operating System, www.cs.vu.nl/pub/amoeba/ (accessed 27 Oct 2012)

[Amr]   D. Amrheim, 'Forget Defining Cloud Computing', http://soa.sys-con.com/node/1018801

[And01]   R. Anderson, 'CORBA Security Service Specification', OMG 2001.
             http://www.omg.org/docs/formal/02-03-11.pdf

[And04]   Anne H. Anderson, 'An Introduction to the Web Services Policy Language (WSPL)', *5th IEEE
             International Workshop on Policies for Distributed Systems and Networks*, Yorktown Heights,
             New York, 7–9 June 2004. http://labs.oracle.com/projects/xacml/Policy2004.pdf (accessed 9 Nov
             2012)

[And08]   R. Anderson, *Security Engineering* (2nd edition), John Wiley & Sons, Inc., 2008

[Anw06]   Z. Anwar, W. Yurcik, R. Johnson, M. Hafiz and R. Campbell, 'Multiple design patterns for Voice
             over IP (VoIP) security', *Proceedings of the IEEE Workshop on Information Assurance (WIA 2006)*,
             Phoenix, AZ, April 2006

[Arc03]   I. Arce and E. Levy, 'An analysis of the Slapper worm', *IEEE Security and Privacy*, Jan./Feb. 2003.
             82–87

[Arg]   Argus Systems Group, 'Trusted OS security: Principles and Practice',
             http://www.argus-systems.com/Products/products.html (accessed 27 Oct 2012)

[Ark10]   B. Arkin, 'Introducing Adobe Reader Protected Mode',
             http://blogs.adobe.com/asset/2010/07/introducing-adobe-reader-protected-mode.html (accessed
             27 October 2012)

[Ars01]   A. Arsanjani, 'Rule Object 2001: A Pattern Language for Adaptive and Scalable Business Rule
             Construction', *39th International Conference and Exhibition on Technology of Object-Oriented
             Languages and Systems (TOOLS39)*, Santa Barbara,, California, July 29-August 03, 2001
             http://www.computer.org/portal/web/csdl/proceedings/t#4

[Arx]   Arx, Digital Signature Solution (Standard Electronic Signatures),
             http://www.arx.com/products/cosign-digital-signatures.php

[Avg05]   P. Avgeriou and U. Zdun, 'Architectural patterns revisited: A pattern language', *Proceedings
             EuroPLoP 2005*, 1-39

[Bac08]   J. Bacon, D. M. Eyers, J. Singh, P. R. Pietzuch, 'Access control in publish/subscribe systems',
             Proceedings Second International Conference on Distributed Event-Based Systems (DEBS), 2008,
             23–34, ACM

[Bad04]   M. Badra, A. Serrhouchni and P. Urien, 'A lightweight identity authentication protocol for wireless
             networks', *Computer Communications* Volume 27, Issue 17, 1 November 2004

[Bad09]   M. Badra and I. Hajjeh, Internet-Draft, (D)TLS Multiplexing, April 2009
             http://tools.ietf.org/html/draft-badra-hajjeh-mtls-05

[bag]   Bagle (computer worm), http://en.wikipedia.org/wiki/Bagle_(computer_worm)

[Bar99]   J. Barkley, K. Beznosov and J. Uppal, 'Supporting Relationships in Access Control using Role Based Access Control', in *Proceedings of ACM Role-Based Access Control Workshop, RBAC'99*, Fairfax, Virginia, US, 1999, 55–65

[Bar00]   P. Barham, B. Dragovic, K. Fraser, S. Hand, T. Harris, A. Ho, R. Neugebauer, I. Pratt and A. Warfield, 'Xen and the Art of Virtualization', *Proceedings of the ACM Symposium on Operating System Principles, SOSP' 03*

[Bar07]   A. Barbir, C. Hobbs, E. Bertino, F. Hirsch and L. Martino, 'Challenges of Testing Web Services and Security in SOA Implementations', in *Test Analysis of Web Services*. SpringerLink, Sep. 2007, 395–440

[Bas06]   D. A. Basin, J. Doser, T. Lodderstedt, 'Model Driven Security: From UML Models to Access Control Infrastructures', *ACM Transactions on Software Engineering and Methodology*, vol 15, No 1, 2006, 39–91

[Bau09]   C. Baun, M. Kunze, 'Building a private cloud with Eucalyptus', *Proceedings of 5th IEEE International Conference on E-Science Workshops*, 2009, 33–38

[BEA11]   BEA Aqualogic Service Bus, http://en.wikipedia.org/wiki/AquaLogic (accessed June 27, 2011)

[BEA]   http://www.bea.com/content/news_events/white_papers/BEA_Itanium_Windows.pdf, page 3

[Bec96]   K. Beck et al., 'Industrial Experience with Design Patterns', *Proceedings of ICSE-18*, 1996, 103–114

[Ben02]   B. Benatallah, M. Dumas, M.-C. Fauvet, F. A. Rabhi and Q. Z. Sheng, 'Overview of Some Patterns for Architecting and Managing Composite Web Services', *ACM SIGecom Exchanges*, vol 3, No. 3, August 2002, 9–16

[Ber01]   H. Berghel, 'The Code Red worm', *Communications of the ACM*, vol 44, No 12, December 2001, 15–19

[Bha04]   K. Bhargavan, R. Corin, C. Fournet and A. D. Gordon, 'Secure Sessions for Web Services', *ACM Workshop on Secure Web Services*, 56–66, 2004

[Bha05]   A. Bhargav-Spantzel, A. C. Squicciarini, E. Bertino, 'New basic technologies for DIM: Establishing and protecting digital identity in federation systems', *Proceedings of the 2005 Workshop on Digital Identity Management*, ACM Press, 11–19

[Bie01]   E. Biermann, E. Cloete and L. M. Venter, 'A Comparison of Intrusion Detection Systems', *Computers & Security*, Volume 20, Issue 8, 1 December 2001, 676–683

[Biz04]   Implementing Pipes and Filters with BizTalk Server 2004 http://msdn2.microsoftwarecom/en-us/library/ms978668.aspx#implpipesandfilters_securityconsiderations

[Biz09]   SOA Patterns with BizTalk Server 2009, http://www.packtpub.com/soa-patterns-with-biztalk-server-2009/book (retrieved on July 13, 2011)

[Bla04]   B. Blakeley, C. Heath and Members of the Open Group Security Forum: Technical Guide: Security Design Patterns, 2004, http://www.opengroup.org/bookstore/catalog/g031.htm

[Bon12]   I. N. Bonilla and E. B. Fernandez, 'Whitelist Firewall pattern', in preparation

[Bou11]   R. Bouaziz, B. Hamid, N. Desnos, 'Towards a Better Integration of Patterns in Secure Component-Based Systems Design', *Proceedings of ICCSA'2011*, Springer

[Box02]   D. Box, *Understanding GXA,* Microsoft Corporation, http://msdn.microsoftwarecom/enus/library/aa479664.aspx (accessed 15 Dec 2009)

[Bra00]   A. Braga, C. Rubira and R. Dahab, 'Tropyc: A pattern language for cryptographic object-oriented software', Chapter 16 in *Pattern Languages of Program Design 4* (N. Harrison, B. Foote and H. Rohnert, Eds.). Also in *Proceedings of PLoP'98*, http://jerry.cs.uiuc.edu/~plop/plop98/final_submissions/

[Bra08a]   F. Braz, E. B. Fernandez and M. VanHilst, 'Eliciting Security Requirements through Misuse Activities', *Proceedings of the 2nd International Workshop on Secure Systems Methodologies using Patterns (SPattern'07).* In conjunction with the 4th International Conference onTrust, Privacy & Security in Digital Business (TrustBus'07), Turin, Italy, September 1–5, 2008, 328–333

[Bra08b]   M. Braendle and M. Naedele, 'Security for process control systems: An overview', *IEEE Security & Privacy,* vol 6, No 6, Nov.-Dec. 2008, 24–29

[Bra09]   F. Braz, *Instrumentalizacao da Analise e Projeto de Software Seguro Baseadaem Ameacas e Padroes.* PhD Thesis, Department of Electrical Engineering, University of Brasilia, Brazil, 2009.

[Bra10]   E. J. Braude, *Software Engineering: Modern approaches* (2nd edition), John Wiley & Sons, Inc., 2010

[Bre08]   R. Breu, F. Innerhofer-Oberperfler and A. Yautsiukhin, 'Quantitative Assessment of Enterprise Security Patterns', *Proceedings of Third International Conference on Availability, Reliability and Security (ARES 2008),* 921–928

[Bro99]   F. L. Brown and E. B. Fernandez, 'The Authenticator Pattern', *Proceedings of the Conference on Pattern Language of Programs (PloP'99),* http://hillside.net/plop/plop99/proceedings/

[Bro05]   K. Brown, *The .NET Developer's Guide to Windows Security,* Addison-Wesley, 2005

[BSI]   Building Security in Maturity Model, http://bsimm.com

[Buc09a]   I. A. Buckley and E. B. Fernandez, 'Three patterns for fault tolerance', *Proceedings of the OOPSLA MiniPLoP,* October 26, 2009 http://www.refactory.com/minisploppapers/FT_Patts.pdf

[Buc09b]   I. Buckley, E. B. Fernandez, G. Rossi and M. Sadjadi, 'Web Services Reliability Patterns', *Proceedings of the 21st International Conference on Software Engineering and Knowledge Engineering (SEKE'2009),* Boston, July 1–3; Boston, 2009

[Buc11]   I. Buckley, E. B. Fernandez and M. M. Larrondo-Petrie, 'Patterns Combining Reliability and Security', *Proceedings of PATTERNS 2011:The Third International Conferences on Pervasive Patterns and Applications,* September 25–30, 2011, Rome, Italy http://www.iaria.org/conferences2011/SubmitPATTERNS11.html

[Buc12]   I. Buckley and E. B. Fernandez, 'Failure patterns: A new way to analyze failures', *First International Symposium on Software Architecture and Patterns,* in conjunction with the 10th Latin American and Caribbean Conference for Engineering and Technology, July 23–27, 2012, Panama City, Panama

[Bus96] F. Buschmann, R. Meunier, H. Rohnert, P. Sommerlad and M. Stal, *Pattern-Oriented Software Architecture: A System of Patterns*, Volume 1. John Wiley & Sons, Inc., 1996

[Bus07] F. Buschmann, K. Henney and D. C. Schmidt, *Pattern-Oriented Software Architecture, vol 4: 'A Pattern Language for Distributed Computing*, John Wiley & Sons, Inc., 2007

[Byr04] E. Byres and J. Lowe, 'The myths and facts behind cyber security risks for industrial control systems', in *Proceeedings of VDE Congress*, 2004

[Cam90] N. A. Camillone, D. H. Steves and K. C. Witte, 'AIX operating system: a trustworthy computing system', in *IBM RISC S/6000 Technology*, SA23–2619, 1990, 168–172

[Cam06] R. Camargo, A. Goldchleger, M. Carneiro and F. Kon, 'The Grid Architectural Pattern: Leveraging Distributed Processing Capabilities', *Proceedings of the International Conference on Pattern Languages of Program Design 5*, 2006, 337–356

[Car12] C. Carroll and E. B. Fernandez, 'Security Aspects of Software Defined Networking', in preparation.

[cc] Common Criteria Portal, http://www.commoncriteriaportal.org/

[Cen10] Centre for the Protection of National Infrastructure, 'Information Security Briefing 01/2010 Cloud Computing', March 2010. http://www.cpni.gov.uk/Documents/Publications/2010/2010007-ISB_cloud_computing.pdf

[Cer03] Cerebit, Inc., 'Safeguarding the Enterprise from the Inside Out', http://www.cerebit.com/download/Cerebit-EnterpriseApplicationSecurity.pdf

[Cer06] CERT Coordination Center, Carnegie Mellon University, http://www.cert.org/, (accessed 15 January 2011)

[Cha01] R. Chandramouli, 'A Framework for Multiple Authorization Types in a Healthcare Application System', in *Proceedings of the 17th Annual Computer Security Applications Conference* (ACSAC), New Orleans, LA, Dec. 11–14 2001, 137–148

[Chat04] S. Chatterjee, 'Messaging Patterns in Service-Oriented Architectures', http://msdn.microsoftwarecom/en-us/library/aa480027.aspx

[Che03] 'Using Security Patterns to Model and Analyze Security Requirements' (with S. Konrad, L. Campbell and R. Wassermann), *IEEE Workshop on Requirements for High Assurance Systems*, (RHAS03), September 2003, Monterey, California

[Che] Checkpoint Software Technologies, Inc. http://www.checkpoint.com/products/softwareblades/ipsec-virtual-private-network.html (accessed 20 July 2010)

[Chi84] R. E. Childs Jr., J. Crawford, D. L. House and R. N. Noyce, 'A Processor Family for Personal Computers', *Proceedings of the IEEE*, vol 72, No 3, March 1984, 363–376

[Chr] The Chromium Projects: Sandbox, http://dev.chromium.org/developers/design-documents/sandbox (accessed 30 October 2012)

[Cisa]   Cisco IOS Software,
             http://www.cisco.com/en/US/products/sw/iosswrel/products_ios_cisco_ios_software_category_home.html (accessed 26 June 2007)

[Cisb]   Cisco Systems: Products and Technologies > Cisco Intrusion Detection,
             http://www.cisco.com/warp/public/cc/pd/sqsw/sqidsz/

[Cit]   http://www.citrix.com/English/ps2/products/product.asp?contentID=15005 (accessed 21 June 2010)

[Coc07]   The Apache Cocoon Project, http://cocoon.apache.org

[Col04]   M. Collier, 'The Value of VoIP Security', July 2004,
             http://www.callcentermagazine.com/shared/printableArticle.jhtml?articleID=22103933 (accessed 10 June 2007)

[Cona]   Connectix Corporation, 'The Technology of Virtual Machines', white paper, San Mateo, CA,
             http://www.connectix.com

[Conb]   'Conficker', http://en.wikipedia.org/wiki/Conficker

[Cra95]   S. Crane, J. Mageeand N. Pryce, 'Design patterns for binding in distributed systems', *OOPSLA'95 Workshop on Design Patterns for Concurrent, Parallel and Distributed Object-Oriented Systems*, Austin, TX, October 1995

[Cre81]   R. J. Creasy, 'The Origin of the VM/370 Time-Sharing System', *IBM Journal of Research and Dev.*, vol 25, No 5, 1981, 483–490

[CRN06]   The Communications Research Network (CRN), 'VoIP loophole aids service deniers?' February 2006

[CTR96]   'Security: Resellers getting the advantage of growth', *Computing Technology Review,* February 1996, 14–17

[Cyb]   Cyberoam, http://www.cyberoam.com/vpn.html (accessed 20 July 2010)

[Dam09]   E. Damiani, C. A. Ardagna, N. El Ioini, *Open source systems security certification.* Springer, New York, NY, US, 2009

[Das98]   F. Das Neves and A. Garrido, 'Bodyguard', Chapter 13 in *Pattern Languages of Program Design 3,* Addison-Wesley 1998

[Dat04]   DataPower, http:///www.datapower.com

[Dat05]   IBM Corporation, WebSphere DataPower XML Security Gateway XS40,
             http://www-01.ibm.com/software/integration/datapower/xs40/ (accessed 25 Nov 2009)

[Day91]   R. A. Dayan et al, *Signaling attempted transfer to protected entry point BIOS routine,* United States IBM (US) Patent 5063496, 1991, http://www.freepatentsonline.com/5063496.html

[DeC02]   S. De Capitani di Vimercati, S. Paraboschi and P. Samarati, 'Access conTrol : Principles and Solutions', *Software – Practice and Experience*, vol 33, No. 5 (April 2003), 397–421

[DeC05]   S. De Capitani di Vimercati, P. Samarati and S. Jajodia, 'Policies, models and languages for access control', in *Databases in Networked Information Systems, Proceedings of the 4th International Workshop, DNIS 2005*, Aizu-Wakamatsu, Japan, March 28–30, 2005, LNCS 3433, Spriger, Berlin/Heidelberg, 2005, 225–237

[Del04]   N. Delessy, E. B. Fernandez, S. Rajput and M. Larrondo-Petrie, 'Patterns for application firewalls', *Proceedings of the Pattern Languages of Programs Conference*, September 2004, http://hillside.net/plop/2004/

[Del05]   N. Delessy and E. B. Fernandez, 'Patterns for the eXtensible Access Control Markup Language', in *Proceedings of the 12th Pattern Languages of Programs Conference (PLoP2005)*, Monticello, Illinois, US, 7–10 September 2005, http://hillside.net/plop/2005/proceedings/PLoP2005_ndelessyandebfernandez0_1.pdf (accessed 18 Sept 2011)

[Del06]   N. Delessy, E. B. Fernandez and M. M. Larrondo-Petrie, 'A pattern language for identity management', *Proceedings of the 2nd IEEE International Multiconference on Computing in the Global Information Technology (ICCGI 2007)*, March 4–9, Guadeloupe, French Caribbean, http://www.computer.org/portal/web/csdl/doi/10.1109/ICCGI.2007.5

[Del07a]   N. Delessy, E. B. Fernandez, M. M. Larrondo-Petrie and J. Wu, 'Patterns for Access Control in Distributed Systems', *Proceedings of the 14th Pattern Languages of Programs Conference (PLoP2007)*, Monticello, Illinois, US, September 5–8, 2007, http://hillside.net/plop/2007/index.php?nav=program

[Del07b]   N. Delessy, E. B. Fernandez and M. M. Larrondo-Petrie, 'A Pattern Language for Identity Management', *Proceedings of the 2nd IEEE International Multiconference on Computing in the Global Information Technology (ICCGI 2007)*, March 4–9, Guadeloupe, French Caribbean

[Del07c]   N. Delessy and E. B. Fernandez, 'Adapting web services security standards for mobile and wireless environments', in *Advances in Web and Network Technologies and Information Management*, K. Chen-Chuan Chang, W. Wang, L. Chen, C. A. Ellis, C-H Hsu, A. C. Tsoi and H. Wang (Eds.), Springer LNCS 4537, 624–633
Proceedings of the 2007 International Workshop on Application and Security service in Web and pervAsive eNvironments (ASWAN 2007), June 16–18, 2007, HuangShan (Yellow Mountain), China

[Del08]   N. Delessy and E. B. Fernandez, 'A Pattern-Driven Security Process for SOA Applications', *Proceedings of the 3rd International Conference on Availability, Reliability and Security (ARES 2008)*. Barcelona, Spain, March 4–7, 2008, 416–421

[Del12]   N. Delessy and E. B. Fernandez, 'The Secure MVC Pattern', *First International Symposium on Software Architecture and Patterns*, in conjunction with the 10th Latin American and Caribbean Conference for Engineering and Technology, July 23–27, 2012, Panama City, Panama

[Dem04]   S. Demurjian, K. Bessette, T. Doan and C. Phillips, 'Concepts and Capabilities of Middleware Security', Chapter 9 of *Middleware for Communications*, Q. H. Mahmoud, ed., John Wiley & Sons, Inc., 2004, 211–236

[DeW09]   B. DeWin, R. Scandariato, K. Buyens, J. Grgoire and W. Joosen, 'On the secure software development process: CLASP, SDL and Touchpoints compared', *Information and Software Technology*, vol 51, 2009, 1152–1171

[dig]   Digital signature, http://en.wikipedia.org/wiki/Digital_signature

[Dod10]   M. Dodani, 'On "Cloud Nine" Through Architecture', *The Journal of Object Technology*, vol 9, no. 3, 2010

[DoD83]   US Department of Defense, *Trusted Computer System Evaluation Criteria*, 1983

[Don76]   J. E. Donnelley, 'A Distributed Capability Computing System', (DCCS) *Proceedings of the 3rd International Conference on Computer Communication*, Toronto, Canada, August 3–6, 432–440

[Dou09]   C. Dougherty, K. Sayre, R. C. Seacord, D. Svoboda, K. Togashi, *Secure Design Patterns,* Technical Report CMU/SEI-2009-TR-010, March 2009; updated October 2009

[Dri03]   F. Dridi, M. Fischer and G. Pernul, 'CSAP – An Adaptable Security Module for The e-Government System Webocrat', *Proceeedings of the 18th IFIP International Information Security Conference (SEC 2003),* Athens, Greece, 26–28 May 2003

[Dri05]   S. Dritsas, L. Gymnopoulos, M. Karyda, T. Balopoulos,S. Kokolakis, C. Lambrinoudakis, S. Gritzalis, 'Employing Ontologies for the Development of Security Critical Applications' I3E 2005, 187–201

[EAP]   EAP-TLS, http://en.wikipedia.org/wiki/Extensible_Authentication_Protocol (accessed 6 Nov 2012)

[Eic05]   M. Eichelberg, T. Aden, J. Riesmeier, A. Dogac and G. B. Laleci, 'A Survey and Analysis of Electronic Healthcare Record Standards', *ACM Comp. Surveys*, vol 37, No 4, Dec. 2005, 277–315

[Ela11]   G. Elahi, E. Yu, T. Li and L. Liu, 'Security requirements engineering in the wild: A survey of common practices', *Proceedings 35th IEEE Annual Comp. Software and Applications Conference*, 2011, 314–319

[Elg06]   A. Elgohary, T. S. Sobh, M. Zaki, 'Design of an Enhancement for SSL/TLS Protocols', *Computers & Security* Volume 25, Issue 4, June 2006

[ElK09]   P. El Khoury, P. Busnel, S. Giroux and K. Li, 'Enforcing Security in Smart Homes using Security Patterns', *International Journal of Smart Home*, vol 3, No 2, April 2009, 57–70

[Ell03]   J. Ellis, 'Voice, Video and Data Network' Academic Press, Amsterdam, 2003

[Elm03]   R. Elmasri and S. Navathe, *Fundamentals of Database Systems* (4th edition), Addison-Wesley 2003

[emp]   Empower Identity Manager, http://www.identitymanagement.com/?_kk=identity%20management&_kt=d37d8c67-315a-4919-abfc-41011051bd9e&gclid=CNrgw7ylnq8CFcNa7Aod90Shaw

[Erl09]   T. Erl, *SOA Design Patterns*, Prentice Hall PTR; 1st edition, 2009

[Ess97]   W. Essmayr, G. Pernul and A. M. Tjoa, 'Access controls by object-oriented concepts', *Proceeedings of 11th IFIP WG 11.3 Working Conference on Database Security*, August 1997

[Euc]   Eucalyptus Systems, Inc, http://www.eucalyptus.com/

[EVI10]   Evidian, 'Proteger la confidentialite: le controle d'acces en hopital', White paper, 2010, http://www.evidian.com

[Ext]   Extreme Networks, http://www.extremenetworks.com/products/OS/

[Fay04]   M. E. Fayad and H. Hamza, 'The Trust Analysis Pattern', *in Proceedings of the Fourth Latin American Conference on Pattern Languages of Programming (SugarLoafPLoP 2004)*, Porto Das Dunas, Ceara, Brazil, August 10–13, 2004, http://sugarloafplop2004.ufc.br/acceptedPapers/ww/WW_1.pdf (accessed 15 Dec 2009)

[Fed99]   Federal Information Processing Standards Publication. 1999. Data Encryption Data (DES), http://csrc.nist.gov/publications/fips/fips46-3/fips46-3.pdf

[Fed00]   Federal Information Processing Standard, 'Digital Signature Standard', 27 January 2000, http://csrc.nist.gov/publications/fips/fips186-2/fips186-2-change1.pdf

[Fed01]   Federal Information Processing Standards Publication, 2001, Advanced Encryption Standard, http://csrc.nist.gov/publications/fips/fips197/fips-197.pdf

[Fen06]   L. Fenster, *Effective use of Microsoft Enterprise Library*, Microsoft .NET Development Series, Addison-Wesley, 2006

[Fer75]   E. B. Fernandez, R. C. Summers and C. B. Coleman, 'An Authorization Model for a Shared Data Base', *Proceeedings of the 1975 SIGMOD International Conference*, ACM, New York, 23–31, 1975

[Fer78]   E. B. Fernandez, R. Summers, T. Lang and C. Coleman, 'Architectural Support for System Protection and Database Security', *IEEE Transactions on Computers*, vol C-27, No. 8, 767–771, August 1978

[Fer81]   E. B. Fernandez, R. C. Summers, C. Wood, *Database Security and Integrity*, Addison-Wesley, Reading, Massachusetts, Systems Programming Series, February 1981

[Fer85]   E. B. Fernandez, 'Microprocessor architecture: The 32-bit generation', *VLSI Systems Design*, October 1985, 34–44

[Fer93a]   E. B. Fernandez, M. M. Larrondo-Petrie and E. Gudes, 'A method-based authorization model for object-oriented databases', *Proceeedings of the OOPSLA 1993 Workshop on Security in Object-oriented Systems*, 70–79

[Fer93b]   E. B. Fernandez, E. Gudes and H. Song, 'A model for evaluation and administration of security in object-oriented databases', *IEEE Transactions on Knowledge and Database Engineering*, vol 6, no. 2, April 1994, 275--292

[Fer94a]   E. B. Fernandez, J. Wu and M. H. Fernandez, 'User group structures in object-oriented databases', *Proceeedings of the 8th Annual IFIP W.G.11.3 Working Conference on Database Security*, Bad Salzdetfurth, Germany, August 1994

[Fer94b]   E. B. Fernandez, E. Gudes and H. Song, 'A model for evaluation and administration of security in object-oriented databases', *IEEE Transactions on Knowledge and Database Engineering*, vol 6, no. 2, April 1994, 275--292

[Fer95]   E. B. Fernandez and R. B. France, 'Formal specification of real-time dependable systems', *Proceedings of 1st IEEE International Conference on Engineering of Complex Computer Systems*, Fort Lauderdale, FL, 1995, 342–348

[Fer97]   E. B. Fernandez and J. C. Hawkins, 'Determining Role Rights from Use Cases', *Proceedings of 2nd ACM Workshop on Role-Based Access Control,* ACM, 1997, 121–125, http://www.cse.fau.edu/~ed/RBAC.pdf

[Fer99a]   E. B. Fernandez and X. Yuan, 'An analysis pattern for reservation and use of entities', *Proceedings of PLoP99,* http://st-www.cs.uiuc.edu/~plop/plop99

[Fer99b]   E. B. Fernandez, 'Coordination of security levels for Internet architectures', *Proceedings of 10th International Workshop on Database and Expert Systems Applications,* 837–841, http://www.cse.fau.edu/~ed/Coordinationsecurity4.pdf

[Fer00]   E. B. Fernandez and X. Yuan, 'Semantic analysis patterns', *Proceedings of the 19th International Conference on Conceptual Modeling, ER2000,* 183–195 Also http://www.cse.fau.edu/~ed/SAPpaper2.pdf

[Fer01a]   E. B. Fernandez and R. Pan, 'A Pattern Language for Security Models', *Proceedings of the 8th Annual Conference on Pattern Languages of Programs (PLoP 2001),* 11–15 September 2001, Allerton Park Monticello, Illinois, US, 2001 http://hillside.net/plop/plop2001/accepted_submissions/accepted-papers.html http://www.hillside.net/plop/plop2001/accepted_submissions/PLoP2001/ebfernandezandrpan0/P LoP2001_ebfernandezandrpan0_1.pdf (accessed 18 Sept 2011)

[Fer01b]   D. Ferraiolo, R. Sandhu, S. Gavrila, D. R. Kuhn and R. Chandramouli, 'Proposed NIST standard for Role-Based Access Control', *ACM Transactions on Information and System Security,* vol 4, No 3, August 2001, 224–274

[Fer02]   E. B. Fernandez, 'Patterns for operating systems access control', *Proceedings of PLoP 2002,* http://jerry.cs.uiuc.edu/~plop/plop2002/proceedings.html

[Fer03a]   E. B. Fernandez, M. L. Petrie, N. Seliya, N. Delessy and A. Herzberg, 'A Pattern Language for Firewalls', *Proceedings of the PLoP Conference, 2003.* http://www.hillside.net/plop/plop2003/

[Fer03b]   E. B. Fernandez and J. C. Sinibaldi, 'More patterns for operating system access control', *Proceeedings of the 8th European conference on Pattern Languages of Programs, EuroPLoP 2003,* http://hillside.net/europlop, 381–398

[Fer03c]   E. B. Fernandez and R. Warrier, 'Remote Authenticator/Authorizer', *Proceedings of PLoP 2003,* http://hillside.net/patterns/

[Fer04a]   E. B. Fernandez, 'Two patterns for web services security', *Proceedingsof the 2004 International Symposium on Web Services and Applications* (ISWS'04), Las Vegas, NV, June 21–24, 2004

[Fer04b]   E. B. Fernandez, 'A methodology for secure software design', *2004 International Conference on Software Engineering Research and Practice (SERP'04),* Las Vegas, NV, June 21–24, 2004

[Fer05a]   E. B. Fernandez and M. M. Larrondo-Petrie, 'Teaching a course on data and network security using UML and patterns', *Proceedings of the Educators Symposium of MoDELS/UML 2005,* Montego Bay, Jamaica, October 2–7, 2005

[Fer05b]   E. B. Fernandez and D. L. la Red Martinez, 'Using patterns to develop, evaluate and teach secure operating systems', *Proceedings of the Congreso Internacional de Auditoría y Seguridad de la Información (CIASI 2005),* Madrid, Spain, 125–130

[Fer05c]   E. B. Fernandez and T. Sorgente, 'A pattern language for secure operating system architectures', *Proceedings of the 5th Latin American Conference on Pattern Languages of Programs,* Campos do Jordao, Brazil, August 16–19, 2005

[Fer05d]   E. B. Fernandez and A. Kumar, 'A security pattern for rule-based intrusion detection', *Proceedings of the Nordic Conference on Pattern Languages of Programs,* Viking PLoP 2005, Otaniemi, Finland, 23–25 September 2005

[Fer05g]   E. B. Fernandez, T. Sorgente, M. M. Larrondo-Petrie, 'A UML-based methodology for secure systems: The design stage', *Proceedings of the 3rd International Workshop on Security in Information Systems (WOSIS-2005),* Miami, May 24–25 2005

[Fer05h]   E. B. Fernandez, T. Sorgente and M. VanHilst, 'Constrained Resource Assignment Description Pattern', *Proceedings of the Nordic Conference on Pattern Languages of Programs, Viking PLoP 2005,* Otaniemi, Finland, 23–25 September 2005

[Fer06a]   E. B. Fernandez and N. Delessy, 'Using patterns to understand and compare web services security products and standards', *Proceedings of the International Conference on Web Applications and Services (ICIW'06),* Guadeloupe, February 2006, IEEE Comp Society, 2006

[Fer06b]   E. B. Fernandez, M. M. Larrondo-Petrie, T. Sorgente and M. VanHilst, 'A methodology to develop secure systems using patterns', Chapter 5 in *Integrating security and software engineering: Advances and future vision,* H. Mouratidis and P. Giorgini (eds.), IDEA Press, 2006, 107–126

[Fer06c]   E. B. Fernandez, M. VanHilst, M. M. Larrondo Petrie, S. Huang, 'Defining Security Requirements through Misuse Actions', in *Advanced Software Engineering: Expanding the Frontiers of Software Technology,* S. F. Ochoa and G.-C. Roman (Eds.), International Federation for Information Processing, Springer, 2006, 123–137

[Fer06d]   E. B. Fernandez, N. A. Delessy and M. M. Larrondo-Petrie, 'Patterns for web services security', in *'Best Practices and Methodologies in Service-Oriented Architectures',* L. A. Skar and A. A. Bjerkestrand (Eds.), 29–39, part of OOPSLA 2006, *21st International Conference on Object-Oriented Programming, Systems, Languages and Applications,* Portland,OR, ACM, October 22–26

[Fer06e]   E. B. Fernandez and G. Pernul, 'Patterns for Session-Based Access Control', in *Proceedings of the Conference on Pattern Languages of Programs, PLoP 2006,* Portland, OR, October 2006, http://hillside.net/plop/2006/

[Fer06f]   E. B. Fernandez, T. Sorgente and M. M. Larrondo-Petrie, 'Even more patterns for secure operating systems', *Proceedings of the Conference on Pattern Languages of Programs, PLoP 2006,* Portland, OR, October 2006, http://hillside.net/plop/2006/

[Fer07a]   E. B. Fernandez, J. C. Pelaez and M. M. Larrondo-Petrie, 'Attack patterns: A new forensic and design tool', *Proceedings of the 3rd Annual IFIP WG 11.9 International Conference on Digital Forensics,* Orlando, FL, Jan. 29–31, 2007 Chapter 24 in *Advances in Digital Forensics III,* P. Craiger and S. Shenoi (Eds.), Springer/IFIP, 2007, 345–357

[Fer07b]   E. B. Fernandez and M. M. Larrondo Petrie, 'Securing design patterns for distributed systems', Chapter 3 in *'Security in Distributed, Grid and Pervasive Computing',* Y. Xiao (ed.), Auerbach Publications, Taylor & Francis Group, LLC, 2007, 53–66

[Fer07c] E. B. Fernandez, D. L. laRed M., J. Forneron, V. E. Uribe and G. Rodriguez, 'A secure analysis pattern for handling legal cases', *Proceedings of the 6th Latin American Conference on Pattern Languages of Programming (SugarLoafPLoP'2007)*, 178–187. http://sugarloafplop.dsc.upe.br/AnaisSugar2007_WEB.pdf

[Fer07d] E. B. Fernandez, J. C. Pelaez and M. M. Larrondo-Petrie, 'Security patterns for voice over IP networks', *Journal of Software,* vol 2, No 2, August 2007, 19–29 http://www.academypublisher.com/jsw

[Fer07e] E. B. Fernandez, P. Cholmondeley and O. Zimmermann, 'Extending a secure system development methodology to SOA', *Proceedings of the 1st International Workshop on Secure Systems Methodologies Using Patterns (SPattern'07).* in conjunction with the *4th International Conference on Trust, Privacy & Security in Digital Business (TrustBus'07)*, Regensburg, Germany, September 03–07, 2007, 749–754.

[Fer07f] E. B. Fernandez, J. Ballesteros, A. C. Desouza-Doucet and M. M. Larrondo-Petrie, 'Security Patterns for Physical Access Control Systems', in S. Barker and G. J. Ahn (Eds.), *Data and Applications Security XXI*, LNCS 4602, 259–274, Springer 2007 *Proceedings of the 21st Annual IFIP WG 11.3 Working Conference on Data and Applications Security,* Redondo Beach, California, US, July 8–11, 2007

[Fer08a] E. B. Fernandez, H. Washizaki and N. Yoshioka, 'Abstract security patterns', position paper in *Proceedings of the 2nd Workshop on Software Patterns and Quality (SPAQu'08),* in conjuction with the 15th Conference on Pattern Languages of Programs (PLoP 2008), October 18–20, Nashville, TN http://patterns-wg.fuka.info.waseda.ac.jp/SPAQU/index.html or http://hillside.net/plop/2008/papers/ACMVersions/spaqu/fernandez.pdf

[Fer08b] E. B. Fernandez, H. Washizaki and N. Yoshioka, A. Kubo and Y. Fukazawa, 'Classifying security patterns', *Proceedings of the 10th Asia-Pacific Web Conference (APWEB'08),* Springer LNCS 4976, 2008, 342–347

[Fer08c] E. B. Fernandez and D. LaRed M., 'Patterns for the secure and reliable execution of processes', *Proceedings of the 15th InternationalConference on Pattern Languages of Programs (PLoP 2008),* colocated with OOPSLA, Nashville, TN, Oct. 2008

[Fer08d] E. B. Fernandez, M. Fonoage, M. VanHilst and M. Marta, 'The secure three-tier architecture', *Proceedings of the Second Workshop on Engineering Complex Distributed Systems (ECDS 2008),* Barcelona, Spain, March 4–7, 2008. 555–560

[Fer08e] E. B. Fernandez and M. VanHilst, 'An overview of WiMax security', Chapter 10 in the *Handbook of WiMax security and QoS*, S. Ahson and M. Ilyas (eds.), CRC Press, Taylor and Francis Group, Boca Raton, FL, 2008, 197–204

[Fer09a] E. B. Fernandez and J. L. Ortega-Arjona, 'The Secure Pipes and Filters Pattern', *Proceedingsof the 3rd International Workshop on Secure System Methodologies using Patterns (SPattern 2009)* http://www.matematicas.unam.mx/jloa/publicaciones/PipesFiltersMay22-09.pdf

[Fer09b] E. B. Fernandez and J. L. Ortega-Arjona, 'Securing the Adapter pattern', *Proceedings of the OOPSLA MiniPLoP*, October 26, 2009

[Fer09c]   E. B. Fernandez, M. VanHilst, D. laRed M. and S. Mujica, 'An extended reference monitor for security and safety', *Proceedings of the 5th Iberoamerican Conference on Information Security (CIBSI 2009)*. Montevideo, Uruguay, November 2009

[Fer09d]   E. B. Fernandez, N. Yoshioka and H. Washizaki, 'Modeling misuse patterns', *Proceedings of the 4th International Workshop on Dependability Aspects of Data Warehousing and Mining Applications (DAWAM 2009)*, in conjunction with the 4th International Conference on Availability, Reliability and Security (ARES 2009), March 16–19, 2009, Fukuoka, Japan, 566–571.

[Fer10a]   E. B. Fernandez, N. Yoshioka, H. Washizaki and M. VanHilst, 'Measuring the level of security introduced by security patterns', *Proceedings of the 4th workshop on Secure systems methodologies using patterns (SPattern 2010)*, in conjunction with ARES 2010, Krakow, Poland, February 2010

[Fer10b]   E. B. Fernandez, K. Hashizume, I. Buckley, M. M. Larrondo-Petrie and M. VanHilst, 'Web services security: Standards and products', Chapter 8 in *Web Services Security Development and Architecture: Theoretical and Practical Issues*, Carlos A. Gutierrez, Eduardo Fernandez-Medina and Mario Piattini (Eds.), IGI Global Group 2010. 152–177

[Fer10c]   E. B. Fernandez, N. Yoshioka and H. Washizaki, 'A Worm misuse pattern', *Proceedings of the 1st Asian Conference on Pattern Languages of Programs(AsianPLoP 2010)*, Tokyo, Japan, March 16–17, 2010, http://patterns-wg.fuka.info.waseda.ac.jp/asianplop/

[Fer10d]   E. B. Fernandez and M. M. Larrondo-Petrie, 'Designing secure SCADA systems using security patterns', *Proceedings of the 43rd Hawaii Conference on Systems Science*, Honolulu, HI, Jan.2010, 1–8, http://ieeexplore.ieee.org/stamp/stamp.jsp?tp=&arnumber=5428672

[Fer10e]   E. B. Fernandez, Carolina Marin and Maria M. Larrondo Petrie, 'Security requirements for social networks in Web 2.0', in the *Handbook of Social Networks: Technologies and Applications*, B. Furht (Editor), Springer 2010

[Fer11a]   E. B. Fernandez, N. Yoshioka, H. Washizaki and M. VanHilst, 'An approach to model-based development of secure and reliable systems', *Proceedings* of the 6th *International Conference on Availability, Reliability and Security (ARES 2011)*, August 22–26, Vienna, Austria

[Fer11b]   E. B. Fernandez, N. Yoshioka and H. Washizaki, 'Two patterns for distributed systems: Enterprise Service Bus (ESB) and Distributed Publish/Subscribe', *18th Conference on Pattern Languages of Programs (PLoP 2011)*

[Fer11c]   E. B. Fernandez and S. Mujica, 'Model-based development of security requirements', *CLEI (Latin-American Center for Informatics Studies) Journal, vol 14, No 3, paper 2*, December 2011 Special issue of best papers presented at SCCC 2010, Antofagasta, Chile

[Fer11d]   E. B. Fernandez, S. Mujica and F. Valenzuela, 'Two security patterns: Least Privilege and Secure Logger/Auditor', *Proceedingsof Asian PLoP 2011*.

[Fer11e]   E. B. Fernandez and S. Mujica, 'Model-based development of security requirements', *CLEI (Latin-American Center for Informatics Studies) Journal, vol 14, No 3, paper 2*, December 2011 Special issue of best papers presented at SCCC 2010, Antofagasta, Chile

[Fer12a]   E. B. Fernandez and H. Astudillo, 'Should we use tactics or patterns to build secure systems?', *First International Symposium on Software Architecture and Patterns*, in conjunction with the 10th Latin American and Caribbean Conference for Engineering and Technology, July 23–27, 2012, Panama City, Panama

[Fer12b]   E. B. Fernandez, 'Wireless network security for health applications', Chapter 15 in *Pervasive Communication Handbook*, S. Shah, M. Ilyas, H. T. Mouftah (eds.), CRC Press 2012

[Fer12c]   E. B. Fernandez, O. Ajaj, I. Buckley, N. Delessy-Gassant, K. Hashizume, M. M. Larrondo-Petrie, 'A Survey of Patterns for Web Services Security and Reliability Standards'. *Future Internet* 2012, *4*, 430–450, http://www.mdpi.com/1999-5903/4/2/430/

[Fer12d]   E. B. Fernandez, David La Red Martinez and J. I. Pelaez, 'A conceptual approach to voting based on patterns', *Government Information Quarterly.* 30, 2013, 64–73

[Fer12e]   E. B. Fernandez and A. V. Uzunov, 'Secure middleware patterns', accepted for the *4th International Symposium on Cyberspace Safety and Security (CSS 2012),* Melbourne, Australia, Dec. 12–13, 2012

[Fer12f]   E B. Fernandez, E. Alder, R. Bagley and S. Paghdar, 'A Misuse Pattern for Retrieving Data from a Database Using SQL Injection', *RISE'12, Workshop on Redefining and Integrating Security Engineering*, part of the ASE International Conference on Cyber Security, Washington, DC, December 12–14

[Fer13]   E. B. Fernandez, E. Gudes and M. Olivier, *Secure Software Systems*, Addison-Wesley (to appear)

[Fer]   D. F. Ferguson, D. Pilarinos and J. Shewchuck, 'The Internet Service Bus', *The Architecture Journal* 13, http://www.architecturejournal.net

[Fla99]   R. Flanders, E. B. Fernandez, 'Data Filter Architecture Pattern', *Proceedings of PLoP'99*, 1999

[For04a]   Forum Systems Inc., http://www.forumsys.com/

[For04b]   B. A Forouzan, *Data Communication and Networking.* McGraw Hill, 2004

[For]   Forum Systems. Sentry: Messaging, Identity and Security
             http://www.forumsys.com/products/soagateway.php

[Fow97]   M. Fowler, *Analysis patterns – Reusable object models*, Addison- Wesley, 1997

[Fow]   M. Fowler, 'Audit Log', http://martinfowler.com/ap2/auditLog.html

[Frea]   http://www.freeradius.org/mod_auth_radius/

[Freb]   FreshBooks, 'Say Hello to Cloud Accounting', http://www.freshbooks.com/ (accessed 30 Sep 2012)

[Fro85]   G. Frosini and B. Lazzerini, 'Ring-protection mechanisms: general properties and significant implementations', *IEE Proceeedings*, vol 132, Pt. E, No 4, July 1985, 203–210

[Ful07]   Mei Fullerton and E. B. Fernandez, 'An analysis pattern for Customer Relationship Management (CRM)', *Proceedings of the 6th Latin American Conference on Pattern Languages of Programming (SugarLoafPLoP'2007)*, May 27–30, 2007, Porto de Galinhas, Pernambuco, Brazil, 80–90

[Gal09]   B. Gallego,-Nicasio, A. Munoz, A. Maña and D. Serrano, 'Security Patterns, Towards a Further Level', *Proceedings of SECRYPT 2009*, 349–356

[Gal10]   J. Galloway, 'Preventing-open-redirection-attacks', http://www.asp.net/mvc/tutorials/security/preventing-open-redirection-attacks

[Gam94]   E. Gamma, R. Helm, R. Johnson, J. Vlissides, *Design Patterns: Elements of Reusable Object-Oriented Software,* Addison-Wesley, Boston, Mass., US 1994

[Gar02]   S. Garfinkel, *Web Security, Privacy & Commerce,* 2nd edition, O'Reilly 2002

[Gar09]   P. García-Teodoro, J. D'az-Verdejo, G. Maciá-Fern‡ndez and E. Vázquez 'Anomaly-based network intrusion detection: Techniques, systems and Challenges', *Computers & Security* Volume 28, Issues 1–2, February/March 2009, 18–28

[Gar10]   J. P. Garcia-Gonzalez, V. Gacitua and C. Pahl, 'Service Registry : a key piece for enhancing reuse in SOA service oriented architecture', *The Architecture Journal*:21, Microsoft, 2010. 29–36

[Gia08]   A. Giani, T. Roosta, S. Sastry, 'Integrity checker for wireless sensor networks in health care applications', *Proceedings of the 2nd International Conference on Pervasive Computing Technologies for Healthcare*, 2008

[Gnu]   GnuPG, The GNU Privacy Guard, http://www.gnupg.org/

[Goe05]   D. Goeke and H. Nguyen, SCADA system security, 2005 http://islab.oregonstate.edu/koc/ece478/05Report/Goeke-Nguyen.pdf

[Gol79]   B. D. Gold, R. R. Linde, R. J. Peeler, M. Schaefer, J. F. Scheid and P. D. Ward, 'A security retrofit of VM/370', *Proceedings of the National Computer Conference (NCC 1979)*, 335–344

[Gol06]   D. Gollmann, *Computer Security* (2nd edition), John Wiley & Sons, Inc., 2006

[Goo1]   Google, 'Welcome to Google Enterprise',http://www.google.com/enterprise/apps/ (accessed 29 Sep 2012)

[Goo2]   Google Inc., https://developers.google.com/appengine/

[Gor09]   S. Gorman, 'Electricity grid in US penetrated by spies', in *The Wall Street Journal Online*, April 8, 2009, http://online.wsj.com/article/SB123914805204099085.html?mod=goog

[Gra00]   C. Grace, IT Journalist PC Network Advisor – Tutorial, 'Understanding Intrusion Detection Systems', http://www.techsupportalert.com/pdf/t1523.pdf

[Gra68]   R. M. Graham, 'Protection in an information processing utility', *Communications of the ACM*, vol 11, No 5, May 1968, 365–369

[Gru03]   A. Grünbacher 'POSIX Access Control Lists on Linux', http://www.suse.de/~agruen/acl/linux-acls/online/ (accessed 25 Sept 2011)

[Haf06]   M. Hafiz, M. Adamczyk and R. E. Johnson, 'Organizing Security Patterns', *IEEE Software*, vol 24 No 4, 52–60

[Haf08]   M. Hafiz and R. Johnson, 'Evolution of the MTA Architecture: An Impact of Security'. *Software – Practice and Experience*, 38(15):1569–1599, Dec 2008

[Haf11]   M. Hafiz, P. Adamczyk and R. E. Johnson, 'Growing a pattern language (for security)'. *Proceedings of the 18th Conference on Pattern Languages of Programs (PLoP)*, 2011

[Hal06]   S. T. Halkidis, A. Chatzigeorgiu and G. Stephanides, 'A qualitative analysis of software security patterns', *Computers & Security*, vol 25, 2006, 379–392

[Hal08a]   S. T. Halkidis, N. Tsantalis, A. Chatzigeorgiu and G. Stephanides, 'Architectural risk analysis of software systems based on security patterns', *IEEE Transactions on Dependable and Sec. Computing*, vol 5, No3, July-September 2008, 129–142

[Hal08b]   C. Haley, R. Laney, J. Moffett and B. Nuseibeh, 'Security requirements engineering: A framework for representation and analysis', *IEEE Transactions Softw. Engineering*, 34(1):133–153, 2008

[Ham73]   K. J. Hammer Hodges, 'A fault-tolerant multiprocessor design for real-time control', *Computer Design*, December 1973, 75–81

[Ham04]   H. S. Hamza and M. E. Fayad, 'The Negotiation Analysis Pattern', *Proceedings of the Pattern Languages of Programs Conference (PLoP2004)*, http://hillside.net/plop/2004/

[Har01]   J. M. Hart, *Win32 System Programming* (2nd edition), Addison Wesley 2001

[Har76]   M. Harrison, W. Ruzzo, J. Ullman, 'Protection in Operating Systems', *Communications of the ACM*, vol 19, No 8, August 1976

[Has02]   J. Hassell, *RADIUS*, O'Reilly, 2002.

[Has09a]   K. Hashizume, E. B. Fernandez and S. Huang, 'Digital Signature with Hashing and XML Signature patterns', *Proceedings of the 14th European Conference on Pattern Languages of Programs (EuroPLoP 2009)*

[Has09b]   K. Hashizume and E. B. Fernandez, 'Symmetric Encryption and XML Encryption Patterns', Proceedings of the 16th Conference on Pattern Languages of Programs (PLoP 2009) http://portal.acm.org/citation.cfm?doid=1943226.1943243 (accessed 10 Nov 2012)

[Has09c]   K. Hashizume, E. B. Fernandez and S. Huang, 'The WS-Security Pattern', *1st IEEE International Workshop on Security Engineering Environments,* Dec. 17–19, 2009, Shanghai, China

[Has12a]   K. Hashizume, E. B. Fernandez, M. M. Larrondo-Petrie, 'Cloud Service Model Patterns', *19th International Conference on Pattern Languages of Programs (PLoP2012)*

[Has12b]   K. Hashizume, N. Yoshioka and E. B. Fernandez, 'Three Misuse Patterns for Cloud Computing', in *Security Engineering for Cloud Computing: Approaches and Tools*, D. G. Rosado, D. Mellado, E. Fernandez-Medina and M. Piattini, Eds. IGI Global, 2012

[Has12c]   K. Hashizume, D. G. Rosado, E. Fernández-Medina, E. B. Fernandez 'An Analysis of Security Issues for Cloud Computing', in revision for the *Journal of Internet Computing*

[Has12d]   K. Hashizume, E. B. Fernandez and Maria M. Larrondo-Petrie, 'A Pattern for Software-as-a-Service in Clouds', accepted for *Workshop on Redefining and Integrating Security Engineering (RISE'12),* part of the ASE International Conference on Cyber Security, Washington, DC, Dec. 2012

[Has12e]   K. Hashizume, E. B. Fernandez and M. M. Larrondo-Petrie, 'Cloud Computing Reference Architecture', in preparation

[Has13]   K. Hashizume, E. B. Fernandezand M. M. Larrondo-Petrie
            'A Reference Architecture for Cloud Computing', submitted for publication

[Hat07]   D. Hatebur, M. Heisel and H. Schmidt, 'A pattern system for security requirements engineering', *Proceedings of ARES 2007*, 356–365

[Hay00]   V. Hays, M. Loutrel, E. B. Fernandez, 'The Object Filter and Access Control Framework', *Proceedings of PLoP 2000*, http://www.hillside.net/plop/plop2k/proceedings/proceedings.html

[Hea06]   C. Heath, *Symbian OS: Platform Security*, John Wiley & Sons, Inc., 2006

[Hey07a]   T. Heyman, K. Yskout, R. Scandariato and W. Joosen, 'An analysis of the security patterns landscape', *29th International Conference on Software Engineering Workshops (ICSEW'07),* IEEE 2007

[Hey07b]   K. Heyman, 'A new virtual private network for today's mobile world', *Computer*, IEEE, December 2007, 17–19

[Hil]   J. Hill, 'An Analysis of the RADIUS Authentication Protocol', InfoGard Laboratories, http://www.untruth.org/~josh/security/radius

[HIP]   HIPAA, http://www.hipaa.org/

[Hip]   Health Insurance Portability and Accountability Act, http://en.wikipedia.org/wiki/Health_Insurance_Portability_and_Accountability_Act

[Hog04]   G. Hogland and G. McGraw, *Exploiting Software: How to Break Code*, Addison-Wesley 2004

[Hog11]   M. Hogan, F. Liu, A Sokol and J. Tong, NIST Cloud Computing Standards Roadmap, Special Publication 500–291, July 2011

[Hol06]   K. J. Hole, V. Moen, T. Tjostheim, 'Case study: online banking security', *Security & Privacy,* IEEE, vol4, no.2, 14–20, March-April 2006

[Hop04]   G. Hoppe and B. Woolf, *Enterprise integration patterns: Designing, building and deploying message solutions,* Addison-Wesley 2004

[How03]   M. Howard and D. Leblanc, *Writing Secure Code* (2nd edition), Microsoft Press, 2003

[How06]   M. Howard and R. Lipner, *The Security Development Lifecycle*, Microsoft Press, 2006

[HP09]   Hewlett-Packard, HP SOA Systinet, 2009 https://h10078.www1.hp.com/cda/hpms/display/main/hpms_content.jsp?zn=bto&cp=1-11-130-27%5E1461_4000_100__&jumpid=reg_R1002_USEN (accessed 15 Dec 2009)

[HP]   Hewlett Packard Corporation, Virtual Vault, http://www.hp.com/security/products/virtualvault

[Hp]   HP Cloud Service, http://hpcloud.com/

[Hug05]   J. Hughes, E. Maler, 'Security Assertion Markup Language (SAML) 2.0 Technical Overview', http://xml.coverpages.org/SAML-TechOverview20v03-11511.pdf

[Hut05]   B. Hutchison, H. Hinton, M. Hondo, 'Security Patterns Within a Service-Oriented Architecture', Dec. 2005, http://www.ebizq.net/topics/woa/features/6535.html?page=6 (accessed 19 Nov 2012)

[IBM04]   IBM Corporation, Web Services Security 2004, http://www.ibm.com/developerworks/library/specification/ws-secure/ (accessed 15 Dec 2009)

[IBM05]   IBM Corporation, WebSphere DataPower XML Security Gateway XS40, 2005 http://www-01.ibm.com/software/integration/datapower/xs40/ (accessed 15 Dec 2009)

[ibm09a]   Security in a Web Services World: A Proposed Architecture and Roadmap, http://download.boulder.ibm.com/ibmdl/pub/software/dw/library/ws-secmap.pdf (accessed 3 Dec 2009)

[ibm09b]   IBM Corporation, Web Services Security 2004, http://www.ibm.com/developerworks/library/specification/ws-secure/ (accessed 7 Dec 2009)

[IBMa]   IBM Cloud Computing: SaaS, http://www.ibm.com/cloud-computing/us/en/saas.html. (accessed 9 Nov 2012)

[IBMb]   IBM Corporation, 'Introduction to Business Security Patterns', white paper http://www-03.ibm.com/Security/patterns/intro.shtml

[IBMc]   IBM Tivoli Federated Identity Manager, http://www-306.ibm.com/software/tivoli/products/federated-identity-mgr/

[IBMd]   http://www.redbooks.ibm.com/redbooks/pdfs/sg246963.pdf, page 29

[Igu06]   V. M. Igure, S. A. Laughter and R. D. Williams, 'Security issues in SCADA Networks', *Computers & Security*, 25(7):498– 506, 2006.

[ILO]   'ILOVEYOU', http://en.wikipedia.org/wiki/ILOVEYOU

[Ima03]   T. Imamura and M. Tatsubori, 'Patterns for Securing Web Services Messaging', *Proceedings Of OOPSLA Workshop on Web Services and Service Oriented Architecture Best Practice and Patterns*, 2003

[int99]   Intel Corporation, *Intel Architecture Software Developer's Manual, vol 3: System Programming*

[ION]   IONA Technologies, 'Artix and Security'. http://www.iona.com/info/aboutus/collateral/Artix%20and%20Security.pdf

[IRP]   Intermediate Routing (Little, Rischbeck, Simon), http://soapatterns.org/design_patterns/intermediate_routing

[jav]   Sun Developer Network, http://java.sun.com/blueprints/patterns/

[Jen07]   M. Jensen, N. Gruschka, R. Herkenhoner, N. Luttenberger, 'SOA and Web Services: New Technologies, New Standards – New Attacks', Web Services, 2007. *ECOWS '07. Fifth European Conference on Web Services*, 35–44, 26–28 Nov. 2007

[Joh85]   H. L. Johnson, J. F. Koegel, R. M. Koegel, 'A secure distributed capability based system', *Proceedings of the 1985 ACM Annual Conference on the Range of Computing: Mid-80's Perspective*, 392 – 402.

[Joo11]   W. Joosen, B. Lagaisse and E. Truyen, 'Towards application driven security dashboards in future middleware', *J. Internet Services and Applications*, November 2011, DOI 10.1007/s13174-011-0047-6

[Jos01]   N. Josuttis, 'Designing a 3-Tier-Architecture' http://www.posa3.org/workshops/ThreeTierPatterns/submissions/NicolaiJosuttis.pdf#search=%22layer%203tier%20architecture%20pattern%20example%22

[Jos05]   A. Jøsang, J. Fabre, B. Hay, J. Dalzieland S. Pope, 'Trust Requirements in Identity Management', *Proceedings of the 2005 Australasian Workshop on Grid Computing and e-research*, ACM Press, 99–108

[Ju10]   J. Ju, Y. Wang, J. Fu, J. Wu and Z. Lin, 'Research on Key Technology in SaaS', in *2010 International Conference on Intelligent Computing and Cognitive Informatics (ICICCI)*, 2010, 384 –387

[Jue04]   J. Juerjens, *Secure systems development with UML*, Springer-Verlag, 2004

[Jur08]   A. D. Jurik and A. Weaver, 'Remote medical monitoring', *Computer*, April 2008, 96–100

[Kai12]   K. Kaighovadi and E. B. Fernandez, 'A Pattern for the Secure Shell Protocol', *First International Symposium on Software Architecture and Patterns,* in conjunction with the 10th Latin American and Caribbean Conference for Engineering and Technology, July 23–27, 2012, Panama City, Panama

[Kar08]   P. Karger and D. Safford, 'I/O for Virtual Machine Monitors: Security and Performance Issues', *IEEE Security & Privacy,* Sep/Oct 2008, 16–23

[Kau02]   C. Kaufman, R. Perlman and M. Speciner, *Network Security* (2nd edition), Prentice-Hall 2002

[Kel97]   M. Kelley, *Windows NT Network Security, A Manager's Guide,* Lawrence Livermore National Laboratory, 1997

[Kie02]   D. M. Kienzle, M. C. Elder, D. Tyree, J. Edwards-Hewitt, Security Patterns Repository, version 1.0, 2002, http://www.scrypt.net/~celer/securitypatterns/repository.pdf (accessed 3 March 2013)

[Kim06]   D. K. Kim, P. Mehta and P. Gokhale, 'Describing Access Control Models as Design Patterns Using Roles', *Proceedings of PLoP 2006*, http://www.hillside.net/plop/2006/Papers/ACM_Version/ (accessed 18 Sept 2011)

[Kin01]   C. King et al , *Security Architecture*, Osborne McGraw Hill 2001

[Kir04]   M. Kircher and P. Jain, *Pattern-Oriented Software Architecture: Volume 3, Patterns for Resource Management,* John Wiley & Sons, Inc., 2004

[Kis02]   M. Kis, 'Information Security Antipatterns in Software Requirements Engineering', *Proceedings of the 9th Pattern Languages of Programs Conference (PLoP2002)* http://jerry.cs.uiuc.edu/%7Eplop/plop2002/final/mkis_plop_2002.pdf

[Kis10]   P. C. Kishore Raja, M. Suganthi and M. R. Sunder, 'Wireless node behavior based intrusion detection using genetic algorithm', *Ubiquitous Computing and Communication Journal,* http://www.ubicc.org/files/pdf/PCKISHORERAJA_88.pdf

[Kod01]   S. R. Kodituwakku, P. Bertok and L. Zhao, 'APLRAC: A pattern language for designing and implementing role-based access control', *Proceedings of EuroPLoP 2001*

[Kov01]   L. Koved, A. Nadalin, N. Nagarathan, M. Pistoia and T. Schrader, 'Security Challenges for Enterprise Java in an e-business Environment', *IBM Systems Journal*, 40(1), 130–152, 2001

[Kum10]   A. Kumar and E. B. Fernandez, 'Security pAtterns for Virtual Private Networks', *Proceedings of the 8th Latin American Conference on Pattern Languages of Programs (SugarLoafPLoP 2010),* Salvador, Bahia, Brazil, Sept 23–26, 2010

[Kum12a]   A. Kumar and E. B. Fernandez, 'Security Patterns for Intrusion Detection Systems', *First International Symposium on Software Architecture and Patterns,* in conjunction with the 10th Latin American and Caribbean Conference for Engineering and Technology, July 23–27, 2012, Panama City, Panama, http://www.laccei.org/LACCEI2012-Panama/TechnicalPapers/TP010.pdf

[Kum12b]   A. Kumar and E. B. Fernandez, 'A Security Pattern for the Transport Layer Security (TLS) Protocol', *19th International Conference on Pattern Languages of Programs (PLoP2012)*

[Lar05]   C. Larman, *Applying UML and Patterns: An Introduction to Object-Oriented Analysis and Design and Iterative Development*, 3rd edition. Prentice-Hall, 2005

[Lau10]   A. Laube, A. Sorniotti, P. El Khoury, L. Gomez and A. Cuevas, 'Security Patterns for Untraceable Secret Handshakes with Optional Revocations', *International Journal of Advances in Security,* vol 3, No 1&2, IARIA, 2010, 68–79

[Law08]   G. Lawton, 'Developing Software Online With Platform-as-a-Service Technology', *Computer,* vol 41, no 6, 13–15, IEEE, June 2008

[lay09]   Layer 7 Technologies, The SecureSpan XML Firewall, http://www.layer7tech.com/main/products/xml-firewall.html (accessed 9 Dec 2009)

[Leh02]   S. Lehtonen and J. Parssinen, 'Pattern Language for Cryptographic Key Management', *Proceedings of EuroPlop 2002*, http://www.hillside.net/patterns/EuroPLoP2002/papers.html

[Liba]   Liberty Alliance Project, http://www.projectliberty.org/

[Libb]   Liberty Alliance Identity Framework, http://www.projectliberty.org/resources/specifications.php

[Lid]   Linux Intrusion Detection System, http://www.lids.org/

[Lip05]   S. Lipner and M. Howard, *The Trustworthy Computing Development Lifecycle*, 2005 http://msdn2.microsoftwarecom/en-us/library/ms995349.aspx

[Liu10]   G. Liu, 'Research on independent SaaS platform', in *Proceedings of the 2nd IEEE International Conference on Information Management and Engineering (ICIME)*, 2010, 110 –113

[Lob09]   L. L. Lobato and E. B. Fernandez, 'Patterns to Support the Development of Privacy Policies', *Proceedings of the First International Wokshop on Organizational Security Aspects (OSA 2009),* in conjuction with ARES 2009. March 16–19, 2009, Fukuoka, Japan.

[Loc]   H. Lockhart, et al., 'Web Services Federation Language (WS-Federation)' Version 1.1. http://download.boulder.ibm.com/ibmdl/pub/software/dw/specs/ws-fed/WS-Federation-V1-1B.pdf?S_TACT=105AGX04&S_CMP=LP

[Loh10]   H. Löhr, A.-R. Sadeghi, M. Winandy 'Patterns for Secure Boot and Secure Storage in Computing Systems', *4th International Workshop on Secure Systems Methodologies Using Patterns (SPattern 2010), Proceedings of ARES 2010: International Conference on Availability, Reliability and Security.*, 569–573, IEEE Computer Society, 2010

[Lop04]   J. Lopez, R. Oppliger and G. Pernul, 'Authentication and Authorization Infrastructures (Aais): a Comparative Survey', *Computers & Security,* vol 23, 2004, 578–590

[Mad05]   P. Madsen, Y. Koga, K. Takahashi, 'DIM frameworks: Federated Identity Management for Protecting Users from ID Theft', *Proceedings of the 2005 Workshop on Digital Identity Management*, ACM Press, 77–83

[Mah]   R. Mahmoodi, 'Three-Tier Architecture in C#', 2005
            http://www.codeproject.com/Articles/11128/3-tier-architecture-in-C

[MAJ]   Microsoft Architecture Journal, 'Identity and Access', Journal 16

[Mar11]   C. Marin, E. B. Fernandez and M. M. Larrondo-Petrie, 'Secure Location-Based Service for Social Networks', *9th Latin American and Caribbean Conference* (LACCEI'2011)

[Mar12]   J. Markoff, 'Killing the computer to save it: Peter G. Neumann', *The New York Times*, October 30, 2012

[McG06]   G. McGraw, *Software Security: Building Security In*, Addison-Wesley 2006

[Mic00]   Microsoft, *Windows 2000 Security, Technical Reference*, 2000

[Mic07]   Microsoft Corporation, .NET Framework Class Library, November 2007
            http://msdn.microsoftwarecom/en-us/library/ms229335.aspx

[Mic11]   Microsoft Corporation, The ASP .NET MVC framework, 2011
            http://www.asp.net/mvc/mvc3 (accessed 6 March 2012)

[Mica]   Microsoft, 'Pipes and Filters', http://msdn2.microsoftwarecom/en-us/library/ms978599.aspx

[Micb]   Microsoft, Windows Azure, http://www.windowsazure.com/en-us/

[Mil05]   A. Miller, 'Trends in Process Control Systems security', *IEEE Security and Privacy,* 3(5):57–60, 2005

[Mor06a]   P. Morrison and E. B. Fernandez, 'The Credentials Pattern*', in Proceedings of the 2006 Conference on Pattern Languages of Programs (PLoP 2006),* Portland, OR, US. October 21–23, 2006
            http://hillside.net/plop/2006/Papers/Library/PLoP2006_Credential.pdf

[Mor06b]   P. Morrison and E. B. Fernandez, 'Securing the Broker Pattern', *Proceedings of the 11th European Conference on Pattern Languages of Programs (EuroPLoP 2006)*
            http://www.hillside.net/europlop/

[Mor12]   S. Moral-Garcia, S. Moral-Rubio, E. B. Fernandez, E. Fernandez-Medina, 'Enterprise Security Pattern: A New Type of Security Pattern', submitted for publication

[Mos05]   T. Moses, 'eXtensible access control markup language (XACML)' version 2.0, OASIS, 2005,
            http://docs.oasis-open.org/xacml/2.0/access_control-xacml-2.0-core-spec-os.pdf (accessed 3 March 2013)

[Mou06]   H. Mouratidis, M. Weiss and P. Georgini, 'Modelling Secure Systems using an Agent-Oriented Approach and Security Patterns', *International Journal of Software Engineering and Knowledge Engineering*, vol, 16, no 3, 2006, 471–498

[Moz]   Mozilla Newsgroup: mozilla.dev.tech.crypto
           http://www.mozilla.org/projects/security/pki/nss/ssl/

[MS03A]   Enterprise Solution Patterns Using Microsoft .NET: Broker Pattern
           http://msdn.microsoftwarecom/library/default.asp?url=/library/en-us/dnpatterns/html/DesBroker.asp

[MS04A]   .NET Remoting Authentication and Authorization Sample
           http://msdn.microsoftwarecom/library/default.asp?url=/library/en-us/dndotnet/html/remsspi.asp

[msd]   Microsoft Patterns and Practices Development Center,
           http://msdn.microsoftwarecom/practices/topics/patterns/

[MSR08]   Microsoft Research, Cambridge, UK, *Samoa: Formal Tools for Securing Web Services,*
           http://research.microsoftwarecom/en-us/projects/samoa/ (accessed 22 Nov 2012)

[MS]   Microsoft Forums: What is TLS/SSL
           http://technet.microsoftwarecom/en-us/library/cc784450(v=WS.10).aspx

[Mui12]   J. de Muijnck-Hughes and I. Duncan, 'Thinking Towards a Pattern Language for Predicate Based Encryption Crypto-Systems', to appear in the Student Doctoral Track of the *6th International Conference on Security and Reliability, SERE (SSIRI) 2012*. DOI: 10.1109/SERE-C.2012.34

[Mul07]   S. Mullan, Programming with the Java XML Digital Signature API, Sun Microsystems March 2007, http://java.sun.com/developer/technicalArticles/xml/dig_signature_api/

[Mul]   MuleSoft, Mule Enterprise Service Bus,
           http://www.mulesoftwarecom/mule-esb-open-source-esb

[Mun09]   J. Muñoz-Arteaga, R. Mendoza, M. Vargas, J. Vanderdonckt, F. Alvarez, 'A Methodology for Designing Information Security Feedback Based on User Interface Patterns', *Advances in Engineering Software*, vol 40, No 12, 2009, 1231–1241

[Mun11]   J. Muñoz-Arteaga, E. B. Fernandez and H. Caudel , 'Misuse Pattern: Spoofing Web Services', *Proceedings of Asian PLoP 2011*

[mv]   MV8000 principles of operation
           http://cid-e17ca7e5bcaa1096.skydrive.live.com/self.aspx/P%c3%bablico/014-00648_MV8000_PrincOps_Apr80.pdf

[Nae07]   M. Naedele, 'Addressing IT security for critical control systems', in *Proceedings of the 40th Hawaii International Conference on Systems Science (HICSS-40),* January 2007

[Nag05]   N. Nagaratnam, A. Nadalin, M. Hondo, M. McIntosh and P. Austel, 'Business-driven application security: From modeling to managing secure applications', *IBM Systems Journal*, vol 44, No 4, 2005, 847–867

[Nak05]   K. Nakayama, T. Ishizaki and M. Oba, 'Application of Web Services Security using Travel Industry Model', *Proceedings of the 2005 Symposium on Applications and the Internet Workshops (SAINT-W'05)*, IEEE 2005

[Net03]   Netegrity, Inc., (now part of Computer Associates), 'A Reference Architecture' http://www.slidefinder.net/a/agenda/32855788 (accessed 12 Nov 2012)

[Net06]   L.-H. Netland, Y. Espelid and K. Mughal, 'Security pattern for input validation', *Proceedings of VikingPLoP 2006*, Helsingør, Denmark

[Neu04]   P. G. Neumann, 'Principled assuredly trustworthy composable architectures,' Final SRI report to DARPA, December 28, 2004

[Nex10]   Nexof, 'Cloud Computing: Platform as a Service (PaaS), http://www.nexof- ra.eu/?q=node/669

[Nic04]   D. M. Nicol, W. H. Sanders and K. S. Trivedi, 'Model-based evaluation: From dependability to security', *IEEE Transactions on Dependable and Secure Computing*, vol 1, No 1, 2004, 48–65

[Nie00]   'Examining VMware', *Dr. Dobbs Journal*, August 2000, 70–76

[Nima]   'F-Secure Virus-descriptions: Nimda', http://www.f-secure.com/v-descs/nimda.shmtl

[Nimb]   Nimbus, http://www.nimbusproject.org/about/

[Nis]   The National Institute of Standards and Technology (NIST), 'Cloud Computing Use Cases' http://www.nist.gov/itl/cloud/use-cases.cfm

[Niza10]   H. A. Nizamani and E. T., 'Patterns of Federated Identity Management Systems as Architectural Reconfigurations', *Proceedings of the Second International Workshop on Visual Formalisms for Patterns (VFfP 2010)*, Electronic Communications of the EASST, vol 31, 2010 http://venturebeat.com/2012/05/24/paypal-partners-with-verifone-equinox-to-accept-mobile-payments-in-store/

[Nok01]   Nokia Inc. copyright, White Paper: 'Combining Network Intrusion Detection with Firewalls for Maximum Perimeter Protection', April 2001 http://www.itu.dk/courses/DSK/F2003/Combining_IDS_with_Firewall.pdf

[NTC01]   *CORBA Security Service Specification*, OMG 2001 http://www.ntcip.org/library/documents/pdf/1105v0102a.pdf

[Nut03]   G. Nutt, *Operating Systems* (3rd edition), Addison-Wesley, 2003

[Oak01]   S. Oaks, *Java Security* (2nd edition), O'Reilly, 2001

[OAS06a]   OASIS, Web Services Security: (WS-Security 2004) http://www.oasis-open.org/committees/download.php/16790/wss-v1.1-spec-os-SOAPMessageSecurity.pdf (accessed 15 Dec 2009)

[OAS06b]   OASIS, Web Services Security: SOAP Message Security 1.1 (WS-Security 2004), 1 February 2006, http://www.oasis-open.org/committees/download.php/16790/wss-v1.1-spec-os-SOAPMessageSecurity.pdf

[OAS07]   OASIS, WS-SecurityPolicy 1.2, 1 July 2007 http://docs.oasis-open.org/ws-sx/ws-securitypolicy/v1.2/ws-securitypolicy.pdf

[OAS09]   OASIS Standard, WS-Trust 1.4
             http://docs.oasis-open.org/ws-sx/ws-trust/v1.4/os/ws-trust-1.4-spec-os.pdf (accessed 7 Dec 2009)

[Oku11]   T. Okubo, H. Kaiya and N. Yoshioka, 'Effective Security Impact Analysis with Patterns for
             Software Enhancement', *Proceedings of Sixth International Conference on Availability, Reliability
             and Security (ARES 2011)*, 527–534

[Ope1]   The OpenSSL Project, OpenSSL, http://www.openssl.org/

[Ope2]   OpenNebula Project Leads, http://opennebula.org/

[Ort03]   J. L. Ortega-Arjona, 'The Shared Resource Pattern: An Activity Parallelism Architectural Pattern
             for Parallel Programming', *Proceedingsof the Conference on Pattern Languages of Programs (PLoP
             2003)*

[Ort08]   J. L. Ortega-Arjona and E. B. Fernandez, 'The Secure Blackboard Pattern', *Proceedings of the 15th
             InternationalConference on Pattern Languages of Programs (PLoP 2008)*

[OS2]   http://www-306.ibm.com/software/os/warp/

[OWAa]   OWASP, Comprehensive Lightweight Application Security Process
             https://www.owasp.org/index.php/CLASP (accessed August 24, 2012)

[OWAb]   Security Analysis of Core J2EE Patterns Project,
             https://www.owasp.org/index.php/Category:OWASP_Security_Analysis_of_Core_J2EE_Design_
             Patterns_Project

[Oza88]   B. M. Ozaki, E. B. Fernandez and E. Gudes, 'Software Fault Tolerance in Architectures with
             Hierarchical Protection Levels', *IEEE MICRO*, vol 8, No. 4, August 1988, 30–43

[Ozg05]   O. Depren, M. Topallar, E. Anarim and M. K. Ciliz, 'An Intelligent Intrusion Detection System
             (IDS) for Anomaly and Misuse Detection in Computer Networks', *Expert Systems with
             Applications*, vol 29, Issue 4, November 2005, 713–722

[Pal]   http://www.palmos.com/dev/tech/overview.html

[Pap03]   M. P. Papazoglou and D. Georgakopoulos, 'Service-Oriented Computing: Introduction',
             Communications of the ACM, vol46, 24–28, 2003

[Par05]   Parthenon Computing, UK (ceased trading 2007)

[Pay]   http://venturebeat.com/2012/05/24/paypal-partners-with-verifone-equinox-to-accept-mobile-
             payments-in-store/

[Paz04]   A. Pazin, R. Penteado, P. Masiero, 'SiGCli: A Pattern Language for Rehabilitation Clinics
             Management', *Proceedings of SugarLoafPLoP 2004*
             http://sugarloafplop2004.ufc.br/acceptedPapers/index.html

[Pei12]   N. Peiravan and E. B. Fernandez, 'XSS Misuse Pattern', in preparation

[Pel09]   J. Pelaez, E. B. Fernandez and M. M. Larrondo-Petrie, 'Misuse Patterns in VoIP', *Security and
             Communication Networks Journal*. John Wiley & Sons, Inc., vol 2, No 2, 635–653, published
             online 15 April 2009, http://www3.interscience.wiley.com/journal/117905275/issue

[Pel10]   J; C. Pelaez and E. B. Fernandez, 'Network Forensics Models for Converged Architectures', *International Journal on Advances in Security*, IARIA, 2010, vol 3 no. 1 & 2, 2010. http://www.iariajournals.org/security/tocv3n12.html

[Per10]   Z. Pervez, S. Lee and Y.-K. Lee, 'Multi-Tenant, Secure, Load Disseminated SaaS Architecture', in *Proceedings of the 12th International Conference on Advanced Communication Technology*, Piscataway, NJ, US, 2010, 214–219

[PGP]   http://en.wikipedia.org/wiki/Pretty_Good_Privacy

[pin06]   Ping Identity Corporation, PingTrust, a standalone Security Token Server, http://www.pingidentity.com/about-us/news-press.cfm?customel_datapageid_1173=1404 (accessed 15 Dec 2009)

[POSA2]   D. Schmidt, M. Stal, H. Rohnert and F. Buschmann, *Pattern-Oriented Software Architecture*: *Volume 2, Patterns for Concurrent and Networked Objects,* John Wiley & Sons, Inc., 2000

[Pri04]   T. Priebe, E. B. Fernandez, J. I. Mehlau and G. Pernul, 'A Pattern System for Access Control ', in *Research Directions in Data and Applications Security XVIII,* C. Farkas and P. Samarati (Eds.), *Proceedings of the 18th. Annual IFIP WG 11.3 Working Conference on Data and Applications Security,* Sitges, Spain, July 25–28, 2004, 235–249

[Pri05]   PrismTech Corporation, Xtradyne's WS-DBC – the XML/SOAP Firewall for Enterprises, 2005 http://www.xtradyne.com/products/ws-dbc/ws-dbc.htm (accessed 15 Dec 2009)

[Pry00]   N. Pryce, 'Abstract Session: An Object Structural Pattern', Chapter 7 in *Pattern Languages of Program Design 4* (N. Harrison, B. Foote and H. Rohnert, eds.). Also in *Proceedings of PLoP'97*

[QNX]   QNX Software Systems, http://www.qnx.com

[Qu02]   Q. W. Qu and S. Srinivas, 'IPSec-Based Secure Wireless Virtual Private Network', *Milcom 2002 Proceedings,* vol 2, 1107- 1112

[Qwi]   QNX, Wikipedia, http://en.wikipedia.org/wiki/QNX

[Rad04]   S. Radhakrishnan, 'Web App Security using Struts, Servlet Filters and Custom Taglibs' http://www.ibm.com/developerworks/web/library/wa-appsec/ (accessed 29 October 2012)

[Rau97]   L. Rau, 'Inferno: One Hot OS', *Byte*, June 1997, 53–54

[Ray04]   I. Ray, R. B. France, N. Li and G. Georg, 'An Aspect-Based Approach to Model Access Control Concerns', *Journal of Information and Software Technology*, 46(9), 575–587

[Rea03]   Reactivity, http://www.reactivity.com

[Ren]   K. Renzel and W. Keller, 'Three Layer Architecture', In *Software Architectures and Design Patterns in Business Applications* http://www4.informatik.tu-muenchen.de/proj/arcus /TUM-I9746.html

[RFC2743]   IETF, 'Generic Security Service Application Program Interface Version 2', update 1 http://www.ietf.org/rfc/rfc2743.txt (accessed 20 Nov 2012)

[Rig00]   C. Rigney, S. Willens, A. Rubens, W. Simpson, 'Remote Authentication Dial In User Service (RADIUS)', June 2000. http://www.ietf.org/rfc/rfc2865.txt

[Riv78]   R. L. Rivest, A. Shamir, L. M. Adleman, 'A Method for Obtaining Digital Signatures and Public-Key Cryptosystems', *Commun. ACM* 21(2): 120–126, 1978

[Rod07]   A. Rodríguez, E. Fernández-Medina, M. Piattini, 'M-BPSec: A Method for Security Requirement Elicitation from a UML 2.0 Business Process Specification', ER Workshops 2007, 106–115
             http://link.springer.com/chapter/10.1007/978-3-540-76292-8_13?LI=true#page-1

[Rod08]   A. Rodriguez, 'RESTful web services: the basics', IBM Developer Works, 2008
             http://www.ibm.com/developerworks/webservices/library/ws-restful/

[Rod]   J. Rodriguez and J. Klug, 'Federated Identity Patterns in a Service-Oriented World', Microsoft Architecture Journal, 16, 6–11

[Ros05]   M. Rosenblum and T. Garfinkel, 'Virtual Machine Monitors: Current Technology and Future Trends', *Computer*, IEEE May 2005, 39–47

[RSA]   RSA Security, PKCS #1: RSA Cryptography Standard
             http://www.rsa.com/rsalabs/node.asp?id=2125

[Rs]   IBM: Real Secure Intrusion Detection Systems by IBM,
             http://publib.boulder.ibm.com/infocenter/sprotect/v2r8m0/index.jsp

[Rut]   Wikipedia: GNU Free Documentation License, 2009
             http://mjrutherford.org/files/2009-Spring-COMP-4704-TLS-Wikipedia.pdf\

[Sad05]   M. Sadicoff, M. M. Larrondo-Petrie and E. B. Fernandez, 'Privacy-Aware Network Client Pattern', in *Proceedings of the 12th Pattern Languages of Programs Conference (PLoP2005)*, Monticello, Illinois, US, 7–10 September 2005,
             http://hillside.net/plop/2005/proceedings/PLoP2005_msadicoff0_0.pdf

[Sal]   Salesforce, 'Salesforce Product Overview', *Salesforce.com*
             http://www.salesforce.com/products/ (accessed 28 Sep 2012)

[Sal2]   Salesfore, 'Force.com: A Comprehensive Look at the World's Premier Cloud- Computing Platform'
             http://www.developerforce.com/media/Forcedotcom_Whitepaper/WP_Forcedotcom-InDepth_040709_WEB.pdf

[Sal3]   Salesforce, 'An Introduction to the Force.com IDE'
             http://wiki.developerforce.com/page/An_Introduction_to_Force_IDE

[Sal4]   Salesforce, 'An Introduction to Environments'
             http://wiki.developerforce.com/page/An_Introduction_to_Environments

[Sal5]   Salesforce, 'About the Force.com Developer Edition Environments'
             http://wiki.developerforce.com/page/Developer_Edition

[Sal6]   Salesforce, 'Secure, Private and Trustworthy: Enterprise Cloud Computing with Force.com'
             http://www.salesforce.com/assets/pdf/misc/WP_Forcedotcom-Security.pdf

[San96]   R. Sandhu, E. J. Coyne, H. L. Feinstein and C. E. Youman., 'Role-based access control models', *Computer*, vol 29, No2, February 1996, 38–47

[SAP09]   webMethods Audit Logging Guide, Software AG 2009
            http://documentation.softwareag.com/webmethods/wmsuites/wmsuite8_ga/Cross_Product/8-0-
            SP1_Audit_Logging_Guide.pdf

[SAP]   SAP Netweaver Identity Manager
            http://www.sap.com/platform/netweaver/components/idm/index.epx

[Sar04]   Sarvega, http://www.sarvega.com/

[sau]   http://en.wikipedia.org/wiki/Information_technology_security_audit

[Sch95]   D. Schmidt, 'Experience Using Design Patterns to Develop Reusable Object-Oriented
            Communication Software', *Communications of the ACM (Special issue on Object-Oriented
            Experiences),* October 1995, 65–74

[Sch99a]   D. C. Schmidt and C. Cleeland, 'Applying Patterns to Develop Extensible ORB Middleware', *IEEE
            Communications Magazine,* 37(4), April 1999, 54–63

[Sch99b]   B. Schneier, 'Attack Trees', *Dr. Dobb's Journal,* December 1999, 21–29

[Sch00a]   M. Schumacher, R. Ackermann and R. Steinmetz, 'Towards Security at all Stages of a System's
            Lifecycle', *Proceedings of International Conference on Software, Telecommunications and
            Computer Networks (Softcom),* 2000, 11–19, http://www.ito.tu-darmstadt.de/publs

[Sch00b]   D. C. Schmidt., M. Stal, H. Rohnert and F. Buschmann, *Pattern-Oriented Software Architecture,*
            John Wiley & Sons, Inc., 2000

[Sch01]   M. Schumacher and U. Roedig, 'Security Engineering with Patterns, *PLoP 2001*

[Sch03]   M. Schumacher, *Security Engineering with Patterns,* Springer, Lecture Notes in Computer Science,
            Volume 2754, 2003, DOI: 10.1007/b11930

[Sch06a]   A. Schaad, 'Security in Enterprise Resource Planning Systems and Service-Oriented Architectures',
            Proceedings of SACMAT'06, ACM, June 2006, 69–70

[Sch06b]   M. Schumacher, E. B. Fernandez, D. Hybertson, F. Buschmann and P. Sommerlad, *Security
            Patterns: Integrating Security and Systems Engineering.* John Wiley & Sons, Inc., 2006

[Sco05]   M. Scodeggio et al., 'The VVDS Data-Reduction Pipeline: Introducing VIPGI, the VIMOS
            Interactive Pipeline and Graphical Interface', *Publications of the Astronomical Society of the
            Pacific,* vol 117, November 2005, 1284–1295.

[sec]   The Security Patterns page, maintained by M. Schumacher, http://www.securitypatterns.org

[Sel12]   L. Seltzer, 'Best Practices and Applications of TLS/SSL', white paper, Symantec Corporation, 2012

[Sel]   Security Enhanced Linux, http://www.nsa.gov/selinux

[SER]   Serenity Project, http://www.serenity-project.org

[SeT]   Secure Tropos, http://www.securetropos.org/

[Sha02]   J. S. Shapiro and N. Hardy, 'EROS: A Principle-Driven Operating System from the Ground Up', *IEEE Software*, Jan./Feb. 2002, 26–33. See also: http://www.eros-os.org

[Sha03]   K. Shanmugasundaram, 'ForNet: A Distributed Forensics Network'. Department of Computer and Information Science. Polytechnic University, Brooklyn, NY. 2003

[Shi00]   T. Shinagawa, K. Kono, T. Masuda, 'Exploiting Segmentation Mechanism for Protecting Against Malicious Mobile Code', Technical Report 00–02, Dept. of Information Science, University of Tokyo, May 2000

[Shi10]   Y. Shiroma, H. Washizaki, Y. Fukazawa, A. Kubo, N. Yoshioka, E. B. Fernandez, 'Model-Driven Application and Validation of Security Patterns', *17th Conference on Pattern Languages of Programs, PLoP 2010*

[Shi]   Shibboleth Project, http://shibboleth.internet2.edu/

[Sid07]   B. Siddiqui, 'Securing Java Applications with Acegi, Part 1: Architectural overvIew and Security Filters', http://www.ibm.com/developerworks/java/library/j-acegi1/index.html (accessed October 29, 2012)

[Sil02]   O. R. da Silva, A. F. Garcia and C. J. P. de Lucena, 'The Reflective Blackboard Architectural Pattern', Rept. PUC-Rio Inf. MCC24/02, Sept. 2002

[Sil03]   A. Silberschatz, P. Galvin, G. Gagne, *Operating System Concepts* (6th edition), John Wiley & Sons, Inc., 2003

[Sil05]   A. Silberschatz, P. Galvin, G. Gagne, *Operating System Concepts* (7th edition), John Wiley & Sons, Inc., 2005

[Sil08]   A. Silberschatz, P. Galvin, G. Gagne, *Operating System Concepts* (8th edition), John Wiley & Sons, Inc., 2008

[Slo02]   M. Sloman and E. Lupu, 'Security and Management Policy Specification', *IEEE Network*, March/April 2002, 10–19

[Smi04]   R. F. Smith, 'Auditing Users and Groups with the Windows Security Log' http://www.windowsecurity.com/articles/auditing-users-groups-windows-security-log.html

[Smi08]   B. Smith, 'A Storm (Worm) is Brewing', *Computer*, IEEE February 2008, 20–22

[SOA01]   W3C, SOAP Security Extensions: Digital Signature, W3C NOTE 06, February 2001 http://www.w3.org/TR/SOAP-dsig/

[Son10]   Sonic Wall VPN Products http://www.sonicwall.com/us/products/472.html (accessed 19 July 2010)

[Sor04]   T. Sorgente and E. B. Fernandez, 'Analysis Patterns for Patient Treatment', *Proceedings of PLoP 2004*, http://jerry.cs.uiuc.edu/~plop/plop2004/accepted_submissions

[Sor05]   T. Sorgente, E. B. Fernandez and M. M. Larrondo-Petrie, 'The SOAP Pattern for Medical Charts', in *Proceedings of the 12th Pattern Languages of Programs Conference (PLoP2005)*, Monticello, Illinois, 7–10 September 2005 http://hillside.net/plop/2005/proceedings/PLoP2005_tsorgente0_1.pdf

[Spa09]   G. Spanoudakis, A. Maña, S. Kokolakis, eds. *Security and Dependability for Ambient Intelligence*, Springer, 2009

[Spe09]   C. Spence, J. Devoys and S. Chahal, 'Architecting Software as a Service for the Enterprise'. Oct 2009

[Sph]   Patterns: SOA with an Enterprise Service Bus in WebSphere Application Server V6
            http://www.redbooks.ibm.com/redpieces/abstracts/sg246494.html

[Spr12]   Springsource Community, 'The Spring Web MVC Framework', 2012
            http://static.springsource.org/spring/docs/3.0.x/spring-framework-reference/html/mvc.html
            (accessed 6 March 2012)

[Sri05]   J. Srivatsa, L. Liu, 'Securing Publish-Subscribe Overlay Services with EventGuard'. *Proceedings 12th ACM Conference on Computer and Communications Security* (CCS), 289–298, ACM, 2005

[Sse10]   R. Ssekibuule, 'Secure Publish-Subscribe Mediated Virtual Organizations', *Proceedings of ISSA*, 2010, http://icsa.cs.up.ac.za/issa/2010/Proceedings/Full/18_Paper.pdf

[Sta03]   W. Stallings, *Cryptography and Network Security: Principles and Practice* (3rd edition), Prentice-Hall, 2003

[Sta06]   W. Stallings, *Cryptography and Network Security* (4th edition), Pearson Prentice Hall, 2006

[Sta12]   W. Stallings and L. Brown, *Computer Security: Principles and Practice* (2nd edition) Prentice Hall, 2012

[Ste02]   J. Steffan and M. Schumacher, 'Collaborative Attack Modeling', *Proceedings of SAC 2002*, Madrid, Spain
            http://www.ito.tu-darmstadt.de/publs/pdf/sac2002.pdf

[Ste05]   C. Steel, R. Nagappan and R. Lai, *Core Security Patterns: Best Strategies for J2EE, Web Services and Identity Management*, Prentice Hall, Upper Saddle River, New Jersey, 2005

[Ste06]   C. Steel , R. Nagappan, R. Lai , Chapter 9 in *Securing the Web Tier: Design Strategies and Best Practices*, Sun, 2006

[Str11]   E. Stratmann, J. Ousterhout and S. Madan, 'Integrating Long Polling with an MVC Framework, in *Proceedings of the 2nd USENIX Conference on Web Application Development (WebApps'11)*, USENIX Association, Berkeley, CA, US, 10–10

[Sum97]   R. C. Summers, *Secure Computing: Threats and Safeguards*, McGraw-Hill, 1997

[Sun04a]   Trusted Solaris Operating System, http://www.sun.com/software/solaris/trustedsolaris/

[Sun04b]   http://sunxacml.sourceforge.net/

[SunA]   Sun Microsystems Inc. Java Cryptography Extension (JCE)
            http://java.sun.com/j2se/1.4.2/docs/guide/security/jce/JCERefGuide.html

[SunB]   Sun Microsystems Inc., *Java SE Security*, http://java.sun.com/javase/technologies/security/

[SunC]   Sun Java System Access Manager, http://www.sun.com/software/products/access_mgr/

[SunD]   Sun Microsystems, http://www.sun.com/software/whitepapers/webservices/wp-getstarted.pdf, http://www.sun.com/software/whitepapers/webservices/wp-implement.pdf

[Suo08]   J. Suomalainen, S. Moloney, J. Kolvisto and K. Keinanen, 'Open House: a Secure Platform for Distributed Home Services', *6th Annual Conference on Privacy, Security and Trust*, 2008, IEEE 2008

[Swa08]   R. E. Sward, K. J. Whitacre; 'A Multi-Language Service-Oriented Architecture using an Enterprise Service Bus', *Proceedings of the 2008 ACM Annual International Conference on SIGAda*, October 26–30, 2008, Portland, Oregon, US

[Sym01]   http://www.symbian.com/developer/

[Sym]   Symantec Antivirus Research Center, http://www.symantec.com/avcenter/index.html

[Tan06]   A. S. Tannenbaum, J. N. Herder and H. Bos, 'Can we Make Operating Systems Reliable and Secure?', *Computer,* IEEE, May 2006, 44–51

[Tan08]   A. Tanenbaum, *Modern Operating Systems* (3rd edition), Prentice Hall, 2008

[Tar02]   P. Tarau, 'Object Oriented Logic Programming as an Agent Building Infrastructure', Oct. 2002, http://logic.csci.unt.edu/tarau/research/slides/oolpAgents.ppt

[Tat04]   M. Tatsubori, T. Imamura and Y. Nakamura, 'Best-Practice Patterns and Tool Support for Configuring Secure Web Services Messaging', *Proceedings of the IEEE International Conference on Web Services* (ICWS'04)

[Tay10]   R. N. Taylor, N. Medvidovic and E. M. Dushofy, *'Software architecture: Foundations, theory and practice',* John Wiley & Sons, Inc., 2010

[Tec11]   techPDF, 'Architecture and Components of Cloud Computing' http://techpdf.co.cc/blog/architecture-and-components-of-cloud-computing/, June 15 2011

[Tem]   E. Tempero, Notes for SOFTENG 325: Software Architecture, Lecture 11 http://www.se.auckland.ac.nz

[Ten05]   J. Tennison, 'Managing Complex Document Generation through Pipelining' http://idealliance.org/proceedings/xtech05/papers/04-03-01/

[The12]   The Apache Software Foundation. The Struts Web Framework, 2012 http://struts.apache.org/, 03/06/12. (accessed 19 Nov 2012)

[Tho97]   R. K. Thomas, 'Team-Based Access Control (TMAC): A primitive for Applying Role-Based Access Controls in Collaborative Environments', in *Proceedings of the 2nd ACM Workshop on Role-based Access Control (RBAC 97)*, Fairfax, Virginia, US, 6–7 November 1997, 13–19

[Tho98]   D. Thomsen, R. C. O'Brien, J. Bogle, 'Role Based Access Control Framework for Network Enterprises', in *Proceedings of the 14th Annual Computer Security Applications Conference*, December 1998, 50–58

[Tok04]   E. Toktar, E. Jamhour and C. Maziero,'RSVP Policy Control using XACML', *Proceedings of the 5th IEEE International Workshop on Policies for Distributed Systems and Networks (POLICY 2004)*, 7–9 June 2004, Yorktown Heights, NY, US.

[Ubu]   Ubuntu, 'UEC Package Install Separate'
                https://help.ubuntu.com/community/UEC/PackageInstallSeparate#Overview

[Uzu12a]   A. V. Uzunov, E. B. Fernandez and K. Falkner, 'Securing Distributed Systems using Patterns: A
                Survey', *Computers & Security,* 31(5), 2012, 681–703, doi:10.1016/j.cose.2012.04.005

[Uzu12b]   A. Uzunov, K. Falkner and E. B. Fernandez, 'A Comprehensive Pattern-Oriented Approach to
                Engineering Security Methodologies', submitted for publication

[Uzu12c]   A. V. Uzunov, E. B. Fernandez and K. Falkner, 'Engineering Security into Distributed Systems: A
                Survey of Methodologies', accepted for the *Journal of Universal Computer Science*

[Uzu12d]   A. Uzunov and E. B. Fernandez, 'An Extensible Pattern-Based Library and Taxonomy of Security
                Threats for Distributed Systems', accepted for the Special Issue on Security in Information Systems
                of the *Journal of Computer Standards & Interfaces*

[Van09]   M. VanHilst, E. B. Fernandez and F. Braz, 'A Multidimensional Classification for Users of Security
                Patterns', *Journal of Research and Practice in Information Technology,* vol 41, No 2, May 2009,
                87–97

[Ver02]   T. Verwoerd and R. Hunt, 'Intrusion Detection Techniques and Approaches', *Computer
                Communications,* Volume 25, Issue 15, 15 September 2002, 1356–1365

[Ver04]   M. Verma, 'XML Security: Control Information Access with XACML'
                http://www.ibm.com/developerworks/xml/library/x-xacml/

[Via05]   W. Viana, J. B. Filho, R. A., 'Secrecy with Session Key: Um Padrão de Criptografia para Evitar
                Ataques de Criptoanálise por Textos Cifrados Conhecidos' (in Portuguese), *Proceedings of
                SugarLoaf PLoP 2005,* http://sugarloafplop2005.icmc.usp.br/papers/9700.pdf

[VMW09]   VMware, Inc., SecureSpan XML Virtual Appliance, 2012
                http://www.vmware.com/appliances/directory/249773 (accessed 15 Dec 2009)

[Voe02]   M. Voelter, A. Schmid and E. Wolff, *Server Component Patterns : Component Infrastructures
                Illustrated with EJB,* John Wiley & Sons, Inc., 1996

[Vor09]   Vordel Limited, Vordel STS, http://www.vordel.com/solutions/security_token_services.html
                (accessed 15 Dec 2009)

[Vuo04]   S. Vuong and Y. Bai, 'A Survey of VoIP Intrusions and Intrusion Detection Systems', *Proceedings
                of the 6th International Conference on Advanced Communication Technology,* August 2004

[W3C01]   W3C, XML Key Management Specification, March 2001, http://www.w3.org/TR/xkms/

[W3C02]   W3C, XML Encryption Syntax and Processing, 10 December 2002
                http://www.w3.org/TR/xmlenc-core/

[W3C07]   W3C, Web Services Policy 1.5 – Framework, 4 September 2007, http://www.w3.org/TR/ws-policy/
                (accessed 15 Dec 2009)

[W3C08]   W3C Working Group, XML Signature Syntax and Processing (2nd edition) 2008
                http://www.w3.org/TR/xmldsig-core

[W3C09]   W3C Working Draft, Web Services Metadata Exchange, 2009, http://www.w3.org/TR/ws-gloss/ (accessed 15 Dec 2009)

[Wal81]   S. Wallach and C. Holland, '32-bit Minicomputer Achieves Full 16-bit Compatibility', *Computer Design*, Jan. 1981, 111–120

[Wan06]   Q. Wang, W. Shin, X. Liu, Z. Zeng, C. Oh, B. K. AlShebli, M. Caccamo, C. A. Gunter, E. Gunter, J. Hou, K. Karahalios and L. Sha, 'I-Living: An Open System Architecture for Assisted Living', *IEEE Transactions on Systems, Man and Cybernetics*, (SMC), Taipei, Taiwan, 4268–4275, October 2006

[Wan08]   L. Wang, J. Tao, M. Kunze, A. C. Castellanos, D. Kramerand W. Karl, 'Scientific Cloud Computing: Early Definition and Experience', in *10th IEEE International Conference on High Performance Computing and Communications, HPCC '08*, 2008, 825–830

[War03a]   J. Warmer and A. Kleppe, *The Object Constraint Language* (2nd edition), Addison-Wesley, 2003

[War03b]   R. Warrier and E. B. Fernandez, 'Remote Authenticator/Authorizer', *Pattern Languages of Programs Conference (PLoP), 2003*

[Was09]   H. Washizaki, E. B. Fernandez, K. Maruyama, A. Kubo and N. Yoshioka, 'Improving the Classification of Security Patterns', *Proceedings of the 3rd International Workshop on Secure System Methodologies using Patterns (SPattern 2009)*

[Wei06a]   M. Weiss, 'Credential Delegation: Towards Grid Security Patterns', *Nordic Pattern Languages of Programs Conference (VikingPLoP)*, 2006

[Wie06b]   C. Wieser, J. Roning and A. Takanen, 'Security Analysis and Experiments for Voice Over IP RTP Media Streams', *Proceedings of the 8th International Symposium on System and Information Security (SSI'2006)*

[Wei08]   M. Weiss, 'Patterns and their Impacts on System Concerns', *Proceedings PLoP 2008*

[Wes03]   Westbridge Technology, http://www.westbridgetech.com

[WeS]   IBM WebSphere V5.0 Security, http://www.redbooks.ibm.com/abstracts/sg246573.html (accessed 9 Nov 2012)

[Whi01]   J. A. Whitaker and H. H. Thompson, *How to Break Software Security*, Addison-Wesley 2001

[wik1]   Wikipedia, 'Scheduler Pattern', http://en.wikipedia.org/wiki/Scheduler_pattern (accessed June 21, 2012).

[wik2]   Wikipedia, 'Ring (computer security)' http://en.wikipedia.org/wiki/Supervisor_mode#Supervisor_mode

[wik3]   Proposed Standard: The Transport Layer Security (TLS) Protocol Version 1.2 http://wiki.tools.ietf.org/html/rfc5246

[wik4]   Wikipedia, 'Publish/Subscribe', http://en.wikipedia.org/wiki/Publish/subscribe

[Won08]   W. Wong, F. Verdi, M. Magalhaes, 'A Security Plane for Publish/Subscribe Based Content Oriented Networks'. Proceedings ACM CoNEXT, 2008

[wor09]   'Worm Evolution', May 2009, http://www.digitalthreat.net/?p=17

[Wre04]   Review: RSA ClearTrust 5.5 Secure Federated Identity Management System
             http://searchsecurity.techtarget.com/Secure-SSO-Single-sign-on-security-for-Web-services-with-
             RSA-ClearTrust-55

[WSE]   Solution Design in WebSphere Process Server and WebSphere ESB
             http://www.ibm.com/developerworks/websphere/library/techarticles/0908_clark/0908_clark.html

[WSO]   WSO2, Identity Server, http://wso2.com/products/identity-server

[WSPL]   http://sourceforge.net/projects/openwspl/

[Xtr04]   Xtradyne Technologies, http://www.xtradyne.com/

[Xtr]   Xtradyne Technologies, 'Xtradyne's WS-DBC, the XML/SOAP Firewall for Enterprises',
             http://www.xtradyne.de/products/ws-dbc/ws-dbc.htm

[Yas04]   A. Yasinsac and J. Childs, 'Formal Analysis of Modern Security Protocols' *Information Sciences*
             Volume 171, Issues 1–3, 4 March 2005

[Yod97]   J. Yoder and J. Barcalow, 'Architectural Patterns for Enabling Application Security', *Proceedings*
             PLOP'97, http://jerry.cs.uiuc.edu/~plop/plop97
             Also Chapter 15 in *Pattern Languages of Program Design*, vol 4 (N. Harrison, B. Foote and H.
             Rohnert, eds.), Addison-Wesley, 2000

[Yos04]   N. Yoshioka, S. Honiden and A. Finkelstein, 'Security Patterns: A Method for Constructing Secure
             and Efficient Inter-Company Coordination Systems', *Proceedings of the 8th International IEEE*
             Enterprise Distributed Object Computing Conference, 2004

[Yos08]   N. Yoshioka, H. Washizaki and K. Maruyama, 'A Survey on Security Patterns', *Progress in*
             Informatics, No 5, 2008, 35–47

[Ysk06]   K. Yskout, T. Heyman, R. Scandariato and W. Joosen, 'A System of Security Patterns', Rept.
             CW469, Dec. 2006, Dept. of Computer Science, Katholieke Universiteit Leuven, Belgium

[Ysk08]   K. Yskout, R. Scandariato, B. DeWin and W. Joosen, 'Transforming Security Requirements into
             Architecture', *Proceedings of Third International Conference on Availability, Reliability and*
             Security (ARES 2008), 1421–1428

[Ysk12]   K. Yskout, R. Scandariato and W. Joosen, 'Does Organizing Security Patterns Focus Architectural
             Choices?', *ICSE 2012*, Zurich, 617–627

[Yua03]   X. Yuan and E. B. Fernandez, 'An Analysis Pattern for Course Management', *Proceedings of*
             EuroPLoP 2003, http://hillside.net/europlop

[Yua11]   X. Yuan and E. B. Fernandez, 'Patterns for Business-to-Consumer E-Commerce Applications',
             International Journal of Software Engineering & Applications (IJSEA), vol 2 No 3, July 2011, 1–
             20, http://airccse.org/journal/ijsea/papers/0711ijsea01.pdf

[Zdu06]   U. Zdun, C. Hentrich and W. M. P. van der Aalst, 'A Survey of Patterns for Service-Oriented
             Architectures', *International Journal of Internet Protocol Technology*, Vol 1, No 3, 132 – 143, 2006

[Zen08] Z. Zeng, S. Yu, W. Shin and J. C. Hou, 'PAS: A Wireless-Enabled, Cell-Phone-Incorporated Personal Assistant System for Independent and Assisted Living', *Proceedings of 28th International Conference on Distr. Comp. Systems,* IEEE 2008, 233–242

[Zha02] L. Zhang, G. J. Ahn and B. T. Chu, 'A Role-Based Delegation Framework for Healthcare Systems', *Proceedings of the 8th ACM Symposium on Access Control Models and Technologies (SACMAT'02),* 02–03 June 2003, Como, Italy, 125–134

[Zha10] Q. Zhang, L. Cheng, R. Boutaba, 'Cloud Computing: State-of-the-Art and Research Challenges', *Journal of Internet Services and Applications,* vol 1, 2010, 7–18

[Zho02] Y. Zhou, Q. Zhao and M. Perry, 'Policy Enforcement Pattern', *Proceedings of PLoP 2002*

[Zir04] C. Zirpins, W. Lamersdorf and T. Baier, 'Flexible Coordination of Service Interaction Patterns', *Proceedings of the 2nd International Conference on Service Oriented Computing (ICSOC'04),* November 15–19, 2004, New York, New York, US

Index of Patterns

Entries in lowercase refer to external citations of patterns.
Entries in uppercase refer to citations of patterns described in this book.

543

Index